CW01189193

THE MAKING OF THE ELIZABETHAN NAVY, 1540–1590:
FROM THE SOLENT TO THE ARMADA

When Henry VIII came to the throne in 1509 the English navy was rather *ad hoc*: there were very few warships as such. Merchant ships were hired when needed by the king, and converted for military purposes, which involved mostly the transport of troops and the support of land armies. There were no permanent dockyards and no Admiralty or other standing institutions to organize naval affairs. Throughout the reigns of Henry VIII, Edward VI and Mary, and the early part of the reign of Elizabeth, all this changed, so that by the 1580s England had permanent dockyards, and permanent naval administrative institutions, and was able to send warships capable of fighting at sea to attack the Spanish in the Caribbean and in Spain itself, and able to confront the Spanish Armada with a formidable fleet. This book provides a thorough account of the development of the English navy in this period, showing how the formidable force which beat the Spanish Armada was created. *The Making of the Elizabethan Navy* covers technological, administrative and operational developments, in peace and war, and provides full accounts of the various battles and other naval actions.

DAVID LOADES is Honorary Research Professor, University of Sheffield, Professor Emeritus, University of Wales, Bangor, and a member of the Centre for British and Irish Studies, University of Oxford.

The Making of the Elizabethan Navy, 1540–1590:

From the Solent to the Armada

David Loades

THE BOYDELL PRESS

© David Loades 2009

All rights reserved. Except as permitted under current legislation no part of this work may be photocopied, stored in a retrieval system, published, performed in public, adapted, broadcast, transmitted, recorded or reproduced in any form or by any means, without the prior permission of the copyright owner

The right of David Loades to be identified as the author of this work has been asserted in accordance with sections 77 and 78 of the Copyright, Designs and Patents Act 1988

First published 2009
The Boydell Press, Woodbridge

ISBN 978-1-84383-492-2

The Boydell Press is an imprint of Boydell & Brewer Ltd
PO Box 9, Woodbridge, Suffolk IP12 3DF, UK
and of Boydell & Brewer Inc.
668 Mt Hope Avenue, Rochester, NY 14620, USA
website: www.boydellandbrewer.com

The publisher has no responsibility for the continued existence or accuracy of URLs for external or third-party internet websites referred to in this book, and does not guarantee that any content on such websites is, or will remain, accurate or appropriate.

A CIP record for this book is available from the British Library

This publication is printed on acid-free paper

Designed by Tina Ranft

Printed in Great Britain by
CPI Antony Rowe, Chippenham and Eastbourne

Contents

	Preface and Acknowledgements	vii
	Map showing the navy's presence in the Channel	viii
	Map showing the English presence in Southern Scotland	ix
INTRODUCTION	The King's Ships	1
CHAPTER ONE	Operations, 1544–1547	19
CHAPTER TWO	The Council for Marine Causes	39
CHAPTER THREE	The Navy of Edward VI	56
CHAPTER FOUR	The Navy of Mary, and of Philip and Mary	79
CHAPTER FIVE	The First Decade of Elizabeth	100
CHAPTER SIX	The Navy and the Maritime Community	124
CHAPTER SEVEN	Money	145
CHAPTER EIGHT	Towards War	164
CHAPTER NINE	War	185
CHAPTER TEN	Epilogue	206
	Bibliography	225
	Index	234

Preface and Acknowledgements

This book is not free-standing. It is, in a sense, a sequel to *The Tudor Navy*, published by Scolar Press in 1992 and now out of print. Some of the same research material has been used, although not usually in the same way. It is also partly the product of an ongoing collaboration with Dr Charles Knighton, whose immensely helpful research contribution I would wish to acknowledge as fully as possible. This collaboration has also produced an edition of some documents relating to the Scottish campaign of 1544, which appeared in volume seven of the *Naval Miscellany*, and two other collections in preparation for the Navy Records Society – one on the navy of Edward VI and Mary, and the other on Elizabethan naval administration. The research which has informed those collections, has also informed this book. I would also wish to acknowledge my debt to the many other scholars who have worked in this field over the years, and whose publications are noticed in the footnotes.

Other debts have also been incurred, most notably to the Leverhulme Trust which granted me an Emeritus Fellowship to support the work of which this is a part. Also to Dr Virginia Murphy of Durham University and Professor Rodriguez Salgado of the LSE, who have translated, checked and verified documents; to Peter Sowden of Boydell and Brewer, who made it happen; to Dr Alex Hildred of the Mary Rose Trust, whose invitation to their Anniversary Conference helped me to pull some thoughts together; and to my wife, Judith, who has become accustomed to my postponing other urgent tasks in order to get back to the Tudor navy.

David Loades
Oxford, September 2008

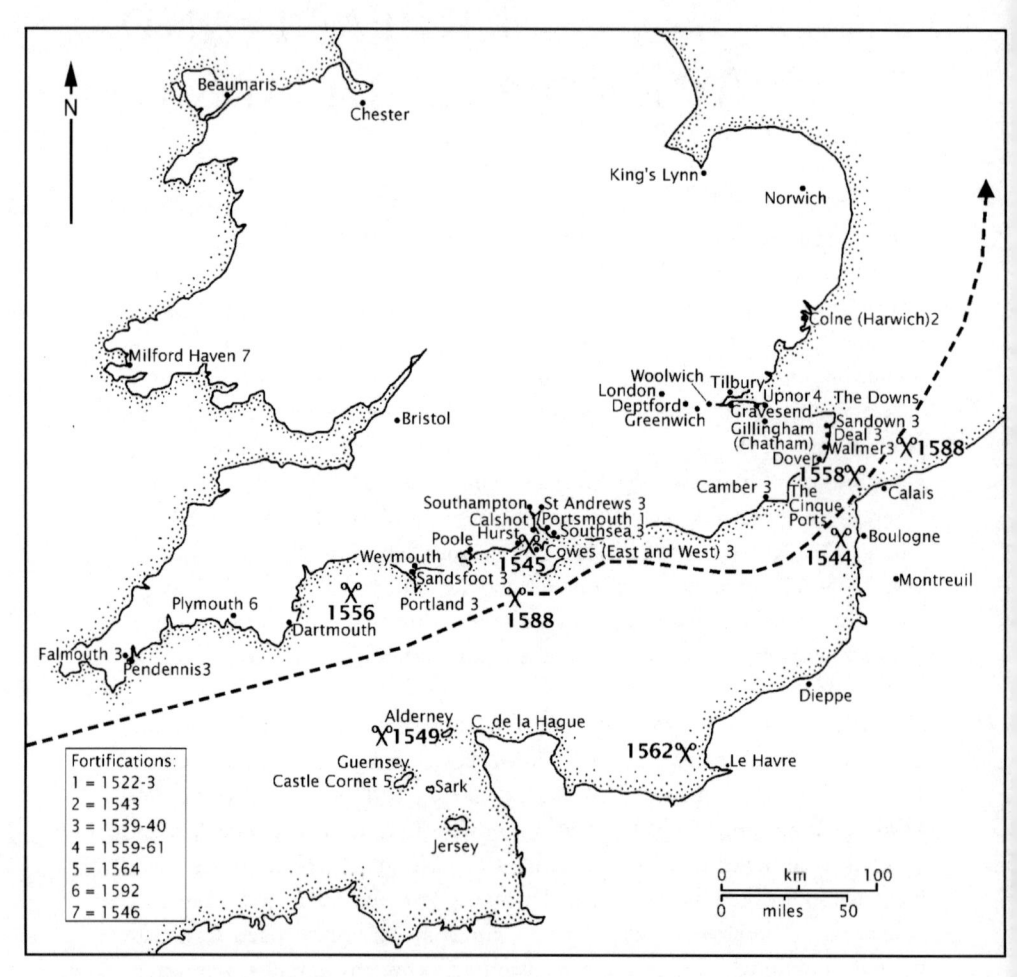

Map showing the navy's presence in the Channel, and the battles that resulted.

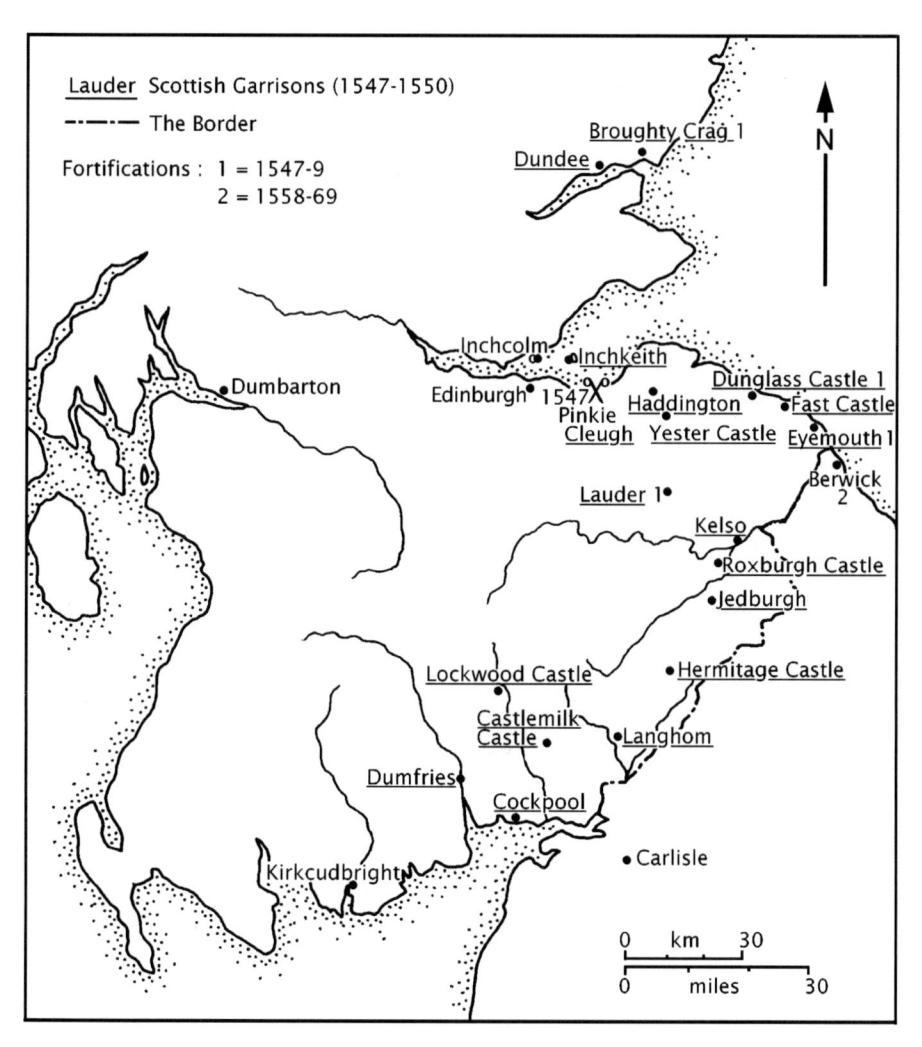

Map showing the English presence in Southern Scotland.

INTRODUCTION

THE KING'S SHIPS

On the eve of the wars with Scotland and France, which were to preoccupy Henry VIII from 1542 to 1546, the English navy was in an embryonic condition. In a sense it had existed since about 1512, when Henry had first gone to war with France, but it lacked an institutional structure and co-ordinated finance. During the years of uneasy peace between 1529 and 1539, when England had been preoccupied with its own internal problems, an observer could readily be excused for not noticing it at all. In 1539, when he had been particularly keen to disparage the English king, the Emperor's ambassador, Eustace Chapuys, had observed that Henry's Great Ships (which he acknowledged to exist) were in such a run-down condition that it would take 'twelve or thirteen months' to get them to sea.[1] When a temporary rapprochement between the Emperor and the king of France had triggered fears of a Catholic invasion in 1539, the king had indeed mobilised his fleet, but he had chosen to spend most of the available money on building a string of artillery forts along the south coast. Docks and storehouses existed at Deptford, Woolwich and Portsmouth, but they were run by skeleton staffs in between mobilisations, and most of the workmen were drafted in as, and when, required.[2] There was an admiralty, but it had nothing to do with maintaining the king's ships. The Lord Admiral was a grandee whose job it was to command the fleet in action and to hold the jurisdiction of the Admiralty Court, a tribunal which administered the Civil Law in maritime disputes.[3]

The Admiralty jurisdiction had developed in the fourteenth century, at which time the 'navy royal' had been an occasional event, without any pretensions to permanence. John and Henry III had possessed galley fleets, designed for inshore and coastal defence, and there had even for a while been a 'galley shed' at Rye and an officer called the Clerk of the Ships to oversee them. However, these highly specialised ships had disappeared with the conflicts which had produced them, and by the reign of Edward III the king owned no more than three or four sailing ships, which were used mostly to import wine for the royal tables or to ferry ambassadors on special missions.[4] Wars were fought on land – as far as possible in France – and a fleet was only needed when a major army was coming or going across the Channel. On those occasions the king 'took up' as many ships as he judged that he needed from the maritime communities of the port towns. Some of these were provided by liberties such as the Cinq Ports on what was known as 'ship service' – a short-term feudal obligation in return for which they held their privileges. This was already becoming obsolete by the time of the Hundred Years War, for the same reason that feudal levies themselves were becoming obsolete. It was reluctantly entered into and bound the mariners to only forty days of unpaid service. For the most part the necessary ships were requisitioned by specially appointed commissioners, and hired at a fixed rate. The men were paid by the king from the time of entering service, and any loss or damage was supposed to be compensated.[5] These requisitions were not popular, because they took ships and men away from their normal commercial occupations for weeks on end, and Henry V (for example) took up most of the ships which he needed in the Low Countries. The big advantage of this was that the captains were more willing to serve; the disadvantage was that foreign 'keels' had to be paid at a slightly higher rate.[6]

It was perfectly possible to use merchant ships in this way, because the only distinctive feature of a warship's design was the castles, fore and aft, which housed the archers and slingers whose job it was to 'soften up' an enemy crew in preparation for boarding. The king kept a store of such castles in a prefabricated form, and specially hired carpenters fitted them to the requisitioned ships before sending them out to fight. After the service was completed, they were removed and returned to store. By the early fifteenth century small guns, called serpentines, might also be mounted in these castles, but they were strictly anti-personnel weapons and had no effect on the structure.[7] Galleys were still used, particularly by the French, but they were not sufficiently seaworthy to go much out of sight of land in northern waters, and were no match for the high-sided cogs when it came to close-quarters fighting. Although the English won some notable victories at sea in the fourteenth century – notably at Sluys in 1340, and the encounter known as 'Espagnols sur mer' ten years later – Edward III never learned to take sea power seriously. Indeed no king of England had done so since the conquest, largely because they were accustomed to holding sizeable parts of France, and always thought of the Channel as a highway rather than a moat.[8] It was not since the tenth century that the 'first English Empire', embracing Wales, Scotland and the Isles, had been held together by sea power. It was only with the renewal of the French war by Henry V in 1415 that something like a royal navy can be discerned for the first time since King Edgar.

Henry built or purchased about thirty ships of various sizes, mostly two-masted balingers, but including his Great Ship the *Grace Dieu* of 1,400 tons, and for a while the Clerk of the Ships was a busy man,[9] but the king's enthusiasm did not outlast the war. No sooner was peace concluded in 1420 than the ships began to be sold off. Wooden ships were expensive to maintain, and deteriorated rapidly, whether in use or not. Henry appears to have had no notion of 'keeping the seas' as a precaution either against piracy or against some sudden attack. After his death in 1422 the run down continued apace, in spite of the fact that there was still fighting in France. By 1430 the *Grace Dieu* had been beached in the Hamble (where its remains can still be seen) and the other Great Ships disposed of. Everything saleable was sold, and by 1452 nothing was left and the office of Clerk of the Ships was discontinued.[10] In fact the king did still own one or two balingers, but they were leased out on a permanent basis and not available for royal service. The French author of *The Debate between the Heralds of England and France*, a tract probably written between 1458 and 1461, could still praise England for being richly endowed with ships and mariners, but he did not have any kind of a royal navy in mind.[11] Henry VI's council was always desperately short of money because the king seemed to be incapable of saying 'no' to petitioners, and that explains the sale of the navy, but it left the problem of keeping the seas unresolved. As the century advanced, piracy became an increasing problem, and merchant communities such as Bristol began to resort to self-help, arming and equipping ships at their own expense to protect their commerce. These private fleets were licensed by the king and were supposed to abide by the terms of their licences, but if they failed to do so no real sanctions were available to the Crown.[12] In fact the council had virtually no control over these private fleets, but they were cheap from the government's point of view, and had a vested interest in guarding the sea lanes. In 1436 licences were issued to merchants of London, Ipswich, Hull and a number of other ports in addition to Bristol. About thirty ships were involved all together, and they were organised into a single fleet under an elected admiral. How this operated is not known, but as a number of the licences were renewed down to 1444 some benefit must have been perceived.[13] Unfortunately such captains were not very careful in selecting their victims. Reprisals against ships from a port known to harbour pirates were considered to be legitimate, but vessels were also taken which had no such connections, and diplomatic 'incidents' often followed. In 1449 one Robert Winnington, who must have commanded a large fleet, captured over a hundred Hanseatic, Dutch and Flemish vessels, an exploit which eventually cost the council £4,500 in compensation.[14]

Another method which the king also resorted to was keeping the seas by indenture. These indentures were similar to those used for noblemen and captains to raise retinues to fight in France. The recipient undertook to raise so many men, or ships, for a given period of time, to pay their initial conduct money, and usually to lead them into action. In return the Crown undertook to pay all the expenses, and eventually did so. The great advantage of indentured men and ships was that they remained under control (more or less). The disadvantage was that they were not cheap, except that in the case of ships the king only paid for them while they were in service, and had no long-term overheads to meet, which would have been the case with a royal navy. In 1435–6 several sums of up to £200 were paid to individuals *pro salva custodia maris*, which suggests small operations of short duration.[15] Unfortunately they still cost money, whether they were effective or not. Both licences and indentures encouraged the growth of private fleets, and ships armed and equipped for fighting began to proliferate. This would have been detrimental to the king's peace even in times of political stability, and the mid-fifteenth century was far from stable. It was one such private fleet, owned by the earl of Warwick and operating out of Calais, which turned the tide of civil war against Henry VI in 1461. Had anything like Henry V's war fleet still been in existence, that would not have happened, and the whole subsequent history of England might have been different.

Edward IV seems not to have taken this point at all. Preoccupied with securing his position within England, sea power remained as much of a closed book to him as it had to most of his predecessors. When first Warwick and then Margaret of Anjou landed troops with hostile intent in 1470, the king made not the slightest attempt to intercept them, and when he returned from his brief enforced exile in 1471 it was in ships borrowed from his brother-in-law the duke of Burgundy. In the event it did not matter because the Lancastrians were so divided and ineffective that the command of the sea became irrelevant, but even at that time, when the Portuguese were beginning a great colonial expansion based on sea power, the king of England did not grasp what it meant to be a Sea King. Edward did indeed purchase some ships of his own, which he used mainly for trading, and leased out from time to time to merchants, but until 1480 when they were not on hire they were in the keeping of Master Mariners appointed for that purpose. In that year he finally resurrected the office of Keeper of the King's Ships, and Thomas Rogers began to keep a systematic record of the five or six modest-sized vessels which then were placed under his control.[16] Rogers was continued in office by both Richard III and Henry VII, but with no very great change in the nature or scale of his duties. By 1485 the 'royal navy' had gone back to being roughly what it was before Henry V's short-lived expansion. Neither Edward nor Richard had used indentures to keep the seas, perhaps for obvious reasons, and the rather perfunctory wars of Edward's reign, against France and against the Hanseatic League (particularly the latter), had been fought at sea by the traditional means. Licences continued to be used, but only (it would seem) because there was no other way of maintaining even a notional control over operations which were going to happen anyway, whether the king willed them or not.

Henry VII was not an innovator, in naval matters or in anything else, but he did make two significant changes. Almost as soon as he had settled his regime by marrying Elizabeth of York, he commanded the building of two large customised warships.[17] These were carracks on the Portuguese model, and were state-of-the-art. Nothing quite like them had been seen in England before. These ships, eventually named the *Regent* (*c.* 600 tons) and the *Sovereign* (*c.* 450 tons), were not the largest ships to have been built in English yards – in fact even the *Regent* was only half the size of the massive *Grace Dieu* – but they were designed for fighting and intended to be armed with guns.[18] Two warships do not make a navy, and apart from this initial effort Henry confined himself to commissioning only a handful of modest-sized replacements for the ageing ships which he had inherited. The point was not to make war, but to make a statement. By deploying these two ships, Henry was signalling that he understood the importance of sea power to a country which was virtually an island. England might still hold Calais, and have a land border with Scotland, but in terms of continental politics, it was an offshore island to be approached only by sea. Secondly they were intended as a deterrent. A king who could command two such ships could summon many others if the need required, and any intended intervention would be encountered at sea before it had any chance to land. Prevention was very much better, and cheaper, than cure, and although Henry's two brief wars – against France in 1492 and against Scotland in 1497 – did involve the deployment of both these capital ships, neither of them is known to have fired a shot in anger.[19]

The other thing which Henry did was to convert the occasionally used anchorage at Portsmouth into an embryonic naval base, by excavating a dock in the vicinity of the present Old Basin and by erecting some basic fortifications at the entrance to the harbour. The reason why he did this was not so much far-sighted planning as because the great carracks were too deep in draft to cross the Hamble bar into the old anchorage. The dock was not a new invention, because such excavations had been made in the past, but it was unusually permanent and was lined with timber as opposed to being a mere hole. The work occupied about six months in 1495 and three months in 1496, and the first period of twenty-four weeks cost a total of £124 2s 3d. A forge and storehouse were also built, and the *Regent* and the *Sovereign* were based there for the remainder of the reign.[20] Henry avoided war as much as possible, and both ships were leased out to merchants from time to time for their proper purposes, but after his death in April 1509, a very different political climate appertained. Henry VIII was looking for a fight from the moment that he ascended the throne. Although this was partly due to adolescent exuberance and dreams of chivalric glory, there were also sound reasons to abandon his father's pacific policy. In the first place, the quickest way for a king to make his mark in the world was by victory on the battlefield. His father had earned the respect of his colleagues the hard way, by long experience and diplomatic graft, but Henry VIII was a young man in a hurry. Secondly he led a nobility which still saw its primary service in terms of warfare. One generation had not been sufficient to alter that habit of mind, and the English nobles, particularly the younger ones, were itching to be led into battle by their glamorous new sovereign. They had also had enough of the sober, suspicious and parsimonious policies of the older Henry. They wanted to be free of bonds and recognisances, and to march off to what they hoped would be glory against the ancient enemy – and of course rich pickings from ransoms.[21]

The king, however, was not so carried away that he proposed to fight France on his own, and it was to be more than two years before Louis XII's falling out with the papacy created the Holy League, which Henry joined with aggressive enthusiasm in December 1511. Meanwhile he had posted his intentions in several ways. The abandonment of his father's restrictive fiscal policies was signalled dramatically by the arrest, trial and execution of two of the old king's most effective 'enforcers', Sir Richard Empson and Edmund Dudley. The independence which he intended to exercise in his personal life was indicated by his sudden decision to marry his sister-in-law, Catherine of Aragon – all scruples swept aside.[22] And his warlike ambitions were expressed in his development of the navy. Like his father, one of his first actions was to lay down two new capital ships, later called the *Mary Rose* (600 tons) and the *Peter Pomegranate* (450 tons). These, however, were not intended as a statement – they were for use. They were built on private contracts and were designed (at least in part) by the king himself.[23] Henry was deeply interested in guns and gunnery, including the use of guns at sea, and it seems to have been at his suggestion that the *Mary Rose* was fitted with a few gun-ports, to allow heavy guns to be mounted on the main deck. These were not numerous – probably no more than three a side – but they were an innovation of great significance for the future. His father's Great Ships were still in service, so by 1510 Henry had four large warships of his own; one of which was equipped with revolutionary big guns. By the time that Henry joined the Holy League, Robert Brygantine, who had succeeded William Commersall as Clerk of the Ships in 1495, had custody of some seven or eight vessels, and had been responsible for rebuilding the *Mary and John* (*c.* 200 tons) after a fire.[24] The immediate prospect of hostilities in 1512 then led to a massive programme of expansion. Within a year the king purchased, built or otherwise acquired no fewer than fourteen ships of over 100 tons, including two massive Genoese carracks, the *Gabriel Royal* and the *Katherine Fortileza*, each of 700 tons.[25]

Fourteen ships were mobilised in April 1512, of which nine were the king's own, the others having been 'taken up' in the traditional manner. Eighteen captains and 3,000 men were mustered at Blackheath on the 16th, and Sir Edward Howard, the newly appointed admiral, was issued with his instructions. He was ordered to proceed to 'The Trade', that is the region of Brest, and to hold the sea against all comers.[26] This was slightly unusual, because although the marquis of Dorset was at the same time taking an expeditionary force to Guienne, Howard was not ordered to escort him beyond Brest, and his operation seems to have been envisaged as entirely separate. In other words the navy was being given its own assignment, without reference to any army royal. At first this appeared to have achieved little. Howard occupied himself 'chasing fishing boats', but he did capture over forty of them in addition to twenty-six Flemish hulks, the cargoes of which would have gone a long way towards paying his expenses.[27] He escorted Dorset down Channel between the 3rd and the 6th June, and held a complete command of the sea, his mobilisation having apparently taken the French completely by surprise. Late in June he retreated to Portsmouth to re-victual and collect five more ships, including the *Sovereign*, and the king seems to have been well pleased with his efforts. It was August before the French response finally emerged – a fleet of some twenty-two warships painfully assembled from the ports of Brittany and Normandy which mustered at Brest. Although he now had almost complete parity with the English, the French Admiral, René de Clermont, seems to have been more concerned to out-face his enemies rather than confront them, and Howard was forced into lengthy and inconclusive manoeuvring. The deadlock was only broken, in a sense, when the *Cordelière*, the 'great carrack of Brest' decided to engage on the 18th, and spectacularly blew up, taking the *Regent*, with which she was grappled, with her. Both ships were destroyed and the loss of life was immense.[28]

For a couple of further weeks Howard continued to raid the Breton coast, and to take prizes, apparently unhindered by French resistance. At the end of August he returned to Portsmouth where the majority of his requisitioned ships were released, and some, at least, of the royal warships brought round to a winter anchorage at Deptford. Other ships continued to be deployed, some to escort the marquis of Dorset home from Guienne in October, and some against the Scots, but Howard's was the main fleet, and the most innovative in terms of its operation. Throughout the winter Henry continued to build and purchase ships, so that when Howard again took to the seas in March 1513 he commanded no fewer than twenty-three of the king's own ships, including the newly commissioned *Henry Grace de Dieu* – the *Great Harry*.[29] All together his fleet numbered about fifty. This time, however, even the somewhat equivocal success of 1512 was not to be repeated. The French were quickly at sea, and deployed a squadron of Mediterranean galleys under the experienced commander Prégent de Bidoux. To these highly mobile nuisances, Howard had no adequate response, and in trying to winkle them out of their lair on the Breton coast in April, he attacked with inadequate support, and lost his life.[30] Much to Henry's annoyance, the English fleet retreated in disarray, and although Howard's brother, Sir Thomas, was quickly appointed in his place, the momentum of the campaign had been lost. Independent naval operations were then suspended and the fleet re-deployed to escort the army royal which the king took over in June, a campaign which culminated in the capture of Tournai. After that the fleet returned to winter quarters, although a small 'Channel guard' continued to patrol during the close season in what appears to have been an innovative attempt to maintain control ahead of the campaigns which were planned for 1514. In the event, although the navy was re-mobilised in February and March, it was not used aggressively, and the war fizzled out in the summer of 1514. Henry had made his mark, and taken Tournai, as well as shattering the Scottish 'second front' at Flodden, and he appears to have been satisfied with his achievement as well as becoming keenly aware of the cost.

Although the navy's role in the war had been significant, and in some ways innovatory, it was what happened afterwards that made the period revolutionary. During the war Henry had, as we have seen, laid up most of his Great Ships for the winter at Deptford, and it was generally expected that, as soon as peace was concluded, most of them would be sold, and a few of the older ones might be scrapped. The last time that the king had actually owned such a large number of ships had been nearly a century before, in the time of Henry V, and that was precisely what had happened in 1420. Henry VIII, however, decided to de-commission them, and keep them on a care and maintenance basis. Thirteen of them, including the *Great Harry*, the *Sovereign*, the *Mary Rose* and the *Peter Pomegranate*, were carefully inventoried in July 1514. Their guns and tackle were then removed and placed in storage, while the ships themselves were moored in the Medway with a dozen or so shipkeepers under the command of the bo'sun to look after each of them.[31] The reason for this innovation is nowhere recorded. It may have been because the design of warships was beginning to diverge from that of merchantmen, and that the former were no longer so useful as load carriers. Ships like the *Great Harry* and the *Mary Rose*, with their gun decks and ports, were seldom leased out, and then more as escorts than as actual traders. It may equally have been that Henry had no intention of keeping the peace for long, and either foresaw or intended their early return to use. For whatever reason, they were kept, and the standing navy may be said to date from that time.

The decision had not been a sudden one, reached as the war ended. A second forge had been opened at Greenwich in 1511, new docks had been constructed at Erith and Limehouse in 1512, and storehouses built at Erith and Deptford.[32] In 1512 a second office had also been created to oversee all this business, that of Clerk Controller, to which John Hopton, a Gentleman Usher of the Chamber, had been appointed. The relationship between the existing Clerk, Robert Brygandine, and Hopton is not entirely clear, but seems not to have been one of line management. Hopton operated principally in the Thames and Medway, while Brygandine was largely confined to Portsmouth.[33] Both were funded directly by council warrants, and both presumably accounted to the exchequer, although the Clerk Controller's accounts do not survive. Between them the Clerk and the Clerk Controller were responsible for all the ships that were 'mothballed', but Henry seems to have kept a few of his smaller vessels in service all the year round, either forming a Channel guard or patrolling the North Sea. Both Scottish and Breton pirates continued to be a nuisance, war or no war, and although the king was not averse to licensing the port town to 'go upon' such pests, he had no intention of reverting to indentures. He intended that force, however deployed, should be a royal monopoly. Consequently, although the level of naval activity was much diminished between 1514 and the next war in 1522, it did not cease altogether. In addition to maintaining shipkeepers, storehouses and docks, a 'pond' was constructed at Erith in 1517 to keep some of the Great Ships 'aflote' but away from the dangers of an open roadstead, and a few new ships were built, including the *Great Galley* in 1515, an oared warship or galleasse in the design of which the king is more than suspected of having had a hand.[34] More intriguingly, Henry commissioned what must surely have been the first royal yacht, the *Katherine Pleasaunce*, a 100-ton pinnace whose first task was to carry the king and queen to his meeting with Francis I at the Field of Cloth of Gold in 1520. For that occasion a number of Great Ships were brought out of retirement to put on a show, but the king chose to travel in his own yacht.[35]

Between 1522 and 1525 England was again at war with France. The fleet was mobilised each summer, and each winter the patrols continued, but little of any significance was achieved, either at sea or on land. Between October 1522 and February 1523 some £2,400 was spent on repairing the ships at Portsmouth, and another £600 on patching up the fortifications.[36] During the campaigning season of 1523 the English navy kept the seas more or less unchallenged, but derived little benefit from this modest success. During the war Henry added two or three medium-sized ships to his fleet, and did not lose any, but the most significant acquisition was a large carrack presented by the Emperor, who may well have had cause to regret his generosity. However, it was significant that he should have made such a gesture, because Henry was now clearly perceived to be a Sea King, whose main strength was in his navy.[37] Ashore, the long-serving Robert Brygandine retired in 1523, and John Hopton died in 1524. The former was succeeded by Thomas Jermyn, who remains an obscure figure, while the latter's office was divided. While Hopton had been responsible for the Erith storehouse as well as acting as Clerk Controller, the former position now went to William Gonson, also described as a Gentleman Usher of the King's Chamber, while the latter was conferred on Thomas Spert, a sea captain of long experience.[38] Gonson was clearly a man of ability, much trusted by Wolsey, who controlled the navy (as he controlled most other things) under the somewhat erratic supervision of the king. Although there seems to have been no declared policy to that effect, Gonson began to receive block warrants from the exchequer, and to pay the actual bills at the dockyards as they arose. Both Jermyn and Spert continued to handle money directly allocated to them, so it would be an exaggeration to describe Gonson as the treasurer, but he was beginning to approach that position. There seems to have been no formal relationship between the three officers, although they must have liaised closely, and each remained directly responsible to the Council – which until 1529 meant Cardinal Wolsey.

The Cardinal did not take competition kindly, and although the Lord Admiral did not have any administrative responsibility, Thomas Howard was rather too effective for his liking. Howard had become earl of Surrey when his father was raised to the dukedom of Norfolk in 1514, and when he became duke in his turn in 1525, he was persuaded to step aside. His replacement was the king's six-year-old bastard son, newly created duke of Richmond. Henry undoubtedly ordered this move, which was why it would have been impossible for Howard to have objected, but the beneficiary was Wolsey.[39] The duke of Norfolk in theory continued in service as Vice-Admiral, but the office was effectively exercised by the Cardinal. He did not do very much with it, and only one ship, the 250-ton *Trinity Henry*, was added to the fleet during his remaining time in power, but he did maintain a programme of repairs and renewals, which kept the dockyards occupied for at least part of each year, and Gonson grew steadily in stature under his patronage. However, late in 1529 the duke of Norfolk, and Wolsey's other noble enemies, had their revenge. The Cardinal failed to find a way out of the morass in which Henry had immersed himself over his marriage, and forfeited the royal confidence in consequence. Although he was also a prince of the church, he was very much the king's man, and when he lost the chancellorship in October 1529, it broke him. He was permitted to retreat to his archdiocese of York, but allowed himself to be inveigled into intrigues with the papacy, which his enemies discovered, and in 1530 he died at Leicester on his way south to face charges of treason.[40] The Admiralty continued for the time being in the youthful hands of the duke of Richmond, but in practice for the next two or three years the work was done by Jermyn, Spert and Gonson, and particularly by Gonson.

However, without the services of his omnicompetent minister, the king was soon struggling. He did not lack advice, but what he received lacked coherence, and practicality. For over two years he tried in vain to fight his way out of the dilemma that his marriage to Catherine had become. Then circumstances conspired to favour him. In August 1532 the aged and obstreperous archbishop of Canterbury, William Warham, died, and this opened the way for the king to find a solution to his 'Great Matter' within the realm. He had already been advised to do this, but could not see a way past the archbishop.[41] Now he was free to appoint a man who would do his bidding – pope or no pope – and he chose Thomas Cranmer, a former Cambridge don who had offered him a treatise in defence of his cause.[42] Inspired by this development, Henry at last had intercourse with his 'mistress' of five years standing, Anne Boleyn, and she fell pregnant. Most important of all, he found a replacement for Wolsey in the person of the Cardinal's former servant, Thomas Cromwell. It was Cromwell who took the fairly obvious step of urging the king to use parliament to solve his problem for him, and once Cranmer had defied Clement VII and pronounced Henry's first marriage null and void, he proceeded to do just that. Although there was acute tension at court, and much opposition in the country, the parliamentary acts against the papal authority worked, and by the autumn of 1533 Cromwell was, in the view of one well qualified observer, 'ruling everything' about the king.[43] He became the king's secretary in about April 1534, and by then had fully assumed Wolsey's mantle of omnicompetence. This, of course, included the navy, and having appraised the existing officers, he came to the same conclusion, and gave his confidence especially to William Gonson.

The navy was not operational for a decade between 1529 and 1539, but the dockyards and a two-year cycle of inspection and repair were maintained through a sort of condominium between Gonson and Spert, in which the former looked after the money, and the latter made sure that the ships were where they were supposed to be. Spert also served as Captain of Portsmouth and one of the bulwarks defending the town bore his name for many years thereafter.[44] Thomas Jermyn remained very much in the background, and when he died at some time in 1537 he was succeeded by the equally obscure Edward More, described as a Groom of the Chamber, but about whom very little is known.[45] It was after Cromwell had assumed his unofficial responsibility that Eustace Chapuys, the Imperial ambassador (who could not stand him), made his disparaging remark about the readiness of the king's ships. Although this observation was contained in a dispatch to his master, Chapuys had made no secret of his opinion for a number of years, and Cromwell knew it. He had been stung into action. Between 1535 and 1539 three new ships were built, and seven rebuilt, including the *Mary Rose*, the *Peter Pomegranate* and the *Great Galley*.[46] Although some of Gonson's accounts survive from this period, they show no sign of this major activity, and it must be assumed that the work was commissioned in private yards directly by the Council, and similarly paid for by direct warrant. Presumably the operation was considered to be too important to be put through the regular accounts, but the result is that we have only archaeological evidence for the work which was done on the *Mary Rose*, and no evidence at all for the others.[47] Whatever Chapuys may have thought, it is reasonable to suppose that by 1539 all the navy's twenty odd ships would have been on something like three months' notice to be ready for sea. The practice of maintaining year-round patrols seems to have continued throughout these years, using the same small ships on a regular basis, so the machinery of mobilisation and supply was kept ticking over, even when there was no international crisis in the offing.

In 1539, however, there was just such a crisis. The Emperor and the king of France apparently resolved their perennial differences at the treaty of Toledo in January, and agreed to break off diplomatic relations with the 'heretic king'. Henry became almost paranoid, convinced that a papally inspired invasion was imminent. He mobilised his fleet, and took up a similar number of auxiliaries, but he did not, interestingly, lay down any new ships. Perhaps he felt that the situation was too urgent for such a medium-term solution. Instead, a series of hastily constructed artillery forts were built along the south coast, and the levies were mustered. It would seem that the king did not think highly of his chances of being able to intercept the threatened invasion at sea. It soon transpired that his anxiety was misplaced. Neither ruler in fact withdrew his ambassador, and the treaty of Toledo was a dead letter. A year later the Emperor and the French king were again squaring up to each other, and Henry was investigating the possibilities of a new Imperial alliance. His fourth marriage, to Anne of Cleves, negotiated partly because of his perceived need for allies in 1539, was already redundant before it happened, and promptly fell apart.[48] Then in the summer of 1540, and for reasons which had absolutely nothing to do with the navy, Thomas Cromwell fell from favour as Wolsey had done. He was promptly replaced as Lord Privy Seal but had no successor as Chief Minister, the king at last deciding to take the reins into his own hands. In the short term this did not make much difference to the fleet. William Fitzwilliam, the earl of Southampton, who had replaced Henry Fitzroy as Lord Admiral on the latter's death in 1536, now became Lord Privy Seal, and took over Cromwell's administrative responsibility in this respect, although not his omnicompetence. He was replaced as Admiral by John, Lord Russell, but that was not really relevant. Spert and Gonson now reported to Wriothesley. Edmund More, the Clerk, had died at about the time of Cromwell's execution, and had been replaced by Edward Waters. Waters, another Gentlemen Usher of the Chamber, was also Gonson's brother-in-law, so naval administration began to have a close-knit, family look about it.[49]

In spite of this, it was also beginning to appear unsatisfactory. Wriothesley did not have Cromwell's expertise, nor his application, and the king, in spite of his undoubted interest in his ships, had a short concentration span and many other things to think about. Nor was the navy doing particularly well in 1540, when the Scots had the east coast under almost constant blockade, and sailed their own warships as far south as the Channel. There was no state of war, and all these operations were strictly unofficial, but the English were being made to look singularly ineffective. In 1533 a new warship, the *Mary Willoughby*, had actually been captured by highland galleys while endeavouring to punish some piratical escapade on the west coast, and the record was altogether unimpressive.[50] Moreover by 1542 continental war was looming again. Francis I and Charles V had resumed their conflict, and Henry was in an aggressive frame of mind, perhaps needing to reassure himself that the warlike king of old was still alive in his corpulent and flagging body. He signed a new treaty with the Emperor, committing himself to a major campaign in the summer of 1543. Cromwell's disappearance also had a number of other knock-on effects. The Privy Council was reformed, to make it more of a working committee and less a rather amorphous body of advisers. This was once attributed to Cromwell himself, but it now appears to have been the king's idea, and its implementation was facilitated by the removal of a Chief Minister who liked to keep all important business in his own hands.[51] After 1540 the Council was more of an institution, with a clerk keeping regular minutes and predetermined times of meeting. Some of the king's offices also underwent a similar transformation. The Office of the Works was created out of the earlier Clerkship, and the Master of the Ordnance was given a board of assistants, including a Lieutenant and a Clerk. These had both been household offices, and now became something much closer to departments of state, with defined responsibilities, salaries, and a management structure.[52] In other words the delegation of specific responsibilities was put on a regular footing – something which would have been very hard to achieve while Cromwell was trying to maintain his personal control of all these functions. By 1545 a similar plan had been drawn up for the navy.

Meanwhile, it was business as usual. When Henry VIII had gone to war with France in 1512, Louis XII had invoked the Auld Alliance, and James IV of Scotland had invaded Northumberland. He had had no particular quarrel with the king of England, who was his brother-in-law, but the opportunity had seemed too good to miss. The result had been disaster and James's own death at Flodden, but Henry had no desire to run the same risk during his new intended campaign. He therefore decided to take out the Scots first. Using some relatively minor border infringements as a pretext, in the autumn of 1542 he launched the duke of Norfolk on a brief but immensely destructive raid into lowland Scotland. Some ships were deployed in support of this operation, but there was no major mobilisation and as a naval operation it was extremely low-key. Nevertheless it had the desired effect. Unable to ignore such blatant provocation, James launched about 20,000 men into the debatable land north of Carlisle, where in November they were caught and routed by a smaller but much better equipped English force commanded by Sir Thomas Wharton and Sir William Musgrave.[53] The battle of Solway Moss was not a bloodbath in the sense that Flodden had been but it did result in the capture of a large number of Scottish noblemen and gentlemen. James IV had not been present at the battle because he was a sick man, and on 14 December he died, leaving his crown to his week-old daughter Mary, with the prospect of a long minority. Fate, as well as victory, had now dealt Henry a strong hand, and he decided to attempt a long-term solution to the Scottish problem by marrying the infant Queen of Scots to his own son Edward, now aged five. To assist in persuading the Scots to accept this unwelcome prospect he had a large number of important prisoners who needed to buy their freedom.

The king, meanwhile, had reshuffled his government in the north. The dukes of Norfolk and Suffolk were recalled to London to prepare for the French campaign which was still intended, and the Warden General of the Marches, Thomas Manners, earl of Rutland, stood down on the grounds of ill health. On 8 November John Dudley, Viscount Lisle, was named as Warden General in his place and dispatched to Newcastle.[54] The news of Solway Moss reached him as he travelled north, and he formally took over his responsibilities on 1 December. Within a fortnight James was dead and the new Warden General was confronted with a chronically unstable regime north of the border. In theory power devolved to the Council of Scotland, but it was not really in control and late in December Henry's envoy in Edinburgh was murdered.[55] On 1 January 1543 James Hamilton, earl of Arran, was named as Protector of the Realm. Henry was doubly indignant, both over the death of his representative and also over the fact that the Council had not consulted him before appointing Arran. However he curbed his temper in the interests of the more important goal, and took oaths from all his Scottish prisoners to uphold the marriage proposal before dispatching them home.[56] Cardinal David Beaton, the protagonist of the French connection, was placed under house arrest. The Scots were not happy under this pressure, but in no position to resist for the time being, and in June Arran sent commissioners to London to negotiate a treaty. This was signed at Greenwich on 1 July, and ostensibly gave the king all that he wanted. In practice, however, this meant little. Although Arran ratified the treaty on 25 August, he was facing increasing intransigence within Scotland. David Beaton's influence remained strong, and the 'assured lords' kept their oaths only while it suited them to do so. In these circumstances, and with a large stake to play for, Henry's attention remained focused on the north, and what had been intended as a side-show took over the main stage. In May he renewed his pact with the Emperor, but effectively abandoned his intention to campaign in France that summer. In September he ordered the duke of Suffolk to mobilise an army to support Arran against his enemies, but then the earl changed sides and the situation became so confused that intervention seemed pointless. An English party, consisting mainly of religious reformers, remained in Scotland, but it was virtually powerless and in December the Scottish parliament repudiated the treaty of Greenwich.[57] A year after Solway Moss, Henry had achieved precisely nothing, except to upset the Emperor considerably by his failure to mount a continental campaign.

In spite of this, the king did not neglect the French war entirely. Optimistically assuming that the difficulties in the north were temporary, in January 1543 he appointed his Warden General to be Lord Admiral. Lisle thus became a member of the Privy Council, and for about three months doubled his responsibilities. This made some sense, as whatever naval activity there was in the first half of that year related mainly to the north-east coast, where four Newcastle ships were appointed to keep the seas between the Humber and the Tweed.[58] By the middle of March a further squadron including some royal ships was stationed in the Downs, and shortly after a third was appointed to the western approaches. By April Lisle was back in London and Lord Parr of Kendal had been briefed to take over his position in the north. As yet no formal hostilities existed between England and France, but 'neither perfite peace nor open warre … but Shippes were taken on bothe sides and merchauntes robbed', as Edward Hall observed. That situation was rectified at the end of June when the French ambassador was given an ultimatum which was timed to expire three days later.[59] War was finally declared on 2 August. This seems to have been almost an afterthought as on 15 June Sir Rhys Mansell as Vice-Admiral had already been instructed to 'go upon' the French, but to refrain from molesting any friendly shipping – which at that point included the Scots. Lisle became preoccupied with the defence of Calais, and according to Chapuys had taken up six or seven ships to reinforce the twelve of the king's own which were to be deployed.[60] On 6 July Mansell fought an inconclusive skirmish with a small French fleet, which seems to have been no more than an encounter of patrols. Individual letters of marque began to be issued in August, and then on 20 December such licence was made general by proclamation in what appears to have been an innovative attempt to mobilise the whole maritime community without resorting to the expedient of requisitioning.[61] It seems to have been assumed that self-interest would provide sufficient motivation, but whether this was the Lord Admiral's idea or the king's is not apparent.

The year 1544 was intended to be the year of major action. Nine new ships were either purchased or built, and the king was committed to launching 42,000 men against the French by 20 June. A full mobilisation of the fleet was ordered as early as February, and in the midst of these preparations, William Gonson died.

Gonson had been the linchpin of naval administration for twenty years, but his death at this crucial stage probably facilitated a reorganisation which would have been necessary in any case. In the short term Richard Howlett was appointed in January 1545 to take over the management of the Erith storehouse, but he did not succeed to Gonson's main unofficial responsibility as 'paymaster' to the king's ships.[62] In the midst of the hectic activity associated with the campaigns both at Boulogne and in Scotland a fundamental rethink was in progress about how the navy should be managed in the future. We do not know who was the driving force behind this, but it is natural to suppose that the new Lord Admiral, John Dudley, played an important part.

INTRODUCTION NOTES

1. *Letters and Papers ... of the Reign of Henry VIII*, ed. J. Gairdner *et al.* (1862–1910), XIV, I, 1510.
2. David Loades, *The Tudor Navy* (1992), pp. 74–102.
3. *Hale and Fleetwood on Admiralty Jurisdiction*, ed. M.J. Pritchard and D.E.C. Yale (Selden Society, 1993). Introduction.
4. N.A.M. Rodger, *The Safeguard of the Sea* (1997), pp. 79–80.
5. M. Oppenheim, *A History of the Administration of the Royal Navy* (1896/1988), pp. 13–15.
6. Ibid., pp. 11–12.
7. TNA E101/20/27. Robert D. Smith, 'Artillery and the Hundred Years War. Myth and Interpretation', in Anne Curry and Michael Hughes, eds, *Arms, Armies and Fortifications in the Hundred Years War* (1994), pp. 151–60.
8. Rodger, *Safeguard of the Sea*, pp. 31–50.

INTRODUCTION

9. Susan Rose, *The Navy of the Lancastrian Kings* (1982), pp. 247–52. The other Great Ships were the *Holighost* (760 tons) the *Jesus* (1,000 tons) and the *Trinity Royal* (540 tons). William Catton became Clerk of the Ships in 1413 (ibid., p. 34).

10. C.F. Richmond, 'English Naval Power in the Fifteenth Century', *History*, 52, 1967, pp. 1–15.

11. *The Debate between the Heralds of England and France*, ed. Henry Pyne (1870), p. 50.

12. David Loades, 'The King's Ships and the Keeping of the Seas, 1413–1480', *Medieval History*, 1, 1991, pp. 93–104.

13. Ibid.

14. TNA E403/784, E28/81. Winnington gave his own account of this exploit in a letter to Thomas Daniel of 25 May 1449. *The Paston Letters*, ed. J. Gairdner (1900), pp. 84–6.

15. TNA E403/724. C.F. Richmond, 'The Keeping of the Seas during the Hundred Years War', *History*, 49, 1964, pp. 283–98.

16. *Naval Accounts and Inventories of the Reign of Henry VII*, ed. M. Oppenheim (1896), pp. 3–6.

17. Ibid., Introduction.

18. Loades, *Tudor Navy*, p. 39. The *Regent* eventually carried over 200 serpentines.

19. *Naval Accounts*, pp. 82–132.

20. Ibid., pp. 143–60.

21. David Loades, *Henry VIII; Court, Church and Conflict* (2007), p. 22.

22. For a full discussion of the circumstances of this decision, see Garrett Mattingly, *Catherine of Aragon* (1942/1963), pp. 93–7.

23. Margaret Rule, *The Mary Rose* (1982), pp. 22–5. The theory that she was originally clinker built is not now generally accepted.

24. Alfred Spont, *Letters and Papers relating to the War with France, 1512–13* (1897), p. 83n.

25. Rodger, *Safeguard of the Sea*, p. 477.

26. Spont, *Letters and Papers*, pp. xii–xiv.

27. Ibid., p. xv.

28. Wolsey to the bishop of Worcester, 26 August 1512. Spont, pp. 49–50.

29. The *Henry Grace de Dieu* (called at that point the *Imperial Carrick* or the *Henry Imperial*) first appears on a list of ships 'appointed to the sea' of February or March 1513. Rodger (*Safeguard of the Sea*, p. 477) is in error in ascribing her building to 1514.

30. Edward Echyngham to Wolsey, 5 May 1513. Spont, *Letters and Papers*, pp. 145–54.

31. D. Loades and C.S. Knighton, *The Anthony Roll of Henry VIII's Navy* (2000), pp. 109–58.

32. TNA SP1/2, f.149. Loades, *Tudor Navy*, p. 68.

33. Ibid.

34. R.C. Anderson, 'Henry VIII's Great Galley', *Mariners Mirror*, 6, 1920, p. 274.

35. *Letters and Papers*, III, no. 558.

36. Estimates of expenditure, 28 February 1523. *Letters and Papers*, III, no. 2073.

37. Known as 'The Spaniard' this ship seems to have been kept for only about a year. Rodger, *Safeguard of the Sea*, p. 477.

38. TNA C66/674, m.13. *Letters and Papers*, IV, i, no. 309.

39. B. Murphy, *Bastard Prince: Henry VIII's Lost Son* (2001), p. 60.

40. For a full discussion of the circumstances of Wolsey's fall, see Peter Gwyn, *The King's Cardinal* (1990).

41. Graham Nicholson, 'The Act of Appeals and the English Reformation', in C. Cross, D. Loades and J. Scarisbrick, eds, *Law and Government under the Tudors* (1988), pp. 19–30.
42. For a full discussion of Cranmer's promotion, see D. MacCulloch, *Thomas Cranmer* (1996).
43. Chapuys to the Emperor, 24 November 1533. *Letters and Papers*, VI, no. 1640.
44. H.M. Colvin, *The History of the King's Works* (1963–76), IV, p. 409.
45. Loades, *Tudor Navy*, p. 81.
46. Rodger, *Safeguard of the Sea*, p. 477.
47. Rule, *The Mary Rose*, pp. 103–48. Loades and Knighton, *The Anthony Roll*, pp. 15–19. M.H. Rule and C.T.C. Dobbs, 'The Tudor Warship Mary Rose; Aspects of Recent Research', in M. Bound, ed., *The Archaeology of the Ship* (1995), pp. 26–9.
48. Retha Warnicke, *The Marrying of Anne of Cleves* (2000).
49. Loades, *Tudor Navy*, p. 81.
50. Richard Boulind, 'Ships of Private Origin in the Mid Tudor Navy: The *Lartigue*, the *Salamander*, the *Mary Willoughby* and the *Galley Blanchard*', *Mariners Mirror*, 59, 1973, pp. 385–408.
51. J.A. Guy, 'The Privy Council: Revolution or Evolution', in C. Coleman and D.R. Starkey, eds, *Revolution Reassessed: Revisions in the History of Tudor Government and Administration* (1986), pp. 59–85.
52. C.S.L. Davies, 'The Administration of the Royal Navy under Henry VIII; the Origins of the Navy Board', *English Historical Review*, 80, 1965, pp. 268–88.
53. M.C. Fissell, *English Warfare, 1511–1642* (2001), pp. 25–6.
54. D. Loades, *John Dudley, Duke of Northumberland* (1996), pp. 51–4.
55. Ibid., p. 52.
56. Gervase Phillips, *The Anglo-Scottish Wars, 1511–1550* (1999). Loades, *Henry VIII*, p. 68.
57. Loades, *John Dudley*, p. 59.
58. *Letters and Papers*, XVIII, i, no. 83.
59. Ibid., nos. 754, 759.
60. Ibid., no. 603.
61. D. Loades and C.S. Knighton, 'Lord Admiral Lisle and the Invasion of Scotland, 1544', *Naval Miscellany*, VII, 2008, pp. 73–5. P.L. Hughes and J.F. Larkin, *Tudor Royal Proclamations*, I (1964), pp. 345–6.
62. Davies, 'Administration of the Royal Navy'.

CHAPTER ONE

Operations 1544–1547

When Viscount Lisle was appointed Lord Admiral in January 1543, Scotland was high on the agenda. As we have seen, he was doubling as Warden General of the Marches at the time, and the active command on the north-east coast was given to Sir William Woodhouse as Admiral of the North Seas. In February Woodhouse was given command of four Newcastle ships which were taken up specifically to 'keep the seas' between the Humber and the Tweed, and his instructions were to take any Scottish ship and any intruding Frenchmen as 'good prizes'.[1] No state of war existed with either of these kingdoms, but the intention was clearly to keep up the pressure on the regency government of the earl of Arran, and to prevent the French from interfering. Whether any such prizes were taken is not clear, but it is likely that Woodhouse was there mainly as a deterrent. The diplomatic situation was delicate, and at the end of April one of Andrew Flammock's captains, serving in the Western Approaches, was reprimanded by the Council for 'staying both friends and foes' – the distinction presumably not being clear to him.[2] The war with France, which eventually came at the beginning of July, was clearly intended before that, and on 15 June Sir Rhys Mansell was briefed as Admiral of a sizeable English fleet in the Channel, which included ten or eleven of the king's own ships. His instructions ordered him to take any French ship which he could find, but not to touch the Scots, who at that point were about to negotiate the treaty of Greenwich. On 20 June the king went to Harwich to view the haven in the Colne where several of his ships were then being prepared, and pronounced himself well pleased with the arrangements.[3]

The first action of the war was fought by Mansell on 6 July, when, as he put it, 'lying in the bottom of the sea', he spied the approach of sixteen sail of Frenchmen, and the following morning between four and five o'clock, he engaged them. After a fierce exchange of artillery fire lasting almost three hours, he endeavoured to close with the enemy, concentrating his attentions upon the *Sacre*, which had become detached from the others. The *Sacre*, however, proved elusive, as Mansell's subsequent account makes clear. She was eventually rescued by her fellows, and the whole French fleet made off, being, as Mansell ruefully confessed, 'very good sailers'.[4] The only achievement of the encounter was the capture of a French hoy with 120 men on board, by the *Less Galley*. The *Minion* sustained some damage in this encounter, and would need new masts, for which she was returning to base. A second French fleet had been spotted, apparently sailing north, but had been too far off to engage. Whether they were heading for Scottish waters is not clear, but probably they were the same as those that were spotted off Holy Island on 13 August.[5] It is not known what they may have achieved. Eustace Chapuys, the Imperial ambassador, reported on 27 July that Henry was stepping up his naval activity, and that six or seven additional ships had been 'taken up'. He reported again to the same effect on 6 September, but it is not known that any further 'enterprise' was attempted that year, and the preparations may well have been connected with the dispatch of 5,000 reinforcements to the garrison of Calais.[6]

Reprisal had for centuries been a recognised means whereby merchants who had been robbed at sea could secure redress against the offenders or their fellow citizens. The procedure of Admiralty Courts (where these existed) was so loaded against foreigners that it was almost pointless to seek a remedy by that route. Letters of reprisal, or of marque, had therefore been issued by the Court of Chancery as early as the reign of Henry III.[7] At some time during the reign of Edward III, and for certain purposes, the issue of these letters had been taken over by the Admiralty Court. On 4 August 1543, Lisle used this recognised jurisdiction in a new fashion by authorising (in the king's name) Miles Middleton, Yeoman of Guard, to arm and equip two ships to the seas at his own cost, to 'go upon' the king's enemies, without any reference to a private agenda. The letters commanded all the king's subjects to aid and assist Middleton in this enterprise, and bound him in his turn to declare all his prizes before the Admiralty Court.[8] There is no reference to any reward, but presumably Middleton got an agreed cut of the profits – if any – of his efforts. Perhaps this rather vague incentive was inadequate, and too few were prepared to follow Middleton's example, but the following December (1544) the king himself took the initiative a stage further. On the 20th he declared (perhaps mendaciously), that

> being credibly informed that divers and many of his most loving, faithful and obedient subjects, inhabiting upon the sea coast, using traffic by sea, and divers others, be very desirous to prepare and equip sundry ships and vessels, at their own costs and charges to the sea for the annoyance of his majesty's enemies ....[9]

He was not only prepared to authorise this enterprise (as Lisle had done for Middleton), but to allow his loving subjects to keep the proceeds of their depredations 'without making any account in any court or place of this realm', and without paying any part or share to the Lord Admiral. This was to authorise piracy on a large scale, and although it seems to have brought out the privateers in numbers, and to have significantly assisted the war effort, it was extremely difficult to rein in once the war was over. For the time being, however, it was a new and effective way of mobilising the maritime community in support of royal policy.

Meanwhile, the English position in Scotland had fallen apart. There was still an English party, led by the earls of Angus and Lennox, but it was too weak to prevent the parliament from repudiating the treaty of Greenwich in December 1543. Henry also realised that Angus and Lennox were loyal to him more out of antipathy to Arran than from any affection for his own policies. In January 1544 his mood was savage, but he realised that there would be little point in targeting the estates of the 'defectors', even where these lay within reach of the border. What was needed was public chastisement on a grand scale. It was therefore determined to launch a direct attack on Edinburgh, an amphibious operation which would involve some 15,000 men. At the end of January the duke of Suffolk was appointed to lead this enterprise, and March was the target date.[10] It was soon apparent that this timetable was too ambitious. Suffolk accepted the mission on 2 February, asking that Lisle be appointed to assist him, but the king then changed his mind. Whatever might happen in Scotland, a campaign in France could not be further delayed. By the beginning of March, Henry had decided that Suffolk was indispensable for the continental campaign, which he intended to lead in person, and the duke was therefore relieved of his command in the north before he had had time to do anything about it. By 21 March the earl of Hertford was back in Newcastle as the new commander, and Lord Lisle had gone to Harwich to mobilise the necessary ships.[11] It was obvious however that several weeks would have to elapse before any campaign could be mounted, and the Scots would have plenty of time to understand what was about to happen. At the same time Stephen Gardiner, the bishop of Winchester, and William Paulet, Lord StJohn, Treasurer of the Household, were commissioned to provide the support services. On 24 March they reported their progress to Hertford. They were assured, they wrote, that 160 ships of various sizes had either departed or were about to depart for the rendezvous at Newcastle, thirteen of which had already set off from London and Colne. Twenty-eight other ships had been victualled for two months, and nineteen more, some as large as 300 tons, were taking on victuals as they wrote. They were also instructed to provide victuals for the whole force which was assembling in the north. 'You may assure yourself', they concluded, 'of a sufficient furniture for your number of men for 56 days in all kinds of victuals, with a great surplusage of certain kinds ....'[12] By the end of March, Hertford had almost all the men that he needed, and a good proportion of the victuals, but only a few of the ships, and one of those (the *Sweepstake*) had run aground at the entrance to the Tyne. She was floated a few days later with minimal damage, but in spite of fair winds, the rest of the fleet did not arrive.

Lisle was apparently doing his best, but either Gardiner and Paulet had been wildly optimistic in their estimate of the ships' preparedness, or the weather in the south was much less kind than it was in the north. It was probably the former, because the commissioners seem to have got their sums wrong in more ways than one. Instead of the 160 ships which they had projected, only 68 eventually set out, 10 of which belonged to the king, 48 were English ships 'taken up' and 10 were 'strangers' ships. It seems that at some point a decision had been made to use fewer and larger vessels, and that may partly have accounted for the delay.[13] It was 20 April before Lisle reached the Tyne with the bulk of the fleet, and by then only heroic efforts had prevented the waiting soldiers from consuming all the victuals provided for the campaign!

Almost the first thing that Lisle did after his arrival was to send a blistering complaint to Henry in the name of all the officers in the north about the quality of the victuals which had been provided. The bread was mouldy, and so badly baked that 'at this present it is no man's meat'. The pipes of salt beef, which should have contained 400 pieces of 2 lbs each sometimes had only a tenth of that number, and many of the pieces were underweight. No doubt there was some truth in this, and the purveyors had been cheating, but if the situation had been as black as it was painted, the expedition could hardly have set out at all. In all probability,[14] Lisle and Hertford exaggerated the deficiencies as part of a political campaign to discredit Gardiner with the king. For the time being they were unsuccessful, and at some time between 21 and 28 April the men (and their victuals) were embarked. On the 28th, Hertford, as the commander of the expedition, issued his orders to the fleet.[15] This was organised in three squadrons, with 'wafters' or scouts attendant upon each. Sea fighting was not anticipated, and the instructions were mainly concerned with signalling systems, and with the establishment of a rendezvous in the event of the fleet being broken up by storms. Every ship was to have its boats in readiness for an amphibious landing. Although the Lord Admiral was at sea in person, he commanded only the 'vanward' of the fleet, and flew his flag on the foretopmast of his ship. Although everyone was aboard by then, the fleet was still struggling to get out of the Tyne because of the contrary winds, and it was 2 May before they eventually succeeded. That, it turned out, was the difficult bit, and they were able to land without any resistance opposite Inchkeith, about two miles from Leith, on the 3rd. Hertford had about 12,000 men with him, and another 4,000 had been sent overland under the command of Lord Eure, who also seem to have encountered no opposition.[16]

Leith was fortified but not strongly defended, and an attempt to meet the English in the field before they reached the town was brushed aside with minimal casualties. This interception was led by none other than Cardinal David Beaton, whose gorgeous apparel and rapid flight were the subject of much mirth on the part of the attackers.[17] The town was comprehensively plundered, the loot being estimated at £10,000 in value, which surprised the English captains, who had apparently expected all Scottish towns to be poverty-stricken. More importantly, two of the Scottish queen's ships, the *Unicorn* and the *Salamander*, were taken in the harbour, and both were to serve with the Royal Navy for upwards of a decade.[18] The fort of Inchgarvie was also taken and razed. On the night of 4 May the English camped within the fortifications, and the fleet unloaded in the harbour the following day. Leaving 1,500 men to garrison Leith, Hertford then set out for his principal target — Edinburgh. The Lord Provost attempted to parley, but his offers were rejected, Hertford's instructions being to destroy the town. The citizens stood to their defence, and the Canon Gate was blown in with a culverin. Lord Hume and the earl of Bothwell had at the last minute sent in reinforcements, but the town was rapidly overrun and only the castle held out, which Hertford had neither the time nor the resources to besiege.[19] The castle guns inflicted a number of casualties on the English, which were glossed over in the official account, but could not save the town from the total conflagration which Hertford ordered. While this assault and destruction was in progress, the English cavalry raided as far as the gates of Stirling, destroying everything in their path, and the warships took and razed as many coastal villages and fortifications as were within reach. The destruction was immense, and very swiftly inflicted. By 15 May the expeditionary force had retreated to Leith again, where it loaded its plunder, including a lot of captured guns, into the ships for their return to Berwick. The army then set fire to the town, and set off home overland, not anticipating any effective resistance — in which they were entirely justified. Edinburgh had fallen on the 8th, and by the time that the force had retreated to Leith the Council in London already knew and sent its congratulations to the commanders — the speed of communications between London and the frontline in this campaign is truly remarkable.[20] Along with their congratulations, the Council also sent instructions for the future deployment of the force. The foreign ships were to be paid off at once, and most of the hired English ships sent back to their ports of origin. Some, however, together with the royal ships, were to join those already deployed in the Channel in preparation for the king's voyage to France. Some of the men were to be placed in the northern garrisons as a safeguard against any possible reprisals, and the rest dispatched to Calais to join the army royal which was already growing there.[21]

By contrast with the relative efficiency of the northern campaign, that mounted against France was a shambles. The naval aspect was unspectacular. Some 150 ships of various sizes were mobilised, including about thirty of the king's own, and between the middle of May and the end of June 30,000 men were transported to Calais. This was a traditional operation on a large scale, and was carried out without a hitch. It was the army which was a shambles. Henry had not troubled to co-ordinate his campaign with the Emperor, so the full impact of an invasion of Picardy was lost; the victualling system (as usual) was defective, and the duke of Norfolk was launched into an ill-considered siege of Montreuil which nearly led to disaster. Henry did not care, because he got what he wanted. On 19 July he laid siege to Boulogne, and after a tough campaign during which the navy not only blockaded the harbour but also bombarded the fortifications, on 14 September it surrendered.[22] By then the duke of Norfolk had extricated himself from Montreuil, but on the same day as the surrender, Charles V, thoroughly disillusioned with the self-serving tactics of his ally, signed a separate truce with Francis I. On 18 September Henry entered Boulogne in triumph, and then promptly returned home, leaving his commanders to pick up the pieces.[23] Fortunately for him, the French were in no position to launch an immediate counter-attack, but such an attack was bound to come, and the king of England was now on his own. In anticipation of such an attempt, the bulk of the army was left in winter quarters in and around the town, and on 30 September Lord Lisle was named as Captain of Boulogne. Lisle was less than delighted, fearing, apparently, that he would lose the Admiralty in consequence. However, no such thing happened, and at the end of January 1545 he was replaced as Captain by Sir Thomas Poynings. Mobilising the fleet for a new campaigning season clearly took priority.

The navy did not suspend its operations while the Admiral was preoccupied with Boulogne. In view of the exposed position of the garrison, the command of the seas during the winter of 1544–5 was doubly important, and at the end of October Sir Thomas Seymour was commissioned as Vice Admiral to ensure that supplies and reinforcements could be sent out at any time. Having resupplied the town, Seymour was then instructed to remain at sea, and to carry out harassing raids on the Normandy coast. However the weather soon made havoc of these careful plans. An easterly gale prevented him from getting to Boulogne, and a French fleet lying at Etaples meant that the Normandy coast was too strong to attack. He sought, and obtained, permission to divert his energies to Brittany, but then discovered another French fleet in the estuary of the Seine. Anxious to redeem his somewhat dented reputation, Sir Thomas decided to attack, only to be frustrated by yet another gale. By the middle of November he was back in the Solent, having achieved precisely nothing, and having failed to provide the 'Channel guard' of fourteen ships which his instructions had stipulated. The king was not pleased.[24]

It was not only at sea that the fleet was in difficulties by the end of 1544. By building, purchase and capture Henry had added eleven ships (eight of them over 200 tons) to his stock in just over a year, and for the first time there are signs that he was having difficulty in manning them. On 8 August, while the king was at Boulogne, an attempt had to be made in London to round up seamen who had taken coat and conduct money, and then disappeared.[25] As the main fleet was already at sea at the time, these were presumably intended to be reinforcements and replacements. By 24 January 1545 the problem had become so acute that the death penalty was decreed for any that 'depart or go from their ships without testimonial signed with their captain's hands, to any place of the land, neither for victual, water, or any other necessaries, nor for any other lawful or unlawful occasion…'.[26]

On the same day a different approach was also tried, when a second proclamation raised the mariners' basic wage from five shillings a month to six and eightpence. This stick and carrot approach seems to have worked for the time being, and for the next ten or twelve years there were no further signs of difficulty. In time of war, even the enlarged navy of Henry VIII was likely to be overstretched, not only in manpower but also in ships. While the main fleet was busy at the siege of Boulogne, private ships had to be hired (and armed) to escort the wool fleet to Calais, and even when the siege was over, Sir Thomas Seymour's responsibilities meant that ships could not be spared to protect distant ports like Bristol and Newcastle.[27] The best suggestion that the king could make in response to requests was that they should arm and send out privateers for their own protection. This was not what privateers were best at, but the ports of Devon and Dorset seem to have taken this route of self-help with some success. In fact the king's general proclamation authorising privateers had been so successful that by April 1545 an attempt was needed to impose some kind of order upon this auxiliary navy. A certain John of Calais was then appointed 'captain of all such adventurers as shall serve his majesty in this war', and those intending to serve were instructed to 'enter themselves with the said captain' at the sign of the Gun in Billingsgate. How many took advantage of this invitation is not known, but given the independent spirit of most of the operators, probably not many.[28]

The year 1545 looked like being a difficult year from the start. In Scotland both Arran and Beaton had been discredited by the English incursion, and that strengthened the hand of the queen mother, Mary of Guise, but although she became powerful enough to impose some control on the regent she did not succeed in replacing him. Then in February his forces won a small but significant victory over the English at Ancrum Moor, and Sir Ralph Eure, the

English Captain, was killed.[29] In spite of the pasting which Edinburgh had received, Scotland was still a potential threat, and could have been a real one if the French had intervened purposefully. However the major forces which were expected on both the east and middle marches in the summer failed to materialise. The complex power struggle between Arran, Angus, Lennox and the queen mother continued, and when Henry faced the great test of a French invasion in July 1545, the Scots did nothing to distract his attention. Francis was, however, wholly committed to the recovery of Boulogne, not so much for its strategic importance as for its symbolic value, and he knew that he could only succeed by securing the command of the sea. His priority therefore became the destruction of the English navy. With this in mind, at some time in March he sent to the Mediterranean fleet for the dispatch of twenty-five galleys, together with their experienced commanders Antoine Escaline and Leo Strozzi.[30] Francis knew perfectly well that in the open sea these vessels would be no match for England's sailing warships, but he did not intend to use them in the open sea, and for operations in coastal waters such as the Solent, they would be ideal. He was also counting on twelve other galleys already in northern waters, six in building at Rouen, and six stationed in Scotland. By April the English had also mobilised, but apart from mounting regular patrols did not attempt to take the initiative, apparently waiting for the French to move. In May the Mediterranean galleys arrived, and for the next six weeks or so Claude D'Annebaut, the Admiral of France, gradually mustered a sailing armada. Somewhere between 120 and 300 ships of various sizes were brought together at Le Havre, Harfleur, and various other ports on the Seine estuary.[31] An army of some 30,000 men was also being slowly assembled. Francis's strategy can be reconstructed fairly easily. He had no intention of launching a large-scale invasion of England, because his objective was the recovery of Boulogne, and the army was intended for that purpose. The fleet, and particularly the galleys, were to launch a massive attack upon Portsmouth, which was the English navy's advanced base. It would be necessary to capture, and probably destroy, the town. Any ships in the harbour would be taken or destroyed at the same time. The sailing warships would then move on to encounter the English fleet, most of which was expected to be at sea, and would now be without a base. D'Annebaut was counting on having enough ships and enough firepower to secure control of the Narrow Sea for long enough to enable the army to attack and overrun the garrison of Boulogne, cut off as it would be from supplies and reinforcements. Henry probably understood his enemy's mind well enough, but he could not afford to take chances, and Commissions of Array were issued on 7 May and 14 June, regional military commands were set up under the dukes of Norfolk and Suffolk, and musters were held right across the south of England.[32]

By early June Lord Lisle had 160 ships and about 12,000 men at his disposal, and at that time the French preparations were still incomplete, so the Lord Admiral decided to attack the Seine in the hope of disrupting or even crippling D'Annebaut's activities. However the wind dropped at the critical moment, leaving his warships becalmed within the estuary and constrained to exchange gunfire at a disadvantage with the French galleys, which were on guard and of course retained their mobility. The conditions then changed abruptly, and as the wind got up, the galleys ran for cover. However this was no help to the English, who then found themselves being driven on to shoals. Lisle consequently stood out to sea with his mission unaccomplished, and returned to Portsmouth.[33] D'Annebaut was unable to take advantage of this retreat because his own ships, apart from the galleys, were not yet ready, but it did mean that he was able to complete his preparations without further disturbance. They sailed eventually on 6 July. The French objective was well enough understood, and Lisle was in a quandary. If he got his fleet to sea, and missed the approaching attack, he would leave Portsmouth exposed. A large army had been mustered and the king was present in person, but there was no guarantee that the town could be held against such a formidable force. If, on the other hand, he kept his fleet in the harbour it would hold a strong defensive position, backed by the fortress guns. Eventually the weather probably made up his mind for him, because as the French approached, the wind blew steadily on shore, which meant that his Great Ships would have had to be warped out, and the risk of being caught in the middle of such a manoeuvre was probably just too great. Consequently, when D'Annebaut entered the Solent on 16 July he found the English fleet waiting for him in Portsmouth harbour. Apart from a skirmish with some of Lisle's scouting vessels off Alderney, he had so far been unopposed.[34]

Taking advantage of the opportunity which the English position offered him, the French Admiral landed some of his soldiers on the Isle of Wight, where they eventually suffered the ignominy of being defeated by the local levies, and on 18 July drew up his fleet in three squadrons in preparation for an attack. This was easier said than done, because by that time the wind had died away completely, and in the flat calm only his galleys retained their manoeuvrability. In spite of holding the tactical initiative, the omens were not good for the French. Although D'Annebaut still had an advantage in numbers, he had actually lost two of his biggest ships before even entering the Solent. The massive 800-ton *Phillippe*, upon which he had planned to display his flag, had burned out at her mooring without ever setting out, the result, apparently, of a disastrous accident. The almost equally large *Grande Maitresse* had sailed with the fleet, but had run aground before she had even left the French coast.[35] In spite of the deliberate pace of his build-up, there was clearly something amiss with D'Annebaut's maintenance programme. However, he eventually got his remaining ships into position, and sent the galleys into the harbour first to try conclusions with the becalmed English warships. Each galley carried one large gun, mounted in the prow where the ram had been in earlier centuries, and was capable of inflicting considerable damage while presenting only a minimal target to the enemy.[36] In this case, although they opened fire, they seem to have achieved nothing. And then a fitful wind sprang up, switching the tactical advantage immediately to the sailing ships. The English fleet began to move out into the harbour, and the galleys were forced to retreat. Thwarted of his intention, and now at a tactical disadvantage, D'Annebaut decided to withdraw.

Just why he declined battle at this point is not clear. It may be that in the absence of his two Great Ships he felt that he was outgunned. The majority of his fleet consisted of quite small vessels, which were troop carriers rather than fighting ships, and with the wind now blowing strongly his galleys were in need of protection. It may also have been that he had an exaggerated respect for the skill of Lord Lisle, who was well known to him, and whose abilities he is known to have appreciated. For whatever reason, he retrieved his battered troops from the Isle of Wight, and moved on down the Solent, heading for the open sea. The English celebrated, as well they might having outfaced a serious threat, but their celebrations were muted because in the course of the confrontation (it cannot be classed as a battle) they had lost one of Henry's favourite ships. The *Mary Rose* was old. She had been built in 1509, as we have seen, and in her original incarnation had been noted as an excellent sailer. However, in about 1536 she had been rebuilt. Her armament had been increased, and a number of new gunports inserted, which had in turn required the reinforcing of her frame.[37] When she went back into service, her firepower was greatly increased, but there are no further references to her sailing qualities, and it must be concluded that the modifications had made her rather cumbersome, and possibly a little top-heavy. When she moved out with her colleagues to confront the French galleys on 19 July 1545, disaster struck. She had, apparently, discharged one broadside, and was coming about to fire the other, when she was struck by a sudden squall. This in itself should not have mattered, and does not seem to have affected her sister ships, but Sir George Carew, the captain, had been a bit too clever, and had brought her about very sharply, causing her to keel over. Normally she would have righted herself quickly, but it was at that very moment that the wind caught her, driving her lower gunports, which were still open from the firing, underwater.[38] As soon as the water began to enter, she could no longer be brought upright, and in a few moments sank like a stone, taking the great majority of her men with her. Of some 500 mariners and soldiers on board, only about thirty escaped – 'drowned like rattens', as one contemporary put it.[39]

As soon as they heard of her loss, the French naturally claimed that she had been sunk by their gunfire, and a mythology began to build up about the *Mary Rose*. Writing a few days later to Sir William Paget, Lord Russell, who had witnessed the sinking, described her as having been 'cast away … by rashness and great negligence', while the Imperial ambassador, Francois van der Delft, who had derived his account from a survivor, attributed it to the 'misfortune and carelessness' of not having closed the gunports.[40] It was only some time later, in what was clearly an attempt to exonerate their kinsman, that the Carew family claimed that shortly before the accident, Sir George had complained of having on board 'a sort of knaves I cannot rule' – implying that the indiscipline of the crew rather than navigational error had been at fault.[41] At first, because she had gone down in no great depth of water, it was believed that the ship could be recovered, and by 31 July a team of Venetian 'experts' had been engaged. The intention seems to have been to pass cables under the wreck, and to have fastened the same to two of 'the greatest hulks that may be gotten'. If this had been accomplished at low tide, as the tide increased, so the hulks would have lifted the ship, which could then have been moved into a position where it would be exposed by the next low water. Whatever the plan, it did not work. In trying to get the *Mary Rose* upright, the salvage team only succeeded in breaking off her masts, and by 9 August Lisle was reporting that they 'could by no means' recover her.[42] Some ordnance was salvaged, and thereafter the wreck was abandoned for over 400 years. Apparently no attempt was made to recover the bodies of those who had drowned.

Meanwhile the French fleet was still lurking a little further down the coast, and D'Annebaut's intentions were uncertain. According to a letter written by Lisle to the king on 21 July he had anchored somewhere within reach of the Isle of Wight, because a further attack on the island was feared.[43] However, unfavourable winds made that unlikely, so he was probably in the lee of Selsey Bill. Lisle contemplated an attack, but did not eventually carry it out. Instead the French were allowed to move slowly along the coast as far as Dover, landing small forces near Brighton and Newhaven, which were quickly repulsed. D'Annebaut then carried out part of his original intention by crossing to Boulogne and landing 4,000 soldiers and 3,000 pioneers to help with the siege. However, he had not secured command of the sea, and if he had intended to blockade the port he was frustrated by the weather. By 10 August an easterly gale left him again upon the Sussex coast, and this time Lord Lisle came after him, looking for a fight. During their earlier encounter at Portsmouth, the French Admiral had organised his ships into three squadrons, with the galleys, rather like cavalry skirmishers, at the front. This was in accordance with the latest tactical thinking, and seems to have been designed with broadside gunnery in mind.

Lisle now adopted a similar method, and his battle orders, issued about 10 August, show him to have been abreast of his rival.[44]

> Item, it is to be considered that the ranks must keep such order insailing that none impeach another .... Item, the first rank shall make sail straight to the front of the battle, and shall pass through them, and so shall make a short return to the midwards as they may, and [are] to have a special regard to the course of the second rank, which two ranks is appointed to lay aboard the principal ships of the enemy, every man choosing his mate as they may ....

We are still a long way from the line-ahead formation and the long-distance bombardment which characterised the Armada campaign. It is clear that close-quarters gunnery, followed by boarding, was still the aim, but ships were no longer thought of as the isolated fighting units which had been envisaged in Thomas Audley's similar instructions fifteen years earlier. They were expected to sail in formation, and to support each other.

Lisle came up with the French somewhere near Brighton on 15 August, and D'Annebaut immediately deployed his galleys, as before. Lisle seems to have had only two proper galleys, and number of small 'rowbarges', so he was initially at a disadvantage. However, as the wind got up the galleys were forced to disengage, and the English recovered the initiative. A complex phase of manoeuvring then followed, in which it appears that the French gained the 'weather gauge' – that is got upwind of their enemies. Whether this cooled Lisle's enthusiasm, or the wind changed, is not clear, but after a desultory exchange of gunfire, he allowed D'Annebaut to slip away under cover of darkness.[45] The cause for the latter's desire to escape, after establishing what looked like a winning situation, was that plague had broken out on his ships. So serious was this outbreak that he had no option but to return to the Seine and demobilise his fleet. The vast expense and effort which Francis had gone to to take advantage of England's isolation had thus fizzled out with nothing accomplished. The English retained command of the sea, and Boulogne remained in English hands. After their abortive encounter off Brighton, although he did not know it, Lisle had undisputed control of the Channel. At first he returned to Portsmouth, and it was about ten days before he realised the advantage which he had been handed. Still having 12,000 men under arms, on 2 September he decided to exploit this situation by raiding the small port of Tréport. There he burned the town and about thirty small ships in the harbour.[46] This was little more than a flourish, a gesture of triumph at the end of a season which had seen both sides make enormous efforts, and which the English had survived more by luck than judgement. By the time that he left Tréport, plague had also broken out among Lisle's mariners, but his problem was nothing like as severe as D'Annebaut's, and by 13 September he had managed to carry out a rapid demobilisation, without spreading the infection right across the south of England. God was definitely on the side of the English in 1545.

The other, and more equivocal, success which the English enjoyed was in the operation of their privateers. Once Henry had given his general blessing to their enterprises, they began to swarm like bees, and because the Emperor was no longer an ally, they did not even have to pretend to be scrupulous about what prizes they took. Any ship heading for a French port, or suspected of carrying French goods, became a lawful target. In January 1545 Charles became so irritated by this behaviour that he seized all the English ships he could lay his hands on, and embargoed further trade.[47] Fortunately for the English merchants the Emperor's orders were not everywhere enforced, but his officials in Spain were zealous, and that led in March 1545 to the so-called 'Reneger incident'. Robert Reneger was a Southampton merchant who traded regularly into Spain and occasionally (illegally) to Brazil. He had frequently complained about the depredations of French pirates, and had been granted letters of marque (or reprisal) at about the same time as Miles Middleton. Over the next two years he is known to have taken several prizes, and to have suffered further losses of his own. Among these were at least two ships stopped at San Lucar in Spain as a result of the Emperor's initiative, and on 1 March 1545, he took his revenge. Lying off Cape St Vincent with four small ships, he seized the *San Salvador*, inward bound from Hispaniola. He claimed that the bulk of the cargo was French-owned, but this was a mere pretext. The ship was carrying (and he must have known that) gold to the enormous value of over 7 million marevedis (about £4,300). This loot, he later alleged, had never been declared to the Emperor's officials, and was therefore unprotected by his authority.[48] There was a diplomatic storm because, in spite of the strained relations between them, relations between England and the Empire had never been broken off. However, the Council accepted Reneger's version of the story, and Van der Delft's representations were rebuffed. Not surprisingly, when Lord Lisle assembled his fleet in April 1545, Reneger and three of his ships were on the payroll. The Council's reaction soured relations with Spain still further. For several years, and without any orders from above, the officials of the Inquisition had tended to regard all Englishmen as 'luteranos' or heretics, on account of Henry's break with the papacy, and merchants had found life increasingly difficult. Then came the Emperor's embargo and the Reneger incident, so that direct trade ceased almost entirely. When Mary began to negotiate to marry Philip of Spain in the autumn of 1553, Simon Renard, then the Emperor's ambassador in England, commented that unfortunately the two nations detested each other because of 'merchants' quarrels'.[49] Robert Reneger cast a long shadow.

On 7 April 1546 Lisle wrote to Lord Paget that, 'Every Spaniard, Portugall or Fleming that comes from the south is robbed by our adventurers, some calling themselves Scots, some wearing visors (masks) ....'[50] By then England faced another season of campaigning on her own against the French, and the costs were mounting alarmingly. The proceeds of the dissolution of the monasteries had been almost entirely dissipated, and the king was in poor health and visibly ageing. Nevertheless another major effort was projected, and in January plans were laid for a fleet of forty-five sail and an army of 20,000. In naval terms, this is less impressive than it appears, because the king had about that number of his own ships by then, nine further large vessels having been built or bought in the course of 1545.[51] In other words, the plan did not include a major take-up of privately owned ships, so it is probable that the intention was primarily defensive. However, musters were ordered, and agents sent to Antwerp and the Baltic in search of naval stores and munitions. Lisle was worried, because in spite of efforts which were being made to protect English trade in the North Sea, the warships could not be everywhere, and French privateers were inflicting considerable damage. It is unlikely that the Admiral's fears on their own had much effect, but by the end of March the king was beginning to change his mind. Probably some hint had been dropped that Francis was willing to settle over Boulogne, and since that was the main bone of contention, peace became a possibility. Negotiations began on 24 April, the English team being led by Hertford, Lisle and Paget, and the French by the Dauphin Henry, and D'Annebaut.[52] Progress at first was hesitant because hostilities had not been suspended, and both sides were looking for an advantage to take into the negotiations. The Dauphin was particularly aggressive, while Hertford had drawn up plans for an attack on Etaples. At the beginning of May supplies were still being shipped into Boulogne, and there were rumours of French naval preparations, of which D'Annebaut denied any knowledge. On the 10th or the 11th Lisle was given permission to withdraw from the negotiations to deal with this situation, which was real enough in spite of the Admiral's disclaimers. A number of French galleys had appeared off Rye, and captured a few small traders. On the 12th or 13th, Lisle attacked them, captured one and drove the rest off.[53] Having thus called D'Annebaut's bluff (if that is what it was), he then blandly returned to the negotiations, which proceeded with renewed momentum.

By this time the two admirals were old sparring partners, and had developed a level of mutual respect which boded well. No sooner was he back at the conference than Lisle confided to Sir William Petre that he found his opposite number 'a very proper man'. On 24 May a ceasefire was finally agreed, and it is clear that although Hertford was the senior negotiator, it was Lisle who was calling the shots on the English side.[54] In spite of some last-minute doubts, agreement had been reached by 6 June, and on the following day the articles were duly signed. Hertford and Paget were then recalled, while Lisle went to Paris for the formal ratification. The so-called Treaty of Camp (from having been signed in a tent) was something of a triumph for the English, and that can be partly attributed to the robust stand which Lisle had taken against the last-minute probe at Rye. Van der Delft believed that Boulogne would be surrendered in return for a French withdrawal from Scotland, but that was not the case. The Boulannais remained in English hands, subject only to the face-saving proviso that it would be handed back to France by 1554 – provided that a ransom of 2,000,000 crowns was paid (about £600,000) and arrears of pensions going back to 1515 were met.[55] Given the state of Francis's finances at the time, this was rightly seen as a virtual concession of sovereignty. Scotland was not even mentioned, except that Henry agreed not to attack again unless fresh provocation were offered. Given that border incursions were of almost daily occurrence, this meant that he had a virtually free hand – and so it was interpreted by Protector Somerset in the following year.

Following the conclusion of this peace, Henry returned his fleet to a peace-time basis, that is to say the majority were laid up at Deptford, one or two at Portsmouth, and a few of the smaller ones kept in commission for a winter guard. That was the situation when Henry died at the end of January 1547, but by then the king had been presented with one of the most remarkable documents of naval history ever compiled. This, which may have been prompted by the general demobilisation of the summer, is known as the Anthony Roll.[56] In form it is an illustrated inventory of all the king's ships, fifty-eight in number, from the *Henry Grace de Dieu* to the *Sun*, a rowbarge of 20 tons. The inventory is not comprehensive, being confined to the 'habillaments of war', and is therefore unlike the rather similar, but unillustrated, inventory which had been compiled in the like circumstances in 1514.[57] The information given for each ship consists of the tonnage, the number of soldiers, mariners and gunners that she was supposed to carry, and then a list of her guns (brass and iron), gunpowder, shot, bows and arrows, munitions (that is, tampons, cartridges, etc), and 'habillaments' generally – that is, spare wheels for carriages, timber for forelocks, and so forth. The compiler of this remarkable record was one Anthony Anthony, at the time Clerk of the Ordnance, a position which probably explains his selection of information to record. It was not a working document, but rather a ceremonial piece, and whether it was in any way solicited we do not know. Anthony appears to have prepared it on his own initiative with a view to attracting some royal patronage, but the king died before he had enjoyed the opportunity to use it for any prestige display.[58] Anthony was eventually promoted to Master Surveyor of the Ordnance, but that was not until January 1549, and whether it was in any way the result of his labour is not known. Anthony was the son of William Anthony, a brewer who had been born at Middleburg in Zeeland and who had died in 1535. He was sometimes described as a Fleming, but was in fact a naturalised Englishman, who took over his father's business, and supplied beer to the royal household. That connection led to his appointment as a Groom of the Chamber, and from 1530 onwards he seems to have acted as a regular purveyor. At the same time he entered into partnership with Henry Johnson, a business associate of his father's, and also apparently a Fleming by birth. Johnson doubled brewing with the office of Surveyor of the Ordnance, and it was through that contact that Anthony came to be involved in the supply of guns, as well as of beer.[59]

Anthony was a man of many parts. On several occasions he was licensed to export beer in large quantities, in spite of complaints by the London Victuallers, and he was a close business associate of Arthur Plantagenet, Viscount Lisle, while the latter was Governor of Calais. In 1533 he became one of the gunners at the Tower of London, a position which he almost certainly discharged by deputy, and in about 1537 he became Clerk of the Ordnance. As such he was mainly responsible for the successful demonstration of a new type of gun before the court, overshadowing his colleague Henry Johnson, although the latter was Surveyor at the time. In addition to these many functions, Anthony also compiled a chronicle of London life between 1522 and 1558, a history which was used by Stow, Holinshed and Burnet, but was never published and has now disappeared.[60] He continued active into Elizabeth's reign, and died eventually in 1563, his final account as Surveyor being submitted by his widow in 1566. Meanwhile his magnificent naval inventory had disappeared into the royal library, where it seems to have remained unnoticed for over a hundred years. In 1680 two of the three rolls comprising the inventory were given by Charles II to Samuel Pepys, who was planning to write a history of the navy. He never wrote his history, and on his death in 1703 the manuscripts passed to his nephew John Jackson. On Jackson's death in 1724 they passed in turn to Magdalene College, Cambridge, where they still remain.[61] The third roll remained in the royal library until it was given by William IV to his illegitimate daughter Mary, who in due course sold it to the British Museum. In 1999 it became part of the British Library's manuscript collection.

Some of the information contained in the Anthony Roll can be confirmed, or modified, from other sources, but the illustrations are unique, and appear to have been Anthony's own work. For many years they were assumed to be accurate, and the only mystery was why the *Mary Rose* was depicted when the ship had actually been sunk a year before the roll was compiled. It is possible that Anthony had begun his work before July 1545, but more likely that he was unaware that attempts to salvage the wreck had been abandoned. The ship was known to have been one of Henry's favourites, and he had been very distressed by its loss, so it may have been that its inclusion as a 'ghost' was a little bit of subtle flattery. The fact that most of the *Mary Rose* has now been recovered, however, has cast serious doubts upon the accuracy of Anthony's representation. The general shape of the ship, and number of masts, seems to be correct, but the distribution of the ordnance bears no resemblance to what the archaeologists have found. There was, for example, only one row of gunports at the main deck level, as opposed to the two which are shown in the illustration. The upper row of gunports, shown without lids, appears to be entirely fictitious, and in the picture there is no sign of the forward-facing cannon mounted in the stern castle which was revealed by the excavation.[62] We do not have the remains of any other ship on the list, so it is impossible to say whether the *Mary Rose*, depicted probably from memory, is less accurate than those which might have been drawn from the life, but it was probably not as they all follow a standard pattern. What is very clear from the roll, however, is the absence of standard design among the warships of the day. They fall into broad categories, but no two are identical. The first ten are large carracks, with tonnage varying from 400 to 1,000. The next eight or nine are smaller ships of similar design, some as small as 80 tons, and known as hoys. These comprise the first roll, but those of the second roll, starting with the *Grande Mistress*, are quite different. They are still sailing warships, but they no longer have the built-up castles of the carracks, having either low castles or no castles at all. Although they are rather squat and clumsy-looking, in profile they resemble the later galleons of John Hawkins's time, and although they have no oars, they seem to be modelled on the galleasses, of which the *Great Galley* of 1515 appears to have been the prototype. The *Great Galley* had been rebuilt as the *Great Barke* in 1538, and appears from Anthony's painting to have been converted into a carrack, but that should probably be taken as poetic licence.

The only oared ship in the second roll is the *Galley Subtle* of 200 tons, which was brand new, having been completed only in 1544.[63] Most of the oared ships feature in the third roll, which contains pinnaces and rowbarges, varying from 80 to 20 tons displacement and carrying no more than three or four guns. Even at the bottom end of the range, however, there are subtle differences in the designs, and it is reasonably certain that not all these ships would have performed equally well, whether in sailing or fighting. In that respect there had been little progress since 1514. What is clear from the roll, however, is that over the course of thirty years the navy had grown greatly in size, from thirteen ships to nearly sixty, and the armament of each vessel (particularly the Great Ships) had been hugely increased. In 1514 the *Henry Grace de Dieu* had carried 182 guns, of which 122 had been serpentines, or light anti-personnel weapons, and twelve might be described as heavy. In 1545 she carried only 151, but 37 of them were big. Similarly the *Mary Rose* had carried only six big guns in 1514, but that had increased to twenty-four by the time that she was lost.[64] These increases reflected a significant change in fighting tactics. Whereas in 1514 even big guns lacked the muzzle velocity to do much harm to the hull of a warship, and the fighting only took place at close quarters, by the 1540s cannon and culverin could be ship killers at a moderate range, which was why the French galleys could plausibly have claimed to sink the *Mary Rose* by gunfire. Thirty years earlier such a claim would have been too ridiculous to be made. The guns of 1545 also had much more uniformity of size and calibre than had been the case earlier, making it plausible to claim that the first synchronised broadsides were probably fired during Lisle's pursuit of D'Annebaut off the Sussex coast.[65] The instructions which envisaged ships manoeuvring in formation also imply co-ordinated gunnery, although nobody specifically described it at the time, and we are dependent for confirmation upon subsequent memories.

The increased size of the navy also meant more widespread deployment. During wartime the fleet could, and did, operate simultaneously in the North Sea, the Channel and the Western Approaches. During the Scottish campaign of 1544, not only were Newcastle and Berwick used as advanced bases, but the Colne, near Harwich, became a regular dockyard, which it remained for about twenty years. Rye and Deal were used as victualling stations, and both Bristol and Dublin were used, as was Newcastle, for local operations. There are no regular accounts for any of the dockyards at this early date, and carpenters and labourers seem to have been hired as they were needed, but there must have been a few clerks and supervisors on the 'ordinary'. There was also at least one Master Shipwright, James Baker, who was paid an annuity amounting to 4d a day in 1538, increased to 8d a day in 1544.[66] When Stephen Vaughn had been appointed as the king's financial agent in the Low Countries in 1538, he had also been instructed to purchase arms and naval stores. English ships could still be largely built out of English oak, but dependence on the Baltic for cables and ropes of various kinds, and upon Norway for mast timber, was growing. The increased size of the navy was responsible for these knock-on effects. The demand for anchorages, dry docks and workmen was growing steadily, and by 1545 it was clear that the ramshackle administration could no longer cope.

CHAPTER 1 NOTES

1. *Letters and Papers*, XVIII, I, no. 225. The *Trinity*, the *Anthony*, the *John Evangelist* and the *Mary Grace*.
2. Loades, *Tudor Navy*, p. 125.
3. Ibid.
4. Sir Rhys Mansell to Lisle, 9 July 1543, Loades and Knighton, 'Lord Lisle and the Invasion of Scotland', *Naval Miscellany*, VII, (2008), pp. 70–1.

5. Sir Ralph Sadler to the duke of Suffolk, 13 August 1543. *Letters and Papers*, XVIII, ii, no. 42.

6. Loades, *Tudor Navy*, p. 125.

7. M.J. Pritchard and D.E.C.Yale, eds, *Hale and Fleetwood on Admiralty Jurisdiction* (Selden Society, 1993), p. 15.

8. Loades and Knighton, 'Lord Lisle and the Invasion of Scotland', pp. 73–5.

9. Hughes and Larkin, *Tudor Royal Proclamations*, I (1964), p. 345.

10. Loades and Knighton, 'Lord Lisle and the Invasion of Scotland', p. 61

11. Sir William Paget to the earl of Hertford, 21 March 1544. Hatfield House, Cecil Papers 231/74. S. Haynes, *State Papers ... of William Cecil, Lord Burghley*, I (1740), pp. 15–16.

12. Gardiner and StJohn to Hertford, 24 March 1544. Cecil Papers 231/97. Haynes, *State Papers,* I, pp. 20–1.

13. TNA SP47/7, no. 15. *Letters and Papers,* XIX, I, no. 643.

14. Hertford, Lisle, Tunstall, Holgate and Sadler to the King, 21 April 1544. BL Add. MS 32654, ff.141–2. Loades and Knighton, 'Lord Lisle and the Invasion of Scotland', pp. 82–3. Lisle and Hertford were political allies against Gardiner in the Council.

15. BL Add. MS 32654, ff.160–61. Loades and Knighton, 'Lord Lisle and the Invasion of Scotland', pp. 85–6.

16. *The Late Expedition Into Scotland* (1544), in A.F. Pollard, *Tudor Tracts* (1903), p. 40.

17. Ibid.

18. Hertford and Lisle to the King, 6 May 1544. BL Add. MS 32654, ff.173–7. *Letters and Papers*, XIX, I, no. 472.

19. *The Late Expedition*, pp. 41–3.

20. Loades and Knighton, 'Lord Lisle and the Invasion of Scotland', p. 64. It is about 500 miles from Edinburgh to London, yet the Council was informed within seven days. Some reappraisal of the efficiency of the Tudor posts seems to be called for!

21. Privy Council to Hertford and Lisle, 15 May 1544, Cecil Papers 231/98. *Letters and Papers*, XIX, I, no. 508.

22. Loades, *Tudor Navy*, pp. 127–8.

23. Loades, *John Dudley, Duke of Northumberland* (1996), pp. 65–6. Instructions to the earl of Hertford, 31 January 1545. *Letters and Papers*, XX, I, no. 121.

24. *Letters and Papers*, XIX, ii, no. 281. Seymour's instructions, 29 October. Ibid., no. 581.

25. From Benjamin Gonson's accounts, 6 August to 28 November 1544, *Letters and Papers*, XIX, ii, no. 674.

26. *Tudor Royal Proclamations*, I, p. 346.

27. Privy Council to the earl of Shrewsbury, 6 Novermber 1544. *Letters and Papers*, XIX, ii, no. 560.

28. *Tudor Royal Proclamations*, I, p. 348.

29. Loades, *John Dudley*, p. 68.

30. Loades, *Tudor Navy*, p. 131.

31. Edward Hall (*The Union of the two noble and illustre houses ...*, p. 863) says 200 sail and 26 galleys, but estimates vary.

32. Loades, *Tudor Navy*, p. 131.

33. Ibid.

34. Ibid.

35. Rodger, *Safeguard of the Sea*, p. 183.

36. For a discussion of the mounting of big guns on galleys, and its effects, see J.F. Guilmartin, *Gunpowder and Galleys. Changing Technology and Mediterranean Warfare at Sea in the Sixteenth Century* (1974).

37. M.H. Rule and C.T.C. Dobbs, 'The Tudor Warship *Mary Rose*, Aspects of Recent Research', in M. Bound, ed., *The Archaeology of the Ship* (1995). S.M. Vine, 'Some Aspects of Deck Construction in the *Mary Rose*', *Proceedings of the Third Annual Conference for New Researchers in Maritime History* (1995).

38. Francois van der Delft to the Emperor, 23 July 1545. *Calendar of State Papers, Spanish*, Vol. VIII, p. 190.

39. C.S. Knighton and D. Loades, *Letters from the Mary Rose* (2002), p. 120.

40. John, Lord Russell, to Sir William Paget, 23 July 1545. *Letters and Papers*, XX, I, no. 1255. *Cal. Span.*, VIII, p. 190.

41. Extract from John Hooker's 'Dyscourse and Dyscovery of the lyffe of Sir Peter Carewe'. Lambeth Palace Library MS 605, ff.16–17. Cited in *Letters from the Mary Rose*, pp. 135–6.

42. Lisle and StJohn to Paget, 9 August 1545. *Letters and Papers*, XX, ii, no. 81.

43. Loades, *Tudor Navy*, p. 134.

44. 'Lord Lisle's Instructions, August 1545', in Sir Julian Corbett, *Fighting Instructions, 1530–1816* (Navy Records Society, 1905), pp. 20–4.

45. Loades, *Tudor Navy*, p. 134.

46. Peter Padfield, *Guns at Sea* (1973), p. 33.

47. G. Connell-Smith, *Forerunners of Drake* (1954), pp. 132 et seq.

48. TNA SP1/200, ff.95–6. Cited by Connell-Smith, *Forerunners of Drake*, p. 141.

49. Simon Renard to the bishop of Arras, 9 September 1553. *Calendar of State Papers, Spanish*, XI, pp. 227–8.

50. *Letters and Papers*, XXI, no. 563.

51. Rodger, *Safeguard of the Sea*, p. 477.

52. *Letters and Papers*, XXI, I, no. 610. Loades, *John Dudley*, pp. 75–8.

53. Van der Delft to Charles V, 15 May 1546. *Letters and Papers*, XXI, I, no. 825.

54. Ibid, nos 881, 909.

55. Loades, *John Dudley*, pp. 78–9. It appears that neither Henry nor Charles V believed that Francis would be able to meet these terms.

56. MSS Pepys Library, Magdalene College, Cambridge, 2991, and BL Add. MS 22047, edited for the Navy Records Society by C.S. Knighton and D. Loades (2000).

57. TNA E36/13, edited with the above, pp. 113–58.

58. 'The Manuscript and its Compiler', *The Anthony Roll*, p. 4.

59. Ibid., p. 3.

60. Bod MS Ashmole 861, pp. 330–50, has extracts, which Burnet used. *The Anthony Roll*, p. 9., n.10.

61. Ibid., p. 5.

62. Stuart Vine, 'The Evidence of the Mary Rose Excavation', in Loades and Knighton, *The Anthony Roll*, p. 16.

63. Loades and Knighton, *The Anthony Roll*, p. 73. John Bennell, 'The Oared Vessels', pp. 34–8.

64. *The Anthony Roll*, pp. 43, 141.

65. Padfield, *Guns at Sea*, p. 33. The evidence for this claim is not conclusive.

66. C.S.L. Davies, 'The Administration of the Royal Navy under Henry VIII: The Origins of the Navy Board', *English Historical Review*, 80, 1965, pp. 268–88.

CHAPTER TWO

THE COUNCIL FOR MARINE CAUSES

The Admiralty, or as it was more usually known, 'the king's council for his marine causes', came into existence gradually as the navy grew in size and permanence. In 1509 the Clerk or Keeper of the king's ships was, as he had been for a quarter of a century, a comparatively minor royal servant who looked after the maintenance of the king's ships when they were not actually in use. He was paid by royal warrant very specifically for jobs which he had actually done, and reimbursed for money which he had really spent.[1] There are some indications that Robert Brygandine, the Clerk at that time, had occasionally been consulted by Henry VII on matters which could be described as 'naval policy', but no sign that Henry VIII did the same. He had his own ideas about ships and the sea. Nor does Brygandine seem to have been involved in the building of new Great Ships. It is not even known exactly where the *Mary Rose* and the *Peter Pomegranate* were built, let alone who was responsible, but the *Henry Grace de Dieu* was built at Woolwich, and William Crane, later the Master of the Boys of the Chapel Royal, was the overseer of the work, while William Bond, Clerk of the Poultry, was the paymaster.[2] The king did not consider it to be inappropriate to make *ad hoc* use of his household servants, whose skills may have had little to do with their ostensible appointments, and whereas Brygandine was certainly involved with ship building at Woolwich, he may not have been on the king's business at the time. When new storehouses were built at Deptford and Erith during the first French war, a special Keeper was appointed. John Hopton operated quite independently of the Clerk. The warrants which the king signed for naval expenditure did not necessarily go to either of these officers, but were sometimes paid directly to the shipmaster, shipwright or purveyor concerned.[3] By 1520 there were docks and storehouses at Erith, Deptford, Portsmouth and Woolwich, but no sort of overall control, either financial or of any other kind – except at the highest level of the Lord Chancellor. When the ships were actually at sea, they were accounted for either by the Lord Admiral (if he was in actual command) or by the Treasurer of the War. In 1513 a special treasurer was even appointed to account for the hire of the extra ships needed, and for the payment of the wages involved.[4] Presumably this was considered to fall outside the remit of the Treasurer of the War.

This situation only began to change when the separate offices of Clerk Controller and Keeper of the Storehouses were created on Hopton's death in 1524. The Clerk Controller's duties were nowhere defined, but William Gonson, the new Keeper, soon began to receive financial warrants which were not directly connected with his obvious duties. Just when this practice began is uncertain, but as early as 1525 he was paying the wages, victuals and tonnage of two London ships which had been taken up for royal service, a function quite unconnected with his official appointment as Storehouse Keeper. In 1532 he wrote to Cromwell that he was seeking the king's ships of war on the east coast 'with money and commissions for fulfilling all things according to the king's pleasure', which also suggests a degree of overall responsibility.[5] A fragment of an account surviving from 1537 shows him paying for shipkeepers and for a trip out on the Solent, as well as for stores and the rent of storehouses. He was also paying money over to the Clerk of the Ships, and there is no indication that any of this was innovative, so this ill-defined treasurership clearly went back to the end of Wolsey's time in power. In 1538 Stephen Vaughn's appointment as financial agent in the Low Countries covered the purchase of arms and sailcloth, and the following year the 'kings merchant' in Danzig was buying naval stores more generally, but these accounts were quite separate from Gonson's.[6] In 1536, in a rather different context, Gonson was placed in charge of the ordnance when the duke of Suffolk went north against the rebels in Yorkshire, and on 4 December Suffolk wrote to the king to allow him to return, because 'we lack him both for putting things in order and for counsel'.[7] The Keeper of the Storehouses was clearly a man of many talents. He was also described as 'Teller of the Exchequer' and was Warden of the Grocer's Company in 1525. When his wealth was assessed for a subsidy in 1541, he was judged to be worth £1,000, which made him one of the richest citizens of London.[8] Clearly handling the finances of the navy was only one of his functions. He was never officially Treasurer of the navy, and money continued to be paid through other channels, but between 1532 and 1537 he spent some £15,589, and was responsible for building the *Galley Subtill*. Another good indication of his increasing importance is the fact that in March 1539 he was paid £500 with the simple instruction that it was to be deployed about 'the affairs of the sea', which was a significant departure from earlier and much more specific requisitions.[9]

By 1540, Thomas Cromwell was presiding over an embryonic naval administration which consisted of three designated officers, four or five dockyard supervisors and at least one Master Shipwright. It had, however, no institutional identity, and no line management apart from Cromwell himself. It was the Lord Privy Seal's fall from power in the summer of 1540 which led to the break-up of what was effectively his personal empire. William Fitzwilliam, the earl of Southampton, became Lord Privy Seal, Sir Thomas Wriothesley and Sir Ralph Sadler split the office of Secretary, and the Privy Council was reorganised as an executive committee. There were other, less obvious consequences which also seem to have followed. The office of the King's Works was reconstituted under a Master, with a regular accounting procedure, and the Ordnance Office and the Admiralty were reorganised. Before 1540 the Ordnance had had a Master, a Clerk and Yeoman, but no structure and only vaguely defined responsibilities. In 1540 a Surveyor was added, and that seems to have marked the point at which something like a department came into existence. The chronology of this development is uncertain, but it occurred some time between 1537 and 1545.[10] The changes in the Admiralty are somewhat easier to date, and occurred between 1544 and 1546. In 1543 John Dudley, Viscount Lisle, became Lord Admiral. Dudley was an experienced soldier who had already served as Vice Admiral since 1537, and he became keenly aware of the ramshackle nature of naval administration during the operations against Scotland and Boulogne which we have already noticed. Then in July 1544 William Gonson committed suicide, although whether this was in any way connected with the onerous nature of his responsibilities is not known. On 17 August, while the king was in France, the queen and Council issued letters appointing his son Benjamin 'to act as treasurer of sea causes after the death of his father ...', which implies that William was officially recognised as holding such a post, although no appointment is recorded.[11] Benjamin kept an account from 5 August to 29 November 1544, which survives. Just how far the rethinking had gone by the end of 1544 is uncertain, but it appears that Benjamin's treasurership was only intended as an interim measure. Early in 1545 he was named as Surveyor and Rigger (a post which did not yet officially exist), Robert Legge, 'Fishmonger of London', as Clerk Controller, and John Winter (who was a Bristol merchant) as treasurer.[12] There seems to have been a debate going on during 1545 about the number of officers required, the division of their responsibilities, and their rates of pay.

These issues were probably resolved by the end of the year, because when official patents of appointment were issued in April 1546, a rather different structure had emerged, and that was almost certainly in place before the patents were registered. The new Council of Marine Causes consisted of six officers, two (or three if we count the treasurership) existed, and the rest were new. Sir Thomas Clere was named as Lieutenant, or Vice Admiral, and he was appointed to preside. Robert Legge became Treasurer,

John Winter having died in November or December 1545; Benjamin Gonson was confirmed as Surveyor and Rigger; and Sir William Woodhouse became Master of the naval ordnance. The Council was then completed by the two officers whose positions certainly existed before, William Broke as Controller and Richard Howlett as Clerk of the Ships.[13] The Keeper of the Storehouses was not named, and seems not to have become a member until later. Individual keepers were appointed for each base, but they did not join the Council. On appointment, each of these officers' remuneration was specified. Before 1545 the Clerk Controller had received £33 6s 8d (50 marks) a year, plus 3s 4d a day for travelling expenses, while the Clerk of the Ships and the Keeper of the Storehouses had each been paid at the rate of £18 5s 0d a year, with 6d a day for a clerk and 3s a day for travelling. If William Gonson received any extra for his unofficial treasurership, it was never specified. After the constitution of the Council, however, these rates were significantly increased. The Controller now received £50 a year, plus allowances which raised his total receipts to £155, while the Clerk was paid £33 6s 8d, with allowances up to £100. The new senior officers were paid proportionately more. The Vice Admiral had £100 per annum as his fee, plus 1s 8d a day for two clerks, 10s a day travelling expenses, which anticipates him travelling with at least two servants and three horses, and £10 a year for boathire. This could have given him as much as £275 a year – out of which he did, of course, have to pay his clerks. The Master of the naval ordnance was not far behind, receiving £66 13s 4d (100 marks) for his fee, 2s 4d a day for three clerks, 6s 8d a day for travel (one servant, two horses) and £8 for boathire – a realisable total of £238. The Treasurer was also paid 100 marks, with other allowances giving him a possible total of £220, while the Surveyor and Rigger actually received rather less than the Controller – £40 and £145.[14] Compared with other royal servants these were generous sums, especially when it is considered that all these men were active in other ways, as merchants and Master Mariners, although the practice of giving them sinecure offices in the royal household seems to have been discontinued. From 1546, therefore, and probably from late 1545, the Admiralty can be classed as Department of State, like the Chancery, the Exchequer or the Court of King's Bench, staffed by salaried officers and with a defined field of competence.

What it did not have was a budget, or ordinary. Although all payments were now made through the Treasurer, and he received block warrants, it was still up to him to indent for whatever money he thought that he needed. Up to a point, expenditure was easy to calculate, because the Treasurer knew how many ships he had on charge, and which ones were due for repair or major maintenance. He also knew how many docks and warehouses he had to rent, maintain and staff. However, beyond that it got difficult, because ships were called into service for political reasons, and these could shift overnight. Storms damaged ships, which would then have to be repaired over and above the normal maintenance schedule, and the king might suddenly decide that he wished to add to his fleet. The advantage of this informal method of funding was that warrants to the treasurer could be drawn on any source which happened to have available funds – the Exchequer, Court of Augmentations, Duchy of Lancaster, or whatever – whereas an ordinary would have to be paid regularly and automatically from the same source.[15] Also, of course, the Council came into existence during wartime, when all notions of ordinary expenditure were in abeyance. Before 1540, in peacetime, William Gonson was accounting for about £4,000 a year, which, since he was not handling all the bills, probably indicates an expenditure of about £5,000. However in the four years from 1543 to 1547 the navy cost almost £200,000, which is ten times the peacetime rate. Of that massive sum £45,230 had been spent on cables, timber and other stores, while £127,846 went on wages, not including the £2,415 expended on coat and conduct money for the musters of seamen. The figures are taken from an overall estimate,[16] and not all this expenditure would have been through the hands of the treasurer of the navy. The wages of men and officers at sea would have been the business of the treasurer of the war, but even so Gonson, Winter and Legge in rapid succession would have paid out some £75,000 over the period of the war – about four times the ordinary rate.

This financial method remained unchanged until 8 January 1557, when the Privy Council, which had been fretting about the navy for over a year, came up with a significant piece of reorganisation. From the time of its creation the Admiralty had been theoretically under the supervision of the Lord Admiral. However, Viscount Lisle, who was effective, was a sea commander rather than an administrator, and his successors after he moved on in February 1547 were rather less effective. The Vice Admiral had therefore been left pretty much to his own devices, and this was not thought to be satisfactory. Just what malpractice was suspected is not known, but it seems to have related to financial control, because the whole Council was taken out of the jurisdiction of the Admiral and placed under that of the Lord Treasurer. This may have had more to do with the marquis of Winchester's desire to control all significant spending departments than with any identified malfeasance, but it was an important step. Winchester had just master-minded the absorption of the Court of Augmentations into the Exchequer, so this was a relatively small matter. However, because of the general insecurity of the international situation, naval expenditure had never retreated to its 1540 level, but instead had run at about £20,000 a year for a decade after 1547. It may well have been in the Lord Treasurer's mind to reduce this, or at least to bring it under central control. The Privy Council solemnly noted that the queen had been 'sundry time troubled with the often signing of warrants' and that her Treasurer would now take over that responsibility. Winchester, it was alleged, had agreed to do that, but only on the condition that

> ... the sum of £14,000 by year ... be advanced half yearly to Benjamin Gonson, Treasurer of the Admiralty, to be by him defrayed in such sort as shall be prescribed unto him by the said Lord Treasurer ....[17]

On that understanding, he would undertake to repair and maintain the queen's ships. It might, he added hopefully, at some point in the future be possible to reduce this ordinary to £10,000 a year.

Nothing happened immediately, because before the ordinary could be introduced, in June 1557, England was sucked into the Franco-Habsburg war, and economy was temporarily forgotten. It was only with the ending of the war in the first year of Elizabeth's reign — and with the marquis of Winchester still in charge — that the ordinary was at last introduced. In March 1559 the new queen signed a warrant dormant for £12,000.[18] Elizabeth did not like the ordinary, because it always had to be found out of the Exchequer, and reduced it first to £6,000 and then to £7,700. She preferred occasional warrants drawn on different sources, and did not mind the trouble of signing them. Winchester's formal responsibility for the Admiralty was never rescinded, but it seems not to have been effective under Elizabeth, and was never claimed by his successor, Lord Burghley.[19]

Meanwhile, the Council as established in 1546 had control of all the support services for the navy, except that of victualling. The supply of food, both for the navy and for armies in the field, had always presented problems, and was usually supervised by specially appointed commissioners, often of some seniority. Before Henry VIII's time, the responsibility for individual ships in royal service lay with the pursers, who bought in provisions for the anticipated length of the voyage, and paid with money drawn from whatever treasurer happened to be responsible.[20] However this could never work for more than one or two ships at a time, and where whole fleets were commissioned a different system had to be used. This was based on the ancient method used to provide for the royal household, whereby locally based purveyors took up supplies on the instructions of the Cofferer. These goods were paid for at 'the king's price', which was significantly lower than the market rate, because it was based upon the traditional feudal right of the king to tax his subjects in kind. This method went on being used to provision the household until Lord Burghley managed to commute all these contributions for cash payments between 1572 and 1595.[21] During Henry VIII's reign these purveyors, plus others who were specially appointed, bought food for the army or the navy as instructed by the king's commissioners. In the case of the navy, every man had a daily allowance:

> Biscuit for one man by the day, a pound of 16oz, or a wheaten loaf of 20oz.
> Beer for one man by the day; one gallon,
> Beef, fresh, for one man by the day; 2lbs.
> Martinmas beef or bacon for want of other beef, for one man by the day, ½lb.
> ...
> The fish day allowance
> Stockfish, for one man by the day; ¼ of a fish.
> Herring for one man by the day, 4 herrings.
> Butter for one man by the day, ¼lb.
> Or else cheese for one man by the day, ¼lb....'

The fish day was normally Friday.[22]

So the commissioners, knowing how many men they had to cater for, could easily calculate how much of these particular foodstuffs they required. Instructions would then be issued to the purveyors in the relevant counties to take up so much of each commodity and to deliver it to the appropriate storehouse, usually at Deptford or Portsmouth. The commissioners, or their agents, were then supposed to check the quantity and quality of what had been delivered before authorising payment. Late in the reign, when small fleets were at sea on routine patrols, and there were no victualling commissions in operation, either the Clerk or the Clerk Controller seems to have carried out these duties. Needless to say, there was fraud. As we have seen, in 1543 Lisle and Hertford complained of being short-changed on the beef with which they had been supplied, '...not doubting but that your Majesty has paid for no less'.[23]

> And also the said Neville saith that there lacketh of the complement of loaf bread, which as appeareth by such books as were delivered to him, should be here in the victuallers 2,300 dozen, which is a great lack ... which we would not believe till we saw it ourselves ....

Sir Thomas Howard had made a very similar complaint in 1513, and it was clearly a permanent problem

At first the establishment of the Admiralty made no difference to this arrangement, although by 1545 the bishop of Winchester had been dropped from the victualling commission. In that year the commission was reconstituted, and was then headed by Lord StJohn, assisted by Richard Southwell (an Augmentations official) and John Ryther (Cofferer to Prince

Edward).[24] For convenience the Customers at the port of Southampton were by this time doubling as the purveyors for Portsmouth, while Edward Baeshe and Richard Wattes in London were being used for Deptford. It was these agents, rather than the commissioners themselves, who were deciding which suppliers, brewers and bakers to use. They were also paying the bills 'up front', and hiring the small ships which were used to carry supplies to the fleet when it was at sea.[25] The commissioners were then authorising their claims, which included a recognised proportion of 'dead pays' – men theoretically provided for who did not actually exist – as their profit margin. This was not the whole story, because the daily allowances, although adequate (indeed generous) in quantity, constituted an uninteresting and ill-balanced diet. Such matters were imperfectly understood at the time, but it was realised that, even when a large fleet was in operation, the pursers of individual ships still needed cash to provide supplements, and that was also provided in the first instance by the agents or purveyors. As we know from the archaeological evidence of the *Mary Rose*, fruit and vegetables were so provided. Also gentlemen officers, who kept their own servants on board, often provided their own somewhat more delicate fare, at their own expense, and that accounts for the appearance of shellfish and chickens among the debris of Henry's great warship.[26]

Whether St John became weary of these duties, or relinquished his commission when he was appointed Lord Treasurer in February 1550, we do not know, but when the war with France was ended by the treaty of Boulogne in March 1550, it was decided not to re-issue the victualling commission. Instead Edward Baeshe was appointed to the newly created post of Surveyor General of Victuals for the Sea, and joined the Council of Marine Causes in that capacity.[27] Baeshe had been the senior London agent, and had in a sense been recognised as the 'Master Victualler' before this happened, as a protest by William Johnson, his equivalent at Portsmouth, makes clear. Baeshe's appointment was not, therefore, entirely unexpected, and it sensibly completed Admiralty control over naval administration. Henceforward all victualling requirements would be issued by the Surveyor General *ex officio*, without special commission. He would advise on the appointment of purveyors or agents, and pay all the resulting bills. For this purpose he was to receive regular tranches of money from the Treasurer, to whom he was expected to account. These accounts survive, and indicate that the system operated with reasonable efficiency.[28] Complaints from sea commanders to the Privy Council about the inadequacy of supplies almost entirely disappear – although that may be because complaints now had to be addressed to Baeshe, and most of his routine correspondence does not survive. This system continued until Baeshe's activities were placed on a contract basis (as we shall see) in 1565.

The finances of the navy were theoretically reorganised in 1557, and in practice from 1559. There were also changes in the membership of the Council. Robert Legge, the Treasurer, died some time in the autumn of 1548 – his last account terminates on 29 September – and he was replaced by Benjamin Gonson, who had been disappointed of his expected promotion by Legge's original appointment. Gonson was replaced as Surveyor by William Winter, the son of that Thomas Winter who had originally been named as Treasurer. Then on 16 December 1552 Sir Thomas Clere was replaced as Vice Admiral by Sir William Woodhouse, and Woodhouse was replaced as Master of the Ordnance by Thomas Wyndham.[29] These new appointments, like the men they replaced, were experienced merchants and sea captains. They belonged to a closely knit community, which married into each other's families, and were also upwardly mobile. Clere and Woodhouse, and subsequently Wyndham and Winter, owed their knighthoods to naval service, while Gonson and Baeshe both died rich men. By the end of Henry VIII's reign naval service was an acceptable career for a gentleman. This had not always been the case, and before 1510 gentleman captains had been rare animals. However, two factors brought about change. First, after the death of the earl of Oxford in March 1513, he was replaced as Lord Admiral by an active sea commander. In fact Sir Edward Howard did not last very long, but he was succeeded in turn by his brother, Lord Thomas Howard, soon to be earl of Surrey, who was equally practical in his approach.[30] This raised the prestige of sea service, and although Howard was succeeded by the infant duke of Richmond, he continued as Vice Admiral to be the operational head of the navy. The second factor reflected the same priority as the first. In 1513 the king appointed several of his elite bodyguard of gentlemen – the Spears – to be captains of warships. Other noblemen followed Lord Howard, like Walter, Lord Ferrers.[31] As fighting opportunities diminished, however, and the size of the navy grew, this tendency became harder to sustain. By 1545, with over 100 ships at sea, Lord Lisle was regretting that there were not enough gentlemen to go around. This was partly because captain was a military rank, and only the larger warships had been accustomed to have them; now Lisle was faced with the challenge of having to provide captains for much smaller vessels, some of which had originally been victuallers, but which needed captains if they were to join the fighting fleet.

> As concerning the mean ships ... I know none other way (I mean those that come out of the West parts and such of London as were victuallers that want captains) but to place them with mean men to be their captains, as serving men and yeomen that be most meet for the purpose ...[32]

The embarrassment was a temporary one. In general Henry's patronage had raised the honour of sea service to a position of parity with that of the army, and his interest in ships and in cosmography had meant that navigation was now considered to be an acceptable part of a gentleman's education.

This social development also had a marked impact on naval discipline. A Master Mariner, or shipmaster, who normally commanded a merchant ship at sea, held the rank of yeoman, which was one of the reasons why the laws of the sea were so draconian. In the interest of safety, the Master's word had to be obeyed.[33] Such obedience was much easier to elicit if it was enforced by the natural authority of a gentleman. So that on a warship, where the Master continued to be responsible for sailing the ship, and assigning duties to the mariners, discipline was the responsibility of the Captain. Originally the Captain had commanded the soldiers which every warship carried, but his social superiority meant that the extension of his duties to cover the seamen as well was natural and inevitable. The Master was not answerable to the Captain for technical aspects of navigation, but in every other respect he was his subordinate. It was not, therefore, irrelevant that the Lord Admiral by 1545 was always a nobleman, or that all the members of the Admiralty were either knights or gentlemen – even Benjamin Gonson who doubled as a merchant. In fact the Council of Marine Causes was a good example of the flexibility of Tudor social distinctions. William Winter, Thomas Wyndham and Benjamin Gonson were all the sons of merchants, as was John Hawkins, Gonson's successor. Richard Howlett, the Clerk of the Ships, had begun his naval career as clerk to John Osbourne, a previous Controller. They all had interests in the city of London, and substantial investments in trade; yet all ranked as gentlemen, and used that status as well as their appointments, if it came to browbeating disaffected suppliers or shipwrights.[34]

This lack of definition could, however, be a handicap when it came to the actual working of the Council. Sir Thomas Wyndham, for instance, went off on a private trading voyage to West Africa in 1557, and did not return. It is therefore of some interest that the original officers do not seem to have had job descriptions, and it was not until 1560 that this defect was remedied. A set of ordinances issued in that year states specifically:

> Forasmuch as since the erection of the said office by our late dearest father King Henry the eight there hath been no certain ordinances established so as every officer in his degree is appointed to his charge ...[35]

This may have been convenient when the said officers were doubling and trebling their careers, but now, 'considering that in these our days our navy is one of the chiefest defences for the preservation of us and our realm ...', a more professional and single-minded approach was called for. This may reflect the queen's own thinking on the subject, because, as we shall see, she was far more interested in the navy than her sister had been, but more likely the administrative flair of Sir William Cecil was responsible. Sir William Woodhouse was still Vice Admiral at that point, and Benjamin Gonson Treasurer, but Richard Howlett, the Clerk of the Ships, died in 1560 and was replaced by William Winter's brother, George. William himself continued as Surveyor and Rigger, but had additionally been appointed Master of the Ordnance after Wyndham's death in 1557. William Broke, the Controller, was to die in 1561, but was still in post at the time of the ordinances. Edward Baeshe was Surveyor of the Victuals, and according to the membership listed, the Clerk of the Store had now been added, although there is no other reference to him in that capacity.[36] By the time that these ordinances were issued the Council had acquired a house on Tower Hill to act as its permanent headquarters, which was another indicator of institutional identity, and it had also assumed responsibility for the newly erected blockhouse at Upnor, which had been built to defend the Gillingham anchorage.[37]

The ordinances start by decreeing that all the officers shall assemble at least once a week at Tower Hill for consultation about naval matters, and shall report to the Lord Admiral once a month. If these reports were ever made in writing, they do not appear to have survived, but a variety of documents which may well have resulted from these meetings do survive, as we shall see, and indicate that a strenuous stocktaking was taking place at the beginning of the new reign. It was also recorded as 'agreed' that all ships not actually in use were to be kept in harbour as economically as possible, and that meant usually at Gillingham under the guns of the new fortress. There was no war in 1560, apart from a land-based intervention in Scotland, but the peace was not secure. The Protestant religious establishment which Elizabeth had created in 1559 had aligned England against the Catholic powers of France, Spain and the Empire in the ideological split which was increasingly obvious, and the freedom to make that alignment might have to be defended at any moment. Hence, no doubt, the timing of these ordinances.

The instructions start with the Master of the Ordnance. He was responsible, not only for the guns, but also for the other 'habillaments of war' which the ships carried. Big guns were stored at the Tower of London, and were ultimately under the control of the Ordnance Office proper, so the Master was responsible for drawing these out when they were required, and for returning them to store when the ship was decommissioned. Small guns, such as hail-shot pieces, handguns and arquebusses, were stored at Portsmouth or Deptford, and remained under the control of the Master, as did the carriages, gunpowder and other equipment, such as body armour. Bows and arrows were also still in use at this point, and the Master was responsible for employing the fletchers and bowyers who kept them in working order. He was instructed to 'make a declaration' of the state of his office to the Vice

Admiral at least once a quarter, which declaration was to include an account of money spent and received, and requisitions for whatever he was going to need during the coming quarter. These working accounts were to be signed by two of his brother officers, and then countersigned by the Vice Admiral. He was also to account formally once a year direct to the Exchequer, which made him the only Admiralty officer not to account through the Treasurer. He was presumably also paid by direct warrant, although that is not clear. All the remaining officers accounted through the Treasurer, who was required to make a weekly declaration of his receipts and payments to the Vice Admiral. He was not supposed to make payments except by warrants signed by at least two other officers, but no such warrants survive, and it is not clear that this instruction was ever observed, although the weekly presence of all the officers at Tower Hill should have made it possible. More importantly, he was supposed to present detailed accounts every quarter, and a number of these quarter books, with every page duly signed by the Surveyor and the Controller, remain among the Rawlinson MSS at the Bodleian Library.[38] Although it is not included in these ordinances, the Master also accounted formally every couple of years or so to specially appointed Audit Commissioners, and these enrolled accounts are still in the National Archive.[39]

The Surveyor General of the victuals was likewise required to make no payments, except by warrants similarly authorised, and we must therefore presume that he set regular payment days to settle accounts with his purveyors. He was also required to keep quarter books, although in his case they do not appear to have survived. He drew his money in regular tranches, or 'prests', from the Treasurer of the navy, and therefore had no direct dealings with the Exchequer. The payments made to the Treasurer, which consisted of regular warrants making up the ordinary (drawn on the Exchequer), contained earmarked allowances for the victualling, as did some extraordinary warrants. It depended on what these latter were supposed to cover. In addition to accounting, the Surveyor was also supposed to present the Vice Admiral with a monthly declaration of the state of his office. Because the navy might also be called into service at short notice, and victuals took time to collect, he was also required to maintain a standby supply sufficient for 2,000 men for one month, and this, of course, had to be constantly renewed.[40] It appears to have been customary to replace these standby rations about once a month.

The main responsibility of the Clerk of the Ships was the purchase of timber, but he was required 'to enter the felling of no timber' without the agreement of three of his brother officers. There was already anxiety in official quarters over the indiscriminate felling of woodland, which had recently led to statutory control,[41] so presumably this measure was intended to ensure that the Clerk did not take more than was strictly necessary. It may also have been designed to

THE COUNCIL FOR MARINE CAUSES 51

prevent him from buying up timber at the 'Queen's price' and then selling it on at a commercial rate for his own profit. There is no evidence of such a practice at this early date, but it was certainly happening by the end of the century, when, if these ordinances were still theoretically in force, they were more honoured in the breach than the observance. The Clerk was to receive his money 'in prest' from the Treasurer, and his accounts were to be scrutinised by at least two other officers before being passed to him. He was not expected to account regularly, and there was no specification for regular reports on the 'state of his office'. The Clerk of the Store was accountable for 'provisions', by which was meant not only foodstuffs but also other materials consumed in use, such as sailcloth, cordage and kitchen equipment. He was required to keep 'perfect books' of all such provisions as came into his hands, with the prices noted. He did not, apparently, handle money, because there is no reference to his receiving 'prests' from the Treasurer, nor was he required to account to him. Instead all his issues were to be witnessed, and he was instructed to account annually to the whole Council, although it would appear that this was a stocktaking of his store rather than a financial account. Once a quarter the store was to be perused, although it is not clear by whom, 'with the remainder a shipboard', and part of his annual account was that 'the waste and expenses of every ship for the whole year ... be seen'. He was also directly responsible for the emergency supplies which the Surveyor of the Victuals was required to provide, because they were to be held in his storehouse. All this Clerk's bills were apparently paid directly by the Treasurer, and were included in his account. None of the working documents from the Clerk's office have survived.

Finally the Surveyor, Controller and both Clerks were collectively responsible for ensuring that the ships were 'from time to time grounded and trimmed' – in other words sent for routine maintenance. It was specified that all ships should be kept 'in that good order and readiness' that at least twelve sail could be 'ready to the seas' in fourteen days, and 'the rest in short time after'. This was no easy requirement, given that the total operational strength of the navy at that point was about thirty-five ships, with several others judged to be so decayed that they were of no practical use.[42] One-third of the navy was supposed to be kept on a fortnight's standby. We have no means of knowing whether this stringent condition was met, because the anticipated emergency did not arise, and the number of ships kept regularly at sea was no more than half a dozen. The document concluded with a few general conditions. Minutes were to be kept of the Council's regular meetings, 'to be entered in a ledger book ... to remain of record', and the officers were to familiarise themselves which each other's responsibilities, so that if one dropped dead, those who remained could pick up his duties in the interim before a successor could be appointed. Moreover their assistants, although not members of the Council, should be similarly briefed in case circumstances should require any one of them to step into his superior's shoes at short notice. The ordinances were to be read publicly once a quarter, and the master copy kept at Tower Hill. Clearly the Admiralty was seen as, and was intended to be, a very busy place.

These ordinances perhaps reflect a slightly higher level of professional expertise than was achieved before Henry VIII's death, but it should not be assumed that the beginning of Elizabeth's reign saw any kind of revolution in the administration of the navy. What it did see was more efficient record keeping, because, as we shall see, the policy deliberations which the Council undertook in March 1559 remain among the State Papers.[43] It may be that these were copies of the minutes, which were sent to Mr Secretary Cecil for his perusal and information. The minute book itself, if it was ever kept, is no longer extant, but Cecil was an avid collector of policy documents, and a compulsive hoarder. The administrative revolution (if it may be termed that) came in 1545–6. This sort of 'government by committee' was also unique in Europe. When Francis I was faced with a similar requirement in France, he created an equivalent of Portsmouth at Havre de Grace, and a multiplicity of local officers, *controleurs, commissaries*, and *tresoriers de la marine*. These were made responsible to a special Secretary of State, but had no coherence as a department.[44] They operated separately, rather as the Clerk and Clerk Controller did in England under the direction of Wolsey or Cromwell, and the French never took the additional step of creating an Admiralty. When it came to mobilising a large fleet, such as that which D'Annebaut led against England in 1545, the admiral had to rely upon co-ordinating the efforts of numerous local controllers, a system which caused both delays and confusion. In Spain a similar system applied, which was one of the reasons why Philip was to find it so difficult (and expensive) to assemble the Armada in 1588.[45] By 1546 the Council for Marine Causes had assumed an *ex officio* responsibility for operations which would hitherto have been dependent upon numerous specific commissions, and it is reasonable to assume that the division of responsibilities so carefully laid down in 1560 had largely been in place from the beginning. The ordinances in other words were more of an *aide-mémoire* than an innovation.

The creation of the Admiralty did not, however, change one important aspect of the navy, and that was the need to 'take up' or requisition privately owned ships. Henry VII had revived the medieval practice of paying bounties of between one and five shillings a ton to private shipbuilders for any vessel over 80 tons, on the condition that they should be available for royal service when required.[46] Although the need for such service diminished with the increase in the number of the king's own ships, it by no means disappeared. Henry VIII continued this system, but raised the limit to 100 tons. His bounties mostly consisted in the remission of customs duties, but they were occasionally paid in cash. Of the twenty or so ships which are known to have been built on this basis, seven were constructed between 1540 and 1547, when the royal fleet itself was at its maximum size.[47] In the spring of 1539 Marillac, the French ambassador, estimated that the whole English warfleet would number 150 vessels, which was more than three times the number that the king possessed, and the number assembled against D'Annebaut in 1545 was no less.[48] Bounties continued to be paid after Henry's death, but the ships so supported constituted only the tip of the iceberg of the ships which were deemed to be available. An incomplete list of 1560 contains the names of seventy-nine ships of over 80 tons, and a much more complete list of 1577 shows 136 over 100 tons.[49] A really large private shipowner, like William Hawkins of Plymouth, might have as many as thirteen vessels, the largest of which was over 500 tons. It was such men (together with the London livery companies) who were first called upon when the Admiralty was in search of auxiliaries. Of course by 1560 there was a considerable difference between a merchantman and a man-of-war, but many of these private ships had been built to serve either purpose. Not only did trading into distant and potentially hostile environments like West Africa require ships which were able to defend themselves, but since 1545 privateering (not to say piracy) had been a lucrative sideline. In other words the privately owned warship, which had virtually disappeared between 1485 and 1545, was now making a comeback, and was to feature prominently during the tense naval stand-offs of the Elizabethan period.

Insofar as there was a revolution in naval strategy at the end of Henry VIII's reign, it consisted in the appearance of these armed merchantmen. Their guns, like the ships themselves, were privately owned, and whereas once upon a time noblemen would have kept armouries in their castles, now big shipowners kept artillery in their warehouses. The implications were different, but a form of private warfare was being waged at sea, the difference being that the protagonists were no longer next-door neighbours or disaffected aristocrats, but shipmasters preying on vulnerable Frenchmen or Flemings. The more the latter responded in kind, the more necessary it was for regular traders to go armed. As we shall see, this was to be an increasing problem during the later sixteenth century. The crews of such ships were also paid on a different basis. Whereas a seaman who shipped on a naval vessel was paid a wage and provided with victuals, the mariner on a merchantman or privateer was paid with an agreed share of the takings, and this might be a much more attractive prospect.[50] It had already forced up the naval base-rate from five shillings a month to six and eightpence, and it would force it up again later. The more piracy and privateering flourished, the tougher became the competition for crews, and although this was a problem which had only just begun to surface by 1547, it was destined to run and run. By the time that Henry VIII died, the navy was big business, because the distinction between peace and war was no longer as clear-cut as it had once been. Not even the king knew whether he was theoretically at war with Scotland or not; peace with France was uneasy; and relations with the Emperor were tense. As the country's first line of defence, no regime could afford to neglect the Admiralty.

CHAPTER 2 NOTES

1. For example on 25 October 1509, Brygandine received £1,175 14s 2d for work carried out on the *Sovereign* in dock at Portsmouth. TNA SP1/2, f.149. *Letters and Papers*, I, no. 1393.

2. TNA, E36/5, ff.131, 152. C.S.L. Davies, 'The Administration of the Navy under Henry VIII', *English Historical Review*, 80, 1965, pp. 268–86.

3. For instance to 'John Browne owner of the Jermayne of Toppesham'. Davies, 'Administration', p. 270. Also 'To John Iseham and George Howard for the wages, victual and tonage for 2 ships called the Barbara and the Mary Barking'. Alfred Spont, *Letters and Papers relating to the War with France, 1512–13* (NRS, 1897), p. x n.

4. Sir Thomas Wyndham, Spont, *Letters and Papers*, pp. 109–21.

5. 15 August 1532. *Letters and Papers*, V, no. 1228.

6. W.C. Richardson, *Stephen Vaughn* (1953).

7. Suffolk to the king, 4 December 1536. *Letters and Papers*, XI, no. 1239. Loades, *Tudor Navy*, p. 76.

8. *ODNB*, sub William Gonson.

9. Ibid. *Letters and Papers*, XIV, ii, no. 781. BL Arundel MS 97, f.65.

10. H.C. Tomlinson, 'The Ordnance Office and the Navy', *English Historical Review*, 90, 1975, pp. 19–39. Davies, 'Administration', Appendix A.

11. TNA E351/2193. William's suicide may have been connected with the execution of his son David, a knight of Malta, for treason in 1541, although the interval seems rather a long one. According to the official account he 'feloniously killed himself' but since he was buried in his parish church, either this is an error, or the crime was hushed up – probably the latter. *Letters and Papers*, XX, i, nos 125–7. *ODNB*.

12. *Letters and Papers*, XX, ii, App. 27.

13. TNA C66/788, mm.27–30.

14. Davies, 'Administration', Appendix B.

15. Loades and Knighton, *Elizabethan Naval Administration* (NRS, forthcoming).

16. TNA SP10/15, ff.23–4.

17. *Acts of the Privy Council*, VI, p. 39.

18. TNA E351/2199. Loades and Knighton, *Elizabethan Naval Administration*.

19. Never formally claimed, that is. Both as Secretary and as Lord Treasurer, Cecil had his fingers in every administrative pie. See D. Loades, *The Cecils; Privilege and Power behind the Throne* (2007).

20. TNA C47/37/14, mm.16, 7–12. Loades, *Tudor Navy*, pp. 34–5.

21. Allegra Woodworth, *Purveyance for the Royal Household in the Reign of Queen Elizabeth* (1945).

22. Bodley MS Rawlinson 846, ff.132–3.. *British Naval Documents, 1204–1960*, ed. J. B. Hattendorf *et al.* (NRS, 1993), pp. 102–3. This document actually dates from 1570, but these allowances had been in use for at least forty years.
23. BL Add. MS 32654, ff.141–2. Loades and Knighton, 'Lord Lisle and the Invasion of Scotland', p. 82.
24. TNA E101/62/40. *Letters and Papers*, XX, I, no. 215.
25. Davies, 'Administration', p. 275.
26. Margaret Rule, *The Mary Rose* (1982), pp. 184–201.
27. TNA E351/2194. M. Oppenheim, *A History of the Administration of the Royal Navy ... from 1509 to 1660* (1896/1988), p. 103.
28. TNA E351/2353 etc.
29. Loades, *Tudor Navy*, p. 153.
30. Spont, *The French War of 1512–13*, pp. xli–ii.
31. Ibid., pp. xxxviii–xxxix.
32. *State Papers of Henry VIII* (1830–52), 7 August 1545.
33. Dorothy Burwash, *English Merchant Shipping, 1460–1540* (1947/1969), pp. 35–81.
34. *ODNB*, sub William Gonson.
35. This document is undated, but can be confidently assigned to 1560. TNA SP12/15, no. 4. Loades and Knighton, *Elizabethan Naval Administration*, pp. 40–1.
36. Ibid.
37. MS Rawlinson A.200. Loades and Knighton, *Elizabethan Naval Administration*.
38. MSS Rawlinson A.200–6.
39. TNA E351/2199 etc.
40. *APC*, VI, p. 39. TNA SP12/15, no. 4.
41. Statute 1 Elizabeth, c.15. *Statutes of the Realm*, IV, p. 377.
42. TNA SP12/3, ff.131–4. *British Naval Documents*, pp. 63–4.
43. *British Naval Documents*, pp. 62–70.
44. Gaston Zeller, *Les Institutions de la France au XVIe Siecle* (1948), p. 333. Robert Doucet, *Les Institutions de la France au XVIe Siecle* (1948), ii, pp. 652–4. Davies, 'Administration', p. 278.
45. G. Parker and C. Martin, *The Spanish Armada* (1988). G.P. Naish, 'Spanish Documents relating to the Armada', Navy Records Society, *Miscellany*, Vol. 4 (1952).
46. B. Dietz, 'The Royal Bounty and English Shipping in the Sixteenth and Seventeenth Centuries', *Mariners Mirror*, 77, 1991, pp. 5–21.
47. Loades, *Tudor Navy*, p. 92.
48. Ibid., p. 131.
49. TNA SP12/11, no. 27. SP12/96, no. 267.
50. G. Connell-Smith, *The Forerunners of Drake* (1954). K.R. Andrews, *Elizabethan Privateering* (1964).

CHAPTER THREE

THE NAVY OF EDWARD VI

When Henry VIII died at the end of January 1547, he left as his heir his son Edward, who was a boy of nine, and a group of men who had formed the majority of his Privy Council, but whose status was now that of executors of his will. What he did not leave was any clear instructions for the formation of a regency government.[1] This was probably because his own mind was not made up, and he regarded his will as a work in progress, rather than from any deliberate intention. However what he had done (or someone had done on his behalf) was to insert a clause empowering his executors to take whatever steps they deemed to be necessary for the safety of the realm. On 30 January the earl of Hertford, the new king's maternal uncle, informed him of his father's death, and brought the boy to London. The following day parliament was informed and the session dissolved. On 31 January also, the executors made certain crucial decisions. They constituted themselves into the Privy Council of King Edward VI, and they created two offices – that of Protector of the Realm and that of Governor of the King's Person – bestowing both upon the earl of Hertford.[2] On 1 February they waited upon the king to obtain his formal assent to their proceedings, and to arrange his coronation for 19 February. The political infighting which accompanied these rites of passage does not concern us here, but one of the consequences of the new arrangements was a distribution of honours and offices, allegedly in conformity with the late king's wishes. The earl of Hertford became duke of Somerset; Viscount Lisle became earl of Warwick and Lord Great Chamberlain; and Sir Thomas Seymour (the Protector's brother) became Lord Seymour of Sudeley and Lord Admiral.[3] Seymour was not content with these arrangements, believing that he should have been made Governor of the King's Person, and applied himself only slackly to the duties of the Admiralty.

Dispatches were sent to the Emperor, the king of France and the regent of the Low Countries, bearing the official tidings of Henry's death, and greetings in the name of the new king.[4] No greetings were sent to the pope, which indicated that Edward's government would continue where his father had left off; and no greetings were sent to the regency government of Scotland, with whom the Protector considered himself to be at war. At the end of May 1546 a group of Protestant rebels had broken into St Andrews castle, murdered Cardinal David Beaton, and dug themselves in. Naturally they looked to England for support, and in September Henry had sent a small fleet of six ships led by the *Pauncey* and the *Minion* to provide them with supplies and munitions. The king was careful not to send any troops, but his fleet orders did include raids on the coast of Fife.[5] Such a gesture was a long way short of open warfare, but sufficient to remind the earl of Arran that his conflict with England was unresolved. The *Pauncey* and her consorts seem to have wintered at Harwich, and no sooner had the pressing business of Edward's coronation been dispatched than Andrew Dudley, the earl of Warwick's brother, was sent to take command of them, '… as well for the annoyance of the Scots bruited to prepare to pass towards France, and for the interruption of such munition as is looked to be brought for Scotland out of France …'.

His instructions were detailed but imprecise. He was to proceed to Holy Island, discharge some of his victuallers there, presumably for the benefit of the garrison, and then to blockade the Scottish coast, keeping a particular eye open for '28 sail of Scots which we hear be directed out of Scotland into France …'.[6] Whether this fleet ever really existed is uncertain, but what the instructions amount to is an order to inhibit any communication between Scotland and France, and to keep the seas northwards from Norfolk. As far as the garrison of St Andrews was concerned, Dudley was to establish communications (if possible), and to put on a display of strength 'to the terror of our enemies and the comfort of our friends', but not actually to do anything which might have been helpful. It was not until March that William Elmes was sent with new instructions, specifically for the re-supplying of the castle, from which it would appear that Dudley had indeed made an earlier attempt, but that his victuallers, inadequately protected by the warships, had been seen off by the Scots. Elmes was instructed to 'encounter' with any such ships as he might find, and particularly to intercept any coming from Iceland.[7] Whether he was successful in either part of his mission is not apparent, nor to what extent he was operating independently of Dudley, whose instructions continued in force. At the beginning of March two Scottish merchantmen were intercepted off Boulogne by the *Bark Aucher*, and one of them was forced aground. Low-key hostilities continued at sea throughout the summer, and Lord Grey, the governor of Boulogne, wrote intermittently to both Somerset and Dudley about ship movements which he considered to be threatening or suspicious.[8]

In spite of this apparent vigilance, however, the English were outmanoeuvred at sea. Somerset was informed on 9 July that a strong force of sixteen or eighteen French galleys had passed through the straits of Dover, heading apparently for Scotland, but had totally failed to do anything about them. By the 13th they had passed Berwick on their way to Dunbar, and on the 25th their commander, Leo Strozzi, laid siege to St Andrews castle. Heavily bombarded and without any succour coming from England, the Castilians surrendered on 30 July.[9] The following day Lord Clinton was briefed to go to their relief. Clinton was provided with twelve warships and six rowbarges, which would have carried a force of about 3,000 soldiers in addition to the mariners. Whoever drafted his instructions knew about the arrival of the French galleys, but did not know about the fall of the castle, as their main thrust was about how to deal with the galleys and break the siege. Only as an afterthought was he instructed to raid the coast of Fife if the castle had already been surrendered. Clinton was also given the task of escorting as far as Berwick the fleet of merchantmen which were carrying the supplies, victuals and munitions for the overland campaign, which was already taking shape, and which must have been decided upon several weeks earlier.[10] The instructions did not in fact reach Clinton until 9 August, by which time he already knew of the fall of St Andrews, and knew also that the secondary purpose, 'to get into his hands the Governor's son', was now as impossible as the first. However, there still remained the task of supporting the army which was then assembling at Newcastle.

From the moment when he assumed power, Somerset had treated Scotland as unfinished business. Although it seems clear that the English were the aggressors at sea, every move was justified as a response to Scottish hostility. Even Clinton's instructions (which were not intended for public consumption) spoke of 'our ancient enemies the Scots' who were supposed to have 'spoiled sundry of our subjects upon the seas …'.[11] The arrival of Strozzi and his galleys off St Andrews provoked a positive frenzy of self-righteous indignation, and the impending invasion was justified as the 'conservation of the treaties of peace and marriage heretofore concluded between our father of most famous memory and the Governor and three estates of that realm …'. This reference to the treaty of Greenwich, which the Scots parliament had repudiated in December 1543, makes the nature of the Protector's purpose perfectly clear. The invasion force which was poised in Northumberland in August 1547 was the natural and coercive sequel to the savage attack of 1544 – it was another stage in the 'rough wooing' which was intended to enforce the unity of the Crowns.[12] The earl of Warwick, as Lord Lieutenant, was already in the north, where he had been supervising the gathering of troops and supplies. On 27 August Somerset himself arrived, and on the 28th, which was a Sunday, the whole force was mustered and inspected. The march commenced the following day, and on the 30th the duke reached Berwick, where Clinton's fleet already lay. Although, unlike 1544, this was an invasion over land, Clinton was in command of a fleet of sixty-five sail, of which thirty-four were royal warships. Since the beginning of March, Robert Legge, the

Treasurer of the Navy, had received £20,690 on twelve separate warrants, most of which had been spent on the assembling of this fleet.[13] An estimate, drawn up in April or May, had presented two alternatives. To transport an army of 15,000 by sea from Berwick to the Firth of Forth would cost £22,810 in a full calendar month, to which would have to be added another £2,000 for the tonnage of 9,000 tons of additional shipping. To transport a similar force over land would cost £24,113 for the same period. In either case the victuals would cost an additional £6,000.[14] So expense was not the deciding factor in the determination to go overland, and eventually the whole cost of the campaign, which lasted just over a month, was £45,912 for the army, and about £20,000 for the navy, which shadowed the soldiers the whole way to Leith and back, but took no part in the action.

William Patten, who wrote a contemporary (and eye-witness) account of the campaign, makes it clear that both sides were expecting the French to intervene, and the main point of having so large an English fleet on the coast was to prevent that. The fact that no such intervention was attempted makes the fleet look rather redundant, but that was not how it was seen at the time. As the army advanced into Scotland, Lord Clinton periodically came ashore to consult with Somerset, but this was mainly about victualling, because it seems that the army was not carrying much in the way of supplies, and was depending upon provisions being regularly landed. On 10 September the two field armies encountered near Mussleborough, the English coming from the south, and the English fleet already stationed in the Firth of Forth, to the north. Patten's account of the battle is long, detailed and circumstantial, and his assessment of the Scottish casualties is exaggerated, but the outcome was a total English victory.[15] The next day the nearby town of Leith was occupied, having been deserted by its inhabitants who had (to Patten's chagrin) taken all their valuables with them. 'Somewhat of woad, wines, wainscot and salt were found ... so nothing else of value', as he commented disgustedly. On the 13th, 'certain of our small vessels', that is the rowbarges, took Kinghorn on the north shore of the Firth, and burned it to the ground. They also took the island of Inchcolm, beyond Leith, but found the abbey deserted. Somerset, alert to its strategic possibilities, then decided to hold and fortify the island in an attempt to 'utterly [deny] the whole use of the Firth itself ...' to the Scots.[16] A garrison of 150 men, commanded by Sir John Lutterell, was installed on the 17th. On the 15th Clinton made a more spectacular strike, attacking the castle and harbour at Blackness. He did not succeed in taking the castle, but managed to cut out the *Mary Willoughby*, the *Anthony* of Newcastle and the *Bosse*, three ships of between 150 and 200 tons, the first two of which had been taken by the Scots on the west coast in 1533. Seven other vessels 'laden with merchandise' they burned at their moorings.[17]

A few days later, on the 18th, Somerset decided to make a more telling strategic use of his victory by establishing a garrison and small naval base at Broughty Crag (now Broughty Ferry), further north on the estuary of the Tay, for the purpose of controlling access to the important towns of Dundee and Perth. On the 20th Clinton and the newly knighted Sir Andrew Dudley approached the castle, the *Galley Subtle* 'going something before the navy', and fired a few token shots. The castle then surrendered, apparently by prior arrangement, and Clinton and his associates landed to inspect the fortifications. According to a report which they sent to Somerset on the 24th, the Italian engineer who accompanied them judged the whole place to be so weak that it would take many weeks of work to make it defensible.[18] This was potentially serious, but there seemed to be no immediate threat of attack, so Clinton decided to leave Dudley with 100 men and six weeks' victuals to begin the work. He also decided to leave the *Mary Hamborough* (a hulk of 400 tons), the *Phoenix* and the *Bark Aucher* to patrol the Firth, and so that their crews could assist the pioneers. Clinton was hopeful that the whole hinterland would 'come in' to the king of England, either out of self-interest or for fear of the warships' guns. As we shall see, that turned out to be over-optimistic. By the time that he received this report, Somerset was on his way home, having reached Lauder on the 19th and found it deserted. On the 23rd he reached Roxborough, and on the 29th crossed the Tweed into England.[19] He had every reason to be satisfied with a campaign which, as far as it went, had been extremely successful. However, the Scottish commissioners who were supposed to come to Newcastle to negotiate peace never turned up, and on 4 October their English equivalents gave up waiting for them and returned south. It was an ominous portent, and indicated that in spite of having been defeated, the Scots were far from subdued. Within a few weeks Lutterell was writing to Somerset from Inchcolm that he could not possibly control the Firth of Forth without the same kind of naval presence which Dudley enjoyed at Broughty Crag. Dudley had loaned him the *Bark Aucher*, but the Scots were assembling ominously to attack him, and he doubted his ability to hold out.[20]

The garrisons were a problem from the start, depending as they did upon naval support, supplies coming in by sea, and occasional somewhat slippery support from local Scots. The *Phoenix*, for example, was running backwards and forwards between Broughty Crag and Holy Island, not only bringing in provisions, but also money to be deployed in bribes, notably £1,000 for Lord Patrick Gray (one of the 'assured lords') who was supposed to be helping the English cause. Gray apparently told Dudley, as he reported on 14 November, that at least 1,000 men were needed at Broughty, and if they could be brought in at once it would save a lot of trouble in the future.[21] Lord Grey of Wilton, Somerset's Captain at Berwick, was much concerned to reinforce Inchcolm, and in response to Lutterell's pleas wrote to Somerset on 26 November, supporting his request for more naval back-up, and also for more guns and powder. In other respects the garrison commander may have been complaining too much, because an independent assessment carried out at the same time judged that he was fully victualled for three months.

Meanwhile, on 22 November, the Scots attacked Broughty with a force estimated at 3,000 men. The town of Dundee, which had submitted to Dudley in October, now supported the attack. The fort would almost certainly have fallen if Thomas Wyndham had not been able to bring a seaborne force from Newcastle in the nick of time. He commanded two warships, the *Lion* and the *Tiger*, and several smaller vessels, bringing both supplies and reinforcements. By landing 300 of the latter close to the town he not only forced Dundee to submit again (for what that was worth), but also raised the siege.[22] It was a temporary respite, because before the end of the year Somerset was already finding that the maintenance and supply of some twenty-four garrisons, stretching from Broughty in the north to Ayton Castle in the south-east and Cockpool in the south-west, was imposing great strains on his limited resources. Strenuous efforts were made during December, but Wyndham was constantly complaining that his ships were damaged, his men sick or their pay inadequate, and early in 1548 the policy for the south-east coast seems to have been re-thought. In February the garrison at Inchcolm was abandoned, and Lutterell was sent to relieve Dudley at Broughty.[23] There he remained out on a limb, with one ship and 200 men; enough (just about) to hold the fort, but not enough to overawe Dundee, which by January 1548 had reverted to a hostile stance. However the politics of the area were complicated, and internal feuding between different Scottish groups enabled the English force at Broughty to survive with occasional support from Wyndham and his ships until 1550, when the earl of Warwick abandoned the whole interventionist policy.

By May 1548 Somerset realised that the situation in Angus was getting out of control, and decided that another major effort would in the long run be cheaper than the war of attrition which was currently being waged. Another long and detailed set of instructions was given to Lord Clinton, putting at his disposal nineteen ships and two pinnaces, led by the *Great Bark* and the *Jesus of Lubeck*. He was to take up any other ships which he might need, and the victuals which were already prepared at Holy Island and Newcastle. He was then to proceed to the Firth of Forth. If a French fleet was already there, he might engage it if he thought fit; if not, he was to ensure that no such fleet arrived. In consultation with Sir Thomas Palmer he was then to install a new fortress at Inchkieth, presumably to replace that abandoned at Inchcolm, and then proceed to the support of Sir John Lutterell.[24] The intention seems to have been to re-impose an English ascendancy on Fife and Angus, and to 'teach a lesson' to those Scots who had reneged on their promises of assistance. However, very little seems to have been accomplished, and on 12 June, reporting to Somerset on his recent return from Haddington to Berwick, Lord Grey noted the arrival of a large French fleet off Dunbar. There were sixteen galleys and five Great Ships – a total of 120 sail.[25] They were on their way to Leith, where a few days later they discharged about 6,000 French troops. While this was in progress several of the galleys (which were not troop carriers) set off for Broughty Crag, hoping to establish French influence there and eliminate Lutterell's garrison. However they too miscalculated the political climate of Angus, and did not achieve their objective. Where Clinton's ships may have been while all this was going on is not at all clear, although it seems likely that they were weather-bound at Newcastle or Holy Island. The important thing is that they were not where they were needed, and thanks to that omission the whole situation in Scotland had been turned around. Following the English victory at Pinkie Cleugh many Scots, particularly those of a reformed persuasion in religion, were willing to do business with the Protector. Although the Scots were not in submissive mood, French influence was at a low ebb, and many nobles and lairds were uncertain where their true interests lay – hence the fluctuating position in Angus which enabled the small garrison at Broughty to survive. Now, with substantial force of French veterans on Scottish soil, the waverers were coming round to that side. Six thousand men would not have been enough on their own to have defeated a full English field army, which was stiffened with German mercenaries for these northern campaigns, but they were quite enough to reduce a few garrisons, and to make sure that the local people withheld their goodwill, and supplies, from the remainder. The galleys may have been disappointed of their objective in Angus, as Lutterell reported with some satisfaction on 20 June, but the presence of French soldiers in their midst did a great deal to restore Scottish morale, and to make Somerset's already difficult task impossible.[26]

The first consequence was the signing of the convention of Haddington on 7 July 1548 between Andre de Montalembert, Sieur d'Esse, the French commander and the Scottish regent. D'Esse clearly had diplomatic status as well as military, and was empowered to sign a marriage agreement committing the young Dauphin to marry the six-year-old queen of Scots. Mary was then promptly smuggled out of Ayr on the west coast on her way to France. The English navy was on the wrong side of the country, and Somerset's whole Scottish policy was in ruins. However, he either felt himself too far committed to be able to withdraw with honour, or he was just too obstinate. Haddington was, apart from Broughty, the main English garrison in the borders, and it was under French siege. An army of over 10,000 men under the earl of

Shrewsbury was assembled at Berwick to go to its relief, and Clinton, who had retreated to Harwich to re-victual, was now instructed to return to the Firth of Forth by way of Holy Island, collecting an additional 1,000 men on the way.[27] The French fleet was still at Leith, and this time he was given specific orders to seek it out and destroy it. Somerset seems to have been getting impatient with his Admiral. However, once again Clinton failed to complete his assigned task. On 10 August he reported that he had found twelve French supply ships and had burned them, but the main fleet had eluded him.[28] Desperate to restore his reputation he blockaded the Forth for several weeks, but the horse had bolted. Shrewsbury forced d'Esse to lift the siege of Haddington, but he did not pursue his campaign with any vigour. No battle was fought and by the beginning of September he had retreated to Berwick and demobilised his force. The French promptly reinvested Haddington, and by the end of the month Clinton had abandoned his blockade and sailed south, allegedly driven by deteriorating weather.

Broughty Crag had been reinforced in August and again in October, but Lutterell was soon complaining in the same vein as Dudley had done about inadequate back-up and supplies.[29] It is not quite clear how many men he had under his command at this point, but it must have been a substantial force, because in November 1548 Somerset withdrew his German mercenaries, and then revictualled the rest for six months. He must have considered the remaining force to be viable, and we do not hear any further complaints from Lutterell. The complex manoeuvres of the late summer and autumn of 1548 can be traced through the extensive correspondence which survives, but are remarkable mainly for their inconclusiveness. There are, for example, repeated references to negotiations with supposedly pro-English lords, such as Lord Ruthven, but nothing ever came of them.[30] The general weakening of the English position must have deterred many such lords from showing their hands. At the same time, relations with France were delicately balanced. Officially, neither side was anxious to extend hostilities beyond Scotland, but neither government was completely in command of its own agents. Threatening gestures were made against Boulogne, and there was an exchange of gunfire in August, occasioned by a dispute over the building of a mole, which the French alleged to be a fortification, and consequently against the terms of the peace.[31] Worse was the escalation of what can only be described as piracy. As the Council admitted to Lord Admiral Thomas Seymour on 7 August, 'we do stand in very doubtful terms with France, and yet there is no plain war …', so letters of marque could not be issued. In principle Scottish ships were legitimate targets, but French were not, but the constant French traffic into Scotland made the whole situation very amorphous. Moreover the discipline of the French captains themselves was far from perfect. On 9 August

Seymour reported that five English crayers had been taken by the French, and he wrote to the Vice Admirals of Devon and Cornwall, authorising them to organise an attack upon the French fishing fleet returning from Newfoundland, by way of reprisal.[32] On 7 September John Graynfyld reported to Seymour that there had been an engagement off Brest, which had resulted in ten French ships being captured, and several others driven ashore, which was probably the result of this permission.[33]

Unfortunately by the end of the year Thomas Seymour's own position was unravelling fast. His wife, the queen dowager, Catherine Parr, died in childbirth during September. Seymour had already been making improper advances to the Princess Elizabeth, who had been removed from the queen dowager's household in consequence. Now he began to approach her again, this time speaking of marriage, which would have been a treasonable offence without the consent of the Council. At the same time he was suspected of trying to raise a party in the House of Lords to get his brother the Protector's patent annulled by statute. He consequently could not afford any imputations against his conduct as Lord Admiral, and he had left himself wide open.[34] Not only had he kept well out of the way when there was work to be done in the North Sea, leaving the whole operation against Scotland to Clinton, as his deputy. He was also more than suspected of collusion with the pirates who he was supposed to be controlling, which had ratcheted up the tensions at sea at a sensitive time in the interests of his own private profit. When he was arrested in January 1549, a number of such charges were brought against him. After his execution in March, Henry II hoped that England would become a prey to internal dissent, and that the war in Scotland would be abandoned. However he seems to have wildly overestimated the amount of support which there was in England for the former Lord Admiral, and Somerset ordered musters in the north during April, for an army to assemble at Berwick on 20 May for a fresh major effort.[35]

Although Lord Clinton does not seem to have deployed more than about twenty of the king's warships at any time during 1548, the whole navy, as it was surveyed in January of that year, numbered fifty-three ships, more or less where it had stood in 1545. The *Artigo* had been sold, and the *Great Pinnace*, the *Mary James* and the *Mary Thomas* had disappeared, probably scrapped, while the *Mary Willoughby* and the *Bark Aucher* had been added by capture. No new ships appear to have been built or purchased in the year following Henry's death.[36] The deployment of these ships in the middle of the close season suggests the anxiety of the times. No fewer than forty-two were at Portsmouth, which was the advanced base and whence ships would be called out should any emergency require it. Six were at Deptford and one (the *Great Harry*) at Woolwich, which were the reserve anchorages. Just four were noted as being 'in Scotland', and of those only the *Mary Hamborough* was of any size.

Nearly all the ships which Clinton is known to have had on the Scottish coast during the autumn were now back at Portsmouth, so presumably the *Mary*, assisted by two pinnaces and one rowbarge, was maintaining a token presence in the Firth of Forth.[37] Robert Legge's last account as Treasurer, which runs from December 1546 to December 1547, shows an expenditure of £41,000, which confirms that the navy was being kept on a war footing during that period.[38] Interestingly, the distribution of this expenditure does not correspond at all with the location of the ships recorded slightly later. A massive £18,824 was spent on timber, cordage and other maintenance supplies at Deptford, while only £1,211 was similarly spent at Portsmouth. Woolwich saw an expenditure of £4,167 and Harwich £3,439, which suggests a good deal of coming and going between Deptford and Portsmouth. The unusually large amount spent at Harwich was because that was the base for the North Sea fleet when it was operating against Scotland. During the same accounting period £6,926 was spent on the wages of officers and mariners at sea, which roughly corresponds to the scale of the known deployment. Of this money £16,287 was received from the Exchequer, £6,317 from the Court of Augmentations, £11,000 from the mint, and the balance from lesser sources.

By the time of Lord Seymour's arrest in January 1549, naval policy had been to some extent rethought. A memorandum of the 22nd of that month suggests that a more limited deployment was intended in support of the Scottish campaign which was planned for that summer. Ten ships are listed 'for the winter season', three of them (including the *Pauncey*) being of 400 tons or more. This was the familiar winter guard which had been mounted in the Channel for more than twenty years. It would require, it was estimated, 1,516 men and would cost £1,175 a month. However, a similar number of ships were now listed 'for the summer season' – rather larger on average, and different vessels; 1,730 men, costing £1,361 a month.[39] No particular assignment was made to either of these guards, and while that was normal in the winter, when the instruction was simply to 'keep the sea', it was very unusual for a summer fleet to be assembled without some defined objective. Perhaps someone was just thinking on paper, but in spite of the fact that musters were held for an expedition, no instructions appear to have been issued to the Lord Admiral. There are one or two problems with these January estimates, because the *Double Rose* and the *Fleur de Luce*, both assigned to the summer guard, are listed as being pinnaces of 50 tons, whereas in the Anthony Roll they appear as rowbarges of 20 tons.[40] Presumably they had been rebuilt and enlarged between 1545 and 1549, although there is no trace of such work in the Treasurer's accounts. This, however, should alert us to the fact that there is much that we do not know about how the navy operated at this time. There were, for example, bases both large and small at Deptford, Woolwich, Portsmouth, Erith, Harwich and Colne. Deptford, Woolwich and Portsmouth were large facilities, and were in operation all the year round, although at different levels. We know that, before the end of Henry VIII's reign, big jobs were undertaken there, and that shipwrights, carpenters, caulkers and other workmen were hired by the week or by the day. However, there must have been clerks and supervisors employed on a longer-term basis to assess the work and to do the hiring. Between the Council for Marine Causes and the casual workforce, there was a stratum of employees about whom we know nothing, and whose existence can only be deduced.

The first time that this silence is broken is in 1548, when there is a 'declaration of such persons as be in ordinary wages'.[41] This lists nineteen named individuals and fourteen unnamed at six different locations, starting with William Holstocke and Thomas Morley who appear from the context to have been employed at Tower Hill itself. Sometimes it is clear what these men are being paid for; for instance at Gillingham there were John Harford, victualler, and Thomas Haynes, clerk; but in other cases their functions are not specified. There were messengers 'riding in post' and purveyors, and unnamed and unlocated shipkeepers. The total for the wages and victuals of this miscellaneous group was £386 18s 10d. We do not know why this list was drawn up, or exactly what it represents, because it cannot be a complete statement of all those who were on the regular payroll. If there were three clerks, a victualler, a purveyor and eleven shipkeepers at Deptford, and three unspecified employees at Harwich, there must have been more than a single clerk at Portsmouth. Unfortunately the Treasurer's detailed accounts do not survive from this period, and the summary accounts do not distinguish between the regular and the casual employees. Given that there were docks, storehouses and forges at several of these locations, and extrapolating backwards from the first Elizabethan Quarter Book, we should probably conclude that a yard like Portsmouth or Woolwich probably employed a dozen or so men on a regular basis.[42] Deptford would have had considerably more, and a small yard like Colne perhaps just two or three. Major repairs or rebuilding might be undertaken at Woolwich, Portsmouth or Deptford, but only minor work elsewhere. Sometimes new building was undertaken in an existing naval yard, but more often it was contracted out to one of the numerous private yards which lined the Thames and the Medway, in which case the bills might be paid directly by the Exchequer without passing through the Treasurer's accounts, which is another source of confusion when trying to reconstruct the manner in which the naval infrastructure operated.

What we can tell from these accounts is that the navy was being maintained on a war footing, even after the war officially came to an end in

1550. Benjamin Gonson's first account as Treasurer runs from 28 September 1548 to 24 October 1551, and shows an expenditure of £66,250 in a little over three years, with no noticeable falling away towards the end.[43] In the course of 1548 most of the 20-ton rowbarges so favoured by the old king were abandoned. Some were either rebuilt or (confusingly) replaced with pinnaces of the same name. Other new pinnaces were built, such as the *Seven Stars* and the *Moon*. Three further pinnaces were acquired in the course of 1549, although whether they were built or purchased is not clear. Apart from the recovery of the *Mary Willoughby*, no new large ships were added, although soon after the outbreak of war with France in August 1549 a French galley of 200 tons, known as the *Black Galley* or *Galley Mermaid*, was taken in action near the Channel Islands.[44]

The hostilities which had this rather unexpected result were the direct consequence of French opportunism, because in July and August 1549 England was convulsed with civil disorder, and Henry II was clearly intent on taking advantage of her anticipated weakness. The rebellions in East Anglia and the south-west had, as far as we know, no naval implications. The only seaport involved was Exeter and there were no naval ships there at the time. When it became necessary to abandon the intended campaign in Scotland, a minimal naval presence was maintained on the Scottish coast, and the garrison at Broughty continued to be supported. The rebellions were first contained and then defeated, using the German mercenaries who had originally been recruited for use in Scotland. The direct consequences were slight, in spite of alarmist reports of the complete collapse of law and order, but the indirect consequences were profound – no less than a complete change of regime.[45] A tense few days in early October saw the Lord Protector overthrown by the Council, and the earl of Warwick emerge as the new leader. The details of this coup do not concern us here, but one aspect of Somerset's alleged misgovernment was his obstinate refusal to accept defeat in Scotland.[46] After the treaty of Haddington and Mary's departure to France, there was absolutely no point in spending resources upon so lost a cause. But Somerset would not see it, and if it had not been for the domestic rebellions would undoubtedly have spent another £50,000 or £60,000 upon a campaign in the Lowlands and up the east coast. Plenty of other charges were brought against him. He had ignored the advice of the Council and governed through his own personal servants; he had favoured the rebellious commons against the gentry, their natural lords; but it was the deployment against Scotland which really united influential opinion against him. Warwick did not immediately emerge as the Protector's replacement, and indeed he never took the title of Protector. There was a power struggle within the Council and it was December before Dudley emerged as the clear victor.[47] Nevertheless, in spite of all this uncertainty, the

French attacks on Boulogne continued to be beaten off. 'Chatillon [the king noted in his Journal] besieged the pier of Boulogne, made in the haven, and after long battery of 20,000 shot or more gave assault to it and were manfully repulsed ....' They then tried 'placing ordnance against the mouth of the haven' to prevent any supplies coming in by sea, but the garrison set upon them by night and dismantled their pieces. A further attempt 'beat divers ships of victuallers', but the English supply vessels kept coming, and 'refreshed divers time the town'.[48] In other words the English retained control of the sea, so that as long as the garrison was prepared to go on fighting, it would not be short of the means to do so.

This was important because the earl of Warwick was a realist. By the middle of October fresh levies had been ordered for the relief of the town, and on the 22nd of that month Sir Thomas Cheyney and Sir Philip Hoby were sent to the Emperor requesting permission to recruit more mercenaries. Charles was reluctant to do business with an heretical government, or to endanger his fragile peace with France, but he eventually agreed to allow the English to take up 5,000 foot and 600 horse in Friesland – provided that they were shipped out direct.[49] It is by no means clear that the whole number were recruited, but at least the shipping condition could be met. By the beginning of November, the English position was thus surprisingly strong, and Warwick, who had no sentimental attachment to Henry's last conquest, began to put out feelers for a deal. The intermediary was a Florentine merchant resident in London, Antonio Guidotti, who contacted Chatillon in Paris. The latter's response was cautious, but positive, and this was the signal for a further round of mind games.[50] By this time the English garrison in Boulogne had been both supplied and reinforced, and the governor, Lord Cobham, was talking bullishly about recovering the outworks (such as Ambleteuse) which had been lost to the earlier French attacks. He knew, and so probably did Warwick, that the besieging French were being troubled by desertions and by inadequate funding, so it was a good time to talk tough. Warwick was also a realist in other ways, because he did not share Somerset's hankering after an Imperial alliance. He knew that England's Protestant religious settlement was always going to make relations with Brussels difficult, and he was prepared to take his friends where he could find them. So when commissioners were appointed on both sides on 8 and 10 January 1550, he allowed a delicate hint to be dropped that he was prepared to discuss a marriage alliance between Edward and the young French Princess Elizabeth.[51] He was prepared, as Somerset had not been, to write off the treaty of Greenwich, and when the fortress at Broughty was overrun by the Scots later in January, he was not prepared to take any steps to recover it.

Negotiations formally began on 19 February, after a number of procedural wrangles in which the two sides jockeyed for position. Opening salvoes were then fired by both sides. The French demanded the unconditional return of

Boulogne, and the English demanded arrears of French pensions going back thirty years. These were mere gestures. The French position was nothing like as strong as they had hoped it would be, and when it became clear that Lord Paget, who was the chief English negotiator, was authorised to sell Boulogne for what he could get for it, a deal was quickly struck.[52] The French were to recover Boulogne, and receive all the military supplies currently in it, in return for 200,000 crown down and another 200,000 on 5 August. Prisoners were to be exchanged and all privateers recalled. Scotland was not specifically covered, because there were no Scots at the negotiations, but Paget agreed to suspend hostilities. This treaty, which was signed on 24 March, has been described as a shameful abandonment of England's interests, but in fact Warwick had got £160,000, which he badly needed, in return for a place of no particular strategic importance which cost a fortune to defend and maintain.[53] In spite of the fact that Scotland was not included, the English abandoned their aggressive stance in the north, and the remaining garrisons, including Haddington, were abandoned. French influence remained paramount, but France was no longer a hostile power, and the Scots reformers were able to spread their message without the taint of being associated with English aggression.

With the coming of peace, it might be supposed that the navy would have been scaled down, but that did not happen, largely on account of the increasingly hostile stance being taken by the regent of the Netherlands, Mary of Hungary. Because the Emperor was increasingly a martyr to gout and other ailments, Mary was effectively in charge of Imperial policy for long periods, and she was anxious to exploit England's supposed weakness. Moreover, after the treaty of Boulogne, English privateers, no longer authorised to operate against the French, were increasingly turning their attention to the Flemings. This was simple piracy, but the English Council seemed to be unwilling (or unable) to control it. In September 1551 Mary wrote to the bishop of Arras, the Emperor's Secretary,

> We must therefore have a port in that country at our disposal, either by force or through friendship. Many people are of the opinion that the kingdom of England would not be impossible to conquer, especially now that it is a prey to poverty and discord …[54]

Charles's ambassadors, first Van der Delft and then Scheyfve, kept up a barrage of complaints and threats, both over piracy and over the king's treatment of his religiously conservative sister, Mary. It is probable that most of this was bluster, because as he faced a renewal of his conflict with France, the Emperor had no desire to add another enemy, but it is more than sufficient to explain why the earl of Warwick did not feel that it would be appropriate to lower his guard at sea.

Warwick had resumed the office of Lord Admiral after Thomas Seymour's attainder, and at the conclusion of the war, on 4 May 1550, he handed it on to

Lord Clinton, who was already an experienced sea commander.[55] This did not result in any change of policy, but there was a certain amount of clarification. On 8 June the Privy Council ruled that all ships not in use should (once their officers and crews had been paid off) be laid up at Gillingham, and on 14 August ordered that all those ships which were currently moored at Portsmouth should be brought round to the Medway.[56] In spite of this instruction, it is clear that the main reserve anchorage continued to be at Deptford, and a further instruction to the same effect in 1559 was similarly ignored, which raises interesting questions about the independence of the Council for Marine Causes. The accounts show that the summer guard was maintained, and we do not know what the mobilisation period for these laid-up vessels was supposed to be. In similar circumstances early in Elizabeth's reign it was intended to be three weeks, but that was ambitious and in 1550 it is unlikely to have been much less than two months. During this period of 'cold war' with the Emperor, only three ships of any size were acquired. The *Gerfalcon* was probably bought, the *Primrose* built and the *Mary Willoughby* rebuilt. The latter two were launched together on 4 July 1551, when the king recorded in his Journal that he had been banqueted by Lord Clinton at Deptford before witnessing the launch.[57] Edward was interested in his navy, but not unduly so. In December 1551 he noted plans for the fortification of Portsmouth harbour, and in August 1552 he visited the work in hand while he was on progress in the area.[58] At about that same time the navy was resurveyed, and this shows that a new *Bark of Bullen* had been acquired, and the little *Trego Reneger* had disappeared, and that the galleys had been laid up permanently as being of no further use. Their crews had been paid off in February 1551.[59]

The most important administrative change to follow the end of the war related to victualling. As we have seen, the custom in peacetime had been for many years that the pursers of individual ships bought in supplies as they needed them from the purveyors who were based in each port. Provisions for the shipkeepers, and for the workmen employed at each base, were organised and paid for by the supervising Clerk. In wartime, when many ships would have to be victualled together, commissioners were appointed with the responsibility for locating and buying in the food needed for the fleet. The purveyors then worked under the supervision of the commissioners, and were paid by them, but the commissioners' remit extended far more widely, and they used agents other than the purveyors to find the necessary supplies. They were inevitably fairly remote figures, and their quality control often left a great deal to be desired. Presumably when a commission was in place the purveyors no longer considered it to be part of their responsibility to ensure that what was supplied was adequate. After the death of Henry VIII, a transitional system seems to have operated, because although Lord Paulet's commission does not seem to have expired until he was promoted to be Lord Treasurer, in fact Edward Baeshe and Richard Wattes, as Surveyors of the Victuals, presented a consolidated account from 1 July 1547 to 28 June 1550.[60] Baeshe had been one of the purveyors based in London for a number of years, and was, as we have seen, already recognised as the 'senior' victualler before his joint commission with Wattes was issued. This commission was exclusive, and all the money allocated to victualling during that three-year period passed through their hands. All together they spent £31,234 11s 3d. In spite of the fact that part of the fleet was based at Newcastle throughout 1547 and 1548, no victualling expenditure there is recorded. Presumably all the provisions were brought up from the south, and indeed the constant references to victuallers plying up and down the coast would seem to confirm that.

Finally, on 28 June 1550, Edward Baeshe was appointed by patent Surveyor General of Victuals for the Sea, and joined the Council for Marine Causes in that capacity.[61] This was a logical extension of the policy previously represented by the joint commission. Baeshe received nearly all his money through Benjamin Gonson, the navy Treasurer, on earmarked warrants from the Privy Council, and accounted to him. One consolidated account survives, running from 28 June 1550 to 29 September 1552, in the course of which he spent £17,572, mostly at Woolwich (with which Deptford was included) – £8,382 – and Gillingham (via Rochester) – £6,137. The other ports for which victualling accounts were rendered were Portsmouth and Dover.[62] There was no base at the latter town, but purveyors were located there and the sum spent (£646) probably represents the revictualling of ships at sea which is known to have taken place in the Downs during the period of the account. It may also be that the appointment of a Surveyor General was intended as an economy measure, by placing in charge an officer who had at once more clout and greater accountability. If such was the intention, it does not seem to have worked. Baeshe's joint account shows an expenditure of over £10,000 a year, while his first solo account is in the region of £8,500, but the first period was mainly one of war, when the expenditure was naturally higher. When the Commission of Enquiry into the king's finances reported in December 1552 one of its specific recommendations was the discontinuance of the office of Surveyor, along with the reduction of 'riding charges' and other extraordinary expenses. It also made vague but ominous noises about 'discharging the admiralty', as part of its brief to increase revenue and reduce expenditure.[63] However the Council wisely decided that the international situation precluded such drastic economies, and eventually none of the recommendations were implemented.

Nevertheless the navy did do something to earn money as well as spend it. For the first time in a decade, naval ships were available for private hire, and of course the Admiralty officials, all of whom doubled as London merchants, had the first call. William Winter and Benjamin Gonson hired two large men-of-war, the *Jesus* and the *Matthew*, for a trading voyage to the Levant in 1552.[64] Such ships were not ideal as load carriers, but were intended rather as escorts to deter the attentions of the Barbary corsairs, which plagued all traders entering the Mediterranean. Of course damage was a risk, and on 6 November the partners entered into recognisances for £1,208 to return the *Matthew* in the state in which she had been hired.[65] What the tonnage charge may have been for such rental is not recorded. At the same time another group of merchants who had (as far as we know) no Admiralty links, hired the *Mary Willoughby* and the *Gerfalcon* for a similar voyage to Spain – again probably for protection rather than as cargo ships. The records are not complete, and other merchants probably did the same. Although some of the navy's strength could be so deployed while the country was at peace, Warwick had no illusions about the fragility of England's position. Friendship with France was theoretically sealed with a marriage treaty between Edward and Elizabeth in June 1551, but the wedding never took place and in fact the alliance depended more upon a common hostility to the Emperor than upon any other shared interest.[66] Warwick not only maintained naval expenditure at around £20,000 a year for the rest of the reign, but also continued to pay a five shillings in the ton bounty to all those who built merchant ships of more than 100 tons, which could be taken up as naval auxiliaries when circumstances required.[67]

It may have been a coincidence, but within a few days of the commission being set up to investigate the royal finances, on 6 August 1552, a fresh survey was conducted into the state of the navy.[68] This identified a total of forty-eight ships, most of which had also appeared in the Anthony Roll of six years previously. Of these, twenty-four were described as 'in good case to serve', with the proviso that they needed to be grounded and caulked once a year 'to keep them tight'. These were presumably the ships whose maintenance programme was up-to-date, which would be consistent with the amount of money then being spent at Deptford and Woolwich. A further seven, including the *Anne Gallant*, which had only been built in 1545, needed to be 'docked and new dubbed to search their trenails and ironwork'. In other words the structure of these ships needed to be investigated, rather in the manner of a motor vehicle now which needs a major service rather than a routine one. Three others were already drydocked 'to be new made at your lordships pleasure', although it is not recorded where they were docked, or why the rebuilding had not been carried out. Presumably funds were short again. All these ships were thought to be basically sound, and the renovation work, where it was needed, was worth carrying out. However, there then followed two short lists of those not thought worth the keeping. First there were four, including the *Unicorn* which had been taken from the Scots in 1544 and the

Christopher which had been bought from Bremen in 1545, which were now 'thought meet to be sold'. With the exception of the *George*, which had been built as a hoy in 1546, these were all large, of uncertain age, and probably rather cumbersome. They were eventually disposed of, but not during Edward's lifetime.[69] Finally, there were five which were simply to be disposed of, presumably by breaking up. This was not quite as negative as it might appear, because every time a vessel was scrapped a great deal of the timber and iron work was salvaged and reused, so that it is sometimes quite hard to tell a breaking-up from a rebuilding. At the end of the list there are three notes, one describing the *Bark of Bullen* as being 'in Ireland, whose state we know not', a second mentioning that the two galleys (the *Subtle* and the *Mermaid*) and the *Brigandine* (which appears to have been a 40-ton pinnace) would need annual repair 'if your lordships pleasure is to have them kept', and a third noting that the *Grand Mistress*, which had been built as recently as 1545, was drydocked but not thought worth the rebuilding.

This document tells us quite a lot about how the navy was being run at the time. Clearly there was a 'core list' of thirty-one ships which were being more or less regularly maintained, and several of which were in regular use. The solitary presence of the *Bark of Bullen* in Ireland indicates the low priority accorded to that area of operations. The *Bark* was probably there to catch pirates, or at least to make a show of doing so, but when troops had been transported to Ireland, as was needed from time to time, local ships were taken up at Liverpool or Bristol for the purpose. The six ships which were listed to be scrapped had presumably not been maintained for some time. Wooden ships deteriorated rapidly, whether they were in use or not, and once they had been allowed to go beyond a certain point would have been prohibitively expensive to renovate. The budget had obviously been tight since 1550. Nor was the list necessarily complete, because we know that the old *Trinity Henry* was laid up at Colne in 1562, and had not been in a usable state for years.[70] Presumably the surveyors in 1552 simply forgot about her.

In other respects, the evidence for naval activity between the end of the war and Edward's death is scrappy. In April 1551 two unnamed ships, one of which may have been the *Bark of Bullen*, were sent to Ireland, which seems to have been a regular, if most unglamorous, posting. Two years earlier, in May 1549, equally unnamed royal ships had actually succeeded in arresting some Irish-based pirates who were brought to England for trial.[71] This piecemeal evidence, and the testimony of the survey, should, nevertheless, remind us that the Irish Sea not only carried quite a lot of Anglo-Irish trade, but was also a back door to Scotland. A minimal naval presence there was the least that any responsible government could ensure. As we have seen, the accounts indicate that summer and winter guards were maintained throughout this period, and this is confirmed by some surviving Council letters. The naval accounts, however, do not reflect the most important maritime development of the reign, because, although it was to have a profound effect upon the later history of the Admiralty, it was initially a commercial rather than a military enterprise. Half a century before, Henry VII had somewhat tentatively backed those Bristol merchants who financed the transatlantic explorations of the Cabots, John and Sebastian. The results had been disappointing, and Henry VIII had not followed his father's example. Individual entrepreneurs, such as William Hawkins, Robert Thorne and Roger Barlow, had tried unsuccessfully to persuade him, but the king's interest in the sea did not really extend beyond fighting the French in the Channel.[72] He had no notion of challenging Spain in the Atlantic, or Portugal in the Far East. No sooner was Henry dead, however, than Sebastian Cabot returned to England. He was by this time an old man, and had been for a number of years Charles V's Pilot Major, based in Seville. Charles was understandably chagrined, and refused at first to believe that Sebastian had come of his own free will. We do not know why he came – it was certainly not for the money – but he seems to have hankered for years for an opportunity to work in England.[73] He brought with him all the secrets of the *Casa de Contratacion*, and his coming transformed the maritime culture of London. In 1549 he was given a pension – a modest 200 marks (£133) a year – and encouraged to transmit his knowledge and enthusiasm to a group of pupils and disciples, who included the young and brilliant John Dee.[74]

For some time both the Merchant Adventurers and the King's Council had been anxious about the excessive dependence of the English cloth trade upon Antwerp. In 1549 the link was still performing very well, and returning large profits, but as relations with the Emperor deteriorated after 1550, it became increasingly vulnerable. A more distant outlet, far beyond the reach of Imperial embargoes, would be extremely useful; and Sebastian had been nursing for years the ambition to find a route to China round the North Cape – what would later be known as the Northeast Passage. In June 1550 he was awarded £200 'by way of the king's reward', and at the same time granted an exemplification of the original patent granted to his father and himself on 5 April 1496, 'touching the discovery of new lands'.[75] In January 1551 the Imperial ambassador, Jehan Scheyfve, who was indefatigably curious about what Cabot was up to, reported that he was working with 'a certain Frenchman' called Jean Ribaut, and some unnamed Englishmen, 'to seek a road to the Indies'.[76] A good deal of spadework was needed, and it was the spring of 1553 before any enterprise was ready to be launched. By then a unique company had been created, consisting of 240 individual shareholders, each of whom had subscribed £25, giving it the large capital of £6,000. The shareholders were mostly London or Bristol merchants, but they also included

Privy Councillors, courtiers and other royal servants.[77] The king himself was not a subscriber, but the strong show of government patronage deterred any potential opponents of the enterprise, and quickly gained the Cathay Company a royal charter of incorporation. On 9 May instructions were issued, probably by Cabot himself, who had to be deterred from accompanying the voyage on the grounds of his very advanced years. Sir Hugh Willoughby was named as Captain General, with Richard Chancellor as Pilot General, and three modest-sized but well found ships were equipped and provisioned for the voyage – the *Edward Bonaventure*, the *Bona Speranza* and the *Confidencia*.[78] These were not owned by the Crown and were probably contributed by London merchants, but there is no doubt that the duke of Northumberland (as Warwick had been since November 1551) was very much behind the enterprise. It set sail on 10 May 1553 and the young king, who believed himself to be convalescent at the time, sat in a window at Greenwich palace to watch it pass. By that time a crisis in the Antwerp cloth trade, provoked originally by the debasement of the English coinage, had resulted in overproduction, and a 'cloth mountain' which urgently needed to be shifted.[79]

Eventually it was not the Willoughby/Chancellor voyage which solved that problem. The ships had barely cleared the Scottish coast when Edward died, and in the political revolution which followed the duke of Northumberland lost his life and the crown was taken by the pro-Imperial Mary. Sir Hugh Willoughby died trying to overwinter on the Norwegian coast, and Richard Chancellor ended up in Russia, via Archangel.[80] As we shall see, the outcome was the Muscovy Company of 1555, which for many years was to conduct a profitable, but not large-scale, trade. What is important about this voyage is not so much its immediate outcome as what it represented: in the first place a much wider vision on the part of the London merchants, who for generations had not been able to see further than the Baltic or the Mediterranean, and secondly the direct patronage and involvement of the Privy Council. Had Edward achieved his majority, he might well have become personally involved. As it was, his Council acted for him and it was to be left to Elizabeth to show a personal interest, but it was the beginning of a maritime outreach which was to have a profound effect upon English history. It is also worth remembering that it was similar adventurers, probing south and west into the Atlantic and down the African coast, and who needed to be armed for their own protection, who provided the training for the long-range privateers of the next generation. The seafaring community, which benefited hugely from these voyages, was the same community which supported the navy, and provided both its manpower and its workforce. Although in a sense the Admiralty was a distinct phenomenon, it cannot really be studied in isolation from the maritime community. Just as the Admiralty officers doubled as London merchants, so mariners served indifferently in the king's ships or in private traders as opportunities offered, and shipwrights worked at Deptford, or Woolwich, or Portsmouth, or one of the private yards, as their services were needed.

While Willoughby and Chancellor were still sailing together into the north-east, Edward's reign had a small naval postscript. A few days after the king died, when Mary had proclaimed herself queen and retreated into Norfolk, the Council in London, affecting not to take her pretensions seriously, sent six royal warships to blockade Yarmouth to prevent her anticipated escape to the continent. There they were visited by Henry Jerningham on Mary's behalf, who, according to one account, persuaded Richard Brooke, the squadron's commander, of the merits of his mistress's cause.[81] According to another account he persuaded the seamen to mutiny in Mary's favour. Whichever way it happened, the ships declared for her, and some of the mariners joined her force, bringing a number of their guns with them. We are told that Mary was greatly heartened by this defection, and that her cause prospered from that moment on. No doubt this is an exaggeration, but it is ironic to think that part of the navy, which Northumberland had been so careful to nurture, should have played a key part in his overthrow.[82]

CHAPTER 3 NOTES

1. There are many discussions of Henry VIII's intentions in drafting this will. See particularly W.K. Jordan, *Edward VI: The Young King* (1967), pp. 54–7; and E.W. Ives, 'Henry VIII's Will: A Forensic Conundrum', *Historical Journal*, 35, 1992, pp. 779–804.

2. *Acts of the Privy Council*, ed. J. Dasent *et al.* (1890–1907), II, pp. 3–4, 17.

3. D. Loades, *John Dudley, Duke of Northumberland* (1996), p. 90.

4. *APC*, II, pp. 489–90. Nobody remembered to write to Venice until 8 March.

5. *Letters and Papers*, XXI, nos 123, 134.

6. TNA SP10/1, no. 23.

7. TNA SP50/1, no. 12. Draft Instructions written by Lord Paget. Elmes is not known to have held any other command.

8. For example, TNA SP68/13, no. 60, dated 8 March 1547. William, Lord Grey of Wilton had been appointed governor of Boulogne on 9 April 1546. He relinquished the command on being appointed Captain General of Horse for the Scottish campaign in August 1547.

9. Jordan, *Edward VI*, p. 245.

10. TNA SP50/1, no. 37. Instructions to Lord Clinton, drafted by William Petre, 1 August 1547.

11. Ibid.

12. Gervase Phillips, *The Anglo Scottish Wars, 1513–1550: A Military History* (1999). Marcus Merriman, *The Rough Wooing* (2003).

13. *APC*, II, pp. 60–120.

14. TNA SP10/3, no. 22. Loades, *Tudor Navy*, p. 142.

15. *The Expedition into Scotland of the Most Worthily Fortunate Prince Edward, Duke of Somerset* ... By William Patten (1548), reprinted in A.F. Pollard, *Tudor Tracts* (1903), pp. 107–27.

16. *Expedition*, ed. Pollard, p. 137. Inchcolm was a house of Augustinian canons regular.
17. Ibid., p. 138.
18. TNA SP50/1, no. 56. The engineer was called Giovanni de Rossetti.
19. *Expedition*, ed. Pollard, pp. 145–6.
20. TNA SP50/2, no. 28.
21. Ibid., no. 36.
22. Andrew Dudley to the earl of Warwick, 30 November 1547. TNA SP50/2, no. 48.
23. Loades, *Tudor Navy*, pp. 144–5.
24. TNA SP10/4, no. 9 (Draft).
25. Grey to Somerset, 12 June 1548. TNA SP50/4, no. 24.
26. Grey to Somerset, 20 June 1548. TNA SP50/4, no. 36. For a full discussion of Somerset's garrison policy in Scotland, and the reasons for its failure, see M.L. Bush, *The Government Policy of Protector Somerset* (1975), pp. 7–39.
27. TNA SP10/6, no. 391. Loades, *Tudor Navy*, p. 141.
28. Clinton to the earl of Shrewsbury and Lord Grey, 10 August 1548. TNA SP50/4, no. 96.
29. Loades, *Tudor Navy*, p. 146.
30. See, for example, Brende to Somerset, 27 July 1548, where he says, 'I shall according to your Grace's commandment, practice with the Lords of Ruthven and Melville in the several purposes …'. TNA SP50/4, no. 83.
31. TNA SP10/9, no. 47. For a discussion of the situation at Boulogne, see W.K. Jordan, *Edward VI: the Threshold of Power* (1970), pp. 118–19.
32. TNA SP10/4, no. 40. The Vice Admirals concerned were Sir Peter Carew and John Grenville.
33. TNA SP10/5, no. 3.
34. Jordan, *Edward VI: The Young King*, pp. 369–82.
35. *APC*, II, p. 298. Loades, *John Dudley*, p. 118.
36. Magdalene College, Cambridge, Pepys Library, MS1266, pp. 145–53. There is a copy in Bod MS Rawlinson C.846, pp. 85–92.
37. D. Loades and C. Knighton, *The Navy of Edward VI and Mary* (NRS, forthcoming), pp. 70–1.
38. TNA E351/2588.
39. BL Cotton MS Otho E.IX, no. 36. PL MS2876, pp. 149–52.
40. *The Anthony Roll*, pp. 92–5.
41. Bod MS Rawlinson 846, pp. 135–7. *British Naval Documents*, pp. 98–9.
42. Bod MS Rawlinson A.200. Quarter Book for 1562–3.
43. TNA E351/2194.
44. W.K. Jordan, *The Chronicle and Political Papers of King Edward VI* (1966), p. 15.
45. For a full discussion of this episode, see Loades, *John Dudley*, pp. 125–40.
46. Bush, *Government Policy*, pp. 37–8.
47. BL Add. MS 48126, f.16. Dale Hoak, *The King's Council in the Reign of Edward VI* (1976), p. 255. Loades, *John Dudley*, pp. 144–5.
48. Jordan, *Chronicle*, p. 16.
49. *Calendar of State Papers, Spanish*, IX, p. 478.
50. BL Harleian MS 284, no. 38. *Cal. Span.*, IX, p. 469.
51. D.L. Potter, 'Documents Concerning the Negotiation of the Anglo-French Treaty of March 1550', *Camden Miscellany*, 28 (1984), pp. 59–180 (pp. 74–5).

52. Ibid. Loades, *John Dudley*, p. 154.

53. For some idea of the costs of defending Boulogne, see the summary of war expenditure contained in TNA SP10/15, no. 11, reproduced in *The Calendar of State Papers, Domestic, Edward VI*, ed. C.S. Knighton (1992), pp. 258–63.

54. *Cal. Span.*, X, p. 377.

55. *APC*, III, p. 24.

56. Ibid., p. 43.

57. Jordan, *Chronicle*, p. 70.

58. Ibid., pp. 138–9.

59. *APC*, III, p. 209. Loades, *Tudor Navy*, p. 153.

60. TNA E351/2353.

61. Loades, *Tudor Navy*, p. 150.

62. TNA E351/2355.

63. BL Harleian MS 7383, f.67. W.C. Richardson, ed., *The Report of the Royal Commission of 1552* (1974), p. 217. See also J.D. Alsop, 'The Revenue Commission of 1552', *Historical Journal*, XXII (1979), pp. 511–33.

64. Loades, *Tudor Navy*, p. 155.

65. *APC*, IV, p. 162.

66. Jordan, *Edward VI: The Threshold of Power*, pp. 127–36.

67. B. Dietz, 'The Royal Bounty and English Shipping in the Sixteenth and Seventeenth Centuries', *Mariners Mirror*, 77, 1991, pp. 5–21.

68. BL Harleian MS 354, f.26. *British Naval Documents*, pp. 100–1.

69. The sale of fourteen vessels of various sizes is recorded in Gonson's account from Michaelmas 1554 to Christmas 1555. TNA E351/2195.

70. Bod MS Rawlinson A.200.

71. TNA SP10/7, no. 12. Warrant for Sir Thomas Woodstock's expenses, 18 May 1549.

72. Loades, *Tudor Navy*, pp. 156–7.

73. *Cal. Span.*, IX, p. 381. Van der Delft to the Emperor, 28 May 1549.

74. D. Loades, *England's Maritime Empire* (2000), pp. 55–9. P.J. French, *John Dee: The World of an Elizabethan Magus* (1973). *Calendar of the Patent Rolls, Edward VI*, I, p. 320.

75. *APC*, III, p. 55. 26 June 1550.

76. Loades, *Maritime Empire*, p. 56.

77. Sir William Foster, *England's Quest of Eastern Trade* (1933), p. 8.

78. John Stow, *The Annals of England Faithfully Collected* … (1592), p. 609. Loades, *Maritime Empire*, p. 57.

79. D.C. Coleman, *The Economy of England, 1450–1750* (1977). Ralph Davis, *English Overseas Trade, 1500–1700* (1973).

80. Richard Hakluyt, *The principall navigations, voyages and discoveries of the English nation* (1589), I, pp. 263–91. Chancellor's account of the voyage.

81. 'The Vita Mariae Angliae Reginae of Robert Wingfield of Brantham', ed. D. MacCulloch, *Camden Miscellany*, 28, 1984, p. 259.

82. The account given by the anonymous author of *The Chronicle of Queen Jane* (Camden Society, 48, 1850) largely supports Wingfield. However, a case brought by Gilbert Grice, at the time the captain of the Greyhound, against the ship's master, John Hurlocke, tells of some strife before the decision was made – not a mutiny, but a disagreement among the officers. TNA HCA 13/9, ff.149–54. J.D. Alsop, 'A Regime at Sea; the Navy and the 1553 Succession Crisis', *Albion*, 24, 1992, pp. 583–8.

CHAPTER FOUR

The Navy of Mary, and of Philip and Mary

On 17 July 1553, two days before her proclamation in London, Mary's Council at Framlingham received the submission of Gilbert Grice, the captain of the *Greyhound*, committed the ship to his keeping, and authorised him to 'bring away' several pieces of ordnance.[1] The chronicles therefore seem to be accurate in substance, although not necessarily in the order of events. Two days later Sir Richard Cavendish was appointed 'to take the government of the Queen's ships', and given instructions which no longer survive. This was a reflection of the uncertainty of the times, because Cavendish, although an experienced sea captain, held no Admiralty office, either then or later. He had, however, been one of the first to declare for Mary, and for that reason she trusted him, not at that time knowing what the attitude of the Admiralty officers in post was likely to be. In the event his responsibility lasted less than a week, and he probably did nothing to discharge it. On 25 July he was replaced by Sir William Tyrell, another notable Catholic loyalist.[2] Tyrell was appointed as Vice Admiral, Lord Clinton, in spite of his close connection with Northumberland, having apparently made his submission and received a pardon. Tyrell's instructions are interesting, and show an immediate awareness on the part of Mary's Council of the need to deploy the navy in support of the new regime. He was instructed to proceed at once to the Narrow Seas with two of the ships already at Yarmouth, the *Greyhound* and the *Jennet*, and to 'ply along the coast as far as Beachy [Head] and so half seas over the channel toward the coast of Normandy'. His main brief was to pursue and arrest pirates, but he was also ordered to arrest any 'suspect persons passing forth of this realm' and to keep a wary eye on any 'ships of power' being sent out by the French.[3] The Council knew perfectly well that Northumberland had been angling for French support in the crisis which had just passed, and that fugitives from his abortive coup may well have been heading in that direction. On 24 September Gonson was paid £867 to be passed on to Edward Baeshe for the victualling of this squadron.[4]

Presumably Tyrell fulfilled his instructions, but we do not know whether he found any pirates, or dissidents heading for France. Henry II was quickly appraised of events in England, and anticipated trouble, but for the time being he instructed his ambassador to make the correct noises, and did nothing. He was locked in conflict with the Emperor, and his main concern was to prevent the notoriously pro-Imperial queen from joining his enemies. The Admiralty also seems to have carried on as though nothing had happened. Benjamin Gonson's declared accounts for the years 1552–4 are missing, but that does not indicate any gap in his responsibilities. We know that the Council authorised warrants to him for over £7,000 between the end of July and December 1553, and that the Admiralty debt, recorded in August, was £2,923.[5] Sir Thomas Wyndham, the Master of Naval Ordnance, had died on a private trading voyage to West Africa during the summer, and was not replaced, but the remaining officers were clearly reappointed. The only sign that all may not have been well came on 25 August when the Great Ship which had been known as the *Henry Grace a Dieu* but had more recently been re-named the *Edward*, burned to the waterline at her moorings in Woolwich, an event which one contemporary attributed to 'negligence and lack of oversight'.[6] Perhaps the Controller had other things on his mind at that point.

The new queen's inexperience showed up in one rather curious episode. Mary did not trust Lord Clinton, in spite of the fact that she had accepted his submission, and wished to replace him as Admiral by Lord William Howard, currently governor of Calais. About the end of October, she apparently wrote to Howard (the letter does not survive), notifying him of his appointment, and requiring him to make way for Lord Thomas Wentworth, who was to replace him at Calais. On 3 November Howard wrote to Clinton about the arrangements for the handover. Clinton was more than a little put out, and responded on the 10th:

> But my Lord, albeit I have of divers men heard that I should forego my said office, and that your Lordship should have it, yet has no such thing been said to me by the Queen's Majesty, nor any of her Highness's Privy Council …[7]

He had, he pointed out, a patent of the office for life, and that could not be lightly overturned. He had received the queen's pardon, and had 'done no fault whereby I ought to forfeit or lose either that or any other thing I have'.

On 14 November, Howard wrote to the Council with some asperity, pointing out that he was already packed and ready to depart from Calais, and that Lord Wentworth was ready to take over. He forwarded Clinton's letter, with the implication that her majesty had really better get to grips with reality. The same day he wrote, rather more circumspectly, to Mary, pointing out the nature of the difficulty which had arisen.[8] We do not know how the issue was resolved, but presumably the queen made it clear that her will was sufficient reason to overturn any patent, no matter what its terms. She had behaved in much the same way over the return of the old religion, because when Sir James Hales attempted to enforce the existing law against the mass, he was arrested by Lord Chancellor Gardiner, and informed that he should pay attention to 'the Queen's proceedings' rather than to the law.[9] Howard joined the Privy Council as Lord Admiral on 3 January 1554, and his patent of appointment was issued on 8 April.[10] There is very little information about the working of the Admiralty during this period, but William Winter, the Surveyor and Rigger, was suspected of involvement in the Wyatt rebellion, which briefly threatened London at the beginning of February. He was arrested on 20 February and spent the next few months in the Tower. He was eventually pardoned on 10 November, and resumed his naval duties.[11] His office had not been forfeit because he had never been tried, but with Wyndham's office vacant, the Council for Marine Causes was operating at only two-thirds strength during the summer of 1554.

In the run-up to the queen's marriage in July 1554 the fleet was on a high alert. On 16 December 1553 Winter was briefed to escort the Imperial ambassadors coming over to sign the treaty, and on 11 January the *Bark*, the *Jennet*, the *Greyhound* and the *Phoenix* were to be 'equipped with speed for Spain'.[12] At that point the prince's early arrival was anticipated, but first rebellion in England and then his own dissatisfaction with the treaty delayed his coming. It was June before he left Valladolid and the fleet was fully deployed. At the end of the month the earl of Bedford was sent to Coruna to escort him to England. The navy was briefed partly to provide an honourable welcome for Philip, and partly to deter the French from interfering. Twenty-nine men-of-war were in commission, manned by a total of 4,034 men.[13] The prince was then further delayed, both by the weather and by his own concerns, and the fleet hung about in the Western Approaches for almost a month. It ran out of victuals on more than one occasion, and tempers were getting short by the time that he actually arrived on 20 July. Although Gonson's accounts from this period do not survive, we do have the accounts of Sir Edmund Peckham, the Treasurer of the Mint, who was specially commissioned on 5 December 1553 to take over the disbursement of all the Crown's revenue while the regular system was overhauled. These show that Gonson received £10,967 between October 1553 and May 1554, and a further £15,159 between May and September, making a total of £26,126 for the full year.[14] We do not, of course, know how much of this was spent, or on what, but the Treasurer's next account, for 1554–5, shows no significant surplus so it is reasonable to suppose that it was all disbursed. Even if Baeshe's victualling expenses were included (as they probably were), this still suggests a level of expenditure which was consistent right the way through the regime change. Scraps of other information support that conclusion. We know, for instance, that one William Watson was paid £649 for a variety of masts and spars brought from Danzig, which included three of 31 yards in length and seven of 30 yards, which would have been suitable for the largest ships, and suggest that the maintenance programme was being fully maintained.[15] A total of fourteen ships were sold during 1554, but this should be interpreted as good housekeeping rather than running down. With the exception of the *Primrose*, which was nearly new and was sold to a London merchant consortium in December for £1,800, all those disposed of were old, and some were very small. The other thirteen fetched a total of £181, which can hardly have exceeded their value as scrap.[16]

Philip was undoubtedly interested in the English navy. Not only was it 'the chief defence of the realm of England', it could also be usefully deployed in support of his father, the Emperor. During the early part of 1555 he had other things on his mind. First the completion of the reconciliation of the church with Rome, followed by the beginning of persecution, and then the queen's supposed pregnancy. At the same time he had more than half an eye on the development of Charles's struggle with France, and by the summer was itching to rejoin his father in the Low Countries. Mary's pregnancy turned out to be a delusion, and as soon as he decently could, at the beginning of September, Philip left for the Low Countries. His going seems to have taken the navy by surprise, or at least to have been quicker than expected, because the escort of thirteen ships which was being prepared in the Thames to escort him was not fully ready. Such ships as were able to go were sent to Dover, but Ruy Gomez, the king's secretary, was forced to bring over six ships from Flanders to make good the deficiency.[17] Philip sailed on 4 September, not overly impressed by English efficiency.

Before he left, the king had set up a 'Select Council' to keep him in touch with English affairs. This appears to have had no formal constitution, but to have consisted of those members of the Queen's Privy Council whom he chose to trust. Before the end of September, it wrote to him about a number of matters, including the state of the navy. It would appear that a number of ships, in addition to those which had constituted part of his escort, had been at sea, probably in the North Sea and the Channel, keeping an eye on the French and the Scots as usual.[18] Mary's marriage to Philip was, of course, strongly opposed by both countries. We know that the *Falcon* and the *Sun* patrolled the Narrow Seas in the autumn of 1554, and that powder was issued to the *Phoenix* and three other ships on 8 December that year, which confirms that these patrols were a matter of routine. In September 1555 the Select Council reported that the ships which had been out, great and small, were 'so battered and torn apart by the force of winds and storms that they can no longer remain at sea'. They proposed to bring them back into the Thames at once for repairs, replacing them with others 'which yet remain intact' to guard the passage between Dover and Calais.[19] In reply, the king approved their plan – indeed he had little option – but observed that it would be better for the repairs to be carried out at Portsmouth. It was difficult, he observed, to get ships out of the Thames, whereas at Portsmouth they would be available as soon as the servicing had been completed. This was particularly relevant because the Emperor was planning shortly to leave for Spain, and wanted twelve or fourteen English ships to escort him as far as Ushant.[20] From the fact that over £6,000 was spent at Deptford during this accounting period, and practically nothing at Portsmouth, it would appear that Philip's instructions were ignored, and the Emperor eventually postponed his voyage, so the escort was not needed. The king's interest is undeniable, but seems to have been largely ineffective. However, the first new naval ships since the *Primrose* were laid down in the autumn of 1555. They were later named *The Philip and Mary* and the *Mary Rose*, and it is at least possible that Philip encouraged this move, although it is highly unlikely that he contributed to the cost.

Mary was more than a little put out by the failure of her Admiralty to provide an adequate escort for Philip on his departure, and on 24 September the Privy Council wrote to Howard to say that the queen had determined on two things. First, to have her navy increased, which may well relate to the two ships mentioned, and secondly to have the existing fleet 'armed and manned against His Majesty's return'.[21] This latter was pure wishful thinking. Not wishing to distress his wife further, when he left Philip had spoken vaguely of returning for the parliament, which was due to meet on 21 October. He probably never had any intention of doing so, and immersed in the affairs of the Netherlands, he soon sent his excuses. He was not in fact to return for another eighteen months. Howard, who was probably aware that such a command was unrealistic, given the number of ships laid up for repairs, and the other demands on his resources, had apparently gone to the Cinq Ports and appealed to the terms of their ancient charter to provide him with the bulk of the escort which the king was going to need. Their answer had been less than helpful, and Howard had appealed to the Council for some clarification of the Ports' responsibilities.[22] The Council responded in the letter referred to, that the Ports were bound to meet the king's summons by providing as many ships as he might require, fully armed and manned at their own expense for fifteen days. After that the king could retain them for as long as he might see fit, but was bound to pay 6d a day for every mariner and 3d a day for every other man in service. The Admiral was to take this answer back to the Ports, and require them to produce twenty-five ships to serve as the king's escort. If they did not comply, the Ports were to be threatened with the loss of their privileges.[23] Another Council memorandum of similar date speaks of only four ships being required and makes no mention of sanctions, so what eventually happened we do not know. In view of the fact that the king's escort was not needed, and the French threat also mentioned turned out to be a chimera, it is probable that the whole matter was allowed to rest.

By the end of 1555 neither the Privy Council nor the queen was satisfied with the state of the Admiralty. Just what was amiss cannot be deduced from the surviving accounts, but at a Council meeting on 11 January 1556 – a meeting at which the Lord Admiral was not present – a comprehensive investigation into the affairs of the navy was ordered. 'First [the minute commences] order is taken for a secret search to be made of all the Queen's ships, as well for the number of men as for victual …'[24] ('secret' in this case apparently meaning without prior warning given to the admiralty officers). It was also ordered that the men and ships appointed for duty, whether in the Narrow Seas or elsewhere, were to be 'suddenly' mustered once a month, and 'tried how they be furnished', for the purpose of 'considering' the expense involved, 'and what prest [advance] is made thereupon'. Victualling was to be reorganised upon a more profitable basis, and order taken for the repairing of the ships, including those already in dock. The nub of the Council's concern seems to have been economy, and it may well be that the hand of the Lord Treasurer, the marquis of Winchester, should be seen behind it.

The implication that the navy was not being properly maintained would seem from other records to be unjustified, although a warrant for payment to Gonson in March 1556 specified that it was for 'the amending, repairing and grounding of the said ships and their boats', which was an unusual proviso, most warrants being granted simply for naval expenses.[25] On the same day the Privy Council also resolved that 'The King's and Queen's Majesties navy should be augmented' and that the *Bark* and the *Peter Pomegranate* 'should this year be repaired'.[26] The impression that the Council was meddling in affairs which its predecessor had been content to leave to the Admiralty is very strong. Apart from this sort of random intrusion, however, the fate of the intended investigation is not known. If it was carried out, then the report does not survive. The only sign of the tightening up which seems to have been intended is that at the end of 1555 Gonson had been over £5,000 in debt (which was about normal), but a year later the debt was only £1,154. He had received £28,385, of which all but £100 had come from the Exchequer, and spent £23,600. Perhaps the Lord Treasurer's fingerprints can be seen in this improvement.[27]

The outcome can be more clearly seen almost exactly a year later, on 8 January 1557, when the Council – again in the absence of the Lord Admiral – issued instructions for the reorganisation of the Admiralty. The most important change was that overall responsibility was transferred from the Lord Admiral to the Lord Treasurer, the latter being merely required to take the Admiral's advice. The reason given was that the queen was tired of signing piecemeal warrants for the navy and wished to transfer the responsibility. The Lord Treasurer, it was recorded, agreed to take this on, on the condition that a budget, or 'ordinary', of £14,000 a year was established, to be paid to Gonson in half-yearly tranches. In return for this, he undertook to ensure that all ships would be made serviceable with 'caulking and new trimming' as necessary; that a programme of systematic rebuilding would be instituted; and that all ships would be kept fully furnished. To achieve this he would be entitled to receive warrants for timber from suitably located royal manors. In addition he would be responsible for victualling the shipkeepers and dockyard workers, and for the maintenance of standby rations for 1,000 men for one month, to be held against an emergency, and renewed as necessary. He allegedly expressed the opinion that when the maintenance and rebuilding programme was up-to-date, it should be possible to reduce the ordinary to £10,000 a year. Gonson and Baeshe were to account separately, and at least once a year.[28] If this was an attempt to economise on the navy, it did not work. No doubt the officers resented the imputation upon their zeal and efficiency, and Gonson went on receiving 'extraordinary' warrants (which presumably the queen still had to sign). In fact it would seem that these reforms were not implemented at all, because within a few months the country was at war with France, and all considerations of economy went out of the window. Nor is there any sign of a block warrant – which would have been necessary for the payment of the planned ordinary – until March 1559, when the war was virtually over and Elizabeth was on the throne.[29] If the Lord Treasurer ever assumed responsibility for the navy, he left remarkably few traces.

It was not often that the navy became involved in the affairs of Ireland, except to convey troops over, but no sooner had the king departed for the Netherlands in September 1555, than a somewhat curious intrusion was planned into the tribal lands of Ulster It began with a request, some time in September 1555, from Sir Edmund Rous, 'late Vice-Trasurer of Ireland', and half a dozen of his colleagues, all of whom had connections with the government in Dublin, to fish the Bann 'whereof they had obtained a lawful lease'. The Council's response to this innocuous-seeming request was to give the petitioners permission to set out with vessels armed and equipped for their own defence, and to 'take any such convenient ground' upon the north parts of Ireland as might seem convenient for their purpose.[30] This was obviously to be no quiet fishing trip. Resistance was expected from 'rebels or enemies of the said realm of Ireland', and the adventurers were enjoined not to trouble any one living peacefully in accordance with the law. They were permitted to borrow ordnance from the royal store on a three-month loan, and were enjoined (as an afterthought) to arrest 'one Cole, a pirate' who had been troubling the queen's subjects in those waters. Some kind of a fortified base in the tribal lands was clearly intended, at least on a temporary basis, and fishing in the Bann may have been a mere pretext.[31] Nothing then happened for several months, and Rous appears to have withdrawn from the project, but on 3 April 1556, recognisances were issued in connection with what was clearly the same scheme. William Piers and Thomas Kent from the original adventurers, this time with London associates, bound themselves in recognisance, not only to fish the Bann, but 'to do certain service' against the Scots who were unlawfully inhabiting that part of Ireland. The point of the recognisance was to bind them not to assail peaceful subjects, or to do anything 'unlawful or prejudicial to their Majesties said realms', nor to break the formal peace with Scotland.[32]

It may be that these conditions were unrealistic, or that the entrepreneurs were unable to raise a sufficient force for their purpose, but again nothing seems to have been done, and between April and June the nature and purpose of the expedition changed again. On the 12th of the month the Irish Privy Council issued a set of instructions to yet another group of men, of whom only William Piers had previously featured, for what was clearly a full-scale military operation. This was to involve four royal warships, the *Mary Willoughby*, the *Jerfalcon*, the *Double Rose* and the *Fleur de Luce*, the first two carrying fifty soldiers each and the others twenty-five. The *Mary Willoughby* was to proceed to the Bann by way of 'the Scottish shore', destroying any galleys (tribal warboats) which she came across. The other ships were to go at once to the Rathins, destroying all the galleys they could find on the Irish coast. They were then to blockade the coast, taking any ship which attempted to enter or leave the Bann, and to keep the seas between Ireland and Scotland. They were to refer back to Carrickfergus for further instructions, and report their doings to the Council. No time limit was set to this enterprise, but it must have lasted at least a month. There were no further references to fishing the Bann, and it seems that that had never been more than a pretext for an armed presence on the Ulster coast.[33] What appears to have started as an officially encouraged private expedition intended to spy out the ground, ended up as a full-blown naval operation. Unfortunately we do not know how successful this operation was, but at least the *Mary Willoughby* escaped the fate which had befallen her in 1533, when she had been captured by Scottish 'pirates' in these same waters.

Fragmentary evidence suggests that the queen was taking the fight against piracy seriously. In late 1555 and early 1556 a fleet of about eight ships was deployed, also looking for the elusive Cole, and for one Stevenson, another

Irish pirate.[34] They do not seem to have been successful. As far as we know, both Cole and Stevenson were just robbers, but there was a political dimension to piracy as well. After the collapse of the Wyatt rebellion in February 1554, a number of disaffected gentlemen took refuge in France, among them Sir Peter Carew and Peter Killigrew. Sir Peter had been Vice Admiral of Devon under Edward, and the Killigrew family had a long record of piracy. Whether they took ships with them, or acquired them in France, is not entirely clear, but with the connivance of the French king they set up in business as pirates, preying on English and Flemish shipping in the Channel. Within weeks Carew was cruising with ships allegedly hired at Rouen, and manned largely by crews of fellow English exiles.[35] By the end of March 1554 the Killigrew brothers were also at sea with three ships, one of which, the 160-ton *Sacrette*, appears to have been given to Killigrew free of charge by Henry II. According to the story which he later told, his original ships had been impounded, whereupon, 'we [Peter and Henry Killigrew] were suitors to the Admiral to be the means to the king that we might have the Sacrett for two years with such furniture to serve her, which was granted us ...';[36] and after the two years were up, they had 'demanded the gift of the said ship' with her ordnance, which was also granted them, and the ship had been conveyed by the French Admiral in Lent 1555. Diplomatic representations were made from the start, but Henry professed a bland ignorance of all such goings-on, and the English Council did not wish to force the issue. Occasionally one was captured. Nicholas Tremayne, for instance, who was a member of another notorious Cornish family, was in prison in February 1555, but he was apparently released in time to get involved in the Dudley conspiracy against the queen at the end of that year.

Henry Dudley (a cousin of the duke of Northumberland, not his son of that name) had spent most of 1555 planning an exile invasion of England to link up with some large but vague gentry conspiracy in the west of England.[37] The French king had originally been planning to support the venture, being anxious to destabilise Imperial control in England, but when he signed the truce of Vaucelles with Philip early in 1556, he withdrew. Dudley then turned his attention to a daring plot to rob the Exchequer of some £50,000 to pay for French mercenaries, but his plot was detected and all those involved were either arrested or running for their lives. This produced further recruits for the pirate fleet, notably Christopher Ashton. By the summer of 1556 this fleet had become a serious menace to both English and Imperial shipping, and on 19 June Edward Wotton, the English ambassador in France, reported that they had taken a number of 'good prizes'.[38] This was not only injurious, it was also an affront to the royal navy which was supposed to be keeping the Channel, and in the middle of July a squadron of about ten or twelve royal ships went in pursuit of them. Seven or eight pirates were caught off Plymouth and a sharp engagement ensued. No account of this battle survives, but it is clear that, formidable as they may have been to their prey, these marauders were no match for the queen's ships. Six of them were captured, including the *Sacrett*, and their crews ended up in prison.[39] Only one or two escaped. Taken to task, Henry claimed that the *Sacrett* had only been loaned to Killigrew for the duration of the Franco-Habsburg war, which was suspended in the summer of 1556, and therefore that its use in this context was a breach of trust. Killigrew, as we have seen, told a different story. The government seems to have treated its prisoners as political opponents rather than criminals. The Tremaynes and the Ashtons remained at large, but Peter Killigrew was released without charge and was shortly commanding a ship in the royal service.

Although this victory greatly reduced the menace of piracy, it did not eliminate it, and it did not touch the danger of exile activity based in France. The truce of Vaucelles broke down in September 1556, and the danger that Henry would consider supporting such ventures again increased. Philip wanted to involve England in the renewed war, claiming that the truce meant that it was not the same war as that from which England had been excluded by the terms of his marriage treaty. The English Council opposed him, arguing that a truce was not a peace, and that the war was the same. Mary supported the war, but was reluctant to act against the unanimous advice of her Council, and this meant that it became increasingly likely that the king would return to help her put pressure upon them. The money also would have to come from Spain, and this meant increasing traffic between England, the Low Countries and Iberia. In February 1557 Ruy Gomez was sent to Spain on the king's behalf, and William Tyrell was briefed to provide the escort 'unto the coast of Spain'. Only one royal warship was apparently allocated to this duty, the remainder of the fleet being made up of armed merchantmen, any of which might be 'taken up' and equipped if they were unlucky enough to be in Plymouth harbour when the instructions arrived.[40] Although some eight or ten royal ships were at sea, constituting the winter guard, there was an obvious reluctance to detach more than the absolute minimum for this duty. By the middle of February Philip had at last decided to return, and the provision of a proper escort had to be considered. Presumably the ships of the winter guard would have been allocated to this duty, but on the 15th the queen wrote to Sir Thomas Cheyney, the Lord Warden of the Cinq Ports, requiring him to provide a certain number of ships for this purpose also.[41] Philip was touchy about his honour, and it may be that he required such a 'spontaneous' demonstration of allegiance. Or possibly it was identified as a service which could be discharged within the charter limit of fifteen days, and was therefore something of a 'test case'.

The king eventually arrived at Greenwich on 20 March at five o'clock in the afternoon, to be greeted with a thirty-two-gun salute, and dutiful cries of 'God save the King and Queen'. The queen was ecstatic, the citizens of London rather less so, realising what his coming portended, and he got straight down to business. He too was reluctant to overrule the Council, at least as long as it remained united, so he set about dividing opinion, using his position to create a 'war party'. On 12 April he admitted to the bishop of Arras that the going was much tougher than he had expected,[42] but then on the 23rd an apparently fortuitous event came to his assistance. A group of English exiles, travelling in two French ships, landed on the Yorkshire coast and took Scarborough castle. They were led by Thomas Stafford, an adventurer with delusions of grandeur, who believed that he had a claim to the English throne. There are a number of suspicious circumstances about this raid, because the English Council had known for weeks that it was coming, and had a fair idea about its target. They were also warned on the 18th that the ships had set off, but they did nothing, either to warn the garrison at Scarborough or to instruct the navy to intercept. The impression is that Stafford walked into a carefully prepared trap, because his small force was mopped up in a matter of days by a local force under the earl of Westmorland which just happened to be in the vicinity on its way to the Scottish border.[43] More importantly, such an act of unprovoked aggression by the French finally overcame the Council's resistance to a declaration of war. Henry consistently denied the slightest involvement, and the chances are that he was right, but nobody in England believed him. The navy had suspiciously stood aside. On 22 May the Lord Admiral was put on standby, and on the 29th he was issued with his instructions for the war which was formally declared on 7 June.[44]

He had twenty ships under his command, of which he was instructed to appoint four to keep the strait between Dover and Calais, to guarantee safe passage for the king's and queen's subjects and their friends. The other sixteen he was to take down the coast as far as Falmouth, and then on or after 7 June (when war would have been declared) to cross to the French coast, and to 'clear the seas' of any enemy shipping which he could catch and overpower. He was to concentrate particularly upon the ports of Le Havre and Dieppe, to prevent any French ships of war from emerging and damaging English or Flemish commerce.[45] A list of these ships, complete with tonnage, manpower and the captains' names survives among the Domestic State Papers, although which were left to guard the strait is not clear. The *Minion*, the *Tiger* and the *Venetian* are marked as 'left behind', but not apparently, for that purpose.[46] It was a formidable fleet, nine of the ships deployed being of 200 tons or more, and seven over 300. At the same time the Lord Admiral was authorised to claim one-third of the value of any prize taken, which was well above the normal going rate. He was also warned in a letter from Sir William Petre, the Principal Secretary, that the French were thought to have mustered twenty ships at Dieppe and sixteen at Le Havre, although the size and power of these remained unknown. A few days later Benjamin Gonson was instructed to prepare additional ships to reinforce the Admiral's fleet.[47] For nearly a month Howard chased shadows in the Channel, or so he claimed. French ships, even quite large ones, would appear on the horizon, and then flee as soon as his own vessels approached. He dutifully reported these encounters, but all they achieved was to give him a clearer sense of his own position. On 22 June he took stock. The four ships guarding the strait were not sufficient, but he could not reinforce them himself 'because he thinketh himself very weak' if the French should emerge in any strength. The reinforcements promised from Portsmouth had not arrived, and there was no sign of the Flemish warships which had been promised. He would stay on station, where he was, until his ships needed re-victualling, which would be about 10 July, and meanwhile he would continue to send pinnaces to spy out the French coast, and to do a little raiding when the opportunity should offer.[48] On receiving this report, the Council noted that this re-victualling would coincide with 'the King's going over', which might have to be reconsidered. On the 27th Howard acknowledged an instruction to convoy ('waft') the merchant ships which were presently due to cross from the Scheldt to the Thames, but reminded the Council that his victuals would not last beyond 9 July.[49]

The earl of Pembroke had already been appointed to lead the expeditionary force which was to accompany the king to Flanders, and the muster of 8,000 men must have been well in hand, because by 29 June the Council had decided to bring forward the date of Philip's departure to 5 July on account of the victualling problem, and had instructed Howard to muster enough ships for their transportation.[50] The Admiral must have had this well in hand, for barely a week later the necessary transports were in place, drawn partly from the Cinq Ports and partly from other harbours in the neighbourhood. Considering the problems which he had earlier encountered with the Ports, this was no mean achievement. At some point between the 29th and the day of departure, Howard apparently took leave from his command to attend a meeting of the Privy Council, because on the latter day the Council wrote to the Lord Treasurer saying that 'this day' they had called him, together with Sir William Woodhouse, the Vice Admiral, and two other Admiralty officers, in order to resolve certain problems which had arisen in connection with the navy. The Lord Admiral, they declared, 'hath shown himself well content to be revoked' from his present command. The letter then proceeded to more detailed matters of deployment.[51] Because no French force had yet appeared in the Narrow Seas, it had been decided to send eight of the ships presently on station there to the north, and to send out three fresh ships to replace them, which was, they admitted, something of a gamble. The rest of the letter concerned the victualling of the ships going north, a matter for which the Lord Treasurer had apparently undertaken to provide.[52] The redeployment to the north was part of a defensive preparation then being made against the Scottish invasion which was anticipated following the outbreak of war with France. This did not eventually happen, because although the queen regent, Mary of Guise, was anxious to intervene, the Scottish nobility would not follow her. How long these ships remained in the north is not apparent, nor just why Howard was relieved of his command. Perhaps he had already fallen out with Philip, who clearly did not trust him. He was replaced in command of the Channel guard by Sir John Clere, and as Lord Admiral towards the end of the year by Lord Clinton, whose patent of re-appointment was sealed on 10 February 1558.[53]

On 8 July three further ships were ordered to sea, and at about the same time Sir John Clere seems to have been transferred from the Channel to the North Sea command, for the specific purpose of protecting the returning Icelandic fishing fleet, presumably against interference by the Scots. He hoisted his flag in the *Minion*, and had eight other vessels under his command.[54] By the 13th the Channel guard stood at thirteen ships, under the command of Sir William Woodhouse in the *Great Bark*. At the same time the officers of Yarmouth, Hull and Newcastle were instructed each to provide two of their largest ships, armed and equipped at their own expense for the royal service. Similar requests for one ship each were sent to Ipswich, Southwold, Lowestoft, Aldborough, Blakeney, Boston, Poole, Weymouth, Exmouth, Dartmouth, Salcombe, Plymouth, Saltash and Fowey; a total of twenty-one ships, if all the demands were met.[55] This would have given Clere the large number of thirty ships, with which he was expected not only to protect the Iceland fishermen, but also merchants returning from Danzig (with naval stores), and to 'annoy' the Scots and any Frenchman who had the temerity to try to reach Scotland. Any prizes taken were to be referred to the queen before being disposed of. Meanwhile, although former pirates such as Peter Killigrew had been recruited, there was a shortage of captains for the Channel guard, and letters were sent 'to certain gentlemen' to supply the deficiency.[56] By the beginning of August the Council was in something of a panic over Scottish intentions, and diverted Woodhouse with part of his Channel fleet to join Clere in the North Sea. Orders were given to Edward Baeshe to divert victuals accordingly. In spite of the summer season even the larger ships were constantly being damaged at sea, and were regularly being called in for repairs. The only orders which survive relate to the queen's own ships – presumably the privately owned ships had to be repaired at their owners' expense.[57]

Meanwhile the army was distinguishing itself, in a modest way, at the siege of St Quentin on 27 August. There was virtually no action at sea – only one rather serious mishap. Clere decided that he would await the returning Iceland fleet off the west coast of Scotland, and proceeded to the Isles of Orkney. There, on 12 August, he very ill-advisedly sought to land, and being resisted, attempted to escape by boat. Caught in the fierce currents of those waters, the boat overturned and Clere and three of his captains were drowned.[58] There was not even a skirmish to justify this loss of life, but presumably Woodhouse took over his command, before returning to the Channel later in the same month. In September the auxiliaries were paid off, and most of the Channel fleet returned to Portsmouth where the crews were discharged.[59] About ten, mostly smaller, ships remained at sea, and they must have been responsible for escorting the troop transports which brought Pembroke's force back from the Low Countries in dribs and drabs during October. Although individual ships are mentioned from time to time, it seems that the French navy did not put in an appearance at any time during the 1557 campaigning season, a fact for which there is no obvious explanation.

The crisis which arose at the beginning of 1558 involved the navy very directly, but as it transpired, as not much more than bystanders. A routine costing, carried out on 29 December, showed five small ships actually at sea in the Channel, with a complement of 400 men, and seven larger ships 'to be equipped', all at a total cost of £2,200 for two months.[60] This seems to have been a regular preparation for the coming campaigning season, and unrelated to any fears respecting Calais. Sir William Woodhouse seems to have been first alerted to the fact that something serious was brewing on 31 December, when an instruction was issued for the preparation of five additional ships 'with all possible diligence'.[61] The earl of Rutland was immediately appointed to take reinforcements to Calais, but musters and other preparations would take weeks, even if the scale was modest and the urgency great. To his credit, the earl set out almost at once, but on 3 January was turned back in mid-Channel by the news that Ruysbank had fallen, and that it was impossible to get into the harbour.[62] If there had been an armed fleet in the harbour at the time, the outcome might have been very different, but there was not, and no reason why there should have been, because Calais was not a normal naval base. What had happened was that the duke of Guise had been beaten in Italy by the duke of Alba, and had been recalled to the north, where he was desperate to redeem his tarnished reputation. Although it was the middle of the winter, he assembled an army of 20,000 men in Picardy, and it was reported that his objective was Hesdin. In spite of the fact that the garrison had been reduced to save money, Calais was thought to be too strong to attack. There had been rumours, but Lord Wentworth, the Lord Deputy, had dismissed them. Then, on 1 January 1558, the duke's forces had overrun Newham Bridge on the frontier of the Pale. In normal circumstances his advance from there would have been painfully slow because of the marshy nature of the ground. However, in early January the marshes were frozen, and he was able to make a lightning strike on Ruysbank which capitulated within hours on 2 January, thus sealing the harbour.[63] The French then turned the guns of Ruysbank against Calais castle, which was the weakest part of its defences, and partly demolished it. After one costly sortie, Wentworth decided that his position was untenable, and Calais was surrendered on the 7th.

Meanwhile, desperate efforts were being made in London to organise a relief force. On the 8th, before the news of the surrender arrived, Woodhouse had been instructed to mobilise any ships which he could find, man them with whatever soldiers might be available, and see if he could force a way into the harbour.[64] The following day this was followed up with an instruction to take up ships for the transport of soldiers, who were being mustered as a matter of extreme urgency. Then, on the night of 9/10 January, there was a mighty storm, and although Woodhouse did not lose any ships, they were all battered into a state of virtual uselessness. At the same time the Council heard of the fall of the town, and although Guisnes was still holding out, the relief operation was cancelled. Woodhouse was instructed to get his damaged ships back to the Thames as soon as possible, leaving such as were still seaworthy to patrol the Channel.[65] The musters were abandoned.

With hindsight, it appears that the loss of Calais was a blessing in disguise, removing as it did a constant source of friction between England and France, and turning the attentions of the English Council outward towards the Atlantic. However, it did not look that way at the time. The psychological shock was profound, and everyone who had been on the ground in Calais was suspected of having betrayed their charge. Philip also found himself blamed, much to his disgust, and his relations with the English Council chilled still further.[66] One of Elizabeth's earliest actions was to attempt to retrieve Calais by intervening in the French civil war in 1562, an adventure which ended with the abandonment of any lingering hope. After 1564, Calais was gone for good.

Meanwhile, there was still a war to be fought, and on 19 January a routine instruction was sent to the Lord Admiral requiring him to prepare such ships as he could for the defence of the realm against both the French and the Scots, 'our ancient enemies'.[67] He was also to arrest as many merchantmen as he considered necessary to make up the strength of his fleets, bearing in mind that many of his own vessels were likely to be out of action for some time, following the great storm. The order to stay all outward bound merchantmen was passed on to the port officials about a fortnight later.[68] On 10 February, as we have seen, Lord Clinton returned as High Admiral, Howard having been formally discharged on the 2nd. Whether this was in any way connected with

Philip's annoyance over the loss of Calais is not known. Probably not, since Howard seems to have ceased discharging any duties before the end of 1557, and all naval instructions during that crisis had been issued to Vice Admiral Woodhouse. However, it was on the king's insistence that Edward Fiennes returned to duty, and there are hints in the records that the queen was not happy with the change. Clinton was not a good enough Catholic for her taste. On 15 March the new Lord Admiral was issued with instructions concerning the disposal of prizes, which the Council obviously thought had been neglected under the previous regime.[69] As the preparations for the new campaigning season proceeded, and perhaps mindful of the theoretical role which the Lord Treasurer had been intended to play in naval matters, the Lord Admiral asked for his assistance in providing victuals for the fleet.[70] Perhaps Baeshe was finding the responsibility too much, or perhaps it was merely a tactful gesture given Paulet's extensive experience in that direction. If the Surveyor General ever had to apply coercion to extract the supplies he needed, the Lord Treasurer's active assistance might be very important.

Philip clearly approved of Clinton. Not only did he write him a fulsome letter on 6 April expressing his confidence in the warmest terms, he also summoned him to Brussels for personal consultations at some time in the same month. While he was in Brussels William Winter (now fully rehabilitated from his former disfavour – again probably by the king's means) assumed command of the fleet at sea, and issued an elaborate code of disciplinary instructions.[71] There was nothing particularly original about this, but it was comprehensive in its coverage; from Divine service on board to the discipline of lights, care of victuals, and orders for the boarding of an enemy. Prize discipline, and what ships should do if unexpectedly separated from their colleagues were also covered. These were not battle instructions of the kind which had been issued by Audley in 1530 and by John Dudley in 1545, but rather they provide an informative guide as to how crews were supposed to conduct themselves at sea. What relation they bore to actual practice is very hard to tell at this distance.

The main objective of the summer campaign in 1558 was intended to be a large-scale Anglo-Flemish attack on Brittany. It was in this connection that letters of summons were sent to eight selected captains, including Walter Raleigh (father of Sir Walter), requiring them to be at Portsmouth by 10 May, to assume command of a similar number of royal ships.[72] On 14 May Clinton was again summoned to Brussels for detailed discussions on the planning of the campaign. The Admiralty, which would be responsible for the mobilisation, appears to have played no part in these consultations; perhaps they were simply expected to obey orders. In informing the count of Feria, his personal representative in England, about these talks, the king expressed the view that the English fleet was 'almost ready' for its main enterprise.[73] At that same time, in the middle of May, there were rumours that Philip would again visit England, and Mary, who took them seriously, was buoyed up with expectancy. However, on the 17th she was compelled to admit that the state of the war and his other 'weighty business' would not permit such a luxury, and that the ships which the Admiral had been instructed to have on standby for such a coming, could be stood down. On the 18th Clinton notified the Council that he was off to Brussels, and leaving William Winter in command of the fleet, as before. Feria was consistently disparaging about the English war effort. Even the queen, he noted on 18 May, was not as keen as he would have expected. The Admiral was a double-dealing crook, but the only man with any influence in military matters. It was, he declared, useless to expect the English to produce an army for the forthcoming campaigning season; the best that could be expected was the 6,000 or 7,000 men already proposed for raids on the French coast.[74] The navy was the only useful military asset that the English possessed. Clinton, meanwhile, continued to discharge his duties. Apart from preparing a force to raid France, he had to secure the Channel and provide escorts for merchantmen, particularly those bringing the arms and munitions which Gresham had purchased in the Low Countries. These duties were reflected in a list drawn up on 22 May, allocating thirteen royal ships and six armed merchantmen to join the Lord Admiral at Portsmouth, thirteen royal ships and one merchant to the Channel guard, and one royal ship with five merchantmen to the escort duties.[75] He also had to provide safe passage for the messengers who were constantly coming and going between the king and the queen, who he recommended should go either via Flushing or Ostend.

By the end of June some 140 vessels had been assembled for the main venture, to link up with thirty or so which were coming from Flanders. A list of fifty-five captains drawn up at the same time probably indicates the number of fighting ships, as distinct from transports and victuallers, which were involved in this enterprise. At about the same time, on 22 June, letters of marque were issued to a further twenty-three captains, to 'go upon' the enemy at their own expense.[76] Clinton issued a set of fighting instructions, similar to those issued by Dudley in 1545, but placing more emphasis upon the duty of captains to obey the Admiral. However, the long-prepared campaign of which so much was expected turned out to be a sad disappointment. The Flemings duly turned up, there was no sign of the French navy, and Clinton landed 7,000 men near Brest at the end of July. Resistance, however, was fierce and the town turned out to be too strong to be attacked. After burning the village of Le Conquet, and suffering rather more casualties than was comfortable, the English re-embarked. Clinton was then trapped in the harbour by adverse winds, and his supplies began to run out. On 3 August the wind changed, and his Flemish allies promptly departed, leaving the Admiral little option but to return to Portsmouth.[77] Anxious to redeem his tarnished reputation, Clinton set out again with a much reduced number of ships to raid the coast of Normandy. This time he got as far as the Channel Islands when a virulent outbreak of sickness again forced him to retreat. By 24 August he was back in Portsmouth, where he promptly fell sick himself. God was clearly not on the side of the English in the summer of 1558.

There were, however, two relatively minor actions which enjoyed more success. The first occurred when John Malen was detached with a squadron of ten ships to assist the Imperial defenders of Dunkirk against a French attack. Before he could get there, the town had been relieved by the count of Egmont, and a battle developed near Gravelines, within sight of the sea. Malen stumbled upon this battle in progress, and in an inspired moment of improvisation brought his ships close into shore, bombarding the French positions. Taken by surprise, and badly mauled by the big guns, the French broke and Egmont was totally victorious. His action earned Malen a special commendation from the queen, and the rank of Vice Admiral.[78] The other action took place far away, on the west coast of Scotland, whither a squadron of nine ships under Sir Thomas Cotton had been sent to the assistance of the earl of Sussex, Lord Deputy of Ireland. The trouble was that the MacDonalds of the Isles were interfering (again) in Ulster, and when royal troops arrived to chastise them, were simply taking to their boats. So Sussex was planning a punitive expedition against the clansmen, for which he needed naval support. Sussex and Cotton left Dublin on 14 September, and in spite of adverse weather landed over 1,000 men on Kintyre. Cotton's big ships, the *Mary Willoughby* and the *New Bark*, could only stand off such a dangerous coast and offer supporting firepower, but the smaller vessels acquitted themselves well. One Irish ship was lost, but considerable damage was inflicted, both on Kintyre and on neighbouring Arran, before bad weather and sickness forced the invaders to retreat.[79] Cotton was back in Dublin by 5 October. The following day the earl of Sussex sent a full report of the expedition to the queen.

Mary's time, however, was running out, and her Council had other things to worry about beyond a war effort which was now visibly on hold. John Malen proposed a sort of commando raid on Le Havre, which the Council approved, but before anything could be done peace negotiations had commenced between the two exhausted principals, and all such adventures were suspended. By the end of the month it was known that the queen's illness was likely to be fatal, and on 7 November Mary finally acknowledged that she would have no child and that her husband was not prepared to fight for the succession. She sent a verbal message to Elizabeth, acknowledging her right to succeed. When the count of Feria returned, he was, in his own words, received

THE NAVY OF MARY, AND OF PHILIP AND MARY

'like one who bears bulls from a dead pope'. The councillors were holding their breath, and looking towards Ashridge.

At about this time, someone drew up another list of the queen's ships. It shows twenty-two ships and five pinnaces – 3,565 men at a cost of £1,435 a month. These were not ships actually at sea, which would have been no more than a quarter of that number, but presumably represented those which were deemed to be 'fit for service', probably about two-thirds of the navy's total strength.[80] In other words the fleet which Mary passed to her successor was much the same, both in size and in preparedness, as that which she had inherited five years before. Philip's role in sustaining this situation was indirect, but substantial. It is very unlikely that the queen would have maintained the momentum of naval policy without his interest – and need. He also bequeathed one other significant gift to Elizabeth. Earlier in 1558 he had invited Stephen Borough, an English explorer and adventurer, to visit the *Casa de Contratacion* in Seville. Perhaps he felt that after Sebastian Cabot's defection it had few secrets left to hide. Borough nevertheless profited hugely from his journey, and returned with a copy of Martin Corte's *Arte de Navegar*. When this was translated into English by his friend Robert Eden in 1561, it played a further large part in promoting that maritime enterprise which was to cause the king of Spain so many problems.

CHAPTER 4 NOTES

1. TNA PC2/5, p. 2 (*APC*, IV, p. 295). HCA 13/9, ff.149–54, 195–8. J.D. Alsop, 'A Regime at Sea'.
2. TNA PC2/6, pp. 5, 6. *APC*, IV, pp. 416–18. Tyrell had been dispatched by Mary to Harwich on 22 July to keep an eye on the town.
3. Ibid.
4. Loades, *Tudor Navy*, p. 161.
5. *APC*, IV, pp. 339–78. TNA SP11/1, no. 14.
6. J.G. Nichols, *The Diary of Henry Machyn*, Camden Society, 42, 1848, p. 43.
7. TNA SP69/2, no. 76(i).
8. Ibid., no. 75.
9. William Cobbett, *State Trials* (1816), I, p. 714.
10. *Calendar of the Patent Rolls*, 1553–4, p. 262.
11. Winter was indicted, but never tried. D. Loades, *Two Tudor Conspiracies* (1965), pp. 95–6.
12. *APC*, IV, p. 383.
13. Loades, *Tudor Navy*, p. 162.
14. TNA E101/63/5, f.7.
15. Bod MS Rawlinson 846, f.166.
16. TNA E351/2195.

17. *Calendar of State Papers, Venetian*, VI, I, nos 200, 204. Loades and Knighton, *Navy of Edward VI and Mary*, pp. 96–7 and n.

18. TNA SP11/6, no. 17. September 1555. Memorial of matters before the Privy Council since the king's departure.

19. Ibid.

20. Ibid. For Charles V's proposed journey see *Cal. Span.*, XII, pp. 40–1.

21. BL Cotton MS Otho E.IX, no. 40, with lacunae made good from PL 2876, pp. 158–9 – a copy made before fire damaged the original.

22. Ibid.

23. Ibid. 'We think it very strange that they answer the matter so slenderly ....'

24. TNA PC2/7, pp. 351–3. *APC*, V, pp. 219–20.

25. Loades, *Tudor Navy*, p. 161.

26. *APC*, V, p. 258.

27. TNA E351/2196.

28. TNA PC2/7, pp. 545, 565–6. *APC*, VI, pp. 39–41.

29. TNA E351/2197.

30. TNA PC2/6, pp. 308–9. *APC*, V, pp. 183–4.

31. Ibid. Loades, *Tudor Navy*, pp. 163–4.

32. TNA PC2/6, pp. 398–9. *APC*, V, pp. 259–60.

33. Dublin, Royal Irish Academy, MS 24 F.17 [Red Council Book, Acts of the Privy Council of Ireland, 1556–71]. Loades and Knighton, *Navy of Edward VI and Mary*, p. 101.

34. Loades, *Tudor Navy*, p. 164. Richard Cole had been sought as a pirate by Edward VI's government, and had been imprisoned in the Tower for a while in 1549.

35. Ibid., p. 164.

36. TNA SP11/9, no. 25. Interrogation of Peter Killigrew, August 1556.

37. Loades, *Two Tudor Conspiracies*, pp. 176–217.

38. Wotton to Sir William Petre, 19 June 1556. *Calendar of State Papers, Foreign*, II, p. 229.

39. Loades, *Tudor Navy*, p. 165.

40. TNA SP11/10, no. 6. The Queen to William Tyrell, 13 February 1557.

41. BL Cotton MS Otho E.IX, no. 37, with lacunae supplied from PL 2876, p. 154 – a copy made before the original was damaged by fire.

42. D. Loades, *The Reign of Mary Tudor* (1991), p. 191.

43. For a full discussion of this episode, see ibid., pp. 304–9.

44. TNA SP11/10, nos 60, 65. King and Queen to the Lord Admiral, 22 and 29 May 1557.

45. Ibid., no. 64, also dated 29 May.

46. This list exists in two parts, TNA SP11/10, no. 67, and SP11/11, no. 37. Lacunae in both parts are supplied from PL 2875, pp. 13–14, a copy made before the original was mutilated. The full muster consisted of 2,880 men – 568 soldiers, 1,988 mariners and 324 gunners.

47. TNA SP11/11, no. 1. This is a draft in Petre's hand. Although he had resigned the secretaryship a little earlier, Petre was still clearly drafting official correspondence.

48. TNA SP11/11, no. 14. Responses to enquiries from the Lord Treasurer

49. Ibid., no. 16.

50. TNA SP11/11, no. 18, corrected from PL 2875, p. 20.

51. Ibid., no. 20, corrected from PL 2875, pp. 22–3. King and Queen to the Lord Treasurer.
52. Ibid.
53. TNA SP11/11, no. 35. *Calendar of the Patent Rolls*, 1157–8, p. 2.
54. SP11/11, no. 35.
55. Ibid., no. 38.
56. 26 July 1557. Ibid, no. 29.
57. Queen to Vice Admiral Woodhouse, 1 August 1557. PL 2875, pp. 28–30.
58. Loades and Knighton, *The Navy of Edward VI and Mary*, p. 123 n. Clere had landed at Kirkwall on 11 August, but finding the natives hostile had beat a hasty retreat, leaving some of his guns behind. There is an account of the incident in J. Strype, *Ecclesiastical Memorials* (1822), III, ii, pp. 86–7.
59. Loades, *Tudor Navy*, p. 171.
60. TNA SP11/11, no. 65.
61. Wentworth had at last begun to take the rumours of attack seriously on 26 December, when he alerted the Council. The earl of Rutland was appointed on the 29th. Ibid., no. 66. TNA SP69/11, nos 699, 701; 69/12, no. 708.
62. TNA SP69/12, no. 712. He had met the *Saker*, returning from a failed mission.
63. C.S.L. Davies, 'England and the French War, 1557–9', in J. Loach and R. Tittler, eds, *The Mid-Tudor Polity, 1540–1560* (1981), p. 172.
64. TNA SP11/12, no. 12. T. Glasgow jnr, 'The Navy in Philip and Mary's War', *Mariners Mirror*, 53, 1967, p. 333 and n.
65. TNA SP11/12, no.18. The Queen to Woodhouse, 12 January 1558. The musters were abandoned on the 17th.
66. *Cal. Span.*, XIII, p. 348. For a full discussion of the correspondence passing at this time, see Loades, *The Reign of Mary Tudor*, pp. 316–21.
67. TNA SP11/12, no. 23.
68. BL Cotton MS Otho E.IX, no. 41 (with lacunae supplied from PL 2876, p. 160).
69. TNA SP11/12, no. 51. For some recollections of the circumstances of the replacement of Howard by Clinton, see *The Letters of William, Lord Paget of Beaudesert, 1547–1563*, ed. B.L. Beer and S.M. Jack (Camden Society, 4th series, 13, 1974), pp. 130–1.
70. Queen to the Lord Treasurer, 27 March 1558. PL 2875, p. 36. Explaining that the Lord Admiral 'had made humble suit unto us' for this assistance.
71. PL 1266, pp. 63–72.
72. TNA SP11/12, nos 69, 70.
73. *Cal. Span.*, XIII, pp. 383–4.
74. Ibid., pp. 385–7.
75. William Winter to Secretary John Boxall, 22 May 1558. TNA SP11/12, nos 11, 11(i).
76. Loades, *Tudor Navy*, p. 173.
77. TNA SP11/13, no. 64. Glasgow, 'The Navy in Philip and Mary's War', p. 337.
78. Glasgow, 'The Navy in Philip and Mary's War', p. 336. TNA SP11/13, no. 51.
79. Glasgow, 'The Navy in Philip and Mary's War', p. 339. TNA SP50/1, nos 36, 37. SP62/2, nos 70, 71. The earl of Sussex to the Queen, 3 and 6 October 1558.
80. PL 2876, p. 153.

CHAPTER FIVE

THE FIRST DECADE OF ELIZABETH

Warfare was very expensive. Over two full years, from 30 December 1556 to 30 December 1558, Benjamin Gonson received £144,941, of which £131,154 came from the Exchequer.[1] According to his own account, he spent £157,638 of which victualling amounted to £73,503 and wages to men at sea a further £43,492. This should have left him with a deficit of over £12,000, but when he commenced his next regular account on 1 January 1559, he acknowledged arrears of only £841.[2] So either the difference had been written off or the statement of his income is incomplete. These accounts cover all but the last three months of the war, when peace negotiations were ongoing and military operations had virtually ceased, so the cost of the navy during the run-up to the war, and while hostilities were active, was some £78,000 a year, more than three times the peacetime level, in spite of the fact that no Navy Royal was sent out. Neither Elizabeth nor William Cecil, now her principal man of affairs, had previously received any detailed information about the working of the Admiralty, and it is not clear that Lord Clinton, who was retained as Lord Admiral, was much better informed. Consequently on 12 December, less than a month into the new reign, a memorandum was drawn up for Cecil's benefit. This showed that at the moment of Mary's death there had been six royal ships and seven auxiliary merchantmen on patrol in the Narrow Seas, carrying a total of 335 masters, mariners and gunners.[3] If these figures are accurate, they must all have been small ships, but we do not know which ones they were. It was essentially a costing estimate for what was actually happening (and had happened) between 1 October and 31 December 1558, and the patrols, which presumably remained constant over that period, would, it was judged, require £3,167. At the same time 184 shipwrights and other craftsmen were currently rebuilding the *Peter* at Woolwich, and the *Jennet* and the *Hare* at Portsmouth, work which it was estimated would cost a further £2,123. By the time that the regular wages and expenses at the other yards were added to these totals, they would have amounted to some £6,000 for the quarter, or £24,000 for the full year – assuming, of course, that the peace negotiations were successful.

THE FIRST DECADE OF ELIZABETH 101

At this time, Cecil was busily accumulating information about every aspect of the job which he had undertaken, and on 20 February 1559 someone, probably the Clerk of the Ships, drew up a checklist of the navy for his benefit, heading it 'The names of all Her Highness's ships and where at present they do remain ...'.[4] This started with three Great Ships, the *Mary Rose*, the *Lion* and the *Philip and Mary* at Gillingham, presumably out of commission. Nine were listed as being 'in the river of Thames', probably at Deptford, with a further eight at Portsmouth. Work on the *Hare* had by this time been completed. Four small ships of between 40 and 70 tons were still patrolling the Narrow Seas, while two, the *Falcon* and the *Phoenix*, were noted as 'presently to be sent northward', reflecting the ongoing anxiety about the intentions of the Scots. The *Peter* and the *Jennet* were still being worked upon at Woolwich and Portsmouth, while the *Hare* had been replaced in dock by the *Sweepstake*. Four further vessels were 'At Deptford, to be repaired' – a total of thirty-four ships displacing some 7,250 tons. In addition it was noted that six merchant ships were 'presently in her Majesty's service'. The memorandum continued with a request to know the queen's pleasure for the future of the ordinary of £14,000, which as we have seen had been allocated in 1557, and a reminder that if any of these ships were to be 'put to the seas in fashion of war', that would count as extraordinary expenditure, not to be met out of the ordinary. Cecil then made his own note in the margin, reminding himself that the *Henry Grace de Dieu* had been burned in 1553, and the *Primrose* sold for £1,800 (of which £800 was still outstanding). He also noted that the *Minion* had been 'given to Sir Thomas Seymour'. This is the only record of such a transaction, and it must have come back to the Crown on his attainder, because it later features in royal service. The *Trinity Henry*, the *Dragon*, and a second (and smaller) *Lion* were noted as decayed.[5]

His appetite thus whetted, Cecil clearly called upon the Admiralty for some forward planning, and the following month a comprehensive set of proposals was drawn up, entitled 'A boke of Sea causes'.[6] This differs from the previous exercise in a number of ways. The former was a report, whereas this is more in the nature of a policy assessment. It is subtitled 'A declaration of an army which may be made as well of the Queen's Majesty's own ships and barks as of her subjects ships and barks, with an estimate of the charges that will grow upon the same ...', and it starts with a list of twenty-one ships 'thought meet to be kept and preserved'. This bears no particular resemblance to the previous list, and several of the ships then appearing no longer feature, either here or in a supplement of ten ships 'thought meet to be continued' only during the doubtful time of peace, and thereafter to be scrapped or sold at the queen's pleasure. Why this should have been so is not known. It is estimated that forty-five merchant ships are available for war service. The tonnage of the first list is 5,350, and number of men required 3,880; of the second list 1,600 and 1,720; and of the third category (unlisted) 7,040 and 4,600. In addition to these it was noted that twenty victuallers of 80 tons 'or thereabouts' would be needed, and that the charges for 'the whole army being furnished' would be £11,363 a month. There was, of course, no question of actually raising such a force in the current political climate, so the exercise is a hypothetical one. It is, nonetheless, interesting in some of its particulars. The first list starts with 'the great new ship' of 800 tons, not otherwise mentioned, and later named the *Elizabeth Jonas*, which was presumably nearing completion by this time,[7] although it is not known when she was laid down. A seaman's pay is given as 8s 6d a month, with 12s for victuals, which presumably represents an average for both mariners and officers, since the former's wage had been raised from 5s a month to 6s 8d in 1545. The tonnage to be paid on ships 'taken up' was 12d a month, and that had not changed for a very long time. The demobilisation cost for such an army was estimated at £4,000.

The second element of the 'boke' was an updating of the pre-Christmas report, showing seven royal ships and eight armed merchantmen as being actually at sea, although they were now carrying 940 men, including 320 soldiers under the command of Sir Thomas Cotton.[8] The estimated monthly cost of this guard was £1,597. The present voyage was scheduled to continue to the end of March, and the queen's pleasure concerning its continuance was requested. Interestingly, the armed merchantmen upon which tonnage was being paid were led by the *Primrose* of London – probably the same ship which the navy had recently sold.[9] The close connections between the Admiralty and the City had more than one way of manifesting themselves! There then followed a third element, similarly dated 24 March, which consisted of a summary of work in progress at Woolwich, Deptford and Portsmouth 'within the compass of the ordinary', which had by then (11 March 1559) been fixed at £12,000.[10] At Deptford five small ships were being worked upon by 170 shipwrights and other artificers and twenty-five labourers. The former, who were lodged and fed as well as receiving wages, cost 12d a day, while the latter, who were paid wages only, cost 7d a day. The total cost, for just over three months, would be £1,816. At Woolwich were eight ships, 150 artificers and twenty-five labourers for a charge of £1,254, and at Portsmouth nine ships, 130 artificers and twenty-four labourers, estimated to cost £1,151. A total of twenty-two ships, about two-thirds of the fleet, were thus undergoing some sort of repair or refurbishment at this point. The remainder were 'aflote' either at Portsmouth or in the Thames, being looked after by a total of 372 shipkeepers and gunners. The latter being paid at a significantly higher rate, the average wage bill per man/month was reckoned to be 20s, totalling £1,195. The total ordinary expenditure calculated for the first half-year was therefore £5,417, comfortably within the limit of £6,000 which was available. These figures are difficult to relate to Gonson's summary accounts, which are differently divided and cover a more extended period, but the impression remains that the totals were massaged to fit, and need to be taken with a pinch of salt.

The three parts of the book were then followed by two brief policy papers, the first for the navy in peacetime, and the second in the event of war. Gillingham was 'the meetest harbour to keep the Queen's Majesty's ships', because it was more secure, required fewer shipkeepers, and was more convenient for 'grounding'.[11] The Admiralty officers had been arguing along these lines for a number of years, and as we have seen had had a disagreement with Philip on the subject. They now recommended that the ten ships presently lying at Portsmouth should be brought around to the Medway, and that the old blockhouse at Sheerness should be refurbished and kept with six gunners to protect the anchorage. It seems that these recommendations were acted upon, because a new fort was built at Upnor later in the same year, and manned as suggested.[12] It was calculated that fitting out the ships needed in the Medway and then moving them to Portsmouth would cost no more than £2,000. If they then remained based in the south during June, July and August, about £1,700 would be added to the cost of their maintenance, so they should be brought back to Gillingham as soon as their tour of duty was completed. The sending out of a 'summer guard' even in peacetime was clearly a well established routine by this time, although the number of ships used would depend on the circumstances. Finally, the officers present a profile of the future navy 'sufficient number for her Majesty to have of her own, which may be made and brought to perfection within five years next following ...', provided that the ordinary was continued – about which there already seems to have been some doubt.[13] This navy was to consist of twenty-four ships of 200 tons and upwards – four of 600–800 tons, four of 500, four of 400, six of 300 and six of 200. In addition there should be four barks of 60–80 tons and two pinnaces of 40 tons – a total of thirty. This blueprint was altogether too tidy, and was never strictly adhered to, but it did form the basis of naval thinking for the next twenty-five years or so, until the growing threat from Spain at sea prompted a significant expansion.

What is clear from these documents is that the navy had been well maintained since the death of Henry VIII. Discounting the rowbarges the total number of ships had declined from 40+ to 30+, but there had been a number of replacements, and the ratio of Great Ships to lesser had actually increased. A structured policy of maintenance, rebuilding and refurbishment was in place throughout the period, with the workforce in each location fluctuating in accordance with demand, but an infrastructure of permanent staff was regularly employed. It seems likely that the later practice of retaining a small number of skilled craftsmen, and moving them from job to job as required, was already being followed, although the absence of names from these summary accounts makes that kind of conclusion elusive.[14] There is more than a suggestion in the Admiralty advice that an ordinary of £12,000 was likely to be inadequate, and that something more in the order of £20,000 would have been appropriate. However, as we shall see, even £12,000 was more than Elizabeth would readily allocate, not because she was mean, but because she preferred a flexible deployment of resources. The queen also knew perfectly well that by choosing a Protestant religious settlement, she was taking an aligned position in the ideological conflict which was now replacing dynastic conflict as the main engine of European politics, and like the duke of Northumberland, would not be able to afford the luxury of lowering her guard. In that respect the peace of Cateau Cambrecis, which ended the Franco-Habsburg war in April 1559, was a non-event. Elizabeth had been forced to concede Calais, but had done so with an exceedingly bad grace,[15] and although Scotland was included in the peace, a powerful French force remained in the north, threatening continued instability.

Then in July Henry II died as the result of a jousting accident. This brought his son Francis II to the throne, and re-opened the whole question of the French recognition of Elizabeth's title. Henry II had accepted her, but Francis was married to her chief dynastic rival, Mary of Scotland. The couple immediately quartered the arms of England with those of France and Scotland, thus laying claim to a triple monarchy extending from the Shetlands to the Mediterranean. It was an insubstantial bid, but a significant and threatening one.[16] Francis was fifteen, and therefore technically of age by French custom, which meant that there was no restraining regency, and his wife's kinsmen, the duke and cardinal of Guise became all-powerful. Their sister Mary was queen regent of Scotland, and even if Francis himself had not been particularly keen, there were still ample grounds to fear aggression in the north. There were therefore plenty of anxieties to justify a careful fostering of naval strength.

Fortunately, Elizabeth was not the only one to fear the Guises. Not only did opposition to them begin to gather in France, threatening the breakdown of royal government which was shortly to ensue, but the Protestant lords of Scotland also came out in open rebellion in the spring of 1559. For a little while it looked as though the Lords of the Congregation would be able to take out the Francophile government of the queen regent without English assistance. But as the summer advanced it became clear that their levies were no match for the French professionals. They suffered a number of defeats and their forces began to evaporate.[17] Equally important, they had no fleet to prevent further reinforcements arriving from France, and for that reason they appealed for Elizabeth's assistance in the autumn of 1559. In spite of the critical nature of their predicament, the queen did not respond at once, hoping, as always, that the development of events would make action unnecessary. That, however, did not happen, and the news that such reinforcements had actually sailed on 13 December forced her hand. On the 16th she ordered Sir William Winter to sea with thirty-four ships, and instructions to intercept any French vessels bound for Scotland. Bizarrely, and quite unrealistically, his instructions enjoined him to act as though on his own initiative – as though anyone would have believed that a large fleet of the queen's ships was acting on anyone's orders but her own![18] Fortunately this extraordinary order rapidly became irrelevant, because the situation on the ground in Scotland was deteriorating all the time, and on the 24th the Council instructed the duke of Norfolk to cross the border with 4,000 men who had already been mustered. He was to advance cautiously, but the object of his intervention was clear. At the same time the French fleet which had created the original alarm was dispersed and driven back by storms. All that actually changed, however, was that Winter's role became open and acknowledged. A second fleet was rapidly assembled in the Normandy ports, with the intention of shipping 10,000 men north 'by Candlemas'.[19] Winter reached the Firth of Forth on 22 January 1560, and immediately cut the lines of communication between the French headquarters in Leith and the army currently deployed in Fife. The latter promptly retreated by way of Stirling, leaving their artillery and much of their supplies behind. Meanwhile the second French relief expedition was similarly frustrated by the weather, and the few French ships remaining in the Firth, two galleys and a hoy, were captured. Encouraged by this success, Norfolk was now allowed to conclude a formal treaty of alliance with the Scottish lords. By this Elizabeth became Protector of the Liberties of Scotland for as long as the marriage between Mary and Francis should endure – an ironic position indeed for a daughter of Henry VIII![20]

Meanwhile the situation in France continued to conspire in her favour. On 16 and 17 March a Huguenot conspiracy against the Guise ascendancy erupted in the tumult of Amboise, and religious discord flared up alarmingly. Realising Elizabeth's anxiety to recover Calais, and afraid that she might seek to intervene in France for that purpose, Philip began to make threatening noises. However, he could not afford to go to war again, and the queen did not want to fight on two fronts, so the episode subsided, but not before the Anglo-Spanish amity which had been so recently proclaimed was exposed as the sham it was. More worrying to her Council than Philip's posturing was, however, Elizabeth's hesitancy about her intervention in the north. Norfolk had already had his orders countermanded once, before he signed his treaty, and it looked as though the same thing might happen again. Then on 28 March William Cecil took the bull by the horns. Taking the enormous risk of acting without the queen's specific orders, or at least any that were publicly acknowledged, he authorised Lord Grey to advance from Berwick with a second and more substantial army.[21] By 5 April Leith was under siege. The siege was a failure, but the die had now been cast. Elizabeth and her Scottish allies continued to have different objectives, because while they were concerned to secure control of the country, she was only anxious to get the French out of Scotland. However, the queen regent, whose health was in rapid decline by this time, and who refused to believe that no more reinforcements would get through from France, refused the negotiations which might have prised them apart. Had the French forces still in the north been adequate, the outcome might have been very different, but in spite of their success in holding Leith, they were slowly dwindling, and nothing short of an Armada could have got through Winter's blockade. With so large a fleet, he was able to operate in relays, sending individual ships back to Holy Island or to Newcastle for re-victualling or repairs as necessary, without losing his grip on the Firth. The fact that Scotland had nothing which could be described as an organised navy at this point, and that the French were increasingly preoccupied with their own affairs, meant that Winter's ascendancy was unchallenged. On 11 June the queen regent died, and the Francophile party soon acknowledged defeat. Elizabeth, who was not much concerned with what the Scots did among themselves, was happy to endorse the Protestant ascendancy which then resulted, whatever the young Queen Mary might think.[22] She was concerned to get the French out, and by the treaty of Edinburgh, signed on 6 July 1560, achieved just that. Both England and France agreed to withdraw their forces. The fortifications of Leith, Eyemouth and Dunbar were to be razed, and Mary and Francis were to cease displaying the arms of England in their achievements.[23] Winter then evacuated the whole French garrison and their dependants in what was probably the most efficient naval operation of the reign, although never really acknowledged. By the time that his fleet was withdrawn in September it had been on station for over nine months – an astonishing achievement by the standards of the time – and had cost £11,294 – a fraction of the cost of the army, which had achieved far less.[24]

The year 1560 had been a year of high anxiety, and the deployment of the navy had reflected that. While Winter was in the north, Lord Admiral Clinton was operating out of Portsmouth, guarding the south-western approaches. Although he had forty-two ships, this was more in the nature of a summer patrol than of a focused operation, since it cost less than £6,000.[25] It was a precaution in case Philip's threats should turn out to have substance. As Clinton had two Venetian captains on his payroll, it is quite probable that the navy's two galleys, the *Speedwell* and the *Tryright*, were sent out with this fleet. They had been taken from the French in the closing stages of the war, and otherwise are not known to have been used. During the same 'cruising season' Sir Thomas Cotton had twenty ships in the Narrow Seas at a cost of £3,500.[26] This was the standard summer guard, and did not signify any heightened expectation of hostility from the French, except, of course, in relation to Scotland. In spite of the operations in the north, England was not officially at war with anyone in 1560, but the heightened level of naval activity required by this vigilance was dramatically reflected in Gonson's accounts. Whereas in 1559 he had expended £21,868, including the building and repair work which we have noticed, in 1560 that had shot up to £84,300.[27] Because there was no war, all the deployment costs were channelled through his account, which gives them this inflated appearance. It also explains why Elizabeth was so reluctant either to follow up the treaty of Edinburgh, or to take any initiative against the Guise ascendancy in France. The Scottish lords were anxious for a closer relationship, and there was unfinished business between Ulster and the Scottish islands, but the queen did not want to know.[28] Her ambassador in France, Nicholas Throgmorton, warned her that Mary and Francis would refuse to ratify the treaty of Edinburgh, and that the Guises were bent on revenge, but his warnings went unheeded. This was partly because in the autumn of 1560 Elizabeth was preoccupied by her relationship with Lord Robert Dudley, and the crisis provoked by the death of Lady Amy Dudley in September, but the queen was quite good at detaching her private feelings from her public concerns, and her lack of interest in further military adventures was almost certainly provoked by concern at the expense involved.[29]

Circumstances also conspired to favour her, because in December 1560 Francis II died. This left Mary a widow at the age of nineteen, and broke the direct link between the Guises and the crown of France. Francis was succeeded by his younger brother, who became Charles IX. Charles was a minor, and that necessitated a regency. Guise pretensions were by this time widely resented, even among the Catholic nobility of France, with the result that the regency was given to the strong-minded queen mother, Catherine de Medici, and Catherine's first concern was to rescue her son from excessive dependence on the Guises. So while Mary was reduced to a political shadow, her kindred were on the defensive, which was all very convenient from Elizabeth's point of view.[30] Rather less convenient was Mary's return to her northern kingdom in August 1561, although Elizabeth did not at first see it that way. Her role as 'Protector of the Liberties of Scotland' had come to an end with Francis's death, and she was not anxious to renew it. To her Mary represented legitimacy in the north, and if she could come to terms with the ascendant Protestant lords, a very welcome stability would result. Mary requested a safe conduct to travel to Scotland by way of England, and that may well have presented a greater problem to Elizabeth's Council than to the queen herself, bearing in mind that the Scottish queen had never renounced her claim to the English throne. While they hesitated, Mary took the initiative, and set off escorted by two ships and two galleys. When this flotilla encountered the English barks patrolling the North Sea, they politely exchanged greetings and passed on.[31] This time there was no question of a renewed French military presence in the north, and that was all that interested the queen of England. Even if it had been offered, the Scots lords were quite strong enough by this time to prevent it.

From a naval point of view, 1561 was a quiet year. The usual patrols operated in the North Sea and the Channel, and there were complaints of piracy, but nothing of note was done. The following year, 1562, however, was different, thanks to the deteriorating situation in France. The duke of Guise had no intention of accepting his exclusion from power by the queen regent, and by February had emerged as the leader of the ultra-Catholics, or *dévots*, whose declared aim was the extermination of all heresy in France. This inevitably meant civil war, because the Huguenots counted among their number not only a large number of seigneurs, but also Princes of the Blood, like the Bourbons, whose following was almost – if not quite – as strong as that of the Guises.[32] By the end of March the prince of Conde and Gaspar de Coligny were in arms, and had seized the strategic city of Orleans. They appealed to their co-religionists in Germany and in England for support, and Nicholas Throgmorton from Paris urged the queen to become involved. Elizabeth's first reaction was to offer mediation, but her overtures to that purpose were brushed aside by Catherine, who seems not to have taken her intention seriously. This left Elizabeth in a quandary, because a Catholic victory would leave the Channel ports in hostile hands, and might easily expose Scotland to renewed Guise attention. On the other hand, if she supported the Protestants, she might just possibly be able to exact Calais as the price of her assistance. Her Council was divided. Both Cecil and William Paulet, the marquis of Winchester, whom she had retained as Lord Treasurer, were opposed to intervention, but others urged it, and the most potent voice on that side of the argument was Lord Robert Dudley.[33] Although it is clear with hindsight that Lord Robert's matrimonial ambitions had disappeared by this time, he did not see it that way, and in spite of his not being yet a Privy Councillor, his word was still influential with the queen.

Whether it was his urging, or the situation in France itself, which finally prompted her to act, we do not know, but on 20 September 1562 Elizabeth signed a secret treaty at Richmond with the prince of Conde. England was to provide Conde with 6,000 men and a loan of 140,000 crowns (£45,000), and in return was to recover Calais.[34] Unfortunately Calais was not under

Huguenot control, and until it became available, Elizabeth was to receive Le Havre as a pledge. The latter, known to the English as Newhaven, was to be handed over at once, and half the 6,000 troops deployed were to garrison it. The terms of this treaty must have been worked out some time in advance, because the queen was able to dispatch the first contingent of troops under Sir Adrian Poynings within a matter of days. In so doing she was careful to explain to the Spanish ambassador that she was not at war with France, and was acting to prevent the spread of unauthorised conflict, rather than to encourage it. He was not convinced.[35] Naval deployment kept pace with this rapidly developing situation. In July, before the Huguenot negotiation reached a climax, there had been the usual eight or ten ships at sea: the *Saker* and the *Phoenix* transporting provisions to Berwick; the *Mary Willoughby* and several others ferrying artillery to Ireland and chasing pirates in the Irish Sea — a fairly normal summer agenda.[36] However on 6 August five other vessels were sent out under Sir William Woodhouse, and this portended an exceptional mobilisation. Woodhouse remained at sea in the Channel throughout August and September, being joined by three other ships on 10 September, and by the *Triumph* and the *Victory* (both new and large warships) on 1 October.[37] This formidable fleet ensured a safe passage for the rest of the promised troops, and the earl of Warwick took over responsibility for Le Havre from Poynings in November. With the onset of winter the larger warships were withdrawn, because there was no sign of the French navy and the Guises do not seem to have commanded the services of any ships. On 1 December it was all change on the Channel guard as the *Triumph* and the *Victory* were replaced with five smaller vessels which maintained full communications with Normandy throughout the winter.

So far, so good, but the war which these forces were designed to support was going from bad to worse. On 26 October the Catholic forces took Rouen, and thus cut Le Havre off from the main Huguenot army, and then in December Conde was defeated at Dreux and taken prisoner.[38] This suited Catherine very well, but she had no desire for a more complete Catholic victory, and took advantage of Conde's imprisonment to start negotiations for a settlement. Her efforts were probably aided by the assassination of the duke of Guise in February 1563, although there is no reason to believe that she was responsible, and by the end of March Conde had come to terms. In return for regaining his own liberty, and securing a modest degree of toleration for his co-religionists, he laid down his arms and abandoned his ally.[39] Warwick had played no part in these unfolding events, but he had been busy in his own fashion. As soon as Poynings had arrived in Le Havre, the French government had declared that all English ships were legitimate prizes for its privateers. However the Catholics were not strong at sea, and little damage seems to have resulted. Elizabeth did not retaliate because she wished to maintain the position that she had no quarrel with the French Crown. However, both the earl of Warwick and the Huguenot governor of Le Havre issued their own letters of marque, and in the absence of French Catholic targets, their privateers turned their attention to the Flemings and Spaniards who were constantly passing, inflicting, it was claimed, untold damage.[40] Whether Elizabeth knew about this, let alone approved it, we do not know. On 8 February she dissociated herself from any such practice, forbidding her subjects from giving aid or succour to the Le Havre 'pirates', but this may have been disingenuous, and was in any case no more than a gesture.[41] Warwick certainly had no authority to issue letters of marque, and how many may have originated with him is unclear. The borderline between piracy and privateering was in any case indeterminate, and made more so by these unofficial wars. Francis Clark, who is alleged to have fitted out three ships and to have taken prizes worth £50,000, was probably an unusually successful pirate, but he may have been given countenance either by Warwick, or possibly by Lord Admiral Clinton. However, he does not seem to have accounted to any Admiralty court, which he should have done if his activities had been in any sense legitimate.[42]

In the absence of more purposeful activity, Warwick had kept his soldiers occupied during the winter of 1562/3 by strengthening the fortifications. However, when Conde settled at the end of March, his position became politically untenable. The French abandoned their differences to besiege him, and by the beginning of June 1563 the port was closely invested. This was not a disaster as long as the sea lanes remained open, but by the middle of the month a more serious enemy had struck – plague. Reinforcements were sent, but they succumbed as quickly as the rest. By the beginning of July a crisis was clearly approaching, and a rescue mission of twenty royal ships was hastily planned.[43] By the time that they got to sea, on 17 and 18 July, Warwick had only 1,200 fit men, and then the mission was held up by contrary winds. Before it could arrive, on 24 July, Warwick lost control of the harbour, and being by this reduced to extreme straits, he surrendered on the 26th, on honourable terms.[44] The fleet returned to Portsmouth, having seen no action at all, and orders were given for most of the ships to go back to their anchorages at Gillingham. The only thing that the English had gained from their ten-month stay at Le Havre was fifteen ships, which, on 5 July, 300 seamen were sent over from Rye to bring back to England. The seamen were paid and victualled for ten days, and seem to have accomplished their mission successfully.[45] On arrival the ships were assessed, valued and eventually sold. The operation of recovering them cost £102 in wages and victuals. Apart from this very modest asset, the queen was left with an empty diplomatic hand, and an additional bill for about £8,000, over and above the costs of the army. Gonson started the year of 1562 with a 'surplusage' (deficit) of £7,728. Over the next two years he received £53,790 and spent (including the costs of the Le Havre adventure) £63,151, leaving him with a surplusage at the end of 1563 of £9,521. Elizabeth's gamble had not only failed, it had been exceedingly expensive, and this was a lesson which she was not to forget.[46]

Just about every serviceable ship in the navy was used during the summer of 1563, and quite a few auxiliaries as well, because a regular presence was maintained in the Irish Sea and the North Sea as well as all the activity relating to Le Havre. Ships were also detached for individual missions, as is clear from instructions sent by the Privy Council, usually to the Admiral in the relevant quarter, but sometimes direct to the captain of the ship concerned. For example on 29 August 1562 Sir William Woodhouse was instructed to send the *Swallow*, presently under his command, to carry Sir Hugh Paulet to Spain on a diplomatic mission.[47] In August 1563, when the Channel fleet had only just returned from Normandy, Ralph Chamberlain had three ships under his command in the North Sea. Gonson's Quarter Book, which survives for 1562–3, also suggests specific missions not otherwise recorded. Six ships were victualled for two months on 13 March 1563, five more on 4 April, a rowbarge on 19 May, and the *Swallow* and the *Falcon* on 25 May.[48] Apart from the last occasion we do not know the identity of these ships, or what specifically they were doing, although it is natural to suppose that they were bound for Le Havre. On 27 June three ships were again 'sent northward', and the main fleet was victualled in batches during July, when events in Normandy were coming to a crisis. After that disaster, in the winter of 1563–4, an unusually strong naval presence was maintained in the Channel, perhaps as a precaution in case the Catholic forces in France should suddenly acquire ships and attack the south coast, or more likely in a vain attempt to regain some military credibility.[49] The *Elizabeth Jonas*, the *Victory* and the *Philip and Mary* were all in service between November and January, and it was most unusual to deploy such large capital ships in the middle of the winter.

The majority of ships in royal service during this period were the queen's own, but the practice of hiring private ships, particularly as victuallers, continued. When Winter was in the north in 1560 he was kept supplied by about fifty small vessels, hired at 12d per ton per month – a total cost of £2,072. One such was the *Anne Gallant* of London, whose service we know about because she was individually discharged at Leith on 11 June.[50] In 1563 the *David of Lubeck* was hired for similar service at the higher rate of 16d per ton which had to be paid for foreign 'bottoms'. Private shipping was also used in the pursuit of pirates, not usually by 'taking up' but by authorisation. This was the same kind of licensed self-help which had been common in the previous century. For example on 14 November 1564 the mayor, aldermen and 'certain citizens' of Bristol were granted a commission out of the Admiralty court to set out certain ships 'for the repressing and apprehending of pirates haunting the seas between Scilly and the port of Bristol …' and the justices of the peace for Devon were ordered to assist them.[51] Such commissions were not numerous, but this is by no means an isolated example. It was clearly felt that their former victims were in the best position to know who these pirates were, and where they were to be found. In peacetime private ships were only hired as a short-term expedient, or when the navy's own available ships were deemed to be unsuitable. In 1569 two large London ships were hired for two weeks to do guard duty in the Thames, presumably as a stop-gap while the appropriate royal vessels were prepared.[52] Usually during this first decade the navy's own resources were adequate for the calls which were made upon them.

As we have seen, it had been normal practice during periods of relative political quiet, for the Crown to rent out its warships to private merchant companies. Originally they had been useful load carriers, but more recently their specialised design had suited them to be escorts into the perilous waters where merchants were now venturing. They had been hired for an agreed rental, and against a bond of indemnity in the event of loss or damage. However in 1561 Elizabeth embarked upon a new strategy when she loaned the *Minion*, the *Primrose*, the *Brigandine* and the *Fleur de Luce* to Sir William Chester for a voyage to Africa. Sir William paid no rental because these ships, together with £500 worth of provisions, constituted the queen's investment.[53] In effect she became a large shareholder, and entitled to one-third of the profits of the voyage. In 1562 Robert Dudley 'borrowed' the *Jesus of Lubeck* for two years. This may have been a conventional hire arrangement, but since he paid only £500 for the two years, it also looks like a concealed investment, although the purpose of the exercise is not known. Better known than either of these ventures, however, is Elizabeth's involvement in John Hawkins's second slaving expedition in 1564. He had carried out a trial run in 1562, using private investment and a contact in the Canary Islands.[54] The results had been promising, and by this time Hawkins had good contacts both in the City and in the court. Robert Dudley, the earl of Pembroke and a syndicate of City merchants backed his venture. More importantly, however, he had the 'Admiralty interest' behind him. Lord Admiral Clinton, Benjamin Gonson (whose daughter Katherine he was to marry in the following year) and William Winter were all among his investors.[55] It may have been this which persuaded Elizabeth to contribute the ageing but still serviceable *Jesus*, and as it turned out the presence of this warship was critical. Hawkins's venture was strictly illegal, but the Portuguese interest in West Africa was poorly policed and he had no difficulty in collecting his cargo. However, in the West Indies it was a different story, and when he arrived in Hispaniola he found the Spanish colonists too much in awe of their own viceroy to be willing to trade. It required a significant display of firepower from the warship to persuade them to do business, and to give them the necessary excuse of coercion.[56] The profits were substantial, but there was a political price to be paid. Don Guzman da Silva, the Spanish ambassador in London, made furious representations, and although he was turned aside with soft answers, Elizabeth was sufficiently worried to forbid Hawkins from setting out again.[57]

Instead an entirely private voyage under Captain John Lovell ensued, and without the benefit of either Hawkins's Canary Island friends, or his warship, it was a complete failure. Elizabeth had allowed Anglo-Spanish relations to deteriorate steadily since the beginning of her reign, but the next disruption was not her fault – or at least not directly so. In 1566 protests against Philip's centralising and persecuting policies in the Low Countries blew up a storm, and the regent, Margaret of Parma, decided that the English were to blame. She imposed an embargo on English trade, which forced the Merchant Adventurers to move their staple to Hamburg, and greatly stimulated the search in London for alternative outlets for the cloth trade. Elizabeth negotiated, and in more than one sense she held a position of strength. It rapidly transpired that the Antwerp merchants were suffering far more from the withdrawal of English cloth than were the suppliers. At a pinch they could always go elsewhere, while Antwerp had no alternative source of supply for a trade which had accounted for almost a third of its turnover.[58] Secondly, although the occupation of Le Havre had ended so disastrously, it had at least demonstrated that France had no navy of any significance. The powerful fleet which had threatened to devastate the south of England in 1545 had disintegrated entirely. This meant that unless, or until, the French ended their internal conflicts, Elizabeth no longer had need of an alliance with either Spain or Flanders to provide security at sea – her own navy was quite capable of providing that unaided.

Within a year the embargo was lifted, but the Merchant Adventurers did not return to Antwerp, which embarked upon a prolonged period of decline. With over 30,000 Dutch Protestant refugees in England by 1567, and the (relatively) amenable Margaret replaced in the Low Countries by the duke of Alba, relations were set to deteriorate further. Meanwhile John Hawkins, counting on his mistress's renewed indulgence, was assembling ships at Plymouth for a fresh venture. He did not have any warships under his command at this point, but several of his vessels were clearly armed, because when an uninvited Spanish squadron attempted to take refuge in the harbour from a storm in the Channel, Hawkins opened fire on them and drove them out.[59] He alleged that they refused to salute the English flag, but who was the aggressor in this encounter remains a matter of opinion.

What it did do was to persuade the queen (temporarily at least) that she had nothing to lose by a further act of provocation. Hawkins's intended private venture quickly became a public enterprise. Not only did Elizabeth provide him with two ships, the *Jesus* and the *Minion*, she also issued him with a royal commission. There was no logic behind this gesture, because the voyage was funded as before by private investors – of whom the queen was one – but it was not an official naval expedition.[60] In spite of his commission, Hawkins's situation was totally ambiguous. His fleet included six ships and about 400 men, many of them impressed into service, which suggests that they did not know whether the voyage was official or not. Even the officers seem to have been uncertain. Having set out at the beginning of October 1567, and after battling with Atlantic storms, Hawkins took at least one Portuguese and two French prizes and acquired a payload of slaves in the usual manner, by dealing with the coastal traders. At the end of February 1568 he left the coast of Africa with (according to his own account) ten ships and some fairly unreliable prize crews.[61] After about two months at sea he reached the island of Margarita, off the coast of what is now Venezuela, where he re-supplied his ships and appears to have traded peacefully, not only slaves but also the English cloth which he had brought along to give an impression of legitimacy to the voyage. From Margarita he proceeded to Borobuta on the mainland, where he spent futile weeks trying to negotiate for a trading licence, while his smaller ships explored alternative outlets along the coast, without very much success. From Borobuta he went on to Rio de la Hacha, where a combination of blandishments and force achieved rather more. Having offloaded most of his remaining slaves, about the end of June Hawkins proceeded to Santa Maria, where a mere gesture of coercion was sufficient to unlock the door, and from there on 13 July to Cartagena.[62] Cartagena was a larger and more important settlement, and the English were not welcome there, so after a few days he moved on again, and being almost out of trade goods began to give serious thought to returning home. His manpower being now somewhat reduced by disease and fighting, he abandoned one of his Portuguese prizes, and released one of the French ones with her crew.

However, heading for the straits of Florida his fleet was caught in a severe storm. One ship, the *William and John*, became separated and sailed straight home, having had, as it turned out, a fortunate escape. After searching for some time for a suitable anchorage in which to repair his battered ships, he was advised at length to try his luck at San Juan d'Ulloa, the port town for Vera Cruz. By this time the *Jesus* was in such a bad way that no further delay was possible, so on 16 September, taking his courage in both hands, he entered the harbour.[63] At first he appeared to be well received, probably because the townsmen did not have the wherewithal to resist. Hawkins landed some men, and took over a part of the shore defences as a precaution. However on the 17th his luck deserted him, because a Spanish fleet turned up, also seeking admission to the harbour, and bearing no less a passenger than Don Martin Enriquez, the newly appointed viceroy of New Spain. With the weather threatening, Enriquez negotiated an ostensible stand-off, whereby the English would occupy one side of the harbour to complete their repairs, while the Spaniards occupied the other half.[64] However the Spanish fleet commander, Fransisco de Luxan, regarded the English occupation of shore defences as an outrage, and began to scheme how to dislodge the intruders. As late as the evening of 22 September the Spaniards had kept up a disarming pretence of friendship, and then suddenly on the morning of the 23rd they attacked. In the confusion which followed, the guns of the *Jesus* wrought terrible havoc on the attackers' ships, but unfortunately the ship herself was unrigged in preparation for repairs, and could not be moved. Realising that he was heavily outnumbered, and having already lost the men whom he had sent ashore, Hawkins resolved to escape with as much of the bullion and other profits of the voyage as he could salvage. According to his own account, Francis Drake in the *Judith* had already fled, an action which Drake denied but which caused a long estrangement between the two men.[65] Hawkins himself managed to extract the *Minion* and about 180 men from the chaos, leaving behind five ships (including the *Jesus*), about fifty prisoners and over 130 dead. The *Judith* sailed straight home and had a relatively trouble-free passage, but the *Minion* was overcrowded and under-provisioned. On the coast of New Mexico Hawkins was compelled to set about 100 men ashore, because the alternative was starvation.[66] They were eventually rounded up by the Spanish authorities. On 16 October he eventually left the coast and struggled eastwards, beset by every kind of storm, disease and malnutrition. Convinced that his men did not have the stamina to reach home, he headed for (of all places) the coast of Galicia. Arriving at the beginning of January he was lucky enough to encounter English merchants, and was able to delay for nearly three weeks about Vigo while he replenished his long-exhausted supplies and nursed some of his ailing men back to health.[67] A few of the more seriously ill he transferred to the care of his new friends. Finally, on 20 January he left Vigo, and, conditions favouring him at last, reached Mount's Bay in Cornwall on the 24th. In no way chastened by his experiences, Hawkins was seething with rage against Spanish treachery at San Juan d'Ulloa, and in March, along with other survivors of the voyage, launched a massive claim for compensation in the High Court of Admiralty. His losses, he swore, amounted to £30,000, but since this included a whacking £5,000 for the *Jesus*, which was a leaky old tub and not even his own, his claim deserves to be taken with a large pinch of salt.[68]

In a sense Elizabeth had learned her lesson, and did not again venture the ships of her navy in this fashion, but in another sense the ill will which Hawkins's misfortune had generated had already been overtaken by events. At the end of December 1568 the queen had borrowed on her own behalf the money which several Genoese bankers were shipping to the Netherlands to pay Alba's army. Their ships had been driven into Southampton by a combination of bad weather and French privateers, and on discovering that the money still belonged to the bankers and not to Alba, she announced that she would take it by way of a loan.[69] Alba was furious and immediately imposed another trade embargo, but the bankers had no grievance and accepted this new deal without demur. It was William Cecil who had masterminded this coup, but he had done so with the queen's full connivance, and her unequivocal support for her minister was sufficient to silence those critics who sought to use the resulting diplomatic crisis to discredit him. It is possible that Drake may have reached Devon in time for news of the debacle at San Juan d'Ulloa to have reached Cecil before he decided upon this stroke, but there is no clear evidence of that and the timing is very tight. Although it looks like cause and effect, there was probably no connection between the losses which John Hawkins claimed and the loss which the duke of Alba certainly endured.[70]

Although the queen could not be persuaded into further investment, Hawkins had in a sense given an acceptable face to piracy – so long as it was in the far off Caribbean. Nearer at hand, it was becoming a plague, largely because it was culturally ambiguous. Reprisals had always been recognised as legitimate. If a merchant's goods had been stolen at sea by mariners from an identified port, then that merchant was entitled to obtain forcible redress from any other ship belonging to that port. If the offenders were English subjects then the victim was supposed to resort first to the Admiralty court, and only to use reprisal if that failed to produce satisfaction, but if the offenders were foreigners and their Admiralty jurisdiction unknown, then reprisal might well be a first resort.[71] Piracy had not even been an offence under the common law until statute had transferred it from the Admiralty court to the jurisdiction of the King's Bench in 1536. Thereafter it was a felony, normally triable by a commission of oyer and terminer, and executions following conviction began almost at once.[72] However, it was one thing to hang a few small fry and quite another to bring to court the major operators, who often doubled as respectable merchants and were frequently in league with the local vice admiral who was supposed to be pursuing them. In the twenty years after 1564 English pirates were alleged to have stolen from Scottish merchants goods worth £20,717, while thefts the other way amounted to £9,268, and there was never the slightest diplomatic excuse for such depredations.[73] In 1576 two notorious offenders named Callis and Court relieved five ships out of Rouen of cargo worth £2,000, which they then sold in Cardiff. Rouen merchants were specially privileged, and the Privy Council acted on this occasion. Callis and Court were arrested and tried in November 1577, but in May 1578 they were released on bonds of £4,000 each on the grounds that they were needed for service in the royal navy. It is not surprising that the victims became cynical – or resorted to self-help.[74]

The commission which we have already noticed authorising self-help from Bristol, was followed up on 24 December 1564 with a series of Privy Council letters, directed to all Vice Admirals and to the corporations of various port towns, ordering the arrest of certain named offenders. The authorities involved were also urged to proceed to see justice done. It was one thing to arrest a pirate, but if he was going to be released a few months later, not a lot had been achieved

> ...sundry and divers piracies and spoils have been committed upon the seas by the Queen's majesty's subjects of the west Parts since the conclusion of the last peace with France, and divers of the apprehended, and not one executed or punished according to their deserts.[75]

Clearly the Privy Council had one rule for its agents, and another for itself. Commissions of oyer and terminer had already been issued, and these sessions were to be convened at once. However, the common law depended upon jury verdicts, and these were not always to be relied upon. On 16 March 1565 the commissioners operating in Cornwall were instructed to send up to Star Chamber the members of the jury which had acquitted one Abers, together with a summary of the evidence. Unfortunately we do not know what happened to them.[76] The real problem was collusion. It was not so much that prominent gentry families like the Tremaynes and the Killigrews were any longer active pirates themselves (the Council had made sure that that would be far too dangerous), but that they tended to look the other way, particularly when stolen goods were being disposed of. They were often also coastal landowners who had on their estates small creeks and inlets which were ideal for smuggling the pirates' loot ashore. They and their families bought goods at knock-down prices, without asking awkward questions, and as justices they did not commit offenders unless their guilt was public knowledge. It was often difficult to know whether the poacher turned gamekeeper was not snaring the odd gamebird on the side. On 1 March 1565 Sir John Chichester and Sir Peter Carew were commissioned to conduct a survey of all the creeks and landing places along the coasts of Devon and Cornwall which could be used for illicit purposes. They were paid £40 for their trouble and expenses, but they could probably have supplied most of the relevant information from their own personal experience. On 16 August in the same year the Council turned its attention from the west coast to the east, ordering the Vice Admirals of Norfolk, Suffolk and Essex to search all the coastal villages for stolen goods.[77] They were also to send out two barks at the expense of the counties to catch and deter the small-time operators who were picking off coastal traders. There was clearly a determination at this point that these orders should be taken seriously because on 8 November further commissions were issued to every coastal county 'for the repressing of pirates and other disorders' committed upon the sea coasts, with a rigorous schedule of instructions. A census was to be taken of all ships and barks, unlicensed sailings were to be forbidden, and a strict account was to be taken of every cargo landed.[78] This all sounds very purposeful, and may have been the result of pressures being applied to the Council from outside, but since the commissioners were those same justices whose laxity was creating the problem in the first place, it is unlikely that very much was achieved.

In 1570 England was locked in a struggle with the duke of Alba, conducted largely in the form of embargoes and ship seizures, as the duke sought to punish Elizabeth for the diversion of his money. He had, however, ignored the pleas of the rebel earls in 1569, having (rightly) no confidence in their ability to destabilise England, and not looking for further military adventures. He did not have the strength at sea to intervene, even if he had had the will to do so. This was also the year of the papal excommunication, when Pius V responded belatedly to the appeals of the same rebels by issuing the bull *Regnans in Excelsis*, releasing Elizabeth's subjects from their allegiance. The consequences of this were potentially severe for the English Catholic community, but did not greatly increase the possibility of invasion.[79] Philip was no more enthusiastic than the duke of Alba about extending his military commitments, especially when domestic assassins might do his work for him; and the Guises also had no strength at sea. England's only land frontier was with Scotland, and although Mary's supporters were still holding out there, following her deposition and flight south in 1568, a small-scale military and naval deployment was sufficient to contain that threat.[80] So 1570 was a year for gathering thoughts, and John Montgomery penned a 'Treatise concerning the navie of England'. Who Montgomery may have been, and what connection he may have had with the Admiralty, is not known. He started off in a discursive historical mode –

> purposing therefore upon good will and zeale to my country to write somewhat concerning the maintenance of our navie, I minde first to speake of the greate troubles that have and might happen to this realme for want thereof ...[81]

– proceeding in the conventional mode to look back to the Romans (who had faced no warlike ships), the Britains (who had possessed none) and the Saxons and Danes, who could each have been frustrated by an appropriate navy. A navy could not only 'spoil' and frustrate any potential invasion, but by attacking the enemy's own land could cause any such invasion to be withdrawn. Great care and thought needed to be given to the building and maintenance of such a navy, because 'goodly ships are not to be had at a becke, or made in a daye …'. Woodlands needed to be carefully managed to ensure an adequate supply of timber, which was not being done, he implied, and cunning shipwrights trained and fostered.

> And concerning the number of our shipps, I meane the Queenes Majesties owne shipps which should allawies lye in a reddynes … I would wishe under correction that they were or might be 40 saylles, all made fitt for the warres and for the fight …[82]

In addition to which there ought to be '40, 50 or more tall merchant shippes to be joined with them' to make up the number of 80 or 100 ships of war, which should be sufficient 'with God's help' to withstand 'any enemy that might come against us'. A far smaller force had been sufficient to expel the French from Leith, and now 'the French durst not attempt anything against us'. These tall merchant ships were being well maintained by voyages, not only to Spain, Italy, Hamburg and Danzig, but to Turkey, Barbary, the Indies, the Islands and Muscovy. It was on such voyages, too, that mariners were trained who could be used on the queen's ships when required. Montgomery then proceeded to survey the ports and harbours of England, speculating (quite accurately) on how many of these tall ships each might be expected to produce if called upon to do so. Nor was the fishing fleet to be forgotten as a training ground for seamen. A large part of the economic activity of the country could be harnessed in one way or another to support this essential bulwark of the country's security. The author then proceeded to survey the forts and bulwarks with which the coast was defended, and to display a thorough knowledge of the armaments which the queen's ships carried, 'cannons, culverins, sakars, minions, falcons and foulers … muskets [and] calivers …'.

The thinking behind this work is conventional enough, and asks for little that was not being already addressed. Its interest lies in the closeness of the link which it displays between the merchant community and the Admiralty. As we have seen, Thomas Wyndham died on a trading voyage, Benjamin Gonson hired naval ships for his own commercial purposes, and Gonson, William Winter and William Woodhouse all invested in Hawkins's second voyage. They all died rich, and although their naval salaries were generous by the standards of the time, that is not the explanation. In fact those salaries were not adjusted in line with inflation, which stood at over 100 per cent between 1546 and 1570, so by the latter date they were not particularly ample. A way around this was found, probably in 1559, by formalising the expenses which each officer was allowed to claim. Instead of claiming for what was actually spent, which had been the original intention, each was allowed a set daily rate, ostensibly for travel, which became in effect a supplementary salary.[83] The Vice Admiral was allowed 10s a day, the Treasurer 6s 8d, and the Controller, Surveyor and Clerk 4s each. An order for warrants of payment, issued at some point before Richard Howlett's death in 1560, shows Woodhouse being paid £48 from 25 June to 28 September, and the others proportionately less. Whether this arrangement was confined to those three months or operated all the year round is not clear. It was probably the former, but even so £48 was a nice little bonus. It should also be remembered that when Woodhouse served at sea, as he did in 1562, he was paid at the rate of 20s a day.[84] In the same quarter mentioned above, William Broke, the Controller, was paid a standardised £18 8s for his 'travel', but a further £39 in diets, fees, boat hire and the wages of two clerks – presumably reflecting what he had actually spent.

As we have seen, William Winter was appointed Master of Naval Ordnance in addition to Surveyor after Wyndham's death in 1557, and the office of Vice Admiral was discontinued when Woodhouse died in 1565. Richard Howlett died in 1560 and was succeeded by George Winter, William's brother, and the original Controller died in 1561, being replaced by William Holstock, hitherto Clerk of the Storehouses. William Winter, Gonson and Baeshe served throughout this period, and Winter probably presided at Council meetings, but the Admiralty was getting smaller, and more in-bred. When Gonson retired in 1577, he was succeeded by his son-in-law John Hawkins. This was not altogether a healthy development, and was to lead to problems later on. The navy itself changed relatively little, because although eleven ships were built, or otherwise acquired, not very much is known about their design. Towards the end of his life, Henry VIII had favoured sailing ships built on the relatively low profile of the galleasse, and this build, which might be termed the 'proto galleon', seems to have prevailed through the 1560s.[85] The *Eleanor* was a galley, given in pledge by the French Huguenots, but the *Triumph* and the *Victory* were newly built Great Ships with many years of service ahead of them. In so far as we can tell from contemporary illustrations, they seem to have been intermediate in design between the old carracks such as the *Great Harry*, and 'Race built' ships such as the *Revenge*. Their performance was never criticised, so presumably they made up in firepower what they may have lacked in speed.

This was also a period of significant but rather obscure development in English gunfounding. As late as 1545 the best guns were still being imported from the continent, but by the 1580s English cast iron guns were among the best, and the cheapest, in Europe. The English culverin had unmatched muzzle velocity, and they were being produced in quantity, not only for the royal armoury, but also for export and for purchase by the owners of privateers and other private warships. By the time of the Armada it was no longer true that if a ship had a fine set of matching guns, they must have been issued from the Tower of London. As the Elizabethan magnates lost their private armouries ashore, some of them transferred them on shipboard, and that had undoubtedly begun to happen by 1570.[86] The queen knew perfectly well that such ships constituted no threat to herself, and encouraged the development of this supplementary navy. Why pay for more warships, when her loyal subjects were prepared to supply them?

CHAPTER 5 NOTES

1. TNA E101/64/1, 'A declaration of all such somes of money as have bene payde oute of the receipt unto Benjamin Gonson …'.
2. TNA E351/2195.
3. BL Add. MS 9294, f.1. T. Glasgow, 'The Maturing of Naval Administration, 1556–1564', *Mariners Mirror*, 56, 1970, pp. 3–26.
4. TNA SP12/2, 20 February 1558/9.
5. The 'gift' of the *Minion* to Sir Thomas Seymour may conceal a more complex transaction. Rodger (*Safeguard of the Sea*, p. 479) notes her as having been 'chartered' from 1550 to 1556 – after Seymour's execution. Ibid.
6. TNA SP12/3, no. 44, ff.131–4. *British Naval Documents*, pp. 62–70.
7. This ship is variously described as being of 800 or 1,000 tons. It was probably built at Woolwich.
8. *British Naval Documents*, pp. 66–7.
9. She was repossessed in 1560, possibly because the purchase price had not been fully paid. Rodger, *Safeguard of the Sea*, p. 479.
10. Bod MS Rawlinson A.200, f.1.
11. *British Naval Documents*, p. 68.
12. H.M. Colvin, *The History of the King's Works*, IV, ii, pp. 478–82. A fort at Sheerness had been suggested in 1551 (*APC*, III, p. 193). The new site at Upnor was purchased by Gonson, and work commenced on 31 October 1559. It was in use by 15 August 1562 (TNA SP12/24, no. 12). It was completed at a cost of £3,621 on 29 September 1564 (E351/3545).
13. Elizabeth reduced the ordinary to £6,000 a year on 1 January 1564, but also relieved Gonson of ordinary victualling charges. Glasgow, 'Maturing of Naval Administration', p. 18. This change had little effect on the Treasurer's overall receipts.
14. For the deployment of these mobile workforces, see Gonson's Quarter Books, Bod MS Rawlinson A.200–2.
15. She threatened to execute her commissioners if they failed to secure the return of the town. Loades, *Elizabeth I* (2003), p. 132.
16. For a consideration of the danger constituted by this move, see Wallace MacCaffrey, *The Shaping of the Elizabethan Regime* (1968), p. 57.
17. Loades, *Tudor Navy*, p. 210.

18. TNA SP12/7, ff.169–71. T. Glasgow, 'The Navy in the First Undeclared Elizabethan War', *Mariners Mirror*, 54, 1968, pp. 23–37.
19. Loades, *Tudor Navy*, loc. cit.
20. Henry had spent much time and effort between 1542 and his death in 1547 in trying to enforce a claim to feudal overlordship of Scotland.
21. For a full discussion of this move and its implications, see Conyers Read, *Mr. Secretary Cecil and Queen Elizabeth* (1955), pp. 164–6.
22. Mary was virtually ignored in the negotiation of this treaty, which was one reason why she consistently refused to ratify it.
23. S. Haynes, *The State Papers of Lord Burghley* (1740), pp. 351–2.
24. TNA E351/2197. Gonson's account from 1 January 1559 to 31 December 1560.
25. Ibid.
26. Loades, *Tudor Navy*, p. 212.
27. TNA E351/2197.
28. For a full discussion of this unfinished business, see J.E.A. Dawson, *The Politics of Religion in the Age of Mary Queen of Scots* (2002), pp. 104–10.
29. Read, *Mr. Secretary Cecil and Queen Elizabeth*, pp. 191–5.
30. J. Wormald, *Mary Queen of Scots: A Study in Failure* (1988). Mary's only value, from a Guise point of view, was to recover an interest in Scotland.
31. Loades, *Tudor Navy*, p. 213.
32. Menna Prestwich, 'Calvinism in France, 1559–1629', in M. Prestwich, ed., *International Calvinism, 1541–1715* (1985), pp. 71–109. N.M. Sutherland, *Princes, Politics and Religion, 1547–1589* (1984), pp. 55–72.
33. Derek Wilson, *Sweet Robin: A Biography of Robert Dudley, Earl of Leicester, 1533–1588* (1981). D. Loades, *The Life and Career of William Paulet* (2008), p. 144.
34. TNA SP70/42, ff.582–3.
35. Loades, *Tudor Navy*, p. 214. Philip offered his mediation. Proclamation dispatching forces to Normandy, 24 September 1562, *Tudor Royal Proclamations*, II, pp. 206–7.
36. Loades, *Tudor Navy*, loc. cit.
37. TNA E351/2199. Bod MS Rawlinson A.200, f.153.
38. Sutherland, *Princes, Politics and Religion*, pp. 37–8.
39. By the peace of Amboise, Conde agreed to accept a limited toleration for Huguenot nobles, which led to a rift with his own following. Sutherland, *Princes, Politics and Religion*, pp. 154–5.
40. Loades, *Tudor Navy*, p. 215.
41. *Tudor Royal Proclamations*, II, pp. 208–9.
42. W. Laird Clowes, *The Royal Navy. A History from the Earliest Times to the Present* (1897), p. 477.
43. Bod MS Rawlinson A.200, f.327. T. Glasgow, 'The Navy in the Le Havre Campaign, 1562–4', *Mariners Mirror*, 54, 1968, pp. 281–96.
44. Loades, *Tudor Navy*, p. 216.
45. TNA E351/2199, m.9d. Bod MS Rawlinson A.200.
46. TNA E351/2199.
47. *APC*, VII, p. 129
48. Bod MS Rawlinson A.200, ff.342–4.
49. TNA E351/2200. Gonson's account from 1 January to 31 December 1564.
50. Bod MS Rawlinson 846, f.120. *British Naval Documents*, p. 101.

51. TNA PC2/9, f.122. *APC*, VII, p. 164.
52. The *Trinity Henry* and the *Grace of God*. PL 1266, p. 176.
53. TNA SP12/17, no. 43. Loades, *Tudor Navy*, p. 221.
54. Harry Kelsey, *Sir John Hawkins: Queen Elizabeth's Slave Trader* (2003), pp. 12–33. The family name of his contact in the Canaries was Ponte (Bridges?).
55. Ibid., pp. 38–45.
56. Ibid., p. 44.
57. Guzman da Silva to the King, 4 February 1566. Ibid., p. 38.
58. Herman Van der Wee, *The Growth of the Antwerp Market and the European Economy* (1963), Vol. III.
59. Hawkins to Cecil, 28 September 1567. TNA SP12/44/13, f.29.
60. Hawkins claimed that his commission was from the queen, and flew the royal standard at his masthead, but in fact it appears to have come from the merchant syndicate which was backing him. TNA SP12/53, f.34.
61. John Hawkins, *A true declaration of the troublesome voyadge of M. John Haukins to the parties of Guynea and the west Indies in the yeares of our Lord 1567 and 1568* (London, 1569). BL Cotton MS Otho E.VIII, f.29.
62. Kelsey, *John Hawkins*, p. 82.
63. BL Cotton MS Otho E.VIII, ff.39–40. Kelsey, *John Hawkins*, p. 84.
64. Ibid., pp. 87–8, based on various original testimonies held in the Archivo de Indias, Seville, in Justicia 902.
65. Hawkins, *A true declaration ...*, f.B.v. Kelsey, *John Hawkins*, p. 90.
66. Job Hortop, *The Rare Travails of Job Hortop* (London, 1591), f.B.3.
67. Kelsey, *John Hawkins*, pp. 97–9.
68. TNA SP12/53, ff.1–7.
69. Conyers Read, 'Queen Elizabeth's Seizure of Alba's Pay Ships', *Journal of Modern History*, V, 1933, pp. 443–64. D. Loades, *The Cecils*, pp. 69–73.
70. Ibid.
71. F.E. Dyer, 'Reprisals in the Sixteenth Century', *Mariners Mirror*, 21, 1935, pp. 187–97.
72. 'An Acte for the punyshment of Pyrotes and Robbers of the see...', statute 28 Henry VIII, cap. 15. Loades, *Tudor Navy*, p. 225.
73. BL Add. MS 11405, ff.91, 103.
74. Loades, *Tudor Navy*, pp. 225–6.
75. *APC*, VII, pp. 180–2.
76. Ibid., pp. 206–7.
77. Ibid., pp. 244, 253–5.
78. Ibid., pp. 278–9.
79. Memorandum by Antonio Guaras, *Calendar of State Papers, Spanish, 1568–79*, p. 249. Loades, *Elizabeth I*, pp. 17–71.
80. Mark C. Fissell, *English Warfare, 1511–1642* (2001), pp. 133–6.
81. John Mountgomerey, 'A Treatise concerning the navie of England ...', BL Lansdowne MS 1225, n.2., f.20
82. Ibid., f.13.
83. PL 1266, pp. 181–2. Copy in Bod MS Rawlinson C.846, p. 123.
84. Ibid.
85. Peter Kirsch, *The Galleon* (1990), pp. 14–16.
86. Loades, *Tudor Navy*, pp. 207–8.

CHAPTER SIX

THE NAVY AND THE MARITIME COMMUNITY

In the sixteenth century the word 'navy' was used to describe the whole merchant marine of the country. The king's (or queen's) ships were the 'Navy Royal'. This was legitimate in the sense that the monarch was by custom entitled to require the service of any ship or ships which he (or she) might choose, just as he could in theory call for as many men as he might require for military service. Lists were compiled every so often of the ships that might be so called on. An incomplete note of 1560 shows seventy-nine, while much more comprehensive surveys were carried out in 1577 and 1582.[1] The former shows 136 vessels of over 100 tons, and no fewer than 656 of between 40 and 100 tons. This last group was relevant because it was from that class that victuallers and other supply ships were recruited, but they do not feature in the other surveys. The survey of 1582 is in many ways the most interesting, because it shows 176 vessels of over 100 tons, of which sixty are attributed to London. Suffolk is listed as holding twenty-seven and Newcastle upon Tyne seventeen. Devon, by contrast, accounts for only seven, and the port of Bristol for nine.[2] Whether these lists were comprehensive, or some principle of selection was used, is not known, but what does emerge very clearly is the overwhelming dominance of the capital in the maritime community. Not all the ships registered in London would normally have worked out of the Thames, but London was the great clearing house, not only for merchandise, but also for shipmasters, seamen and gunners. Those who were commissioned to recruit mariners for the navy in times of emergency always looked first to the great city. In places like Deptford and Rotherhithe almost the whole adult male population would have been connected in one way or another with the sea.

Elsewhere the maritime community is hard to define. Waterways penetrated far inland, and in a sense all those who worked them had a connection with the sea. Boats of up to 15 tons burthen, quite big enough to act as coastal traders, could go up-river as far as Bedford, and King's Lynn was described as the 'gateway to a fifth of England', via the various tributaries of the Ouse.[3] Merchants who regularly shipped a portion of their goods either overseas or along the coast were likely to be part-owners of trading ships, and often bequeathed such shares in their wills. Where they were navigable, rivers were much to be preferred to roads for moving any bulky goods, and bargemen or wherrymen would normally have transhipped such goods at inland ports such as Norwich or Gloucester before moving them on inland. Yet it is important to make distinctions. Any landsman could go to sea if he so chose. The demand for mariners always exceeded the supply, and all he would need to do was to get himself to a seaport, where shipmasters and bo'suns were always on the lookout for recruits, or offer his services to one or other of the naval commissions, which might be operating far from the sea. If he was able-bodied he was unlikely to be refused, however inexperienced he might be. He would learn on the job, and it might be a hard process, but he was likely to see a bit of the world, and come back with the rudiments of a trade. However, it would be unrealistic to count everyone who had at some time in their lives been to sea as a part of the maritime community, just as it would be unrealistic to include every merchant who had at some point used a seaborne carrier. The maritime community consisted of those who normally earned their living from the sea, and these were the craftsmen who built and maintained the ships, as well as those who regularly sailed and commanded them. They formed an identifiable group of trades, and some of their records survive.[4]

Shipwrights, for example, were quite distinct from house-carpenters, and had their own guilds, particularly in places like Rotherhithe, Deptford and Portsmouth, where they regularly supplied craftsmen for the royal dockyards. These were not livery companies, and their records are patchy, but we know from circumstantial evidence quite a lot about their structure. Normal apprenticeship regulations applied. A boy would be bound at some time between the ages of eleven and eighteen, and normally served for seven years. Thereafter he was most likely to work as a journeyman, because he would not have had access to the capital needed to establish his own yard. Most such yards were jointly owned, but even buying a share would have needed resources beyond the reach of most workers.[5] If he was skilful enough, or had enough confidence in his skill, he might work as an independent master, and several such feature in the naval Quarter Books. Apart from the ownership of a yard, the pinnacle of this trade was to be a Royal Master Shipwright, but there were never more than two or three of these at a time. The first was James Baker, retained in 1538 on an annuity of 4d a day. By the reign of Elizabeth his son Mathew was earning three times as much.[6] Wherever there were yards, and this applies to the Humber and the Tyne as well as the Medway, there were communities of shipwrights, belonging to their local guild, and working as the opportunities presented themselves. The royal yards, and no doubt the private ones as well, employed a few masters on a regular basis, and hired the others as they were needed. In the naval Quarter Books, where the men are named, we find the same people working as shipwrights at one time, or as caulkers, labourers or night watchmen at others.[7] It was presumably more important to stay employed than to be fussy about the nature of the job. The guilds were friendly societies rather than trade unions, and do not seem to have indulged in collective bargaining. Whether the topmakers, oarmakers and other tradesmen who are described in the accounts were actually separate trades, or whether they were all shipwrights wearing other hats, we do not know. They do not seem to have had their own guilds. In the royal yards the men worked in gangs, each under the supervision of a master, but these seem to have been appointments rather than grades. Every yard had one or more master labourers, but there was no trade structure for such workmen.[8]

Wherever there were a number of yards, there was a related community. The men may normally have worked as shipwrights, but they can also be found selling and transporting timber to the yards, or supplying victuals. Their wives provided lodgings for skilled workers who had been brought in from outside, and laundered the bed sheets, which the yard seems to have provided – for both of which services they were separately paid.[9] The decision over when, and how, to hire outside labour was probably made by the Clerk of the yard, but the actual recruitment would have been the job of the Master Shipwright, who was expected to have contacts and influence within each community. Deptford had its own community, but for Woolwich the men seem to have come from Rotherhithe, and similar men might be sent as far as Bristol or Falmouth if there were special jobs to be done. Shipyards and boatyards were widely distributed around the coast, and similar communities would have existed, not only in large centres like Plymouth or King's Lynn, but also in much smaller places such as Fowey or Southwold. The use of London labour in distant places was not because local workmen did not exist, but either because they were deemed to lack the specialist skills required, or perhaps because of some special understanding between the relevant royal master and the Rotherhithe guild. Unlike some of the tasks mentioned, sail making was definitely a distinct craft, with its own structure, albeit on a modest scale. Sailmakers must also have congregated around the ship yards, but not very much is known about them. The navy bought canvas in bulk, but the work of converting it into sails seems to have been farmed out and was not separately accounted.[10] Perhaps the merchants included that in the price of the canvas as it was delivered. Ropes and cables were purchased regularly for the yards, and the merchants were paid for delivering them, but of sails as such there is no mention. When all these various crafts are added together, they form a large proportion of the maritime community. A glimpse can be obtained of the size of the fleet they were maintaining from the 1577 return, but most of the ships they would have built and serviced would have been coasters, and would not even have reached the limit of 40 tons.

Other crafts of a more general nature also had individual specialists who worked for the dockyards. There were blacksmiths who made everything from nails to anchors; ropemakers, especially at Deptford and Ratcliff; plumbers who provided the pipes and sounding lines; coppersmiths who made nails and pots; and basket weavers whose containers carried everything from victuals to ballast.[11] The same names appear over and over again in the accounts, but what proportion of their annual turnover this work represented is not known. Although they serviced the navy, they were no more part of the maritime community than were the workers in the brewhouses and bakehouses which converted grain into bread and beer, the farmers who grew the grain, or the innkeepers and others who catered for the leisure hours of the workforce.

As we have seen, seafaring recruited a lot of casual labour, some of it voluntary, some of it less so if the recruiting commissioners were having difficulty in filling their quotas. However, there was also the regular and organised trade of mariner, to which most masters and other officers belonged. Whereas the ordinary seamen who crewed the vessels plying up and down the coast or across the Channel learned their skills on the job, often beginning as ships' boys, these tradesmen were the elite. They were the members of one or other of the shipmans' guilds which existed in every seaport town, and would have served a regular apprenticeship, or undergone some other form of recognised training. Local shipmans' guilds are known to have existed at King's Lynn, York, Bristol and Rotherhithe.[12] There were many others, but none of their records survive. The York guild, we are told, had traditionally supported the pageant of Noah in the Corpus Christi celebration, and had decreed that every master 'sailing with a freeman' was to contribute 2d to the expense. Those sailing as 'Fellows' were to pay 1d.[13] So we know that there was a distinction between a 'Master' and a 'Fellow', but we do not know what it was, and we also know that most masters would have found employment in the town's own ships. The Bristol ordinances from 1445 are rather more complete. Here there were three classes of membership, 'Master', 'Yeoman' and 'Servant'. Servants were simply workers hired by a member; yeomen were what would in other contexts have been called journeymen; while masters were those 'knowen able in cunning of his craft', who had been duly examined by the wardens, and were 'within the said place of fraternity' – in other word, full members. It was possible to be a servant without any qualifications at all, while to become a master required further examination beyond the level of the apprenticeship.[14]

Just what kind of training this involved is not clear, but probably a degree of literacy and some knowledge of celestial navigation, at least when such knowledge began to become available after about 1500. In which case it would have been equivalent to that provided by the more prestigious and better known institutions – the Trinity Houses. There were three of these, at Newcastle, Hull and Deptford Strand, of which the last is the best documented. The intention in each case was the same, the instruction of master mariners in the faith, and in the higher levels of their craft. The pious founders had chosen this practical method of safeguarding the lives of those who chose to expose themselves to the perils of the sea. The Trinity House at Deptford had been founded originally in the fourteenth century, but was reorganised in 1515, when the petition for its licence declared that the masters and mariners of the king's navy (in the sense of the merchant marine) wished to found a guild for the reformation of the said navy.[15] Young men, it was alleged, were pretending to act as pilots without any training whatsoever, to the danger of themselves and others. As a result there was a serious shortage of skilled mariners, '… and so this your realm, which hitherto hath flourished' was potentially left destitute. The House was duly licensed to provide a remedy, and in due course its qualifications acquired a special status. They were the best thing of their kind until the advent of Gresham College and the private navigational schools of the later Elizabethan period. The House was also given control over all pilotage and buoys in the Thames estuary, and became synonymous with the government's attempts to improve the safety and quality of inshore navigation.[16]

Merchant companies which ran, or aspired to run, their own long-distance fleets also sometimes conducted their own training schemes. The Muscovy Company, for example, in the instructions drawn up for its first voyage in 1557, laid down that 'the grommets and pages [should] be brought up according to the laudable order and use of the sea, as well in learning of navigation as of exercising of that which to them appertaineth …'.[17] Just what form of tests were applied (if any) to ascertain whether these standards had been met, we do not know, nor whether any qualification so obtained would have been recognised outside the company. Both grommets (adolescents) and pages (boys under fourteen) were a form of cheap labour – as was always the case with apprentices – and in the royal navy were paid at two-thirds and half the rate of an adult seaman.[18] There may well have been many such schemes, because a statute of 1563 specifically authorised not only merchants and shipowners, but fishermen, gunners and shipwrights to run their own apprenticeship schemes if no guild was available, provided that they registered in the nearest corporate town. How many such schemes there were, and how many boys and young men may have been involved, it is impossible to say. But they would all of them have been entitled to see themselves as part of the maritime community. However, just what counted as a professional seaman seems to have been a matter of some doubt. When the East Anglian ports were asked in 1536 how many seamen they could muster, they counted about 550. Since more than twice that number would have been required to man the deep sea fishing fleet alone, they can only have been counting those who had passed some kind of apprenticeship. In 1543 Dorset reckoned that it had only 285, presumably using similar criteria. In 1565 Yarmouth (Norfolk) counted 400, and in 1570 Devon reckoned that it could muster 1,500. So either their officials were being more conscientious or a different standard was being applied.[19] In 1582, as a part of the nation-wide survey which we have already noticed, it was thought that the whole country could assemble 13,000 seamen, 2,300 fishermen and 1,000 Thames watermen. A somewhat more sophisticated survey taken at about the same time distinguished between 'skilled masters' and other seamen. Norfolk, for example, had 232 of the former and 1,570 of the latter, while the comparable figures for London were 143 and 2,281. The total counted on this occasion was 15,454, not vastly different from the 16,300 of the 1582 list.[20] So making an informed guess at the numbers of shipwrights and other craftsmen who should be included, we are probably looking at an adult male community of some 30,000, which should be approximately tripled to take account of dependants – about 90,000 in a population of something like 3 million. However, this does not include the 'casual labour', so we are probably looking at a maritime community which was about 3.5 per cent of the whole.

However, all such figures present problems. Not only is it hard to decide who should be counted as a mariner, the same problem also applies to the category of 'fisherman'. In 1528 about 160 ships set off from the East Anglian ports for the Newfoundland Banks. Assuming that most of these ships were small, and carried a crew of no more than ten to twenty, that would still have required a workforce of nearly 2,000 men. This trade fluctuated wildly for a variety of reasons, and in 1549 only forty-four ships set out. After 1570 there was a recovery, and by 1593 the fleet again numbered 111, of which fifty-five came from the single port of King's Lynn. These would have required crews to the number of about 1,400. Yet as we have seen the 1582 census counted only 2,300 for the entire country.[21] If we count only 'deep sea' fishermen that figure may not be wildly inaccurate, but a great many other people earned their living by fishing who never intentionally went out of sight of land. Those who fished the estuaries, or caught crabs and lobsters along the coast, were equally earning their living from the sea, and when we bear in mind that there were flourishing communities all around the south and south-west coasts, as well as East Anglia, the total figures begin to look sadly inadequate.

The government also recognised the fishing fleet as one of the principal training grounds for seamen, and after the Reformation had made the old fasting (or fish) days irrelevant when it passed a series of statutes for maintaining Fridays (and sometimes Wednesdays) as fish days for the preservation of the industry. Such acts were passed in the thirteenth, twenty-third and thirty-fifth years of Elizabeth's reign.[22]

Fishermen had their own guilds, and ran their own apprenticeship schemes, and although these were very localised, they could be important in major centres such as Yarmouth or Lowestoft. There are very few references to 'Master Fishermen', but the masters of most boats must have come into that category, because it required relatively little capital to own a small fishing smack, and they were often handed down from generation to generation in the same family. Although fishermen were notoriously individualistic, and journeymen were accustomed to bargaining for their own conditions, the masters tended not to be self-employed, even when they owned their own boats. Instead they worked in established relationships with the fishmongers or other merchants who marketed their catch. Quick and assured sales were essential because in the days before refrigeration fish did not keep, and a time-consuming search for a market could have been disastrous. The boundary between fishermen and the rest of the maritime community was porous in the sense that the former often took service not only on merchantmen but also on the royal ships, but it was less so in the opposite direction, as fishermen tended to be very jealous in defence of their 'mystery', and did not welcome unqualified intruders.[23]

The Council was not alone in recognising the importance of the fishing industry. When John Dee came to write his *Perfect Arte of Navigation* in 1577, he had it very much in mind. Dee was primarily concerned with the royal navy, which he believed should consist of at least sixty 'tall ships' kept regularly at sea and circumnavigating the British Isles. This was part of a scheme which he was anxious to promote for the restoration of a 'British Empire', covering England, Wales, Scotland, Ireland, the Hebrides, the Orkneys and (hopefully) some outposts in the New World.[24] Dee's plan was far more ambitious than anything which actually existed. Although according to the survey of the same year the queen could call upon some 250 ships, fewer than forty of these were her own, and no more than half that number were ever at sea at the same time. What Dee was advocating was maintaining the navy on a permanent war footing. However, even in the crisis year of 1588 the queen did not have as many as sixty ships regularly at sea. The fleet which sailed against the Armada numbered over 130 sail, but that was only at sea for about three months. Moreover the costs for that year amounted to £91,000, and that was not sustainable over any length of time.[25] Dee realised this perfectly well. If implemented, he calculated that his scheme would cost £200,000 a year, which was probably not far out, and took it into the realms of fantasy. It was to be paid for by enforcing a tax of 10 per cent on all foreign fishermen venturing into English waters.[26] If the queen had really had sixty ships regularly at sea, enforcing such a tax might not have been out of the question, but where Dee got his figures for the number of fishermen involved, we do not know. He had excellent contacts in every section of the maritime community, but the thought that foreign fishermen were relieving the country of stocks worth some £2 million pounds in every year beggars the imagination. Dee continued to be a respected figure, both at court and in the London merchant community, but of these ideas, no more was heard. However his extravagance should not blind us to the fact that the principle of having royal ships constantly at sea had long since been accepted, together with the need to put an adequate administrative structure in place to support them.

As we have seen, there was a regular need to recruit both men and ships for the royal service, and to have an adequate system of managing such recruitment. Fortunately in the 1560s one James Humphrey, a junior clerk in the Admiralty, put together a collection of standard letters and forms which he used for these purposes.[27] In so far as these were dated, they vary from 1560 to 1568 and appear to be examples which were actually used. One is a precept, dated 20 March 1568, and directed to the constables or their equivalents 'to give warning to all mariners and seafaring men within their precinct ...' to appear before the queen's commissioners at the time and place specified.[28] The commissioners then 'took up' as many as they required of the most suitable, whose names were then recorded and certified to Humphrey. The constables were then instructed to notify the selected men to report to Chatham on a given day, and were sent a sum of money (in this case 4s) for each of them as 'prest and conduct money'. At the same time a note of instruction was sent to each named individual containing his 'joining' orders. In the example eight men were named from somewhere in the Ipswich area – we do not know exactly where.[29] No doubt this model represents an ideal, but it gives an authentic glimpse of how recruitment actually worked, at least in peacetime. Perhaps the most interesting feature is the delivery of notes of instruction to the seamen themselves. Was the ordinary mariner able to read, or expected to do so, or was it assumed that some literate friend would interpret his orders for him?

No doubt most seamen served for one specified voyage, at the end of which they were paid off, and given notes signed by the master or purser of the ship in which they had served, certifying their status in order to protect them against charges of vagabondage as they made their way home. Their pay should have included conduct money 'according to the distance of miles', so they should have had no need to beg. The example given is made out in the name of Thomas Woodless, and is signed, not by the purser of the *Great Bark*, but by George Winter, the Clerk of the Ships.[30] Nevertheless the principle is the same. Also given is an example of a 'sick note', the special discharge of one 'William

Patche of Essex, mariner', who is laid off because he is no longer able to serve. This is simply a passport, with no mention of payment having been made, and is signed by no less a person than William Winter, the Surveyor of the Navy. Whether Patche had actually been paid for the service which he had discharged, and why his note was signed by William Winter, we do not know.[31] Perhaps it was a specimen rather than a real example. The Quarter Books confirm that these models were generally followed. Very often the recruiting commissioner was the master of the ship concerned, and he would make use of his contacts in his home area to raise sometimes as many as twenty men in a single operation. Master gunners were used in the same way to recruit other gunners, and captains and ensigns of infantry to raise the necessary soldiers.[32] Individual cases like William Patche were not separately recorded, but for the rest, wages and conduct money (both coming and going) seem to have been paid as required. The proper discharge of such obligations was a part of the relationship which the navy had with the maritime community, and the system seems to have worked well enough in normal circumstances.

Two things disrupted the smooth running of this system of recruitment. A seaman's pay was not generous – 6s 8d a month, rising to 10s in 1586 – but it was normally reliable, and victuals were provided.[33] However, privateers paid their men with a share of the plunder, and if there were many privateers taking good prizes, the counter-attraction of such service might prove too much. Once the situation was gearing up for war after 1580, both the demands of the navy and the attractiveness of privateering increased, so recruitment became competitive and difficult. Compulsion might be resorted to, and on occasion even the gaols were raided. The other problem was the breakdown of the money supply. A naval wage of 10s a month only retained any attractiveness if it was reliably paid, and when many ships were to be discharged at once, the money might run out. This notoriously happened when the Armada fleet was demobilised, a situation complicated by the fact that an outbreak of plague required the discharge to be rushed. Not only were many men sick, many were sent home with nothing better than IOUs to be shown for their time afloat. Sheer necessity meant that many of these were discounted long before they could be honoured, and the money eventually went to the village moneylenders.[34] Such failures did not improve relationships, and although on the whole the patriotic enthusiasm of the maritime community remained high, by 1600 naval recruitment was distinctly difficult.

Ships were required as well as men, and although some of these may have been earmarked by the receipt of a bounty, not many were built on those terms in the early Elizabethan period. Most of the ships known to have been constructed with the help of a bounty were not laid down until after 1593.[35] Normally ships were 'taken up' by negotiation between the Admiralty and the officers of a port town or a merchant guild. Once an agreement had been reached, it would be down to the officers concerned to decide which ships would actually serve, and for how long. The terms were standard and involved the government paying tonnage (a hire charge) and all the running expenses and wages while in service. If a ship was lost or damaged, compensation was due to the owners, and these conditions had not changed for many years. Foreign vessels seem to have been taken up on an *ad hoc* basis, whenever they happened to be in the right place at the right time. They were more expensive, at 16d a ton, and might involve diplomatic disputes with their owners, so they tended only to be taken for specific tasks and for short periods. Not surprisingly, none of these negotiations are represented in Humphrey's book of forms, because he would have been too junior to be a party to them, but there are a few certificates of discharge. These are non-standard, and were probably included as an *aide-mémoire*. One is a passport for a hulk, the *David of Lubeck*, discharged by the Lord Admiral, and requires the recipient 'quietly to permit the said … hulk to pass by you with let or hindrance …'.[36] This was presumably directed to the captains of any royal ships which the *David* might encounter, or possibly as a protection against privateers. The second is a similar passport to enable an Irish crayer to pass to its home port of Waterford in safety. In this case there is no mention of service, and it seems to have been simply a safe-conduct. The third is more interesting in that it records the discharge of the *Anne Gallant* of London, which had been carrying victuals to Leith, and the certificate mentions that two of her original crew of nine men and a boy had been stayed 'to serve the queen's Majesty in her Highness's ships now present here'.[37] Whether this was with their own consent or not is not mentioned.

Another of Humphrey's documents is a complete schedule of naval wages, which is undated but was drawn up before the general rise of 1586, so it is probably contemporary with the others. This lists thirty-one different classes of mariner, from the 'Master of a Great Ship' who was paid 40s a month, through the pilot (16s 8d), the steward (11s 8d), the master gunner (10s) and the ordinary seaman (6s 8d) down to the boy at 3s 4d. All together there were twelve different levels of pay, and an appended note reveals that an ordinary seaman's pay was always rounded down rather than up. So if he served one day he was paid 3d, but if he served three days he got 8d, not 9d, and if he served for a week he received 20d, not 21d.[38] Although it was Benjamin Gonson's responsibility to make these payments, Humphrey obviously kept this list beside him to make sure that any sums for which he was acting as agent were accurately discharged. If Humphrey was typical of the Admiralty clerks of the period (and there is no reason to suppose that he was not), it was a conscientious and well disciplined service.

Another link between the navy and the wider community was provided by the victualling service. At the beginning of Elizabeth's reign this was under the control of Edward Baeshe, who had been appointed Surveyor General of Victuals for the seas in June 1550. By the terms of the Privy Council shake-up of 1557, he was supposed to account independently of Gonson, and at least once a year. He probably did account annually, but there is a gap in the surviving sequence from 1552 to 1561, and he was still receiving his money through Gonson as late as 1563. This was to change, as we shall see, in 1565. Baeshe employed his own purveyors and other agents, and how they operated in the earlier part of the reign we do not know. It seems that Baeshe worked out a quota system on a county basis, as a rough guide to what his agents might reasonably demand, and by 1587 this had reached a high level of definition.[39] In that year he submitted to the Council an 'Opinion ... declaring out of what shire the wheat, malt, oxen, butter and cheese is to be had' – these being the staple items which he was expected to supply. For a navy of 10,000 men for one month, he reckoned he would need 5,600 quarters of wheat, 7,000 quarters of malt, 3,900 oxen (for conversion into beef), 400 barrels of butter and 600 hundredweight of cheese. Noting that some of this could be 'borrowed' in an emergency from the 'composition corn for her Majesty's household', he went on to provide a detailed breakdown of how these quantities could be made up. Norfolk, for example, could be expected to deliver 800 qtrs of wheat, 1,000 qtrs of malt and 100 barrels of butter; while Suffolk was set down for the whole 600 cwt. of cheese, and 300 barrels of butter, but only 100 qtrs of wheat and 200 of malt. All together twenty-eight counties were assessed, excluding the far north, which was expected to feed the garrisons on the Scottish border. These sorts of allocations were clearly no new idea in 1587, and were based upon a reasonable judgement of the agricultural capacity of each county, but how long they had been in use we do not know. Even by 1560 Baeshe was running a large-scale operation, with a headquarters on Tower Hill, numerous clerks and other servants, storehouses at St Katherine's (London), Ratcliff, Rochester and Portsmouth, and bakehouses and brewhouses both there and at Deptford. All these had to be maintained and staffed at a considerable cost, as can be seen from the Quarter Book entries from 1562–3, and from the brief reports which he produced for the benefit of the Council.[40] Although he was a member of the Council for Marine Causes he was clearly operating largely on his own, and was applying directly to the Privy Council for instructions regarding the victualling of specific ships. On 24 October 1563, while he was still receiving the bulk of his money from Gonson, he reported that although he had received £1,600 towards the ordinary costs of victualling the ships in harbour, £650 was still owing, and that this could not be covered from the ordinary allocation of £12,000. On 17 December he reported that £900 remained unpaid for the costs of harbour victualling.[41] The impression given by these letters is one of constant struggle to keep up with the changing demands of the Council, and of a constant shortfall in the ordinary revenue.

It may have been in an attempt to provide him with some support, or at least someone to share his burden, that he was issued with a new patent in 1563, jointly with John Elliott. However, if this was an attempt to restructure his responsibilities, it was of short duration, because in 1565 his whole task was redefined when he was placed under contract.[42] This must have been issued with his agreement, and the reasons for his compliance may lie in the silences rather than in the text, because on the surface it appears to be a very unattractive bargain. By its terms he was obliged to provide victuals at the fixed rate of 4½d for every man/day ashore and 5d at sea, and the numbers to be catered for were to be specified by the Council. His ordinary allowance, which would not vary from year to year, was laid down as £1,981 4s (paid at £165 2s a month). Hitherto he had indented for money on Gonson's ordinary in accordance with his own estimate of his requirement, so this represented a considerable loss of flexibility. At the current prices, which fluctuated somewhat from year to year, but showed an inexorable tendency to rise, such sums would have given him no profit margin at all. It must therefore be presumed that, although this is not mentioned in the contract, there would have been an agreed inflation of the specified numbers over and above those actually to be catered for. This practice, known as 'dead pays', was standard in calculating the payments made to military captains for the remuneration of their soldiers, and indeed for captains of ships at sea. Dead pays were calculated at a fixed proportion, which was normally mentioned in the accounts, so the absence of any mention of such a system here probably indicates that it was open to negotiation from year to year. That might explain why Baeshe found the contract acceptable. The ordinary formed only a small part of the Surveyor General's annual turnover. In peacetime, or in times of undeclared war such as the Newhaven campaign of 1563, he was required to victual ships at sea, in accordance with instructions received from the Council. Under the terms of the contract both the numbers of men and the duration of the service were to be specified, and Baeshe would receive extraordinary warrants to cover the costs – a separate warrant for each instruction. Presumably the same level of dead pays was acknowledged. Gonson's account for the two years 1562–3 (before the contract was introduced) shows Baeshe spending £19,311 13s 7½d.[43] This included Newhaven, and his usual expenditure was between £6,000 and £7,000, including the ordinary. At the same time, by the terms of his contract, Baeshe also had to assume responsibility for the storehouses in every port, to pay rents as appropriate, and to maintain the standby provision for 1,000 men specified in 1557.

Just what the Surveyor General was expected to supply for his 5d per man/day was also laid down in a schedule which had probably been worked out in the 1540s, but was also included in the terms of his contract.[44] The daily ration for every man was a pound of biscuit and two pounds of beef on Sunday, Monday, Tuesday and Thursday, while on Wednesday, Friday and Saturday he received a quarter of a stockfish (dried cod), one-eighth of a pound of butter and a quarter of a pound of cheese. Fresh herring were acceptable as an alternative to stockfish. Such a diet, while undoubtedly adequate in quantity, would have been exceedingly monotonous, and not particularly nutritious. It was not directly Baeshe's business, but it should be understood that individual pursers normally supplied dietary supplements in the form of 'herbs', onions and fresh fruit, sometimes drawing on money which was officially given them for other purposes, and sometimes on the private resources of the captain, in whose interest it was to keep his men as healthy as possible for as long as possible. When ashore, the men were probably intended to obtain such supplements out of their regular pay, which was why the shore-based allowance was only 4½d a day. Pursers, who had hitherto been given lump sums, to be used at their discretion, were now expected to invoice Baeshe for their expenditure on firewood, candles, dishes and cans, and they, too, were on a tight rein. They were not expected to spend more than 4d a month for every man on board, plus 8d for every man's 'necessaries by the month' and 2s to every ship for 'lading charges'. Presumably the 'necessaries' might include supplementary food, as well as drugs and the occasional luxury. It was all in theory very tight, but in practice it may have been rather less so, because although Baeshe complained regularly, and had his contract adjusted from time to time, he nevertheless contrived to die a rich man.[45]

One form of adjustment was by way of loans. Baeshe was originally given a £500 'float' to enable him to pay outstanding bills to suppliers. This was increased to £1,000 in 1569, and to £2,000 by 1576, at which point he was proposing to pay off £1,500 of his debt in instalments of £100 a year, leaving the original £500 to his successor.[46] The original somewhat hand-to-mouth method of paying suppliers as they invoiced, and then reclaiming via extraordinary warrants, was replaced with a system whereby the money was obtained in advance in accordance with laid-down estimates, and the suppliers were paid when what they actually delivered had been checked and verified. In theory this should have led to a marked improvement in deliveries, but it did depend upon the warrants being met on time, which was not always done, hence the need for the loans. It was also recognised that commodity prices were rising, and in 1573 the allowances were increased to 5½d per man/day in harbour and 6d at sea. Even so, this did not leave much margin – if any – and Baeshe's report and request for instructions of April 1574 contains a number of ongoing complaints.[47] Nothing was to be had except for ready money, he must have his instructions and money in advance, and he needed letters from the Council authorising him to use the Crown's right of purveyance – that is to say to take up provisions at 'the Queen's price', because although this would be below the market rate, it showed the same tendency to increase Although this was not a time of war, he had obviously been asked to produce an estimate for twenty-four ships for a month 'in warlike manner', and this he judged would cost £4,200, plus £200 for the transporting of the victuals to where they were needed, based on a month of twenty-eight days and a cost of 6d per man/day. 'Because', he concluded, 'in this dear year I shall not be able to victual according to the bargain, that I may have your favourable report to Her Majesty for recompense upon just proof made of the loss ….'[48] Wheat, he declared, was costing 30s a quarter, beef 2d a pound (exclusive of casks and salt), butter 4d a pound and cheese 2d a pound, so that victualling a seaman in port was going to cost at least 8d a day. Moreover he was having to purchase the casks he needed out of his own resources, 'and other necessary things of no small charge which I am to bear by my hard bargain'.[49] His woes were increased in 1576 when his storehouse at Portsmouth burned to the ground, but in spite of its hardness he never attempted to escape from his contract altogether, and we should probably take his protests with a pinch of salt.

In July 1586, when he was already an old man and within a year of his death, Baeshe drew up and sent to the Lord High Admiral a memorandum outlining his career. He had served 'in the said office' (Surveyor General of the Victuals), 'by the space of forty years' (actually thirty-six), and twenty-one years of that under contract. Although the rate of his allowance had been raised, he had lost some £2,800 by the 'restraint of traffic' between 1568 and 1573, and at that time had attempted to 'deliver back his licence' – a gesture for which there is no contemporary record. Now, however, he has had enough. All commodities are so expensive that he can no longer function even within the terms of his revised contract. He therefore wishes to give the six months' notice required by his 'bargain', which, because he had already notified his intention on 7 May, would expire on 6 November.[50] He was no longer able to travel as he had earlier, and although he regretted the decision, he really would have to give up. He had, he declared optimistically, saved the Crown £1,000 a year during his time in office, and he hoped that his resignation would be taken in good part. Although by this time his designated successor, James Quarles, was already in place, and had been since 1582,[51] the old man was not to escape so easily. He had in effect made himself indispensable and his request was politely refused. He died, still in office, the following summer.

Privateering was half-way between piracy and war. It was also an effective way of mobilising the maritime community in the service of the Crown.

Before 1585 the only privateers properly so-called were those who had operated under letters of marque issued either by William of Orange or by the leaders of the French Huguenots. However, it would be difficult to find any other description for the ships which sailed with Hawkins or Lovell to the New World. Similarly Francis Drake was a privateer when he sailed around the world between 1577 and 1580, returning with a huge booty to a hero's welcome. In spite of the enormous risks, it was seldom difficult to find crews for such enterprises, provided that the captain had the right credentials. The Spaniards and Portuguese always regarded these adventurers as pirates, but at home they were clearly distinguished from the operators who plundered coasters or lay in wait for crayers crossing the Irish Sea.[52] This was a distinction shared by the Privy Council, which did its level best to get the latter treated like common criminals, but who indulged the former to the extent of investing in their enterprises. In one sense the outbreak of war made very little difference. Unlike 1544, or 1557, no proclamation was issued authorising letters of marque until September 1597, by which time, presumably, the maritime community was deemed to be in need of some encouragement.[53] Before that, no encouragement had been needed, and any enterprising skipper who could make a show of attacking Spanish shipping was entitled to describe himself as a privateer. In theory all such ships operated under the authority of the Lord Admiral, and were suppose to declare their prizes in his court, but in practice only a minority did so. High-profile operators like the earl of Cumberland had little option, but less conspicuous captains did not usually trouble themselves about such niceties.

This could be a nuisance, because what constituted a lawful prize was by no means clear. A Spanish ship, for example, carrying a French-owned cargo from the Baltic to Brittany was a legitimate target, but whether its captors were entitled to seize the cargo was much more problematic. Such a case would have been rare, but a Dutch ship carrying an Italian cargo from Seville to Antwerp was much more likely, and again should have presented a thorny problem for the Admiralty court. As a rule of thumb, privateers took any Spanish ship and whatever was in her, and anything which looked like a Spanish cargo, irrespective of the nationality of the carrier. As a result, Dr Julius Ceasar, the judge of the Admiralty court, was besieged with complaints from French, Italian and Hanseatic merchants that their ships and cargoes had been plundered on the excuse that they had had dealings either with Spain or with one of the Spanish dependencies, usually Naples or Flanders.[54] It is perhaps not surprising that most privateers landed and sold off their plunder surreptitiously, without going anywhere near the Lord Admiral. That way the profits could be promptly divided between the takers and the members of the maritime community where such goods were sold. At the same time, even with only a minority of prizes being declared, the income to the Crown was substantial. In 1590 Dr Ceasar declared, 'her majesty hath gotten and saved by these reprisals, since they began (that is over the last five years) above £200,000 ...', which was the equivalent of about nine months' ordinary income, or one parliamentary subsidy.[55] It was only when political embarrassment eventually outweighed her greed that Elizabeth felt inspired to rein in her privateers. In 1591 and again in 1592 the plundering of friendly ships (which included the Scots) was prohibited, and it may have been for that reason rather than as a spur that official letters of marque were advertised in 1597. Obviously the ambiguous status of operators who claimed to be privateers without any authorisation was at last causing difficulties which had to be addressed.

Part of the problem was caused by the fact that, although the Admiralty court was a part of the queen's government, it was also (a relic of the medieval situation) a private franchise in the hands of the Lord Admiral.[56] Ceasar knew that a regular judicial circuit was needed, on the same lines as the Assizes, to deal with 'such great personages' as considered themselves to be above the maritime law. Unfortunately these same 'great personages' were also the pillars of their communities, and in other respects the upholders of law and order. A document of instruction, drawn up for the Admiralty Solicitor in 1601, reveals that the remedy was clearly perceived:[57] the indictment of all those who had taken ships to sea since 1585 without letters of authorisation, or who had disposed of prizes in the same way; and the enforcement of the existing statutes defining the duties of Vice Admirals, and the arrest of all private and unauthorised men-of-war. The Lord Admiral should himself sign and seal all compositions for offences, or fines and forfeitures. Unfortunately, such reforms would have required not only the application of a formidable political will, but also the deployment of considerable resources. Apart from anything else, if the Admiralty franchise were to be abolished and the anachronism removed, the Lord Admiral would have to be compensated for his loss of income. In 1601 neither the will nor the resources were available, so nothing was done. And substantial profits, which should have accrued to the Crown, went instead to the entrepreneurs who put these ships to sea, and the coastal communities which helped them to dispose of their plunder.

Paradoxically, the war had turned many erstwhile pirates into privateers, so while this auxiliary navy flourished on the fringes of the law, ordinary piracy ceased to be a serious problem. Perhaps with 200 vessels lurking off the coast of Spain and reducing her trade to a trickle, there were few resources left to spare for the traditional sport of plundering their fellow countrymen. For whatever reason, by 1598 the good times for ordinary pirates were over. Their main 'sustainers' like Sir John Killigrew and Sir John Perrott were dead, and Sir John Wogan, the Vice Admiral of South Wales, had been successfully prosecuted for complicity. Lord Howard of Bindon had squeezed the pirates out of Dorset, and their traditional refuges further west were becoming daily less secure.[58] The more the maritime community displayed its patriotic credentials by putting its energies into privateering, the more effective ordinary discipline became. The Killigrews had fortified Pendennis castle as late as 1571, but by the end of the century such an action would not have been tolerated. The indiscipline of the privateers was clearly an ill wind which blew some good, both in terms of the war effort and in terms of governing the country The war effort, of course, benefited in several different ways. Not only did these private warships decimate the enemies' trade, they also fought in regular actions alongside the royal navy. The most conspicuous of such collaborations was that which resulted in the capture of the great Portuguese carrack the *Madre de Dios* in 1592, by a fleet made up of a royal squadron under Sir John Burgh, a number of the earl of Cumberland's privateers and a few freelance operators.[59]

George Clifford, earl of Cumberland, was the most substantial of the privateers. His flagship, the appropriately named *Scourge of Malice*, weighed in at 900 tons, which made her the second largest of all the English warships, and his private fleet numbered over a dozen vessels.[60] He aimed to run his operation like a major business, but his overheads were so large that he probably did not make any profit at all. However his service to the country entitled him to the generous consideration which he received from his mistress. His ships formed the second largest private contingent in the fleet which went against the Armada, only outnumbered by the City of London. In August 1592 the *Scourge* was not engaged, and the command of the fleet rested with Burgh, so the queen's investment in the enterprise was the largest, which was to be important as things fell out. In January 1592 the London merchants received from Elizabeth an advance of £6,000 in prize money for the ships captured by London privateers during the previous year. The original intention was to fit out another West Indies expedition under the command of Sir Walter Raleigh, but this was changed upon receipt of information relating to the arrival of the East Indies fleet.[61] Once at sea, the English fleet divided. Raleigh handed over one part to Sir Martin Frobisher, and the other to Sir John Burgh. Frobisher was to cruise off Cape St Vincent, while Burgh lurked in the Azores, both with the intention of intercepting the five Portuguese carracks due from the Far East. Cumberland's squadron may originally have been separate, but on receipt of the news of the potential prey, joined forces with the others, attaching themselves mostly to Burgh, who also had the *Dainty*, belonging to Sir John Hawkins, under his command.

Of the five ships which were supposed to be coming, one probably never set out at all, and a second was lost in the Mozambique Channel, so three eventually made it into the Atlantic.[62] One of these was sighted by Frobisher on 7 July, but eluded his clutches and arrived safely. The other two, the *Santa Cruz* and the *Madre de Dios*, were encountered by Burgh. In attempting to escape, the *Santa Cruz* ran ashore during a storm, and the crew successfully unloaded her before setting the ship herself on fire. Burgh landed a party who successfully dislodged the shipwrecked men, but how much of the cargo they recovered is not clear, and the impression given is that it was of small value. That left the *Madre de Dios*, which was literally chased into Burgh's path by Cumberland's ships a day or two later. By this time he seems to have had seven ships under his command, representing the queen, Cumberland, Hawkins and the City of London. They were all well gunned, and good sailers, but they were far too small to put men aboard the Great Ship, which displaced an estimated 1,500 tons. The combat lasted a day and a night, as the Portuguese struggled to shake off their tormentors, and the English struggled to get aboard. Eventually, by laying one ship completely athwart the carrack's bow, they succeeded in bringing her to a halt, and at that point a boarding party was successful.[63] Once boarded, the crew showed no appetite for a fight, and the cargo was taken intact. The prize was eventually brought in to Dartmouth on 7 September, to the universal amazement of the people there, who had never seen a ship even half that size before. What happened then is a matter of some dispute – it depends which of the several accounts you read.[64] The cargo, mostly of jewels and spices, was of enormous value, and there could be no question of avoiding the Admiralty prize jurisdiction. The declared value was £150,000, but that was after the privateering crews (and probably the royal ones as well) had filled their pockets with the most valuable and portable items. The true value was probably nearer £250,000. Sir Robert Cecil, sent down post-haste from London, managed to retrieve part of the missing plunder before it was physically removed, but a lot of small fortunes were made in the early days of September 1592.[65] Elizabeth insisted upon retaining the bulk of what was declared and recovered – far more than the scale of her investment in the voyage would have justified – and the chances are that the main private investors (London, Cumberland and Hawkins) barely covered their costs. However, as an illustration of both the strengths and the weaknesses of the English privateering system, the capture of the *Madre de Dios* could hardly be bettered.

By the mid-1590s the days of (relatively) easy pickings in the West Indies were over. The colonies were now fortified to a degree which would not have been thought necessary before, and the failure of the last collaborative venture between Hawkins and Drake in 1595 cost the lives of both adventurers and sustained a heavy financial loss. Nevertheless skill and daring could still reap rewards, as William Parker's successful raid on the Bay of Honduras in 1594 demonstrated.[66] During the last decade of the war the large-scale practitioners like Cumberland were operating at a loss, but smaller professionals such as William Winter junior, Robert Crosse and Thomas Fenner, who kept up their attacks on a modest scale over a number of years, were still returning a profit. One thing, however, is quite clear. By the end of the century, and in spite of some opinions to the contrary, the war at sea could not remotely pay for itself. What it could do (and did) was to sustain a high level of interest in the maritime community, where the privateers not only returned a modest profit, but provided exceptionally good training for skilled mariners and gunners, so that the fighting potential of that community was substantially increased. It remained to be seen whether the navy could absorb that potential once the war was over.

CHAPTER 6 NOTES

1. TNA SP12/11, nos 27 and 296.
2. TNA SP12/156, ff.88–90.
3. N.J. Williams, *The Maritime Trade of the East Anglian Ports, 1550–1590* (1988), p. 57.
4. Some of these are preserved in the Archive of the Worshipful Company of Shipwrights.
5. Loades, 'The English Maritime Community, 1500–1650' (forthcoming).
6. Bod MS Rawlinson A.200, f.46 etc.
7. Ibid., various.
8. For instance, William Ally, regularly employed at Deptford in 1562. Ibid., f.34 etc. He was also called 'the keeper of the plug'.
9. E.g. 'To Eve Symson, Anne James, Avis Walters ... and 17 other persons of Deptford, Greenwich and theresabouts ... for the lodging of 189 of the aforesaid shipwrights, caulkers and others in 95 feather beds ... at 2d every man the week ... .£13 5s 1d.' Ibid., f.48.
10. Ibid., f.22. The purchase of large numbers of sail needles suggests that the sails may have been made up at the yard, although by whom is not clear.
11. E.g. 'To Thomas Edes of London, basket maker, the same day for the price of 6 dozen of baskets for ballast ... at 18d every dozen ... 9s. 0d.' Ibid., f.24.
12. Dorothy Burwash, *English Merchant Shipping, 1460–1540* (1969), pp. 66–7.
13. Ibid.
14. *The Little Red Book of Bristol*, ed. F.B. Bickley, II (1900), pp. 190–1.
15. M. Oppenheim, *A History of the Administration of the Royal Navy, 1509–1660* (1988), p. 92.
16. Ibid. For a full examination of apprenticeship and its implications, see Cheryl A. Fury, *Tides in the Affairs of Men. The Social History of Elizabethan Seamen, 1580–1603* (2002), pp. 1–44.
17. Richard Hakluyt, *The Principal Navigations, Voyages and Discoveries of the English Nation* (edn. 1907), I, p. 378.
18. Pepys Library MS 1266, pp. 189–91. *Elizabethan Naval Administration*, 4 (j).
19. Williams, *Maritime Trade*, p. 222.
20. Ibid.

21. TNA SP12/156, ff.88–90. *British Naval Documents*, pp. 107–9.
22. *Statutes of the Realm*, III, pp. 545, 668, 857.
23. G.V. Scammell, 'Manning the English Merchant Service in the Sixteenth Century', *Mariners Mirror*, 56, 1970, pp. 131–54.
24. *RSTC* 6459, p. 3 et seq.
25. Loades, *Tudor Navy*, p. 192.
26. Dee, *Perfect Arte of Navigation*, loc. cit.
27. PL MS 1266, pp. 171–91. *Elizabethan Naval Administration*, section 4. For Humphrey himself, see the introduction.
28. PL 1266, p. 171. *ENA*, 4 (a).
29. PL 1266, pp. 172–3. *ENA*, 4 (b) and (c).
30. PL 1266, p. 175. *ENA*, 4 (e).
31. PL 1266, p. 174. *ENA*, 4 (d).
32. Bod MS Rawlinson A.200, ff.345–59.
33. TNA SP12/142, no. 19. For a discussion of the dating of this pay rise, see *ENA*, section 5, introduction.
34. On wages (or the lack of them), see Fury, *Tides in the Affairs of Men*, pp. 93–101.
35. B. Dietz, 'The Royal Bounty and English Shipping in the Sixteenth and Seventeenth Centuries', *Mariners Mirror*, 77, 1991, pp. 5–20.
36. PL 1266, p. 176. *ENA*, 4 (f).
37. Ibid., p. 178. *ENA*, 4 (h).
38. Ibid., pp. 189–91. *ENA*, 4 (j).
39. TNA SP12/107, ff.39–40. *British Naval Documents*, pp. 109–11.
40. Bod MS Rawlinson A.200. TNA SP12/25, no. 48, SP12/26, no. 3. Hatfield House, Cecil Papers 154/36. *ENA*, 6 (a–c).
41. Cecil Papers 154/36.
42. BL Cotton MS Otho E.IX, ff.99–102, 116–19, with lacunae supplied from PL 2876, pp. 161–8. *ENA*, 6 (e). The full text of the contract.
43. TNA E351/2199.
44. BL Cotton MS Otho E.IX, f.99. A slightly different version, allowing a 'wheaten loaf of 20 oz' as an alternative to biscuit, and ½lb of 'martinmas' beef or bacon as an alternative to fresh beef, is contained in Bod MS Rawlinson 846, ff.132–3. *British Naval Documents*, p. 102.
45. TNA SP12/191, no. 28 (ii). *ENA*, 6 (f).
46. *ENA*, section 6, introduction.
47. TNA SP12/95, no. 81. *ENA*, 6 (g).
48. Ibid.
49. Ibid.
50. TNA SP12/191, no. 28 (i).
51. BL Lansdowne MS 62, f.132. Oppenheim, *History*, p. 142.
52. Harry Kelsey, *Sir Francis Drake: The Queen's Pirate* (1998). K.R. Andrews, *Elizabethan Privateering* (1964), pp. 3–5.
53. Hughes and Larkin, *Tudor Royal Proclamations*, III, pp. 183–5.
54. At least eleven English privateers were sailing under letters of marque from Dom Antonio, the Portuguese pretender. Andrews, *Elizabethan Privateering*, p. 202. Loades, *Tudor Navy*, pp. 271–2.

55. Ceasar to Howard, 18 December 1590. BL Lansdowne MS 157, f.434.

56. For a full discussion of this issue see *Hale and Fleetwood on Admiralty Jurisdiction*, ed. M.J. Pritchard and D.E.C. Yale (Selden Society, 1993).

57. BL Lansdowne MS 145, f.15. Loades, *Tudor Navy*, p. 272.

58. R.G. Marsden, 'The Vice Admirals of the Coasts', *English Historical Review*, 22, 1907, pp. 468–77.

59. C.L. Kingsford, 'The Taking of the Madre de Dios, Anno 1592', in J.K. Laughton, ed., *Naval Miscellany*, II (Navy Records Society, 1912), pp. 85–122.

60. R.T. Spence, *The Privateering Earl: A Life of George Clifford, Earl of Cumberland* (1995).

61. Kingsford, 'The Taking of the Madre de Dios'.

62. Ibid.

63. Ibid.

64. Francis Seall, a captain for the earl of Cumberland, wrote the main account, but there are others from Sir John Burgh, John Hampton, and Captain Thompson of the *Dainty* (made to Hawkins).

65. Loades, *The Cecils*, pp. 200–1.

66. Andrews, *Elizabethan Privateering*, pp. 172–3.

CHAPTER SEVEN

Money

One of the purposes of compiling the 'Book of Sea Causes' in 1559 had been to facilitate a realistic estimate of how much the navy should cost in the future. Expenses had skyrocketed during the war which was then coming to an end, and a difficult balance had to be struck between the demands of economy and the need to maintain a realistic deterrent against aggression. Lord Treasurer Winchester had proposed an ordinary of £14,000, to be reduced eventually to £10,000, for the peacetime navy, and it was upon that calculation that Elizabeth based her standing warrant for £12,000 in March 1559, almost immediately after receiving the Book. This was intended to cover the costs of the navy in harbour. That is the wages of the shipkeepers who looked after the vessels at their moorings, and their victuals; the wages and victuals of the workmen carrying out routine maintenance; the wages of the permanent staff; and the costs of 'riding' – that is, carrying messages to and fro between the officers and the Privy Council.[1] However the relationship between ordinary income and expenditure was never straightforward. In 1562 Gonson's ordinary income matched the warrant – £12,000 – however his ordinary expenditure was £13,565. This shortfall was more than covered by the fact that his extraordinary spending only amounted to £4,190, while his extraordinary income was £12,376.[2] Allowing for the fact that he started with a 'surplusage' (deficit) of £7,728, he should have ended the year with a deficit of only about £1,100. However he accounted for 1562 and 1563 together, and the latter year showed quite a different pattern. This time (although the warrant was still in force) he received only £9,630, whereas his expenditure classed as ordinary shot up to £23,470.[3] This would suggest that much of the preparation for the Newhaven expedition was passed on the ordinary budget because it involved repairs of a nature which would have had to be carried out anyway, but were brought forward because of this campaign. Gonson was granted extraordinary warrants to the total of £19,000, and spent £18,390, but this made only a very small dent in his ordinary deficit. When he accounted in December 1563, his 'surplusage' had gone up to £9,521.[4]

These two years, for which we have both the Quarter Book and the Declared Account, raise some interesting questions. Most noticeably, the distinction between the ordinary and extraordinary budgets was either very blurred, or was not being made. The flexibility which was obviously being practised helps to explain Elizabeth's lack of enthusiasm for the ordinary, and the changes which were to be made to it over the following years. Secondly, in spite of what was being said about Gillingham being the most convenient anchorage for ships out of commission, it is clear that Deptford was still by far the busiest yard. In 1562, £7,882 14s 6d was spent there, as against £1,725 14s 4d at Gillingham, and £725 16s 0d at the 'advanced base' of Portsmouth. In 1563 the discrepancy was less marked, but still considerable – £11,760 12s 6d at Deptford, £7,203 8s 11d at Gillingham and £1,457 5s 6d at Portsmouth.[5] Although Portsmouth was the assembly point for the Newhaven fleet, it is clear that most of the work was being done at Deptford and Gillingham. The same fleet required increases in the costs of conduct money, and more obviously in the prests given to Edward Baeshe for victualling – £2,032 in 1562 and £11,975 in 1563. Roughly speaking, the navy cost £17,755 in 1562, when it was doing no more than routine patrolling, and £41,860 in 1563, when it was (partly) mobilised. The contrast may help to explain the queen's extremely cautious attitude to naval deployment over the next few years. The Newhaven campaign had not only accomplished nothing, it had cost about £28,000 for the navy alone, over and above the costs of the army, which came to about £180,000, and the heavy loss of life.[6] In addition to receiving £21,630 over these two years by virtue of the standing warrant, Gonson also received a further £21,526 on occasional warrants from the Exchequer, £6,000 from the sale of Crown lands and £1,000 from the queen's Privy Purse, in addition to other sums from the Court of Wards, the Privy Seal loan (which subsequently absorbed the Privy Purse contribution) and the sale of the *Jerfalcon*.

Even when the ordinary was fully operational, it never provided enough to cover a minimal definition of ordinary expenditure, and it was a regular charge on the Exchequer's permanently stretched resources. On 1 January 1564 it was reduced to £6,000 a year, and then restored in 1567 to £7,695, where it remained until it was reduced again to £5,714 at some time in the 1570s,[7] ahead of John Hawkins's 'bargains'. However it was always a somewhat notional figure and its relation to ordinary expenditure is hard to perceive. The Council nevertheless did its best to ensure that Gonson received enough money to keep the navy going, being aware that his credit resources were limited, and for that reason obtained from him careful costing estimates before the Newhaven campaign commenced. In October 1562, and basing his calculations on the accepted average figure of 9s 4d per man/day for wages and victuals, he declared that the cost of sending 460 officers and men to sea for one month in the *Hart*, the *Swallow* and the *Willoughby* would be £727 6s 8d.[8] The following month he estimated that the cost of sending five smaller ships to sea for the same time and containing 280 men, would be £521 6s 8d.⁹ Exactly what use the Council made of these figures is not clear, but they were part of the armoury of information available to it. Gonson seems to have done his best to keep his employers up to date with the state of his finances, in addition to the rendering of his regular accounts. One note from early January 1565 lists several items of expenditure amounting to £5,797, against which income of £1,533 is to be set, leaving a running debt of £4,264.¹⁰ Several other notes of the same date list the detailed comings and goings of other sums of money – discharged obligations and unpaid bills – which give some idea of the regular diligence of the naval treasurer in the discharge of his duties. The impression is one of constant anxiety about the state of the debt.

In spite of this care, the sums which Gonson actually received year by year fluctuated considerably. In 1565, 1566 and 1575 the total was actually less than the theoretical ordinary, while in 1574 and 1577 he received more than he spent. His peacetime income peaked at £21,471 in 1564, but that was probably due to the 'clearing up' operation after the Newhaven campaign. Otherwise expenditure tended to rise, naturally, in years of high political tension. In 1569, for example, he spent £17,800 'extraordinarily' because of the trouble with the Low Countries and the fear of foreign intervention in the rebellion of the earls.¹¹ In 1570 he received £5,780 on his ordinary, and £17,553 extraordinary, a figure which seems to have been based on his expenditure the previous year. After 1571 a serious attempt was made to sort out the confusion between ordinary and extraordinary expenditure, and that distinction was made in the accounts. In no year did ordinary expenses exceed the income, and normally there was a comfortable surplus, but this was achieved by redefining what was meant by ordinary spending, rather than by increasing the income. Having struggled with these problems for nearly thirty years, Benjamin Gonson died in 1577 and was succeeded by his son-in-law John Hawkins.¹² Hawkins, of course, had his own links, both with the Council and with the court, and immediately proposed a reformed method of funding the navy. This may have been based on Baeshe's agreement for victualling, but more likely on the farming of particular customs which the government was also experimenting with at that time. His proposal was accepted, and in 1579 he entered into a contract with the queen, undertaking to maintain twenty-five ships to a specified standard, but not to repair them or to provide shipkeepers, in return for £1,200 a year.¹³ At the same time Mathew Baker and Peter Pett, the queen's master shipwrights, received similar contracts for £1,000 a year each, in return for which they undertook to ground and careen the same ships at specified intervals (which varied with the size of the ship) and to carry out certain specified repairs. The ordinary appears to have been suspended.

In spite of their seemingly straightforward terms, these 'bargains' caused endless confusion and fierce recriminations. Some parts of the naval maintenance programme were now sub-contracted to those very officers who were supposed to oversee the whole operation. Accusations were inevitably made that those with contracts were seeking to maximise their profits by shifting work which they should have undertaken onto colleagues without contracts, who would be paid as and when extraordinary warrants were made available. So serious did the quarrels become that in January 1584 the Council initiated an enquiry, and Hawkins succeeded by some creative accountancy in convincing the enquirers that he had saved the Admiralty over £10,000 during the five years since his system was introduced.[14] The Treasurer was exonerated of any malpractice, and given a fresh contract to carry out virtually all the work conventionally listed as ordinary in return for £4,000 a year. This seems to have been an attempt to resolve the quarrels by shifting all the contract work from Pett and Baker onto Hawkins, at the same time giving him £800 over and above the previous 'bargain' payments. This made the situation worse, because not only did it invite creative definitions of what could be classed as extraordinary, it added Pett and Baker to the roll of complainants. They denied that Hawkins's contract could be honestly discharged, and accused him of default and negligence on a massive scale.[15] The charges were never proved, but it seems that Hawkins did keep his contract expenditure well below £4,000 a year by using extraordinary warrants. There was technically nothing improper in this, but the furore did not subside and in June 1587 someone (who was not Hawkins, but was clearly well informed) drew up an assessment of the past and present arrangements.

This starts with the warrant dormant for £5,714, which had been introduced at some unknown date after 1570. It then proceeds:

> For which sums there was performed these things following:
> The wages of shipkeepers
> The ransacking and keeping of the ships in harbour, till they come to be new built or drydocked.
> The grounding of the said ships as was fit for them, and as their time came about to continue them in harbour, some in three years, some in two years, and others of the lesser sort once a year. For this service all kind of ironwork and stuff was provided.
> The mooring of ships in harbour
> The wages of the gunners at Upnor castle.
> The wages of clerks &, keepers of the plugs at Chatham, Deptford, Woolwich and Portsmouth.
> The fees of shipwrights, porters, messengers and suchlike.

> The rent for storehouses.
> Fees for the keeping of houses at Woolwich and Portsmouth.
> Repairing of houses at Deptford, Woolwich, Chatham and Portsmouth.
> The watch at Chatham and Deptford ....[16]

There had also been, the author noted, 'an extraordinary charge which passed by warrant', of £2,500 for the new building and repairing of ships in dry dock – a kind of ordinary extraordinary. This all makes the 'old system' look a great deal more tidy and systematic than we know it was, but the argument was for further change, because the memorandum continues that the charge was 'now greatly increased' since the introduction of Hawkins's bargains. Construing some rather imprecise language, it appears that Hawkins's £4,000 was being paid in addition to the old ordinary rather than instead of it, and because of the increasing pressure being placed on the navy by the deteriorating international situation, the whole situation was beginning to get out of control. The old ordinary was now (in a sense) extraordinary, and the only remedy was to cancel the existing arrangements, including the warrant dormant, and start again.

> Certain of her [Majesty's] council and some others to join with the Lord Admiral in commission to see how this charge may be settled, and a new warrant dormant made for such a sum as should be by them determined ...[17]

A few months later, Hawkins surrendered his contract and the system which it represented was abandoned, partly no doubt because of the intensive work needed to put nearly forty ships on a war footing, but partly also because the whole regime of which it was a part had become befouled by confusion and acrimony. On 1 January 1589 the ordinary was restored at £7,268 per annum, and it was increased ten years later to £11,000, but the distinction between ordinary and extraordinary appears to have remained flexible, or rather the earlier flexibility was restored.[18] In the Armada year of 1588 the navy cost some £92,000, all of which was found by extraordinary warrants on whatever sources of money might be available.

As we have seen, this came from all over the place, but the large sums which were needed by 1587 could only be found in the Exchequer, because it was there that the parliamentary subsidies and such foreign loans as could be raised came to rest. At Michaelmas 1578 there was £247,810 in the hands of the tellers, and that had actually increased by 1585. However, by the end of 1587 that sum was down to £154,000, and by the end of 1588, to £55,000. By 1590 it had disappeared.[19] The cost of war was truly formidable. Between

1558 and 1588 Ireland had absorbed £940,993, without any large-scale fighting. Over the three years since 1585 forces in the Netherlands had cost £343,118, and subsidies to (largely ineffective) allies a further £233,299.[20] It is not surprising that Lord Burghley fretted about the navy's dead pays, or investigated discrepancies in the victualling returns. Against this could be set the subsidy of 1585, which yielded £155,000 over three years, was repeated in 1587 and doubled in 1589 – and extraordinary revenue of some £620,000 over about six years.[21] In addition there were windfalls, like the capture of the carrack *St Philip of Spain* in 1585, which yielded over £108,000. Unlike the *Madre de Dios*, this was mainly a naval capture, and the money (or at least £47,000 of it) went into the royal coffers.[22] It was never enough. In the Armada year, Hawkins received £80,666, which left him with a deficit of over £11,000. This was picked up in an expenditure of £59,399 in 1589, and at the end of that year his 'surplusage' was down to £5,147. However in 1590 new expenditure again came to over £60,000 . The economies which Hawkins had been endeavouring to practise between 1579 and 1587 were blown completely away, and the Treasurer was forced to argue his case in competition with the likes of Sir John Norris and the earl of Essex.[23]

A small contribution to this headache was caused by the decision in 1586 to raise naval wages. On 28 December 1585 Hawkins wrote to Burghley, proposing that the common seaman's rate should be raised from 6s 8d (where it had been since the 1540s) to 10s: 'The [present] wages being so small, causeth the best men to run away, to bribe, and to make mean to be cleared from the service ....'[24] All the officers' rates would then be raised in proportion, adding something like 30 per cent to the wages bill. In spite of that, Burghley was convinced, and wrote a memorandum in June of the following year, accepting the proposals. Perhaps it was also necessary to convince the queen, because there was a delay of over a year in implementing the changes. However, in December 1587, just in time for the key mobilisation which it was realised would be necessary, the new schedule was issued.[25] The Lord Admiral was now to receive £3 6s 8d a day, and was to pay other Admirals and Vice Admirals at his discretion. Other officers were paid according to the size of the ship in which they served. In the top category, which carried over 400 men, the master was to receive £3 2s 6d a week, the purser £1 a week and the master gunner 15s a month. In the next category down (250–400 men), the master got £3, the purser 16s 8d, and the master gunner, as before 15s a month. There were four other categories, going down to ketches and small barks, where the master was paid only £1 a month. The ordinary seaman at all levels received 10s a month, plus, of course, his victuals – which doubled the bill, but was differently paid.

After signing his contract in 1565, Edward Baeshe's declared accounts survive in full, plus one Quarter Book for 1563 and a fair amount of supporting material.[26] By about 1560 he had been provided with a headquarters on Tower Hill (Chatham), and storehouses at Ratcliff, St Katherine's and Rochester, for which he had to assume financial responsibility by the terms of his 'bargain'.[27] After 1565 he was provided with his ordinary directly from the Exchequer in regular tranches, and with such extraordinary warrants as he was deemed to need. This seemingly straightforward situation, however, concealed a number of snags. He no longer had access to the household purveyors, but rather used his own deputies in each county, and in 1574 was constrained to write to the Council to know the extent of his planned obligations in advance, so that letters could be sent into the counties requesting that the necessary quantities of provisions be made available.[28] He had obviously been asked to provide an estimate for 6,200 men for one month, which he had done – £4,790 – but he needed to know whether he was supposed to be providing for three months or two, and when the provision was due to commence. If he was supposed to be providing for three months, then he needed to have two months' supplies 'in hand' at the commencement of the period – or six weeks if the provision was for two months. It was also provided in his contract that if he was required to provide for more than 3,000 men at a time, then additional 'commissioners of provisions' would be appointed. Baeshe seems to have had his reservations about this assistance, and preferred that they should work alongside his own operation, rather than being part of it, perhaps because of the confusions which might arise over payments. Nevertheless when a really big mobilisation was required, such as that which took place ahead of the Armada campaign, such commissions were issued, and Baeshe was constrained to work along with them. On 21 February 1587 Lord Hunsdon, the Lord Lieutenant of Norfolk, wrote to the sheriff, the justices of the peace, the deputy lieutenants and 'the Queen's commissioners for the restraint of corn and other provisions' within the county,

> You shall understand that Edward Baeshe, General Surveyor of the Queen's Majesty's Victual for the Sea causes is especially commanded with all expedition to make ready a great proportion of victuals for the whole navy ....[29]

The allocation for Norfolk had been 1,000 quarters of wheat, 1,000 quarters of malt and 100 barrels of butter, but Hunsdon had negotiated for this to be reduced to 500 quarters of wheat and 60 barrels of butter, on the condition that these were made available immediately. Consequently Baeshe was sending down his purveyor 'with all speed' to have these commodities sent to London. Money would be paid immediately upon receipt. It may be that

Hunsdon was expecting something less than enthusiastic compliance, because he added at the end of his letter

> Also you shall understand that the said Edward Baeshe [has] commission of purveyance from her Majesty which he will not put in execution if the provisions may be otherwise reasonably had.

The commission of purveyance was not a part of the Surveyor General's normal armoury, and reflects the urgency, as well as the scale, of the challenge. It would have entitled him to take up the provisions at household prices, whereas otherwise he would have had to bargain in the open market – hence his earlier lamentation about nothing to be had 'except for ready money'.[30] Hunsdon suggested in his letter that 24s a quarter would be a reasonable price for the wheat.

No doubt similar letters were written to other counties, employing the same stick and carrot approach. We do not know how such missives were received in other counties, but in Norfolk Hunsdon's fears seem to have been realised, because a month later he wrote again:

> Much marvelling that you Mr. Sheriff and the residue of the Justices and commissioners are so careless of her Majesty's great service [there] being (as I am informed) so great store in your shire.[31]

As a result Baeshe's purveyor duly arrived, armed with the queen's commission. This time he demanded 500 quarters of wheat and 600 of malt, the butter having been obtained from Suffolk. Whether this was met in full, and how promptly, we do not know, but if a similar effort was required to extract victuals from every county, for a cause which everyone recognised to be real and urgent, it must have been a protracted and wearisome business.

Baeshe retired on 30 June 1587. His successor James Quarles, 'one of the officers of our household' (he was Chief Clerk of the Kitchen), had been appointed by patent in survivorship to take over from him as long before as 1582, which perhaps suggests that, in spite of his protestations, Edward was not all that keen to hand over the reins until ill health forced his hand.[32] He died in the following year. When he handed over his stock on 1 July 1587, although the Armada was still expected that summer, it contained only 12,040 lbs of beef and 2,300 stockfish, which would not have been enough even for the reserve which he was supposed to keep and renew. We do not know how much wheat, malt, butter and cheese there may have been, so it is hard to relate this information to the strenuous efforts which had earlier been made with the counties, but it looks as though the tactics had not been particularly successful.[33]

In 1586 Baeshe had spent £8,636, but in 1587 Quarles disbursed no less than £29,563, which suggest that there was a good deal of leeway to be made up. With the single exception of 1580, when he had spent £11,932, this was the most that the Surveyor General had disbursed since 1563. Otherwise his outgoings had varied from £1,843 (1566) to £7,484 (1569), averaging about £4,000 a year.[34] During his tenure of the office, from 1587 to 1595, Quarles spent on average about £20,000 a year. His largest expenditure, not surprisingly, was in 1588, when it came to a staggering £59,221, and the smallest was in 1593, when he disbursed £9,872.[35] The colossal expenditure in the Armada year not only reflects the enormous efforts which must have been made, but casts some doubt upon contemporary complaints that the supplies were inadequate. Complaints against Quarles, and against Marmaduke Darrell, who took over from him in 1596, were endless, and far more vociferous than they had ever been against Edward Baeshe, but how far these were justified, and how far an expression of the querulousness which was spreading outward from the court, is another matter. Some at least of the complaints against Quarles were the work of a disgruntled junior officer who coveted his post. There was certainly no reduction in spending, and Darrell disbursed an average of about £25,000 a year between 1596 and the end of the reign, peaking at £40,945 in 1602.[36] Of course all these were years of war, and the parallel costs of the Treasurer of the navy ranged from £29,391 in 1586 to £90,813 two years later.

John Hawkins died at sea in 1595, leaving his accounts in a mess. He had not, apparently, submitted a declared account since 1586, as all those from 1587 to 1595 were submitted after his death by his executrix. She must have been well served, and it is reasonable to suppose that Roger Longford, who became Acting Treasurer (without formal appointment) after Hawkins's death, had in fact been keeping the accounts for several years, and was able to produce them in the form required when they were at last sent for.[37] In 1598 Fulke Greville was appointed as Treasurer, and the annual accounts then continue without a break to the end of the reign. Apart from the Armada year, once Hawkins's contracts had been abandoned, the Treasurer's expenditure varied from £22,269 (1593) to £76,513 (1597), averaging around £45,000.[38] The £63,290 which Gonson had spent in 1563 remained a record until 1588, and was only twice thereafter exceeded. The sequence of accounts show no notable decline in expenditure during the period of Hawkins's bargains. Although 1579 and 1583–5 were relatively low (£7,486 and £8,663), both 1578 and 1580 rose over £14,000, which puts them among the highest since the Newhaven campaign. All one can say with confidence is that the navy became vastly more expensive after 1585, which was only to be expected, and that the Exchequer had to find the bulk of the money.[39] When the naval administration had been reorganised in 1557, Lord Treasurer Winchester had specified a supervisory role for himself, more because he wanted to control the spending departments than because he was specifically interested in the navy, but this never seems to have been effective. He was not responsible for the surveys taken in 1559, and when in 1564 he was commissioned to take the accounts of several officers who had been responsible for the Newhaven campaign, Gonson was one of them, without any suggestion that he should have accounted to him anyway. In 1568 he actually requested Sir William Cecil to send him a warrant for extraordinary naval expenditure, so that he could sign it.[40] If he had been in control his own office should have generated such a warrant, so this small episode raises some interesting questions about who was doing what. It is possible that Cecil, as Secretary, had assumed responsibility for the issue of such warrants, which would suggest that day-by-day budgetary control rested with him rather than with either the Lord Treasurer or the Lord Admiral. If that was the case then the function probably returned to the Lord Treasurer's office when Cecil succeeded Paulet in 1572. On the other hand, Paulet seems to have been responsible for the drafting of a memorandum written probably in 1570, pleading for more resources for the navy, so the nature of his relationship with the Admiralty remains uncertain.[41] What is clear is that Lord Burghley, formally or informally, did exercise a supervisory function. It was he who refused to accept John Hawkins's resignation as Treasurer during the fracas of 1586–7, and who kept the office effectively in abeyance from 1595 until 1598.

Burghley was not entirely incorruptible, but his standards of financial probity were high, and after Hawkins's bargains were abandoned, he made sure that a reasonable level of honesty was maintained. After his death in 1598, his supervisory function seems to have reverted to the secretary, an office then held by his younger son, Sir Robert Cecil, rather than to have passed to his successor as Lord Treasurer, Sir Thomas Sackville. Sir Fulke Greville, who was Treasurer of the navy from 1598 to 1604, has been described as 'honest but weak', and it was during his incumbency that the systematic embezzlement of naval resources began, an abuse which became much worse under his successor Sir Robert Mansell.[42] So bad had the situation become by 1608 that a special Royal Commission was appointed to investigate – but that takes us far outside the period. However, by the time that the old queen died in 1603 naval finances were undoubtedly corrupt, and the fact that £103,000 was spent in 1602 (£62,000 by the Treasurer and £41,000 by the Surveyor General) does not indicate that the service was in a flourishing condition.

Not only was the removal of Lord Burghley's oversight conducive to malpractices, the investigation later blamed the negligence of the chief officers in not meeting regularly. 'They should', the commissioners declared, 'at the House at Chatton Hill (instituted for the same purpose) meet, there to resolve all such business as shall tend to the best benefit and good of his Majesty's affairs in the same Navy Royal.'[43] This raises the question of what procedures the Admiralty was following during the later part of Elizabeth's reign. When Sir William Woodhouse died in 1565 the office of Lieutenant or Vice Admiral was discontinued, and who presided over meetings of the Council for Marine Causes thereafter is not entirely clear. It was probably the Surveyor, Sir William Winter, who was the most senior officer, and who was also Master of the Naval Ordnance from 1557. Benjamin Gonson, although equal in seniority, was not equal in status, and his successor John Hawkins would not at first have challenged. Perhaps the trouble really began with Winter's death in 1589, when the Mastership of the Naval Ordnance was discontinued. His successor as Surveyor, Sir Henry Palmer, was a good seagoing officer, but lacked Winter's experience of naval management.

Between 1589 and 1595 it is probable that Sir John Hawkins became *de facto* chairman, and that was why his accounts got into arrears. His temporary successor would not have been in a position to exercise any leadership, and between 1596 and 1598 the only officers fully in post would have been the Lord Admiral himself (who had no gift for administration), Palmer, Marmaduke Darrell, the Surveyor General of the Victuals, William Borough, the Controller, and the Clerk of the Ships, Benjamin Gonson junior, the son of the former Treasurer.[44] It may well have been at this time that the meetings fell into disuse, and that a lack of firm leadership had the deleterious effects which were later noted. For this the queen herself must also bear a share of the responsibility. The Admiralty officers were, after all, her servants. Preoccupied as she was with the need to save money, she should have been alert to the fact that it was corruption at least as much as the needs of the war which raised the bills for the navy to such unprecedented heights between 1597 and 1602.

The accounts can also tell us other things about the ways in which the navy operated. Upnor castle, for instance, was built to defend the Gillingham anchorage in 1559–60, and was fully operational by the end of the second year, but it was built on rented land, which was not purchased by the Crown until 1568.[45] In 1563 there was still a modest establishment near Harwich, called Colne, which cost £33 6s 0d for the year, and where that leaky old wreck the *Trinity Henry* was still being kept in dock. By 1566 that base had been closed down, and the ship disposed of. Woolwich was the other casualty of this period. It was not closed down, and significant work continued to be done there from time to time, but whereas in 1562 £751 was spent there, and £944 in 1563, by 1570 the ordinary was no more than £12.[46] Admittedly this had recovered to £95 2s 3d by 1578, but as a London base for the navy it had clearly lost out to Deptford, where in 1563 no less than £19,707 was disbursed. The year 1563 was a high spending year, and that level was not maintained. In the economical year of 1566, when only £6,244 was spent overall, Deptford's share was £247. Such fluctuations were normal, as we have seen, and in 1570 the yard had a permanent staff of seventeen, including a clerk of the cheque, a clerk of the reports, two purveyors, two master shipwrights – one of them the Venetian Augustine Levello – a 'Keeper of the Plug' and a 'Porter of the Woodyard'.[47] In 1595, when £59,000 was spent all together, £5,631 of it was at Deptford. However the main development was the growth of Gillingham, or Chatham as it was becoming known. Overshadowed by Deptford between 1559 and 1564, thereafter it became the major spending yard, £6,257 being spent there in 1567, £3,133 in 1570, £3,680 in 1584 (out of £8,515 in a quiet year), and £12,328 in 1595.[48] The Council also seems to have established its headquarters there, the Quarter Book for 1570 showing a rent of £5 for 'a house at Tower Hill wherein the officers of her Majesty's ships do meet and confer from time to time, touching her Highness's weighty affairs ...'.[49] By this time the Woolwich ordinary showed nothing but a keeper for the storehouse, and Portsmouth the same, plus a 'Keeper of the plug'. The extraordinary pattern is somewhat different. For example the Woolwich payments for 1578 came to £2,798, a year in which the total payments, ordinary and extraordinary, totalled £14,938.

Quarter Books survive from 1562–3, 1570, 1574, 1578 and 1601, because they were passed down through the Gonson family and eventually came into the possession of Samuel Pepys.[50] In addition to showing the detailed breakdown of receipts and expenses, they also enable some reconstruction of where work was being carried out. For example at Gillingham in 1570, wages and victuals were accounted for shipwrights and others repairing the *Antelope*, the *Jennet* and the *Primrose*, '... and [working] upon the new building and new making of the *Bull* and the *Tiger*, her highness's old ships in the fashion of galleasses'. This employed over 200 men for a total of more than 20,000 man/days.[51] At Portsmouth in the same year seventy men worked for a total of 3,598 man/days repairing the galley *Eleanor* (which was normally kept there), and a painter was paid £5 for 'beautifying and garnishing' the captain's cabin and for picking out in gold the queen's name and the crown upon the stem and sides. At Deptford a new ship was being built – unnamed but probably the *Foresight* of 300 tons – which kept Mathew Baker and 138 craftsmen busy for 9,146 man/days. This ship was launched in September, and seventy-four mariners were specially recruited for four days to finish her rigging and trimming. William Lizard of London was then paid £49 16s 0d for 'garnishing' her, which presumably meant similar gilding and painting, and for setting up the royal arms.[52] All this work, which would have been classed as ordinary in 1563, had now become extraordinary, which is one of the reasons why the totals are so hard to compare. Nor is it altogether clear why some expenditure is classed under the extraordinary of the base concerned, while some is more generally classified as 'Sea Causes Extraordinary' – a category which had earlier been reserved for operational expenses. In 1563 the wages paid to those who had sailed to Newhaven (£6,664), or had tried to recover the ordnance from the *Greyhound* 'lost on the bar of Rye' (£32), were so classified, but not the building and repairing of ships.[53] By 1570 all sorts of miscellaneous expenses were placed under this heading, including the cutting of a new mast pond at Gillingham, with four divisions for 'the better preserving' of the trees which had usually been imported from Scandinavia. Nineteen ships were also rigged and provisioned for the seas, all from Gillingham. In 1574 there was little action at sea, and between twenty-six and twenty-eight ships were in the anchorage in each quarter of the year. By this time the Senior Clerk was being paid (on the ordinary) at the rate of £6 13s 4d a quarter, which indicates the greater level of responsibility which he was being asked to assume.[54] It is not surprising to find a number of shipwrights also paid on the ordinary, together with their travelling expenses when they were sent on distant jobs, but various items of equipment such as pump hoses and stop-leathers were purchased with the same money, and it is hard to avoid the conclusion that the Senior Clerk was simply using whichever fund happened to be most convenient.

The 1574 Book is incomplete, showing no totals for ordinary receipts or payments. The Woolwich and Portsmouth ordinaries appear to be unchanged from 1570, but Deptford reveals a change of practice. Whereas in 1563 the wives of shipwrights and other workers were being paid for providing lodgings, by 1574 rent was being paid for several houses which were used for accommodating the visiting workmen, although how the laundry bills were then met is not very clear.[55] No extraordinary expenditure is recorded for either Woolwich or Portsmouth, but because of the nature of the account it would be unwise to assume that there was none. We can learn from other sources that the total income for the year was £14,157, and the total expenditure £12,883 – a figure which includes £2,964 for victualling. This presumably means that the income figure includes Baeshe's money as well as Gonson's, so the comparison with other years since 1565 is not exact.

There is also an incomplete Book for 1578, the first year of Hawkins's service. This shows an extraordinary income of £13,938, and a total of 'all expenses and charges extraordinary' of £9,221.[56] However other sources give the total income at £14,276, and extraordinary expenditure at £8,727, so it is very difficult to make sense of these conflicting figures. The one thing that we can be sure about is that Gillingham continued to advance at the expense of its rivals. Twenty-two different ships were anchored there at various times of the year, and the practice of shipkeeping seems to have changed since 1563. Whereas in that year a large ship like the *Elizabeth Jonas* (800 tons) would have retained a crew of five officers and twenty-six seamen, in 1578 the *Triumph*, which was even larger at 1,000 tons, had only four officers and thirteen seamen. Shipkeepers were not paid the full rate, but a master still cost £6 11s 5d a quarter, and an ordinary mariner £1 1s 11d. Perhaps this was simply an economy measure, because all the crewmen are listed by name, and are unlikely to have been 'dead pays'.[57] Smaller ships, like the *Achates* of 100 tons, were kept in 1578 by three officers, but only two seamen. In the second and third quarters of the year about 130 shipwrights and other workmen were employed about caulking and repairing 'her majesty's ships against the winter weather', and two new ships, the *Revenge* (500 tons) and the *Scout* (120 tons), were fitted out.[58] Half a dozen bricklayers were also employed to reconstruct the hearts and furnaces which lay in the bowels of every ship of any size, and the beakhead of the *Dreadnought* was repainted. In this same year yet another mast pond was dug at Chatham (Gillingham), big enough to hold two or three small ships if necessary, and a number of repairs were carried out to the buildings there. This involved the employment of tilers and house-carpenters, who were quite distinct from the workmen employed on the ships. Gillingham, however, appears to have had no dry dock, and when the *Hope*, the *Philip and Mary* and the *Antelope* were judged to be in need of docking, they had to be moved to Deptford. Rather surprisingly, the *Philip and Mary* retained its original name until it was rebuilt as the *Nonpareil* in 1584.[59] The extensive programme of docking carried out in this year probably reflects the new priorities of Mr Treasurer Hawkins. It also threw a lifeline to Woolwich, which as we have seen was seriously underused a few years earlier. In 1578 the *Elizabeth Jonas* was docked there. We do not know the nature of the work carried out, but it took six workmen fourteen days to open the dockhead and let her out. The docks at Woolwich (or at least that particular one) were obviously of the old-fashioned variety, because in that same year we find the first reference to dock gates being installed. This was at Deptford and cost £150, which was a lot of money but removed the need for the expensive and time-consuming business of 'digging out'. Thereafter all the docks constructed seem to have been of the new design, which was universal by the end of the century.[60]

Meanwhile the *White Bear* was also docked at Woolwich, and the 300-ton *Jennet*, built originally in 1538, was broken down into a lighter. The galley *Eleanor* continued her lonely existence at Portsmouth, where her maintenance costs and the wages of her shipkeepers were virtually the only charges against the ordinary. The distinction between ordinary and extraordinary expenditure seems by this time to have become totally arbitrary. Work on the ships at Deptford appears under both headings, and whereas opening the dock at Deptford was classed as extraordinary, opening a similar dock at Woolwich was ordinary. Shipwrights' wages and 'emptions' – the purchase of things such as timber and nails – appear in both categories, and the repair of the *Triumph* at Woolwich, which seems to have been routine, was nevertheless classed as extraordinary. The only category which remained consistently distinct was 'Sea charges', and in 1578 these related mainly to the service of the *Lion*, the *Elizabeth Bonaventure*, the *Dreadnaught*, the *Swiftsure* and the *Foresight* upon the coasts of Ireland in what was probably an attempt to frustrate the pirate 'galleys of Kisimul', which were a perpetual nuisance to any trader operating in the Irish Sea.[61] In the absence of further Quarter Books, detailed expenditure is hard to track. There was, for instance, a destructive fire at Portsmouth in 1576, but we do not know how long it took to make good the damage – only that it had been done by 1585.[62] In 1574 the suggestion of 1559 was finally taken up and the Edwardian bulwark at Sheerness was rebuilt. In 1585, on the outbreak of war, it was decided that Upnor and Sheerness were inadequate safeguards, and a chain was placed across the entrance to the Medway. This was a complicated and expensive operation. The chain was anchored to great piles at one end and tensioned at the other by being passed over two great wheels. Even so, it required the support of five lighters. The 'back way' into Chatham by way of St Mary's creek had already been blocked with piles in 1574 to prevent any flank attack on the anchorage.[63] If the Dutch had attacked the Medway eighty years sooner, they would have found their task a great deal more difficult.

The outbreak of war also required further precautions with financial implications. Two pinnaces were to be kept at Sheerness on standby, presumably to alert the Council of any sudden attack, and the largest ships, which were anchored downstream nearest to the chain, were required to carry lights at night. In 1585 the Council ordered that the principal officers of the navy (excluding the Lord Admiral) should take it in turns, a month at a time, to sleep on board one of the larger ships in order to supervise the shipkeepers.[64] Whether this showed a lack of confidence in the junior officers, or was a means of making sure that the members of the Admiralty earned their allowances, is not clear. Additional wharves and storehouses were also built at Chatham, Deptford and Woolwich in anticipation of having larger numbers of ships at sea, and a 'ropehouse' was constructed at Woolwich by one Thomas Allen. This seems to have been for the manufacture rather than the storage of ropes, and may have been an attempt to make England more self-sufficient in this important commodity. If so, it seems to have failed because Russian rope went on being purchased in quantity, and Allen's name does not appear again.[65]

A ship building and replacement programme had been in place after a fashion since the 1530s, and Elizabeth continued to build and rebuild steadily throughout her reign. There were already ships on the stocks when she came to the throne, and others were laid down at the rate of about one a year from then for the next twenty-five years. In the early part of the reign this was mostly done by direct labour in the royal yards, under the supervision of Peter Pett or Mathew Baker, who would also have been responsible for the design. The *Triumph* had been built in this manner in 1562 at a cost of £3,788.[66] After Hawkins became Treasurer, however, most of this work was contracted out, which was consistent with his enthusiasm for internal contracts which we have noticed. It may also have been one of the reasons for his perpetual disagreements with Pett and Baker, that he was taking away from them work to which they felt entitled. The reasons for this shift may not have been entirely financial, because there are good reasons to suppose that Hawkins wanted to exercise a controlling influence over the design of these ships himself. That would have been difficult had they been in the hands of Pett and Baker, whom the Treasurer may well have thought rather conservative in their ideas. By putting the work out in this way, it may be that he was trying to bypass his rivals. The *Lion* was so contracted in 1582 for a price of £1,440, and the *Nonpareil* was rebuilt in 1584 for £1,600.[67] It is likely that these costs were exclusive of the rigging, which could probably be done more economically in-house, and with which Pett and Baker need not have been involved. However, this interpretation of Hawkins's motivation is little more than speculation, because the 'Fragments of English Shipwrightery', which is almost certainly by Baker and was written about 1586, shows that he had embraced the newer principles of design, and the ship described is 'race built'.[68] Baker also had an interest in more than one private yard himself, and in 1590 built the *Merhoneur* under contract for £3,600, plus two smaller vessels, the *Quittance* and the *Answer*, for £1,400 each. In 1594, when he built the *Adventure* in a royal yard using direct labour, he claimed that it cost the Crown far more – but his testimony was hardly impartial.[69] It is also possible that by then Hawkins was disillusioned with the contract system, and no longer believed that it saved the money which he had once claimed.

As we have seen, very few ships were purchased by Elizabeth – only five between 1560 and 1592, and that included the re-possession of the *Primrose*. So the outlay in that fashion was minimal, about £100 a year over the whole period. There were, however, some which were acquired in other ways. The galley *Eleanor*, for example, came as a pledge from the French Huguenots, while two other galleys, named the *Speedwell* and the *Tryright*, were taken as prizes at the end of the war in 1559. The *Tiger* was exchanged for the *Sea Dragon* in 1584, and the *St Andrew* and the *St Mathew* were taken from the Spaniards at Cadiz in 1596. The galleys were little used, and the *Speedwell* and the *Tryright* disappear from the records in 1580. They came back into fashion at the end of the century, and four new ones were built in 1601, but the reason for this change of mind is unknown. Early in the reign the *Eleanor* remained immobile at Portsmouth, and the only sign of galley use was the retention of the Venetian shipwright whom we have already noticed. Elizabeth may have been hard up, and desiring to economise, but she did not do so by forcing her subjects to sell their vessels to her at cut prices. With the exception of the *Ark Royal*, which began life as the *Ark Raleigh*, she did not acquire any ships in that fashion. The goodwill of the maritime community, and its willingness to deploy ships in her service when really needed, was too valuable an asset to compromise. Of course the costs of royal investment in semi-private adventures did not pass through the naval accounts, and these need to be borne in mind when calculating the costs of seaborne enterprise. Frobisher's voyage of 1589 cost £11,000, that of Frobisher and Hawkins in 1590, £17,000, while the outlay on the Cadiz expedition (which was an act of war, in spite of being privately financed) was a massive £78,000.[70] Of course against this was to be set the prize money which was the objective of such investment – £46,672 from the *St Philip* in 1587, £80,000 from the *Madre de Dios*, and a number of smaller windfalls. It is impossible to complete the sums, or to form any idea of the balance, but the chances are that Elizabeth lost more than she gained by these adventures.[71] However, the point was not entirely financial. However important money may have been, the queen's collaboration with her subjects in expeditions of this kind had a political point which went far beyond the sums which the Lord Treasurer was forced to present.

All together, in the course of her reign, Elizabeth put something like £1,350,000 into her naval accounts, irrespective of the sums invested in other ways.[72] She spent rather more, but for a country which had spent eighteen years at war – a war in which the navy had been in the front line – it was a comparatively modest sum. Henry VIII's conquest of Boulogne, and its retention for four years, had cost £1,013,022, and the English government ended up with nothing to show for the expenditure. Elizabeth's navy had played a major part in saving the independence of the country, and that was value for money.

CHAPTER 7 NOTES

1. For an example of 'riding charges', see MS Rawlinson A.200, ff.147–9.
2. Ibid., various. The totals are my own.
3. TNA E351/2199. *Elizabethan Naval Administration*, section 3.
4. Ibid., m.10d.
5. MS Rawlinson A.200. My own calculations.
6. F.C. Dietz, *English Public Finance, 1558–1640* (1964), pp. 11–12, citing TNA AO 283/1069.
7. T. Glasgow, 'The Maturing of Naval Administration, 1556–1564', *Mariners Mirror*, 56, 1970, p. 18. Loades, *The Tudor Navy*, p. 183.

8. TNA SP12/25, no. 13. *ENA*, 5 (a).
9. Ibid., no. 66. *ENA*, 5 (b).
10. BL Cotton MS Otho E.IX, ff.120–4. *ENA*, 5 (c).
11. Oppenheim, *Naval Administration*, p. 161.
12. *ODNB*.
13. TNA SP12/132, nos 88–91. S. Adams, 'New Light on the "Reformation" of John Hawkins: The Ellesmere Naval Survey of 1584', *English Historical Review*, 105, 1991 pp. 97–111. Loades, *Tudor Navy*, p. 184.
14. PL 2875, p. 60. Copied by one of Pepys's clerks from an original in the State Papers, which does not survive. *ENA*, 5 (d).
15. Oppenheim. *Naval Administration*, pp. 162–3.
16. 27 June 1587, 'Summary of the arrangements for the ordinary and extraordinary …', TNA SP12/202, no. 35, *ENA*, 5 (h).
17. Ibid.
18. TNA SP12/218, no. 16. SP12/270, no. 26. Oppenheim, *Naval Administration*, p. 163.
19. Dietz, *Public Finance*, p. 55.
20. TNA SP12/209, no. 14.
21. Dietz, *Public Finance*, pp. 54–5.
22. TNA SP12/204, no. 46. BL Lansdowne MS 70, f.82. Oppenheim, *Naval Administration*, pp. 165–6.
23. Ibid., p. 161. Loades, *Tudor Navy*, pp. 280–1.
24. TNA SP12/185, nos 33 and 33 (ii). *ENA*, 5 (e).
25. Bod MS Rawlinson A. 171, ff.310–13. *ENA*, 5 (g).
26. TNA E351/2353–2884 (Declared Accounts). BL Harleian MS 167, ff.1–38 (Quarter Book).
27. BL Cotton MS Otho E.IX, ff.99–102, 116–19. With lacunae supplied from PL 2876, pp. 161–8. *ENA*, 6 (e).
28. 20 April 1574. TNA SP12/95, no. 81. *ENA*, 6 (g).
29. Bod MS Tanner 241, pp. 28–9. *British Naval Documents*, pp. 111–12.
30. TNA SP12/95, no. 81.
31. Bod MS Tanner 241, pp. 30–1. Loades, *Tudor Navy*, p. 206.
32. Oppenheim, *Naval Administration*, p. 142. BL Lansdowne MS 62, f.132.
33. Oppenheim, *Naval Administration*, loc. cit.
34. Ibid, p. 161.
35. Ibid.
36. Ibid.
37. TNA E351/2223–32. Declared Accounts, 'J Hawkins per executrix'. Longford was simply appointed 'General Paymaster of Marine Causes'.
38. Oppenheim, *Naval Administration*, p. 161.
39. Dietz, *Public Finance*, pp. 153–5.
40. Loades, *The Life and Career of William Paulet, First Marquis of Winchester* (2008), p. 157.
41. Ibid.
42. A.P. McGowan, *The Jacobean Commissions of Enquiry, 1608, 1618* (NRS, 1971), introduction.
43. Ibid.

44. Loades, *Tudor Navy*, p. 276. The younger Gonson was succeeded in 1600 by Peter Buck.
45. Ibid., p. 190. For Colne, see MS Rawlinson. A.200.
46. Oppenheim, *Naval Administration*, p. 161.
47. Bod MS Rawlinson A.201.
48. Oppenheim, *Naval Administration*, loc. cit.
49. MS Rawlinson A.201, f.41.
50. For the descent of the papers which came into the hands of Samuel Pepys, see *ENA*, General Introduction (by C.S. Knighton).
51. MS Rawlinson. A.201, f.106. Loades, *Tudor Navy*, p. 188.
52. Ibid. For the significance attached to this 'garnishing', see S. Rodgers, 'The Symbolism of Ship Launching' (Oxford D.Phil., 1983).
53. MS Rawlinson. A.200. E351/2199, m.10.
54. MS Rawlinson A.202.
55. Ibid.
56. MS Rawlinson A.203.
57. Ibid.
58. Ibid.
59. Rodger, *Safeguard of the Sea*, p. 479. The *Philip and Mary* had been launched in 1556 as a celebration of the Anglo-Spanish union, which was looking very frayed by 1584.
60. Loades, *Tudor Navy*, p. 189. Rodger, *Safeguard of the Sea*, pp. 335–6.
61. Loades, *Tudor Navy*, p. 190.
62. The fire cost Edward Baeshe £240 in lost provisions. E351/2374.
63. BL Add. MS 9294, f.58. TNA E351/2210.
64. Loades, *Tudor Navy*, pp. 190–1.
65. Ibid., p. 191.
66. MS Rawlinson A.200, ff.26–33. Ibid., p. 193.
67. Oppenheim, *Naval Administration*, pp. 128–9.
68. Pepys Library, MS 2820. Peter Kirsch, *The Galleon* (1990), pp. 116–21.
69. McGowan, *Jacobean Commissions*, pp. 252–3. Rodger, *Safeguard of the Sea*, pp. 336–7.
70. TNA SP12/256, no. 107. Oppenheim, *Naval Administration*, p. 164.
71. Ibid.
72. Ibid., p. 161. My calculation.

CHAPTER EIGHT

Towards War

One of the few positive things to come out of the Newhaven campaign was the realisation that Elizabeth no longer had to fear the French navy. The formidable fleet that had confronted her father in 1545 no longer existed.[1] Consequently a close relationship with Spain was neither necessary nor desirable. Anglo-Spanish relations had not been good since the 1530s, and Mary's marriage to Philip had made the situation worse. In so far as they wanted employment in Philip's armies, English aristocrats might proclaim themselves to be 'Spanish', but that was sheer opportunism, and the rest of the country did not share their profession. Mary had been deeply troubled by this hostility, and Elizabeth had made it perfectly clear to the count of Feria that she felt no obligation of gratitude to Philip at the time of her accession. 'She trusts', Feria wrote, 'in the people'.[2] The king's proposal of marriage to her in January 1559 was undertaken solely in the cause of duty. She was still officially an ally in an ongoing war, and he knew perfectly well that, left to her own devices, she would take her country back into heresy. This he hoped to prevent, but was hugely relieved when she turned him down. His proposal was made in the course of duty, but he had placed the onus for refusal upon her. Thereafter the queen had played a double game. Neither her intervention in Scotland in 1560 nor that in France in 1563 were directly hostile to Spain, but both were contrary to Philip's interests. On the other hand she issued proclamations against the French pirates who were attacking Spanish shipping, and in September 1563 even ordered her subjects to defend Spanish ships which came under such attacks.[3] There were crises in relations with Philip's agents in the Low Countries from 1563 to 1566, and again from 1568 to 1572, but in both cases the king himself gritted his teeth and refrained from any retaliation more formidable than a trade embargo. However Elizabeth realised that in backing Hawkins in 1568, she had sailed a shade too close to the wind, and thereafter drew back from similar commitments. Illicit English voyages to the Caribbean continued, but the queen was not involved, except in so far as she made no serious attempt to stop them.

All together there were thirteen such voyages between 1570 and 1577. They varied in their outcome, but were not for the most part very successful, and did not make any pretence of carrying out legitimate trade. The first two independent voyages of Francis Drake in 1570 and 1571 may be taken as typical. He kept away from the main harbours and centres of population, preying instead upon the virtually unarmed barks which plied along the coasts of Panama and Mexico and between the small island colonies of the Caribbean. From the second of these voyages he came back with booty which the injured colonists claimed to be worth 40,000 ducats (about £13,000).[4] Of course this was not all profit, but the shareholders presumably saw a reasonable return on their outlay. The queen was not in any way involved, but was kept up to date with his exploits via his friends at court. He was 'out' again in 1572–3, and on that occasion enjoyed a far more striking success, although one that cost the lives of two of his brothers. Operating in loose collaboration with French Huguenot corsairs, he ambushed a mule train near Nombre de Dios and relieved it of a small fortune in silver bullion, so much indeed that neither he nor his allies were able to carry it all away.[5] The Huguenots were partly motivated by revenge, because the viceroy of the Indies had destroyed their colony in Florida in 1562 with a heavy loss of life, and the *cimarrones*, or escaped slaves, who collaborated with them had their own reasons for hating the Spaniards. How much of the booty from this expedition found its way to England is not clear, but one estimate is 50,000 pesos, or about £20,000. It was certainly enough to maintain Drake's credit, and to fill his coffers. By 1575 he was a very rich man.[6]

These raids left Philip with a dilemma. In global terms they were mere pinpricks, but the lurking presence of the queen of England gave them political significance. The king's servants in the New World began to suspect that behind these probing attacks there was a serious intention to challenge Spain's hegemony in the Americas by the establishment of English colonies at strategically located sites beyond the present range of Spanish settlement. Their reaction to the French colony in Florida had been motivated by a similar fear. Such suspicions were not entirely misplaced, because Richard Grenville did indeed produce such a scheme in 1574, and Spain came to know about it when John Oxenham was captured in Panama in 1577.[7] However, the queen had refused to license it, and for settlement – as distinct from mere robbery – the royal authority (and money) was certainly needed.

In the later 1570s Elizabeth was trying to have her cake and eat it. At one level she was anxious to placate Philip, and perhaps to persuade him to withdraw his support from the Guises in France, but at the same time she was countenancing the piratical activities of men like Francis Drake. One of the reasons for this was that the queen's view of the world had been changed by the action of Pope Pius V in 1570. The rebels in northern England who had set out to depose her in 1569 had appealed for aid to the duke of Alba in the

Low Countries, and to the pope. Alba had not been interested in so flimsy a venture, but Pius had responded in 1570 with the bull *Regnans in Excelsis*. By the time that this bull was promulgated it was too late to help the rebels, but it declared Elizabeth deposed and absolved all her subjects of their allegiance to her.[8] In theory it also obliged all Catholic princes to co-operate in carrying out the sentence, and this meant primarily the king of Spain. It also meant, of course, that any Englishman who recognised papal authority became a potential traitor. From being a nuisance and an embarrassment, English Catholics had now become a serious threat, and possibly a Spanish fifth column. This had the effect of making patriotism a Protestant monopoly, and giving those who went raiding in the Caribbean an additional cover for their activities. They could now claim to be striking a blow for the godly Reformation. By 1580 it was quite reasonable to regard war with Spain as inevitable, sooner or later, and to exploit whatever advantages circumstances seemed to offer.

The queen blew hot and cold. Grenville was in a sense unlucky, because when he had approached her she had been in a cautious mood, and such moods were bound to pass. When a further group of speculators approached her in 1577, she was much more responsive. This time the proposal was not for a colony or colonies, but rather for a voyage through the straits of Magellan to explore the western coast of South America.[9] Elizabeth knew perfectly well that the Spaniards were already settled on the west coast, although not in the same numbers as on the east coast, and that this voyage would inevitably mean conflict. She sanctioned it nevertheless, only insisting that she remain as a private shareholder. The proposers asked for the loan of the royal ship *Swallow*, which would have been an unequivocal symbol of her participation, but that she refused. Francis Drake was by this time the obvious man to command such an expedition, and when the Spanish ambassador found out, he was understandably convinced that another act of provocation was afoot.[10] Elizabeth's only direct intervention was to insist that Drake's flagship (which he owned himself) should be named the *Pelican*. Since the pelican was one of her favourite emblems, the implication was clear, although it might have been too subtle to be picked up by the Spaniards. This extremely well known, and well documented, voyage began on 15 November 1577, and came to grief almost at once in a storm off the Cornish coast. Drake had been negligent and the ships had been badly loaded, so that one was badly damaged by the time that they got into Falmouth. While the captain took out his annoyance on his subordinates, the whole fleet had to return to Plymouth for repairs, and it was 13 December before they finally got under way.[11]

January 1580 saw them at Cape Blanco on the Moroccan coast, where they took, looted and eventually abandoned several small Spanish trading vessels.

Although no formal instructions had been issued, or apparently received, everyone who sailed on this voyage knew that its main objective was piracy, and Drake's hand was considerably strengthened when, among the Cape Verde Islands, he took a large Portuguese merchant ship, the *Santa Maria*, and her experienced pilot Nuno de Silva. De Silva knew the South American coast in a way that neither Drake nor any of his officers did, and this was to prove an enormous asset.[12] However, the ship itself was a mixed blessing, because Drake put Thomas Doughty, the captain of his soldiers, on board to command her, and from that separation arose misunderstandings which resulted in a bitter quarrel between the two men. There are a number of accounts of this developing animosity, which reflect no credit upon either of the protagonists, and Drake subjected his nominal second in command to a series of humiliations, dismissing him eventually to the 'command' of the tiny *Swan*, a victualler and support vessel.[13] Drake struck the Brazilian coast in April 1578 and headed south, his relations with Doughty worsening all the time. At the end of June he had reached Port San Julian, where he decided to winter before tackling the Magellan straits. He also decided to settle with Thomas Doughty, who, for some reason which does not emerge clearly from the accounts, he had concluded was guilty of both mutiny and necromancy. Claiming an authority which he did not in fact possess, on 30 June he went ashore and put his subordinate on trial.[14] The evidence was circumstantial and inconclusive to everyone except Drake, but the trial was conducted in due form, and the verdict delivered by an open show of hands among all those present. The judgment, inevitably, was guilty, and Doughty was duly executed.

Why Drake proceeded in this ruthless and vindictive fashion has never been satisfactorily explained, but it is clear that he had become paranoid about any challenge to his authority, and of this Doughty had undoubtedly been guilty. Drake's men were now genuinely frightened of him, and that may have been part of the point. His expedition had a difficult and dangerous route ahead, and anything less than unquestioning obedience could well have been fatal. However, they also admired him, and ruthlessness suited the image of a successful pirate. He would not spare them, but he would not spare himself either in the months which lay ahead. Accidents, decay and abandonment had by this time reduced the fleet to just three vessels, the *Pelican*, the *Marigold* and the *Elizabeth*. They quitted Port San Julian on 17 August and entered the strait of Magellan on the 21st. Their passage was relatively uneventful, although it seems that many men died from disease and malnutrition.[15] Drake took symbolic possession of an island which he named Elizabeth Island, and the crews restocked their larder by massacring large numbers of penguins. However, when they emerged safely on 6 September they ran straight into a South Pacific storm. Over the next few days, the

Marigold was lost, and the *Pelican* and the *Elizabeth* became separated. Drake himself seems to have been driven far to the south and east, and may even have rounded Cape Horn before he was able to resume his proper course.[16] The *Elizabeth* re-entered the strait of Magellan, and there Thomas Wynter waited for three weeks for Drake to appear. When he did not do so, Wynter set out for home, concluding that his captain had been lost. Drake subsequently accused Wynter of desertion, but at the time there was probably a strong feeling of mutual relief at this enforced parting.

It was 28 October before the *Pelican* (now renamed the *Golden Hind*) was able to resume its journey north.[17] Drake had now just one ship and about eighty men. Zig-zagging his way up what is now the coast of Chile, on 25 November he reached the island of Mocha. He was then among the Spanish settlements, and an attempt to land near Mocha was repulsed with loss. In spite of this setback, he decided to attack the small town of Valparaiso, which he did on 5 December, using some Spanish-speaking crewmen as a subterfuge to gain admission to the harbour. This time he was much more successful, and relieved the settlers of one ship and of gold which was later valued at 200,000 pesos.[18] This was the kind of thing that Drake did best, and the enthusiasm of his men is understandable. Continuing his journey north, he stopped at Bahia Salada, which was then uninhabited, a circumstance which enabled him to careen and rearm the *Golden Hind* without interference from the settlers. The nearest town was Copiapo, but that was several miles away and virtually deserted at the time. Continuing north, his next stop was Tarapaca, where he found only a handful of Spaniards, but two well loaded merchantmen from which he took wine, food, and 3,000 pesos' worth of silver.[19] By this time Drake's fleet numbered four ships and a pinnace, far more than could be reliably crewed, and about 9 February he decided to cut his losses and abandon the three captured ships, which was duly done once everything of value had been taken out of them. Although his crew was now reduced to about seventy men, Drake continued to take whatever opportunities offered, capturing some ships at sea, and even managing a successful raid on Callao, which was the port for Lima, the principal city of Peru. At Paita, a few miles north of Callao, he took another ship loaded with gold and silver to the value of 22,000 pesos. All together on the whole of that coast, he met with no opposition from armed ships, and only sporadically from men ashore.[20] The west coast was completely unprepared for marauders such as Drake, who with one ship and a handful of men was able take pretty much what he pleased.

He continued until he reached the small port of Guatulco, on the coast of what is now Mexico. From there he was expected to head for Acapulco, and thence north in search of the western end of the strait of Anian, which should in theory have led back to the Atlantic. In fact there was no strait of Anian, and there is very little evidence that Drake was seriously looking for it. Instead he spent some time on the coast of what is now upper California, although the story that he took possession of it in the name of Queen Elizabeth appears to be a myth.[21] From there he sailed west for the Moluccas, going apparently by the southern route taken by the Manilla galleons. Allegedly he was out of sight of land from the end of August 1579 until the end of November, and when he did make a landfall it was at Palau in the Philippines. The Moluccas offered nothing in the way of Spanish colonies to attack, and very little in the way of shipping. There were, of course, spices, but Drake was not a trader and was unwilling to part with any of his specie. More welcome to him were places like 'Crab Island' where he was able to careen his ship, which was very foul after so long at sea. Then on 8 January 1580, while looking for a way out of the islands into the Indian Ocean, the *Golden Hind* stuck fast on a reef. Drake jettisoned cargo, and even some guns in an attempt to lighten her, but nothing availed. Turning to God for aid, he ordered his chaplain, Francis Fletcher, to hold a communion service. With an incredible lack of common sense, Fletcher then preached that their predicament was a punishment for Drake's treatment of Thomas Doughty. The captain was livid, and immediately placed his chaplain under restraint, whereupon a gale sprang up and blew the ship off the reef.[22] Drake immediately interpreted this providential intervention as Divine support for his action, and seems to have acted as his own chaplain for the remainder of the voyage.

Having jettisoned so much cargo, the *Golden Hind* was obliged to stop again on the southern coast of Java to replenish her supplies. This they were able to do in the most generous and satisfactory way. The people were friendly and hospitable, and their food plentiful, although a little on the expensive side. It was the first stroke of good luck that the expedition had enjoyed since leaving the coast of Peru. From Java to the Cape of Good Hope was an uninterrupted passage of two and a half months at sea, but after their last stop the men were in good heart and in reasonable health. In fact they did not stop until 22 July 1580, by which time they had reached Sierra Leone on the coast of Guinea, where they took on firewood and fresh water.[23] Thereafter Drake may, or may not, have stopped at La Rochelle to recruit additional seamen – the sources are inconsistent.[24] What is clear is that he reached Plymouth at the end of September after an epic journey which had lasted almost three years, bringing with him one ship, a fraction of the men he had started out with, and an extremely valuable cargo of gold and silver bullion. The officially declared value of this was £307,000, but the true total was about £600,000. This gave his ordinary investors a 4,700 per cent return on their outlay of £5,000, and his extraordinary investor, the queen, some £300,000, enough to pay off her whole foreign debt and still leave £42,000 over to be invested in the new Levant

Company.[25] It is not surprising that she was so enthusiastic, or that she had considered sending out a search party when her captain was so long delayed.

Drake's circumnavigation had been a magnificent achievement of seamanship and sheer bloody-mindedness. It is doubtful if anyone less driven or less ruthless could have accomplished it. It was not a feat of exploration, because he had opened up no new lands, and had not even sailed uncharted seas. Nor had he opened up new markets, or the way for colonial developments. What he had done (apart from bringing back a fabulous plunder) was to make a statement of intent. Having been overshadowed by the Iberians for generations as navigators, cartographers and ocean-going seamen, the English were now ready to compete on equal terms. Drake's plunder was very welcome, both to his shareholders and to the queen, but the political significance of his voyage was very much greater. No ocean in the world was now safe from English freebooters, and where English pirates went, the navy was very likely to follow. The king of Spain read the omens and was deeply disturbed. There would soon be no place that was safe from the heretics, their traders, and their guns.

Spanish complaints about Drake's depredations had preceded his return. An agreement had been negotiated in 1579, during his absence, for the mutual return of plundered goods, but in this case the English Council had no intention of honouring it. A variety of excuses were made for non-compliance, but the main point was that the bulk of what had been taken was Spanish Crown property, and not covered by the agreement.[26] When the news of Drake's return reached her, the queen publicly announced that she had been greatly embarrassed by his activities. However, this was for the benefit of Mendoza, the Spanish ambassador, and privately Elizabeth expressed her pleasure. In October Drake was received at court, and spent some six hours closeted with the queen, setting out the events of his voyage. On his return to Devon he was in theory allowed to keep £10,000 of his plunder, but appears to have retained as much as £40,000, to which a blind eye was turned. He brought the *Golden Hind* round to the Thames, where the queen knighted him on the deck. He was now both a national hero and an even richer man. He purchased Buckland Abbey and spent a lot of money on its refurbishment, but clearly had no intention of settling down. Plans were soon being canvassed for another voyage, perhaps to the West Indies, perhaps to the Pacific. There was even talk of a trading post in Brazil. However, little was achieved. Drake did not sail himself, and Edward Fenton's voyage of 1582, aimed at the East Indies, disintegrated through poor leadership and did nothing.[27] In material terms, the piratical exploits of these years were of little significance. Only ten Spanish ships were taken between 1578 and 1581 and (Drake apart) the plunder was negligible. In 1582 the entire English merchant marine contained only twenty ships of 200 tons and over – at least that was what was declared, and such vessels would have been difficult to conceal.[28] Even Drake had done little to undermine Spanish power in the New World. It was the threat which mattered, and that threat began to turn Philip's thoughts in the direction of war with England.

Meanwhile the general political situation became ever more tense. In 1580 Sebastian, the king of Portugal, died, leaving no direct heir. However his indirect heir was Philip, who promptly occupied the country and took over its extensive colonial empire. He was challenged by an illegitimate pretender, Dom Antonio, known as the Prior of Crato. Antonio was supported by the rebel Dutch, by the French Huguenots and by everyone else with a desire to embarrass Philip. Elizabeth received him at court and gave him a modest sum of money, but little else.[29] He raised a fleet, consisting of French, Dutch and renegade Portuguese ships, but it was defeated at Terciera by the marquis of Santa Cruz on 26 July 1583. The few English ships involved were not there with the queen's blessing. Bernardino de Mendoza at the same time was bearing himself with a high hand, Drake being the main theme of his persistent complaints. The queen retaliated by demanding an explanation of Spain's recent involvement with the rebellious Irish, and declared that she would not receive the ambassador again until such was forthcoming.[30] Mendoza asked to be recalled, claiming that his presence in England was now useless, but Philip kept him at his post, apparently as a pressure point, and encouraged him to become involved in plots to overthrow the English government. These focused on Mary, Queen of Scots, who was playing a double game. On the one hand she was negotiating with Elizabeth for the possible establishment of a condominium in Scotland with her son James, a plan which she claimed would settle the chronic instability of that country.[31] At the same time, however, she was negotiating with Philip for his protection, and for the education of her son in Spain. In 1583 a plot was hatched in Paris, in which the prime movers were agents of the duke of Guise, for the assassination of Elizabeth and her replacement with Mary. This was to be accomplished by a joint Spanish and Guisard invasion, backed by an English Catholic rebellion. Both the nature of the plan and his own disposition prompted Mendoza to become deeply involved, and he communicated with Francis Throgmorton, a young and indiscreet recusant whose role it would be to mobilise his co-religionists. Unfortunately, the Council was already aware of Throgmorton and his predilections, and he was arrested towards the end of 1583.[32] Subsequent interrogations revealed the extent of Mendoza's involvement, and in January 1584 he was expelled. Philip consequently had no diplomatic representation in England as the crisis came to a head.

Elsewhere the tide was running strongly in Philip's favour. In 1583 the duke of Parma captured the ports of Dunkirk and Nieupoort, which enabled the king to re-establish a North Sea squadron, and effectively re-opened communications by sea between Spain and the Netherlands. In May 1584 the maverick duke of Anjou died, leaving the Huguenot leader Henry of Navarre as the heir to the French throne, with the inevitable consequence that civil war was resumed in France. The country ceased to be a factor in Spanish calculations. Finally in July 1584 the Dutch rebel leader William the Silent was assassinated. There is no reason to suppose that Philip was directly involved in this, but it suited his purposes admirably. The Dutch were temporarily leaderless and demoralised, and it seemed that sooner rather than later the duke of Parma would be able to claim a complete victory.[33] This left Elizabeth in a painful dilemma. Either she must aid the Dutch swiftly and substantially, which would inevitably mean war with Spain, or she must wait in the hope that Philip would be satisfied with crushing the Dutch and would not want to take the war further. Rightly or wrongly she was already convinced that the king of Spain would eventually turn his fire on her, and she therefore decided – if she could – to rescue the Dutch. Lord Burghley expressed the situation succinctly:

> Although her Majesty should thereby enter into a war presently, yet were she better able to do it now, while she may make the same out of her realm, having the help of the people of Holland, and before the King of Spain should have consummated his conquests in these countries ... and shall be so strong by sea ... as that her majesty shall in no wise be able ... neither by sea nor land to withstand his attempts ...[34]

In August 1584 she began to negotiate with the representatives of the United Provinces, and a year later by the treaty of Nonsuch bound herself to provide 4,000 infantry, 400 cavalry, and 600,000 florins a year, and to send a naval squadron to the West Indies.[35] There was no mention of Spain, and formal war was never declared, but by then the die had been cast.

The contrast in resources between the two kingdoms at this point was ludicrous. Between 1571 and 1580 Philip received 12 million ducats (about £3,300,000) in silver from the Americas, and over the following decade the figure was 18.7 million (£4,800,000), an average of over £400,000 a year. This was only a part (and not the largest) of his income, which was mainly derived from the taxation of Castile.[36] In 1577 alone his total income was some 8.7 million ducats, or rather more than £2 million. By contrast Elizabeth's ordinary revenue in the early 1580s was about £300,000. A parliamentary subsidy, when granted, added about £150,000, but might be spread over several years. By extremely frugal management, and with the assistance of windfalls like Drake's treasure, by 1584 she had accumulated a reserve equivalent to about one year's ordinary revenue, enough to sustain the navy on a war footing for about four years.[37] On the other hand, England's ships and guns were superior and her machinery for mobilisation far more efficient than her rivals'. No one – not even Philip himself – knew how large his income in 1585 was likely to be, but it would be about ten times that of the queen of England. In spite of the fact that the English militia had been reorganised in the 1570s, Spain's army was far larger, and far more efficient than anything which Elizabeth could have deployed against it. Only at sea did England have the edge, and it was consequently at sea that the Council decided to wage war.[38]

In 1584 John Hawkins had proposed a scheme for privateering under the flag of Dom Antonio, just about the only way in which the pretender could be useful, using Plymouth as a base, and deploying 'a certain leader', by whom he appears to have meant himself. By November this had developed into a plan for an expedition, probably to South America, backed by the queen and a similar circle of investors to those who had supported the circumnavigation.[39] No doubt the outcome of that adventure had provided encouragement. However, by this time the projected command had been shifted from Hawkins to Drake, possibly because of his superior track record, or perhaps because of the queen's favour. This plan would probably have been implemented in the summer of 1585 in any case, but on 26 May Philip himself provided a pretext.

For some reason, which may have had more to do with the desire to seize grain cargoes than with any deep-laid political plot, all British, French and Dutch shipping in Spanish ports was seized and their cargoes confiscated.[40] The pretext given was that the ships were intended to serve the Spanish Crown in a forthcoming expedition, but no such expedition seems to have been in prospect and the whole affair is to an extent mysterious. The majority of the ships seized were in fact Dutch, but the outrage caused in the City of London was significant. Up to that time the majority of the merchant community had been in favour of accommodating Spanish interests, and hostile to those councillors who were known to be seeking war, a fact of which both Lord Burghley and the queen herself were well aware. This stroke, however, alienated them, and they became sympathetic to the idea of a naval conflict. Between them they owned most of the big ships in the English merchant fleet, so this change of attitude was important. Their ships would not be at sea, or otherwise unavailable, if the queen needed them. Whether the expedition which Drake eventually led out on 14 September was a response to the Spanish action, or independent of it, is a matter of some dispute.[41] The voyage had, as we have seen, been set up in the previous year, when the queen had pledged £10,000 and two ships as her investment. This would have made it a private venture, like the circumnavigation. In February 1585 the queen upped her investment to

£20,000, but there was no sign of active preparations, and by April she seems to have changed her mind about the whole enterprise. Then came Philip's action, and after about a month of hesitation, on 1 July Elizabeth issued orders for a rather different kind of expedition. Drake was now commissioned by the queen, and instructed to proceed to the Vigo to negotiate the release of those ships which were still being held.[42]

This, however, was not the whole story, and the fact that it took another two and a half months to get the ships to sea also requires some explanation. There seems to have been a lot of debate as to what the commander was supposed to do after issuing his ultimatum at the Vigo. If the ships were released, should he come straight home? If they were not released, what then? Should he go in search of the American treasure fleet, or should he raid Santo Domingo or Cartagena?[43] Characteristically no written instructions were issued, and what verbal orders he may have received are a matter for conjecture. It is quite possible that Elizabeth was dithering, and she may have changed her mind more than once. The whole delay is expressive of uncertainty, as is the fact that in spite of the long period of gestation, some of the designated ships were still not ready. Eventually Drake seems to have simply cut the Gordian knot and to have set off, without formal instructions, or even adequate provisions.[44] It is quite possible that Elizabeth had been counting on that happening, because no steps were taken to prevent him. Drake carried his flag on the *Elizabeth Bonaventure*, and the other ships included another *Elizabeth*, the *Mathew*, the *Leicester* and the *Tiger* – in all, twenty-nine ships and about 4,000 men. The royal navy was represented by the *Elizabeth Bonaventure* and the *Aid*, and the City of London by the *Primrose*.[45] After taking one or two small prizes on the way, and augmenting his supplies, Drake reached the mouth of the Vigo river on 27 September. The governor of Bayona was compliant, and agreed to release the ships as required, but there then followed a sequence of misunderstandings about the acquisition of supplies, which resulted in some skirmishing, and then in renewed negotiations. Eventually a settlement was reached, not without some damage to the town, and Drake remained in the Vigo for about a week taking on the supplies which he needed – long enough as it transpired to miss the treasure fleet, which made harbour during his stay.[46] This may have been the result of the fact that he knew another English fleet was lurking off Terciera for that purpose, or possibly because he mistrusted his chances against the powerful escort ships. According to one account it was 6 or 8 October before he even realised that he had missed his target. In spite of having accomplished his ostensible mission, Drake showed no sign of returning home. Instead he sailed to the Canaries. Having been met with a cannonade at the entrance to Palma harbour, the fleet passed on to the island of Hierro, where they did actually land, but to little purpose. Drake and Christopher Carliell, the captain of his soldiers, took advantage of this landing to issue new and tighter instructions for the guidance of landing parties, but nothing else was achieved.[47] They then proceeded by way of Cape Blanco on the African coast to Sao Tiago in the Cape Verde Islands, a settlement of some 600 persons which they raided successfully, coming away with many guns and with a huge quantity of food, which more than set them up for the voyage ahead. So far there was nothing to distinguish this voyage from its predecessors. San Tiago was set ablaze, as was the neighbouring settlement of Praya, and at least two English seamen were hanged for what the captain deemed to be criminal offences. Quarrels among the officers also endangered discipline, but fortunately there was no Thomas Doughty among the dissidents on this occasion. On 18 December the fleet made its landfall in the West Indies.[48]

By this time there was much sickness among the men, and reaching the island of St Christopher on Christmas Day, Drake tried putting some of them ashore in the hope of improvement. Instead about twenty died in the space of four days, and the only consolation was that they were no longer a danger to the remainder of the crews. On 31 December the fleet reached Santo Domingo, and took the town in a night attack.[49] It was poorly defended, having no fortifications and a garrison of only about 150 men. In the confusion the galley slaves who were held in the town were freed, and promptly joined the attackers, plundering whatever they could lay their hands on. Having taken the fortress, which surrendered the next day, Drake sat down to negotiate a ransom, drawing his ships up in a defensive formation in the harbour. He need not have worried; there were no resources on the island capable of dislodging him. After about three weeks, he finally became convinced that the colony could not possibly muster the million ducats he was demanding. He had applied as much coercion as was possible, and eventually settled for 25,000 ducats, plus all the loot which they could remove from the houses which had not been set ablaze.[50] There has been a good deal of misunderstanding about the capture and ransom of Santo Domingo. From the English point of view it was an easy victory, but a disappointing outcome. There was no great battle, and no Spanish regular soldiers, only a modest, and not very courageous, militia. From the Spanish point of view it was not a great defeat, but it was a major humiliation.[51] During so long a stay ashore, there were inevitably disciplinary problems among the English soldiers and sailors, and some of the officers quarrelled so fiercely that they fought duels. Drake used the cathedral as a gaol for offenders, but remarkably only one man appears to have been hanged — for murder. At Santo Domingo Drake reorganised his fleet, abandoning one or two of his original ships which had become leaky and unseaworthy, and helping himself to replacements, two of which he named the *New Years Gift* and the *New Hope*. The remaining ships which he had found in the harbour were towed out to sea and set on fire.[52]

From Santo Domingo Drake eventually took his fleet directly south to the coast of the mainland, and being warned off Rio de la Hacha, headed instead for Cartagena. Although one of the principal cities of the Indies, Cartagena actually had a smaller population than Santo Domingo, and was similarly unfortified, although there was a fort at Boqueron, some distance from the town.[53] The bay upon which the town was situated was sheltered, and could be entered only through two narrow channels. For some reason these were not defended, and the fort was easily cut off, although two galleys and a galleass were positioned in the inner harbour so that their guns could be brought to bear on the intruders. The defenders numbered about 600, including 200 Indian bowmen; the attackers had rather more than twice that number.[54] Drake arrived in the outer harbour at about noon on 9 February 1586, and after surveying the situation decided upon a simultaneous attack on the town and the fort. He landed his men at 2 a.m. the next day on the beach about four miles from Cartagena and advanced on the town; at the same time the attacking party for Boqueron set off for their target in pinnaces which the fleet carried for just such operations. Although the Spanish had been expecting the attack to come where it did, and had laid ambushes, these turned out to be ineffective, and instead the Spanish militia fell back on the town as Carliell and his men advanced. It was still dark when battle was joined at the entrance to Cartagena itself. In theory the defenders were strongly placed and, supported by the guns of the galleys, should have been able to mount a withering fire. However the gunners in the battery upon which the Spanish principally relied were too slow to reload and were swiftly overrun. There was some fierce hand-to-hand fighting, with casualties on both sides, and then the defenders broke and ran back into the city. There was some house-to-house fighting, and further casualties, but this did not last long and the Spaniards were driven out of Cartagena into the neighbouring countryside.[55] The galleys, in attempting to escape, ran smack into the battle which was still raging for Boqueron, and when one of their magazines exploded, in the confusion they both ran ashore and were abandoned.

Meanwhile the fort was proving a much tougher proposition. The first two attacks were repulsed, and Drake was on a seriously short fuse before the resistance was finally overcome. The main advantage of this second battle from the English point of view was that it tied down a significant part of the defending force, which was thus unable to come to the assistance of Cartagena when its defences crumbled. By mid-morning on 10 February it was all over, and Drake was able to bring his ships into the inner harbour. The number of casualties is uncertain, because both sides tried to minimise their losses, but it appears that no more than thirty of the attackers died in the actual fighting, and the Spanish lost even fewer – but they did not count the Indians.[56] Far more Englishmen succumbed to disease, and possibly to wounds, over the following weeks while Drake occupied the town and sought to negotiate a ransom. Although he held a number of influential prisoners, these were no more successful than they had been at Santo Domingo; his demand for 500,000 ducats being met with an offer of 25,000. Every time the negotiations stalled, Drake burned another part of the town, but such coercive tactics proved unavailing. Only when he accidentally or deliberately (the accounts differ) blew up the newly constructed cathedral was a settlement reached. Drake eventually obtained 107,000 ducats, plus the separate ransoms of some houses which stood outside of the town, and whatever loot he could find.[57] It seems that this latter included quite a lot of silver which mysteriously disappeared from his lodgings, and that the declared ransom was a great deal less than what was actually paid. In spite of his heroics, and his genuine leadership qualities, Drake was less than honest when it came to money. Perhaps it was that which made him such a successful pirate.

The declared ransom was not a great return for the 200 or so English dead who were eventually left behind in Cartagena. Nor was morale good when the time for departure came. His captains declared that they had only 700 men fit for duty, with perhaps 150 sick, although these figures are more than a little doubtful since it is unlikely that the mortality level had reached anything like 75 per cent.[58] The booty was disappointing, and the cities of the Indies were clearly not what they pretended to be in terms of their wealth. Drake wanted to go on and attack Nombre de Dios or Panama, but his officers had had enough, urging him to return home 'with the honour already gotten'.[59] Discipline was also a major problem. The men had had too little to do in Cartagena, and had got into bad habits. A few were hanged, and Drake's reputation for ferocity was augmented, but such a regime would not answer at sea and they had a long voyage ahead of them. He first moved his ships (and their occupants) away from the town while they were careened and repaired, and did not eventually leave the bay until 14 April, from where he went via the Cayman Islands to Cabo San Antonio at the extreme western tip of Cuba. The million ducats which Drake had apparently promised the queen as the profits of the voyage must have looked a very distant prospect indeed. Having taken on fresh water, with considerable difficulty, the fleet then sailed towards Havana. This time he did not have an attack in mind, and indeed had stowed most of his artillery below decks, closing and locking the gunports.[60] As his ships approached the port of Havana they came under fire, but Drake did not respond, choosing instead to anchor in a nearby estuary. There is some doubt about what his plans may have been at this juncture, because apparently a

Spanish fleet was expected, and some of the English officers wanted to lie in wait for it. This, however, would have meant reactivating the guns, and that Drake was apparently reluctant to do. Instead he sailed off towards Florida, where he reached the small Spanish settlement of San Augustin on 27 May.

San Augustin was not seriously defended, and the few guns which Drake had kept in service were sufficient to intimidate the settlers into leaving. As soon as they had gone the local Indians looted the place, but they were no match for Drake's men, who stripped the settlement of guns, tools and everything else of value, including 6,000 ducats of the king's money.[61] By the time that he had finished, there was nothing left for the fugitives to return to. This modest success was almost the final flourish of the voyage. Almost, but not quite, because Drake continued up the coast of what was later to be Virginia, and made contact with the newly planted English settlement of Roanoake. The governor, Ralph Lane, and his colleagues were in a bad way, and asked for his assistance. He offered them supplies, and the use of one of his smaller ships. However a fierce storm destroyed his intended gift, and a few days later the colonists were so demoralised that they asked for a passage home. This was readily granted and the embryonic colony was abandoned.[62] From Roanoake Drake set his course for home, arriving at Plymouth on 28 July 1586. From the investors' point of view the voyage had been a failure, and the plunder was not even sufficient to cover their outlay. However, there was another side to the story, because although in theory this had not been an act of war, in practice it was quickly exploited as a great triumph over Spain. *The Summarie and True Discourse of Sir Francis Drakes West Indian Voyage* was swiftly published and translated into several languages.[63] Treating the truth cavalierly, it presented Drake as a Protestant hero of gigantic proportions, fighting against the tyranny and bigotry of Catholic Spain. The propaganda victory more than compensated for the poor results of the actual voyage, and elevated El Draque to the status of a bogeyman among the Spaniards themselves. From King Philip's point of view, Sir Francis had graduated from being a nuisance to being a substantial threat, and that was good news to Queen Elizabeth.

Provoking the king of Spain had not, however, been the only sign of approaching war. The death of the duke of Anjou had, as we have seen, led to a renewal of civil war in France. The Spanish-backed Catholic League was on the offensive, and very much aware that English sympathies were with its Huguenot opponents. On 31 December Philip signed with the League the treaty of Joinville, pledging mutual support both in France and in the Netherlands.[64] The English Council did not know that, but feared a pre-emptive strike by the Guisards, and on 23 December 1584 ordered the mobilisation of a fleet of thirty-five ships, including eleven warships.[65] The attack did not materialise, and the order was countermanded, but not before much work had been done to prepare the ships for sea. Consequently, when relations with Spain took another turn for the worse early in 1585, more ships were ready than would normally have been the case. Nor was Drake the only captain at sea in the summer of 1586. Henry Palmer aboard the *Foresight* is described as the Admiral of the Narrow Seas in that year, and on 6 August John Hawkins was issued with instructions for what can only be described as an Atlantic patrol.[66] The orders themselves do not survive, but he appears to have commanded eighteen or twenty ships, of which five belonged to the queen. Four of these, the *Nonpareil*, the *Revenge*, the *Hope* and the *Lion*, were over 500 tons, so he would have mustered considerable firepower. The exact purpose of this operation is not clear. It may have been in support of the Huguenots at La Rochelle, and if it was intended to protect them against a seaborne assault, then it may well have succeeded. According to the Venetian ambassador it was intended as a preventive measure against French Catholic privateers, although the ships seem rather large for that purpose.[67] It may well have been that the earlier alarm about a possible Guisard attack had not gone away, or had been renewed. The main objective cannot have been any attack on Spanish shipping, because in spite of being at sea for two and a half months, Hawkins took only a handful of prizes, just three of which came during the peak month of September.[68]

Two things emerge from this. Firstly, in spite of being in a state of acknowledged although undeclared war with Spain, the naval expenditure for 1586 was still a little short of £30,000 – less than half what had been spent in 1563, and more like a third in real terms.[69] This was partly because the £20,000 which Elizabeth had eventually invested in Drake's expedition did not pass through the naval accounts, and partly because the maritime community was squarely behind the queen in the struggle which she had now undertaken. Not only had the London merchants invested substantially in Drake's voyage, but they were also contributing ships both to Hawkins's patrols and also to Palmer's. Secondly, England's war effort depended heavily, not only on the willingness of parliament to vote extraordinary revenue, but also on the ability of private shipowners to fight as naval auxiliaries. The earl of Cumberland with his fleet of privateers, and his great warship, the *Scourge of Malice* stands as the symbol of this spirit.[70] Sir Walter Raleigh and the earl of Leicester both sold their private warships to the queen for notional sums, and other courtiers continued to curry favour by fitting out their own ships for the royal service. For a number of years at least, this was a genuinely national war, and was seen as a struggle for the survival, not only of England, but also of the Protestant faith in northern Europe. In this respect the alliance with the Dutch was both timely and effective. The earl of Leicester made a mess of his mission to the Low Countries, but the English soldiers did better than they are normally given credit for, and the intervention was sufficient to see the United Provinces through their immediate crisis.

By the autumn of 1585, although he had declared no official war, Philip had decided that the time had come to settle accounts with the troublesome islanders, heretics and pirates. As early as the end of 1583 the marquis of Santa Cruz had impressed upon him the feasibility of an amphibious strike against England. The king had consulted the duke of Parma, who advised that it would be better to complete the conquest of the Netherlands first, and the plan was dropped for the time being.[71] However the advent of a new and zealous pope in the person of Sixtus V, and Drake's appearance at Bayona in September, fired the king with a new ambition. On 24 October 1585, while Drake was on his way from Galicia to the Canaries, Philip wrote to the pope, accepting his suggestion for an attack upon England, but pointing out that it would take time, and would be very expensive. He asked for the papal blessing – and for money.[72] The news which arrived over the next few weeks confirmed him in his resolution. English forces were building up in the Low Countries and Drake was wreaking havoc in the Caribbean. On 29 December Philip returned to the plans which Santa Cruz had put forward two years before. Parma was now informed that the king's intention was to launch a major assault on England, and he was invited to contribute his thoughts as to how that could best be accomplished. By the end of April 1586, both Parma and Santa Cruz had submitted plans for the proposed operation. The latter was by far the most elaborate, envisaging a full-scale seaborne invasion direct from Spain. This would involve an army of 55,000 men, complete with their artillery and equipment, which would require a fleet of 150 ships (some 77,250 tons) for transport and escort. This enormous number would be made up of forty Italian merchantmen and thirty-five from the Biscay ports, while the fighting ships would come from the Spanish crown (twenty-five galleons) and the crown of Portugal (twenty galleys and galleasses).[73] The role of the Armada itself would be purely defensive – to get the army to the point of disembarkation and to cover it while that took place. The ultimate objective was left vague, but it seems that the conquest of a significant part of England was planned, to knock the country out of the war, and hopefully to bring about a regime change. The landfall of this formidable force was also left indeterminate, and could have been anywhere from Milford Haven to Margate. Parma's plan was altogether more modest. First, the Netherlands must be secured, partly by military and partly by diplomatic means, to make sure that France did not take advantage of the situation. Once that was done, a force of 30,000 foot and 500 horse could be shipped across to Kent in a flotilla of seagoing barges, an exploit which he reckoned would take about ten to twelve hours.[74] Naval support from Spain was a secondary consideration. It would be useful if enough ships could be spared from their duties in the Atlantic, but clearly was not felt to be necessary.

Neither of these plans was particularly realistic; Santa Cruz's because of the enormous deployment of resources which it would require, and Parma's because it took no account of any possible intervention by the English navy. The latter was also handicapped by the long delay which it underwent in its submission. Having been asked for in December, it was April before it was dispatched and June before it was de-coded and reached the royal desk. Having read both proposals, Philip then turned them over to Juan de Zuniga, his senior adviser, who shortly after came up with his own plan. This involved a scaling down of Santa Cruz's proposed force to a more manageable level, and using Ireland as a launching pad for the final assault on England, meanwhile accepting Parma's suggestion of a landing in force in Kent.[75] If this plan had been followed the English would have had to cope with two simultaneous invasions of approximately equal strength. It was also clear, Zuniga argued, that an operation of this scale and complexity could not be launched in a hurry. It was July 1586 when he submitted his opinion, and he suggested that the Enterprise of England should be launched in either August or September 1587. Having absorbed all this advice, Philip then formulated the final plan. He cut out the Irish stage of the operation, decreeing instead that the force from Spain should proceed directly to rendezvous with Parma's forces in Flanders, and that there should then be a single co-ordinated landing, which would be protected from English naval interference by the Armada. Zuniga, Parma and Santa Cruz were all informed of this definitive scheme, but none was invited to comment on it, because it was the royal decision. Santa Cruz was then placed in command of the preparations, with a view to launching the attack in 1587. It was a poorly kept secret, as Parma complained. Everyone in the Low Countries was talking of the Empressa which was to be launched against England, and of course the English Council knew exactly what was going on.[76] It remained to be seen what they could do about it.

CHAPTER 8 NOTES

1. The French still maintained a formidable presence of pirates and privateers, the latter operating under both Huguenot and Guisard permissions, but the king no longer had the power to assemble a Navy Royal.

2. 'The Count of Feria's Dispatch to Philip II of 14 November 1558', ed. M.-J. Rodriguez Salgado and Simon Adams, *Camden Miscellany*, 28, 1984, p. 331.

3. P.L. Hughes and J.F. Larkin, *Tudor Royal Proclamations*, II, p. 235.

4. I.A. Wright, *Discourses concerning English Voyages to the Spanish Main, 1569–1580* (1932), p. xix. Loades, *Tudor Navy*, p. 223.

5. Diego Calderon to the King, 14 May 1573 (AGI Panama 11, f.208). Harry Kelsey, *Sir Francis Drake: The Queen's Pirate* (1998), p. 63.

6. Ibid., p. 66.

7. TNA SP12/95, no. 63 is Grenville's petition to the queen; R. Pearce Chope, 'New Light on Sir Richard Grenville', *Transactions of the Devonshire Association*, 49, 1917, pp. 210–82.

8. Raphael Holinshed, *Chronicles etc.* (London, 1577, 1587), p. 252. For a comment on the effect of this sentence, see the memorandum by Antonio de Guaras, *Calendar of State Papers, Spanish, 1568–79*, p. 249.

9. The plans for this voyage are controversial and uncertain. The best guidance is probably provided by BL Cotton MS Otho E.VIII, ff.8–9 (which is badly damaged). For a discussion see K.R. Andrews, *Drake's Voyages: A Reassessment of their Place in England's Maritime Expansion* (1967), p. 50; and Harry Kelsey, *Sir Francis Drake*, pp. 76–9.

10. See Valderrama to Antonio de Guaras, 20 August 1577. TNA SP94/8, f.101.

11. Drake berated and dismissed the man mainly responsible, who appears to have been called James Stydye (BL Harley MS 540, f.93v), but he should have paid more attention to such matters himself.

12. De Silva subsequently wrote an account of his experiences (AHN Inquisition, libro 1048), which is discussed in Zelia Nuttall, *New Light on Drake: A Collection of Documents relating to his Voyage of Circumnavigation, 1577–1580* (Hakluyt Society, series 2, 34, 1914); and in K.R. Andrews, 'The Aims of Drake's Expedition of 1577–80', *American Historical Review*, 73, 1968, pp. 724–41.

13. Kelsey, *Sir Francis Drake*, pp. 99–100.

14. John Cook's account, BL Harley MS 540, f.100. Francis Fletcher's account, BL Sloane MS 61, f.7. The issue of whether Drake's commission did or did not include such powers is discussed by Kelsey, *Sir Francis Drake*, pp. 106–8.

15. This information is derived from Francis Fletcher's account. The scale of the mortality is not known.

16. These manoeuvres are reconstructed in detail by Kelsey, *Sir Francis Drake*, pp. 117–20.

17. *The World Encompassed by Sir Francis Drake* (London, 1628), p. 34.

18. There are several accounts of this raid, both English and Spanish, which are discussed in detail by Kelsey, *Sir Francis Drake*, pp. 140–3.

19. Griego, quoted in Sarmiento de Gamboa, 'Relacion de lo que el corsario fransico hizo y robo en la costa de chile …'. Cited by Kelsey, *Sir Francis Drake*, p. 148.

20. BL Harley MS 280, f.85.

21. Ibid., f.87. There are various accounts of this incident, not all of them consistent. The brass plate which Drake is alleged to have left behind is now generally regarded as a much later hoax.

22. BL Harley MS 280, f.81.

23. Ibid., f.87.

24. Kelsey, *Sir Francis Drake*, p. 204, citing an uncorroborated Spanish account.

25. 'The regester of Suche as is dellevered unto Xtopher hanes …', TNA SP12/144, no. 17, f.42. Rodger, *Safeguard of the Sea*, p. 245.

26. The agreement covered only privately owned property, which could be sued for through the Admiralty court in the usual way.

27. Elizabeth Donno, ed., *An Elizabethan in 1582: The Diary of Richard Maddox, Fellow of All Souls* (Hakluyt Society, series 2, 147, 1976). For a fully documented account of Fenton's misfortunes, see E.G.R. Taylor, ed., *The Troublesome Voyage of Captain Edward Fenton, 1582–3* (Hakluyt Society, series 2, 113, 1959).

28. TNA SP12/156, ff.88–90. *British Naval Documents*, pp. 107–9.

29. *Calendar of State Papers, Spanish, Elizabeth*, III, pp. 45, 49, 126, 142.
30. Loades, *Elizabeth I*, pp. 219–20.
31. J.B. Black, *The Reign of Elizabeth* (1959), pp. 325–8.
32. Raphael Holinshed, *Chronicle* (edition 18-7-8), IV, p. 536.
33. For a discussion of this crisis, see Jonathan Israel, *The Dutch Republic* (1995), pp. 216–20.
34. Rodger, *Safeguard of the Sea*, p. 247.
35. Geoffrey Parker and Colin Martin, *The Spanish Armada* (1988), p. 101.
36. Rodger, *Safeguard of the Sea*, p. 248, citing various sources.
37. F.C. Dietz, *English Public Finance, 1558–1641* (1932), pp. 53–5.
38. Loades, *The Tudor Navy*, pp. 207–8.
39. The original intention was apparently a voyage to the Moluccas. TNA AO1/1685/20A. It was only in February 1585 that the objective was switched to the West Indies. Mendoza, by this time in Paris was, as usual, well informed. M.A.S. Hume, ed., *Calendar of Letters and State Papers Relating to English Affairs ... in the Archives of Simancas*, Elizabeth, III, pp. 531–2.
40. The Admiralty court in London was promptly besieged with claims for heavy losses. M. Oppenheim, *Sir William Monson's Naval Tracts* (Navy Records Society, 1902), I, p. 125.
41. For a discussion of this point, see Kelsey, *Sir Francis Drake*, pp. 240–1.
42. TNA AO1/1685/20A.
43. Kelsey, *Sir Francis Drake*, p. 241. Loades, *Tudor Navy*, pp. 233–4.
44. Drake seems to have been in the habit of under-provisioning his ships. The point may have been that on a long voyage even the most durable of food (the biscuit) deteriorated, and it was better to pick up fresh provisions as he went. This need also gave him an excuse to conduct raids which were not otherwise planned.
45. Kelsey, *Sir Francis Drake*, p. 243. There are some doubts about both the size of the fleet and the number of men. Monson, *Tracts*, I, p. 124, gives 22 ships and 2,300 men. I have followed Kelsey at this point.
46. Loades, *Tudor Navy*, p. 234.
47. BL Harley MS 2202, ff.57–8.
48. 'Record kept aboard the ship *Tiger*', BL Cotton MS Otho E.VIII, f.233.
49. There is a full description of this capture, based on several sources, in Kelsey, *Sir Francis Drake*, pp. 258–61.
50. Cristobal de Ovalle and others to the King, 24 February 1586 (AGI Santo Domingo 51, ramo 9, no. 87, f.3), cited by Kelsey, *Sir Francis Drake*, loc. cit.
51. Ibid.
52. 'Record kept aboard the ship *Leicester*', BL Harley MS 2202, f.65.
53. There is a contemporary sketch map showing the location of the fort in Walter Bigges, *A Summarie and True Discourse of Sir Francis Drakes West Indian Voyage* (London, 1589).
54. Kelsey, *Sir Francis Drake*, pp. 267–8.
55. Letter of Tristran de Orive Salazar, 11 March 1586 (AGI Patronato 266, ramo 50, no. 12, ff.1–2), cited by Kelsey, *Sir Francis Drake*, p. 268.
56. Ibid. At least 100 Englishmen died in the weeks following the attack.
57. 'The Discourse and Description of the Voyage of Sir Francis Drake and Mr. Frobisher', BL MS Royal 7 C.XVI, f.171.

58. Walter Bigges, 'Resolution of the land captains, what course they think most expedient to be taken ...'. Richard Hakluyt, *Third and Last Volume of the Voyages ... of the English Nation* (London, 1600).

59. 'Record kept aboard the ship *Leicester*', BL Harley MS 2202, f.69.

60. Testimony of Pedro Sanchez, trans. Irene Wright, *Further English Voyages to Spanish America* (Hakluyt Society, series 2, 99, 1951), p. 169.

61. Kelsey, *Sir Francis Drake*, p. 275.

62. Bigges, *Summarie and True Discourse*, pp. 34–6.

63. *RSTC* 3056.

64. Parker and Martin, *The Spanish Armada*, p. 97.

65. Oppenheim, *Sir William Monson's Naval Tracts*, I, p. 125.

66. Bod MS Rawlinson 192, f.210. Drake, Hawkins and Palmer were all commissioned as Admirals in that year. *Acts of the Privy Council*, XIV, p. 206.

67. *Calendar of State Papers, Venetian*, VIII, p. 214. 24 October 1586.

68. Loades, *Tudor Navy*, p. 237.

69. Oppenheim, *Naval Administration*, p. 161. There had been an inflation of some 40 per cent over the intervening years.

70. R.T. Spence, *The Privateering Earl* (1995).

71. Parker and Martin, *The Spanish Armada*, p. 110. The king wrote, 'there is little to be said about the English idea; one should keep away from such distant things ...' (AGS, Estado 946/43).

72. Ibid., p. 111, citing AGS Estado 946/247–8, the king's letter to the pope of 24 October 1585.

73. Ibid., p. 112.

74. Or eight hours with a favourable wind. Ibid., p. 115.

75. Ibid., p. 117, citing Parma's letter (AGS Estado 590/126).

76. Eleven new ships were commissioned in 1586, and two more in 1587, including the *Vanguard*, the *Rainbow* and the *Ark Royal*. Oppenheim, *Naval Administration*, p. 161. Monson, *Tracts*, I, pp. 138–9. Expenditure went up to £44,000. Loades, *Tudor Navy*, p. 239.

CHAPTER NINE

WAR

Elizabeth had plenty of information from spies in Lisbon and Madrid about the preparations for the Armada, but she could not be certain that it was aimed against her. Her spies could see what was going on, but did not have access to those circles where policy decisions were discussed and made. So this great fleet could have been directed against France, or England or the Low Countries – the last being the most plausible. However, subsidiary information filtering through from places like Florence and Venice was not reassuring.[1] Three new ships were laid down in the royal yards, work was resumed on the fortifications of the south coast, and known Catholics in England were disarmed. At the same time Elizabeth re-activated the negotiations which had been going on with the duke of Parma since the summer of 1586. There was never the smallest chance that these negotiations would succeed, because even if Parma had been serious about them (which is doubtful), there was no possibility that Philip would change his mind. The duke was no doubt puzzled by these advances, but seems to have calculated that if he could appear to respond favourably, Elizabeth might be induced to pursue her defensive preparations less assiduously.[2] The queen herself might indeed have reacted so, but neither Cecil nor his fellow councillors allowed themselves to be deceived. Naval expenditure rose to £44,000, most of which was spent in the dockyards, and in December 1586 Robert Flicke of London was licensed to put out his own fleet for the purpose of intercepting the *flota*, or Spanish treasure fleet. Flicke achieved nothing, except perhaps to stimulate the queen into a similar activity.[3] Meanwhile, in December 1586 Zuniga died, and Santa Cruz got into increasing difficulties as he tried to find enough ships, guns and money for his purpose. The duke of Parma began to doubt the soundness of the whole idea, and only Philip remained relentlessly enthusiastic.

Meanwhile the accounts from Drake's West Indies cruise were in total confusion. He had lost about 40 per cent of the men who had started with him, but the rest still had to be paid, and most of his plunder was not in cash. He sought Lord Burghley's help and eventually the very large sum of £57,000 was allocated to him. His investors received about 15s in the pound, but many of the bills were still unpaid two years later.[4] All together the hides, copper, lead, iron and guns which he had brought back were valued at £67,000 (£46,000 net), but this was only what was declared. It seems that tens of thousands of pounds in ransom money and other loot was never revealed, partly to throw Spanish complainants off the scent, and partly to ensure that the unofficial payout was more substantial than the official one. Much of it probably ended up in Drake's own hands, but the investors would also have received enough to have stifled any possible complaints.[5] The queen did not want to know. No doubt she had also received a share, and the only people left thoroughly dissatisfied were the victims – but this was war and they were hardly entitled to complain. Drake's return, the stories of his exploits, and the increasingly alarming tidings from Cadiz and Lisbon, convinced Elizabeth that she really was at war. If she did not do something, the new year, 1587, was likely to see an assault against England which would certainly be the biggest since 1545. Meanwhile the Babington plot had been uncovered, which not only sealed the fate of Mary, Queen of Scots, but also revealed that Philip had more than one way of attempting to deal with his enemies. Protestant England was under siege.[6]

Vigilance was everything, and no sooner had Drake returned than John Hawkins set out. Perhaps the queen expected some knee-jerk reaction from Philip's commanders in the Atlantic, or perhaps she was just taking sensible precautions. Hawkins led five of the queen's galleons up and down the Channel for about a month, and then sailed to the coast of Spain. His instructions are unknown, but it seems that he was just required to register a presence – to demonstrate that Drake was not the only English Admiral at sea.[7] He may have been hoping to intercept some of Philip's American treasure, but if so he was unlucky. Drake himself was hardly back in harbour, and a long way from winding up the affairs of his West Indies voyage, when he started to plan another venture. The Spaniards thought that he was going back to the Americas but the chances are that as the Babington plot was unravelled the first thought was for another Channel or Atlantic patrol. Whatever his initial intention, he was soon diverted to the Low Countries, on an unsuccessful mission to try to solicit aid for Dom Antonio. The Dutch did not want to upset their protector, but were far too hard-pressed themselves to offer any assistance in such a matter.[8] So after a meeting on 13 November, the Estates General merely said that they would leave the decision to the individual towns. Needless to say, nothing happened. Perhaps Drake had been planning to lead an expedition in Dom Antonio's interest himself. He seems to have been on friendly terms with the pretender, and rumours were soon flying that he had sworn to put his friend on the throne of Portugal. More realistically, on 18 March 1587 he signed a contract with a consortium of London merchants for a pillaging voyage, with half the proceeds to the Crown, and half to the investors, who would provide most of the ships.[9] The remaining ships were to be supplied by the queen, and would constitute her investment. The *Elizabeth Bonaventure*, the *Golden Lion*, the *Rainbow* and the *Dreadnaught* were named, all of them over 400 tons, and sufficient to make this an equal partnership between the Crown and the City. No formal instructions were issued, and the objectives of the fleet seem at this point to have been vague. However, Drake got his sailing orders on 27 March, and when his fleet assembled at Plymouth a few days later it numbered sixteen ships and seven pinnaces. Warned that Her Majesty was having second thoughts, he set off at once, on 2 April, announcing his departure with a characteristic flourish,

> The wind commands me away … our ship is under sail. God grant that we may so live in his fear as the enemy may have cause to say that God doth fight for Her Majesty as well abroad as at home …[10]

No sooner was he safely at sea than the queen effectively revoked his commission, causing her Council to instruct him to 'forbear to enter forcibly into any of the said King's ports', confining his attention to ships at sea. However he never received this countermand, and perhaps it was intended that he never should.[11] It is not clear when the resolution was made, but 'forcibly entering' at least one of Philip's harbours was exactly what he had in mind. By the time that he set off he had decided to attack Lisbon, and to inflict as much damage as possible upon the Armada which was assembling there. In retrospect it looks like an obvious move, but only Drake seems to have thought so at the time.

On 16 April he arrived in the Tagus, only to discover that the harbour was well fortified and well nigh impossible to enter. At the same time he received tidings that the other half of the great fleet was lying at Cadiz, virtually unprotected. In a fit of last-minute inspiration, he switched targets and arrived off Cadiz on the afternoon of the 19th, taking the city (and the fleet) completely by surprise.[12] As it turned out, the information which he had received was not quite accurate, in that very few of the Armada ships themselves were in the harbour. What was there was the bulk of the supplies and munitions which Santa Cruz had been collecting with so much pain and difficulty – rice from Milan, biscuit from Malaga, cheese from the Baltic, pitch, cordage, timber and sailcloth from Scandinavia. There were tents and knapsacks for the troops, 12,000 pairs of shoes and leather canteens, arquebuses, pikes and muskets.[13] Cadiz was the supply base from which the Armada was to be equipped, and the preparations were at a critical stage because everything was supposed to come together over the next four months. Drake flew no flags, and at first his ships were mistaken for the squadron of Juan Martin de Recalde which was expected back from a patrol on the Biscay coast. He announced himself by firing on the royal galleys which were drawn up to defend the harbour, his longer-range culverins inflicting heavy damage and forcing the defenders to retire out of range.[14] The only other resistance was offered by two large sailing ships, an armed Genoese merchantman and a Biscay galleon, both of which were swiftly captured and set on fire. Most of the vessels anchored in the outer harbour were completely helpless, having shipped their sails, and sent their crewmen ashore. In many cases their cargoes were still aboard, and Drake's men helped themselves to everything movable before sinking or setting fire to the ships. The few ships which were manned cut their cables and headed for the inner harbour, where they expected to be sheltered by the guns of the fort at Puerto Real.

Skirmishing continued throughout the following night, but the Spanish galleys were no match for the English warships, and suffered further losses, and although the guns of the fort were brought to bear, they inflicted little damage. Meanwhile, ashore, the duke of Medina Sidonia had arrived with several thousand reinforcements and secured the town from any possible English landing.[15] If Drake had been contemplating an attack upon Cadiz itself, he was now effectively deterred, and turned his attention instead to the inner harbour. This turned out to be tricky, and the *Edward Bonaventure* (one of the London ships) ran aground. However Puerto Real again proved an ineffective defence, and although the galleys again put up a spirited resistance, Drake was able to complete his mission of plunder and destruction. He took a few of the ships, and burned the rest, to the number of about two dozen, dividing the extensive plunder as best he could between his own vessels in order to avoid overloading. When he was ready to leave, at about noon on the 20th, his luck at last ran out and the wind failed. While he was becalmed in the harbour mouth, the defenders sent out a number of small fireships. The current carried these among the English, but they were too small for their allotted task, and Drake's men had no difficulty in fending them off. Finally, about twelve hours later, the wind got up and Drake sailed out into the bay, smack into the path of another squadron of Spanish galleys.[16] The outcome was as before. Although a further failure of the wind gave the oared vessels an advantage, they were so heavily outgunned that they had no option but to break off the engagement and retreat. In addition to inflicting enormous damage on Santa Cruz's preparations, Drake had taught Philip a salutary lesson – that galleys were quite useless against heavily armed English warships, even in confined spaces and in the absence of wind. When the Armada eventually set out, its few galleys did not even get across the bay of Biscay.[17] The Spaniards reckoned their losses at Cadiz at 172,000 ducats (about £60,000), but many of the ships were not Spanish, and were not included in this valuation. All together, although the town had not fallen, Drake's attack had inflicted a damaging and humiliating reverse on Santa Cruz. It had put back his preparations by at least twelve months, and with costs running at something like 300,000 ducats a month, there was a serious danger that even Philip's massive income would not be able to cope.

On leaving Cadiz, Drake made an attempt to intercept the Biscay squadron for which he had originally been mistaken, but by the time that he got to Cape St Vincent he knew that Recalde was already safe in Lisbon, and changed his plans. After making an unsuccessful attempt to land at Lagos he took the nearby village and castle at Sagres on about 6 May and was able to use that as his base for the next three weeks or so.[18] Apart from taking a few small passing traders, from Sagres he was able to sally forth to Lisbon on 11 May, where he exchanged messages with Santa Cruz, but did not attempt to penetrate the defences, which were on a state of high alert. On 17 May he sent two of his prizes back to London, and requested permission to stay at Sagres for the time being.[19] Meanwhile his cruising was producing no very positive results and his men were falling sick. On the 20th he sent a number of them back to England and requested reinforcements. However before he could receive a response to either of these requests word reached him of the approach of a large carrack from the East Indies, and he set off in the direction of the Azores to intercept it. On the way, and in the midst of a storm, one of his ships deserted. This was the *Golden Lion*, and the story of its defection is complicated, involving another falling out between Drake and his second in command William Borough.[20] Borough was not a party to the mutiny, but he was on board the *Golden Lion*, and that was sufficient pretext for Drake to convene a drum head court and sentence him to death. If Borough had been within reach, he would have shared the fate of Thomas Doughty. However, he was not within reach, and after Drake had also returned, a commission of inquiry cleared him of all charges.[21] Sir Francis's reputation was dented, more by the perceived malice with which he had pursued his subordinate than by the charges themselves, but that could not disguise the magnitude of his achievement.

With his fleet now reduced to nine ships, and half his men sick, on 8 June Drake arrived off Sao Miguel in the Azores, and the following morning sighted the sail of a big ship. After a short pursuit he surrounded and boarded his prize, which offered only light resistance. She turned out to be the *San Felipe*, the king's own ship, bearing a cargo of oriental goods, including silks, velvet and porcelain. There were also some slaves, who were put ashore on Sao Miguel. Still troubled by sickness, which some described (implausibly) as plague, and satisfied that he now had enough plunder to placate his investors, Drake brought his prize back to Plymouth on 26 June.[22] There are no further references to the mysterious sickness, but Sir Francis was soon playing his usual game with the accounts of his enterprise. An inventory was duly declared, and a dividend allocated, but there is more than a suspicion that much of the plunder simply disappeared – some into the pockets of the seamen, but most into Drake's own. One of Mendoza's English informants wrote of as much as 300,000 ducats (£100,000) in cash having been taken from the *San Felipe* and never declared.[23] Her Majesty, who at that point was trying to revive her futile negotiations with Parma, was alleged to be 'greatly offended with him'. However, disgrace is relative, and Drake continued to be received at court (bearing gifts) even while Burghley was writing of his disfavour. It must be suspected that much of this talk was designed to suggest to Philip that the English were falling out among themselves, and that their greatest captain might not be in a position to oppose his designs. However, the diplomatic network, probably better informed, had stopped referring to 'Drake the pirate'. He had now become the Captain General of the English Navy.[24]

Meanwhile some response to the humiliation at Cadiz was called for. On 23 June, when Drake had already quitted the coast, the Council of War ordered Santa Cruz to sea, ostensibly to protect the treasure fleet, but really to make sure that the English did not come back. During the whole of the Cadiz business and its aftermath, Philip had been ill with what he described as his 'cold', but which was probably a strain of influenza. He was over fifty years old, and slow to recover from such setbacks.[25] However, he had rallied sufficiently to endorse the Council's order, and on 13 July decreed that all the ships which had been assembling at various ports in Andalusia, should be concentrated at Lisbon. He was still hoping, in spite of Drake's depredations, to launch his attack against England that year. Once he was fully back in charge, Philip pressed this agenda hard. In late September he issued orders that Santa Cruz was to 'sail in the name of God straight to the English Channel', and to rendezvous with Parma off Margate.[26] Unfortunately such instructions were totally unrealistic. In the first place Santa Cruz did not return from his escort duties until 29 September, and then his ships were badly in need of repair; and in the second place the duke of Parma had gone off the whole idea. The king would no longer listen to his remonstrations, but if he could not get his troops together to play their part, then the whole scheme would fall flat. As Philip issued his orders in the autumn of 1587, he seems to have become increasingly detached from reality. In early December he even suggested that the duke should launch a surprise attack on Kent, without any kind of seaborne support at all, and on the 24th wrote indignantly to know why his orders had not been carried out.[27] Parma was equally incensed by such nonsense, and used his privileged position with the king to respond angrily that he was being expected to achieve the impossible.

Although Philip was not, apparently, prepared to face the fact, the preparations for his Grand Armada were in total disarray. The provisions which Drake had destroyed had to be replaced, and that required not only time, but very large sums of money. Although the necessary ships were now assembled at Lisbon, the damage to Santa Cruz's key squadron during its late summer *excursus* had not been trivial, and that also required time and money to remedy. The troops and seamen who had been assembled were consuming victuals faster than they could be collected. They were raw conscripts who required a lot of training, and they had to be paid. Whatever the king might think, and whatever orders he might issue, there was not the slightest chance of getting the Armada to sea before the spring of 1588.[28] The sheer frustration of this seems to have caused another crisis in Philip's health, and he took to his bed over the Christmas, fuming (quite unreasonably) against his incompetent servants. It was 20 January before he was fit enough to conduct business again. It is not surprising that he was frustrated, because a stock-taking on 13 February revealed a sorry state of affairs indeed. The Armada was a shambles of unseaworthy ships, rotting supplies and demoralised men.[29] To make matters worse, typhoid had broken out in the camps, and deaths and desertions had reduced their number from 12,600 to 10,000 since 20 January. Among the dead was the marquis of Santa Cruz himself – little mourned according to his contemporaries. He had been a great sea captain, but was an unamiable character and an absolutely useless administrator. His death enabled the king to make his only unequivocally sound decision of the whole enterprise. He appointed Don Alonso Perez de Guzman, duke of Medina Sidonia, to take over the command.[30]

Medina Sidonia lacked combat experience, particularly at sea, but he was not a military novice, and he was an absolutely first-rate organiser. He was also convinced that the whole Armada venture was misconceived, as well as malfunctioning.[31] However his cogent arguments were intercepted by the Council of War, and the king (who was ailing again in February and March) never saw them, so that his attempts to refuse the honour being done him were dismissed as conventional modesty. God, he was reminded, was undoubtedly on the Spanish side. As if to demonstrate this fact, the duke of Parma took the port of Sluys in December 1587, and the English and the Dutch fell to bickering, which resulted in the recall of the earl of Leicester in the same month.[32] Medina Sidonia then proceeded to work his own kind of miracle on the shambles at Lisbon. By a combination of extremely hard work and quite exceptional qualities of leadership, he turned the situation around. The damaged ships were repaired, and new ones were drafted in including some very large merchantmen, seized by embargo. The galleons and armed merchantmen of the India Guard were recruited in April, the Armada having been given priority over all other considerations.[33] Between February and May the number of ships increased from 104 to 130, and by the end of May they were all seaworthy. The troops similarly had been augmented from

10,000 to nearly 19,000, and adequate food had been squeezed out of the reluctant country. Morale had been restored to a remarkable degree, a circumstance which owed a lot to effective religious propaganda, but probably rather more to adequate feeding. However, so favourable a situation would not endure any prolonged period of inactivity, and on 28 May Medina Sidonia seized the moment, and led his fleet down the Tagus to the open sea.[34]

Not everything was inch perfect even after this remarkable transformation. Guns had had to be scraped together from all over the empire. Many of them were unsuitable for use at sea, some were old and all were inefficiently mounted.[35] Enormous efforts had been made to provide enough powder and shot, but the latter, like the guns, had had to be scraped together. As a result much of it was ill matched to the artillery, and when it came to the point proved to be useless. Sea gunners were virtually an unknown breed in Spain, and all the Armada guns were manned by soldiers who had no experience of fighting at sea. More seriously, soldiers had prestige from decades of successful combat, and this rubbed off even on the recently recruited, with the result that the fighting men tended to despise the mariners as mere labourers whose job it was to bring the real men where the real work was to be done.[36] This did not make for harmonious shipboard relations, and the bickering was disruptive. Understandably, Medina Sidonia had grown in confidence as a result of his success in getting the Armada to sea, and no longer believed that his mission was impossible, but unfortunately the logistic realities had not changed. All his captains had been provided with up-to-date charts of the Sussex coast, but that did not alter the fact that Spain did not control an adequate deep-water anchorage, should one be needed. Sluys was the best available, but that was too small and in the wrong place. Nor had the basic military reality changed, that both the English ships and the English guns were better adapted to fighting at sea than their Spanish equivalents. Just before the Armada had set off an anonymous commentator had observed,

> Unless God helps us by a miracle, the English, who have faster and handier ships than ours, and many more long range guns, and who know their advantage just as well as we do, will never close with us at all, but stand aloof and knock us to pieces with their culverins, without our being able to do them any serious hurt. And so we are sailing against England in the confident hope of a miracle ...[37]

Events were to prove him absolutely right. Worse still, he was not the only person counting on miracles. Medina Sidonia and Parma had not agreed any arrangements for their rendezvous, and when this deficiency was drawn to the king's attention, he responded that since his forces were fighting in God's cause, no doubt He would provide an answer when the need arose.[38] In other words, the Armada was sailing into battle under a variety of handicaps, without any firm plans for getting Parma's troops across the North Sea, and with no idea where it could anchor if their synchronisation was anything less than perfect.

Medina Sidonia's instructions, issued on 1 April 1588, were an infuriating mixture of theological exhortation and practical instructions which were tactically sound, but strategically worthless. He was merely ordered to lead his fleet directly to 'Margate Head', and there to 'join hands' with the duke, as though the latter would have been waiting for him upon the sands. The king was perfectly well aware of the dangers from long-range English gunnery, but unable to suggest a remedy, adding simply, 'you will have to take such precautions as you consider necessary in this respect'.[39] The Captain General was no doubt suitably grateful. First, however, he had to get his fleet within range, and that proved to be difficult. Once they were clear of the Tagus, contrary winds slowed the progress of the ships, and the big hulks – the troop transports – proved to be even slower and more cumbersome than had been expected. The slow progress meant that the rations were disappearing at an alarming rate, and in spite of all precautions some of what had been shipped turned out to be rotten. Medina Sidonia's optimism, which had waxed as the Armada got to sea, waned again rapidly. Messages were sent ahead into Galicia, asking for replenishments to be available, and after taking two weeks to struggle from Lisbon to Coruna, off Cape Finisterre the fleet was hit by a mighty gale.[40] Some ships got into Coruna swiftly, but others were widely scattered and took a long time to get back together. On 24 June the Captain General wrote to the king, suggesting that the adverse weather might be a sign from the Almighty that he was not entirely supportive of their efforts. Perhaps they should call the whole thing off? Meanwhile the battered ships had to be repaired and revictualled, and this was a task at which the duke was expert. While awaiting a response to his dispatch, he threw himself into this accustomed work with his usual enthusiasm.

When the king's reply arrived in early July, it was incisive.

> If this were an unjust war, one could indeed take this storm as a sign from Our Lord to cease offending him. But being as just as it is, one cannot believe that he will disband it .... I have dedicated this enterprise to God .... Get on then, and do your part ...[41]

If they remained at Coruna they would be sitting ducks for an English counter-attack. The only possible way was forward. Given the immense amount of time, effort and money which had been invested in the Armada, and its present vulnerability, this at last made strategic sense, and on 21 July Medina Sidonia led his great fleet to sea again. It had been an ill wind which blew no good, because while the fleet had been cooped up in Coruna, Drake and Lord William Howard (the Lord Admiral) had indeed attempted a pre-emptive strike. On 4 July the royal navy had sallied forth with the intention of repeating the exploit at Cadiz the previous year. If, however, one was looking to the weather for a sign of Divine approval, in this case one would have had to conclude that God was on the side of the Spanish. First there were storms off the Scilly Isles, then more gales off Ushant, and finally (still sixty miles from the Spanish cost) a dead calm. When the wind returned it was from the south and their victuals were running dangerously low. They returned, on the same wind which was bringing the Armada north.[42]

Before leaving Coruna, the Captain General had called a council of war, and resolved that the fleet should advance in the same crescent formation which the galleys had used at Lepanto. Since his fleet orders were purely defensive, this made good sense. He had no intention of attempting to destroy the English fleet, because his orders were to proceed directly to a rendezvous with Parma at Flushing – or wherever he happened to be.[43] He was not to attempt any independent landing on the English coast, but to hold his fleet together for the main purpose.

Meanwhile Drake and Howard were for a few days at a disadvantage. They had only returned to Plymouth on the 22nd, and were completely out of victuals. Fortunately for them, Medina Sidonia did not know that, and advanced in a leisurely fashion, dictated by the slow pace of his *urcas*. By 30 July, when the Armada was level with Plymouth, Howard's deficiency had been made good, and he managed to warp his fleet out of harbour against the wind. That night, under cover of darkness, he led the main part of his fleet across the front of the Armada to gain the weather gauge on the right; at the same time Drake, with a second squadron, was able to take up a similar position on the left.[44] Realising what had happened, on the morning of the 31st Medina Sidonia consolidated his crescent formation in three divisions and prepared for battle. All together the Spanish fleet spanned over two miles of open sea, and even the English were impressed. 'We never thought', wrote one observer, 'that they could ever have found, gathered and joined so great a force of puissant ships together and so well appointed them ....'[45] Between galleons, hulks and galleasses they numbered about 130 sail. But as time was to prove, only a minority of these were fighting ships.

Against them Howard mustered 105, of which nineteen were royal warships and forty-six large auxiliaries, provided by the City of London or by private owners. The remaining forty were smaller vessels of various provenance, but all suitably armed.[46] At the same time fifteen galleons and about twenty smaller ships were stationed in the Narrow Seas under the command of Lord Henry Seymour, to make sure that the duke of Parma did not make any independent attempt to get his troops across. During the whole period covered by this campaign, that is between March and October 1588, Elizabeth had a total of 197 ships in service. Of these thirty-four constituted the royal navy proper, while fifty-three were 'taken up' or requisitioned in the traditional fashion.[47] These were mostly large ships, of over 200 tons, and on them the queen paid tonnage. A further twenty-three were described as 'coasters', and seem to have been smaller ships similarly requisitioned. However almost half the total was provided by voluntary contribution – a measure of the extent to which the queen had her subjects behind her in this struggle. The City of London sent thirty, and a further thirty-four were owned by private individuals, bearing revealing names like *Galleon Leicester*, *Galleon Dudley* and *Bark Hawkins*.[48] Medina Sidonia had more large ships, but most of them were hulks and the very largest ships on both sides (at about 1,000 tons) were well matched. The traditional notion that the Armada ships were much larger than the English was based on differences in the calculation of tonnage between the two sides; overall the discrepancy was small.[49]

Battle was joined off Plymouth on 31 July, but it was a one-sided and inconclusive business. The only remarkable thing about it was that the English apparently attacked *en ala*, that is in line ahead. If this was so (and there is no reason why the Spanish observers should have been mistaken) it is the first recorded use of what was later to become a classic battle tactic.[50] Howard's ships sailed along the Armada formation, firing their culverins at a range to which the Spanish could not hope to respond. The worst affected was the *San Juan*, commanded by Juan Martinez de Recalde, which led the rearguard, and she only suffered about twenty casualties. However, that was not the whole story, as two large ships became crippled, one by an explosion on board and the other by collision. These, the *San Salvador* and the *Nuestra Senora del Rosario*, were eventually abandoned in the interest of maintaining the whole fleet's momentum. The *San Salvador* was largely evacuated, but the *Rosario* was simply left behind in a crippled state, with all its officers, crew, armaments and baggage still on board.[51] The first prize was picked up later the same day by Sir John Hawkins, and the latter the following night by Sir Francis Drake. Drake was later accused of having abandoned his position in the agreed attack formation in order to secure the *Rosario*. As she was still fully manned and armed this was no easy matter. However, once he had contrived to get aboard, Sir Francis managed to persuade Don Pedro Valdes of the hopelessness of his position, and he surrendered. About 50,000 ducats of the king's gold, which was being carried to pay the troops, disappeared into the pockets of the English seamen, and, as usual, Drake was accused of appropriating more than his fair share – which no doubt he did.[52] In the aftermath of the engagement, and not happy with the manner in which some of his captains had responded to the English bombardment, Medina Sidonia re-organised his fleet into two divisions, each retaining the same crescent formation, and made it clear that he would deal severely with any captain who abandoned his position.[53]

As he entered the Channel, about 29 July, the Captain General had sent a pinnace to warn the duke of Parma of his approach. The message, however, never arrived, having fallen victim to some English (or possibly Dutch) scouting vessel which would have been on the lookout for just such an attempt. Having received no reply, on 1 August he sent again. It was now getting very urgent that he receive some positive information about the proposed link-up. This message arrived, but was not treated with the urgency which it deserved.[54] Meanwhile, on the morning of 2 August, both fleets lay becalmed a few miles to the west of Portland Bill. Fitful winds thereafter, which gave the weather gauge first to one side and then to the other, largely dictated the fortunes of the subsequent battle. Howard was frustrated in attempting to get his squadron between the Spaniards and the coast, but was able to engage with the rearguard, while at one point Martin Frobisher in the *Triumph* became cut off and was subject to a determined attack until Howard was able to come to his assistance.[55] It was an untidy engagement, and like all the others, inconclusive. The English gunners were outfiring the Spaniards by about ten to one, but inflicting remarkably little damage for such a lavish expenditure of powder and shot. By the end of the day, Howard's ships were running out of both, and it had become clear that, although they could sail rings round them, they could not sink or critically damage the large Spanish ships. Tactically, the victory of these days lay with the Armada, because when the English guns fell silent, it simply resumed its formation and sailed on to the east, bruised but by no means bowed.[56]

However, strategically Medina Sidonia's advantage was less clear, because the Isle of Wight was now on his port quarter, and he had a critical decision to make. Not having heard anything from Parma, he did not know what kind of a reception to expect in the Low Countries. Should he ignore his orders and seek to anchor in the Solent, perhaps taking the Isle of Wight as a precaution, until he received some definite news? Or should he proceed on regardless, hoping for the best? In the event, Howard made up his mind for him. Having replenished his ammunition supplies and re-organised his fleet, he knew perfectly well that the Armada was considering entering the Solent, and deployed three squadrons under Drake, Hawkins and Frobisher to prevent that from happening.[57] At this point the Captain General was handicapped by the fact that some of his ships began to straggle, and piecemeal battles developed as the English tried to cut them out, while their fellow captains sought to rescue them. With these untidy battles to distract him, and the English deployed to prevent his access to the Solent, the moment passed. The wind took the Armada east of the Needles during the night of 3/4 August, and the English, having disengaged from the main body of their opponents, made a furious and unexpected attack upon the right wing. This onslaught had the effect of pressing the whole fleet towards Selsey Bill and the Ower banks, and of forcing Medina Sidonia to move his own ship and its accompanying squadron to support his right wing.[58] As a result he had no option but to sail on to the east, or risk being driven ashore. He probably would not have made the Solent even if it had not been for this fierce intervention, but it certainly settled his options as to where to head next. On the morning of 6 August the Armada came in sight of Boulogne, and at 4 o'clock that afternoon dropped anchor in the Calais Roads. The fleet was substantially intact, its manpower only slightly reduced, and it was ready for its rendezvous with the duke of Parma. The Captain General sent word of his arrival ashore, and awaited a response.

This came earlier than was expected, on the evening of the same day. However it soon became apparent that this was not a reply to his latest missive, but to the one before.[59] It had been written three days earlier, and announced that Parma would not be ready to embark until Friday, 12 August – in six days' time. If Calais had been a safe anchorage, this would have been no more than a nuisance, but as things were, it spelled disaster. The Armada had survived, but it had not secured command of the sea, and indeed Howard's fleet, having been reinforced by the squadron which Seymour had been keeping in the straits, was now stronger than ever.[60] Their unexpected shortage of ammunition had been no more than a temporary setback, because operating so close to their own bases, they could be (and were) re-supplied. Medina Sidonia was in despair. To windward, and just out to sea, lay the English fleet, while to leeward were the Flanders banks – treacherous shallows from which the Dutch had removed all the buoys and other markers. There was no way in which the great ships of the Armada could get any closer to Parma's likely point of embarkation, and between Parma and the fleet lay a powerful squadron of Dutch flyboats, heavily armed and flat-bottomed to operate in the coastal shallows.[61] If he was ever to get to sea at all, the duke would have to fight his way out against this formidable opposition. The Captain General had made all sorts of baseless assumptions about Parma. He had overestimated the size of the force at his disposal, although on this point he had been warned, he had assumed that his own advance would have been known to the duke, and he had believed that the army of Flanders would be already embarked and awaiting his arrival. He also seems to have been totally unaware of the existence of the Dutch fleet. Partly because of the weather conditions, partly through enemy action, and partly from sheer complacency, there had been a total breakdown of communications between Parma and Medina Sidonia. These chickens were now coming home to roost.[62]

The English Admiral knew about the Dutch, but he did not know the state of Parma's preparations, or whether he would make an attempt to force his way out of Dunkirk. He also knew that the French governor of Calais had proved unexpectedly welcoming to this great fleet, and had entertained many of its officers ashore. Quite what this portended he did not know, but it was an ominous sign. There was no time to be lost if the present tactical advantage was not to be wasted. Now reinforced to about 140 ships, Howard held a council of war on board his flagship on the morning of 7 August, and it was decided to attack that night, using fireships.[63] The conditions were ideal for such a stratagem. Both the wind and the tide were setting from the west; the Armada was anchored in a tight formation; and just to leeward lay the Flemish banks, waiting to receive any ship which tried to take evasive action. Eight small vessels were swiftly prepared, crammed with combustibles and mounted with double-loaded guns, at a total cost of just over £5,000, one of the best investments, as Michael Oppenheim observed, that Elizabeth was ever to make.[64] The Spaniards knew about fireships. They had used them themselves with devastating effect at Antwerp only a few years earlier, but how to counter them was another matter. When the attack came, Medina Sidonia ordered certain of his small ships to intercept the floating infernos and to tow them aside. He then instructed all captains to slip their cables, moving out of the way of the fireships. When the danger had passed they were to return as nearly as possible to their original anchorages. These instructions were sensible enough, but following them was another matter. Two of the fireships were intercepted and neutralised, but the other six got through, and faced with these terrifying threats most of the captains just cut their cables and ran. Only five vessels, including the Captain General's flagship the *San Martin*, were able to recover their original positions.[65] The rest were scattered to leeward and in imminent danger of running aground.

 At dawn, Howard attacked, with an enormous advantage which would have been even greater if he had not been diverted by an attempt to take the galleass *San Lorenzo* which had run ashore under the guns of the Calais fort.[66] As it was he wasted some two hours on this escapade, which gave Medina Sidonia just enough time to recover some of his wandering fleet. The battle which followed, known as the battle of Gravelines, lasted nine hours and was fought along the fringes of the shoal waters between Gravelines and Ostend. It was a sea battle the like of which had never been seen before, because on this occasion the English moved in close, and got the maximum advantage out of their superior firepower. Its formation broken, the Armada was hammered mercilessly, and both its ships and its men suffered terribly. Some six or eight ships were so badly battered that their crews were forced to run them ashore and abandon them; one or two were sunk outright; and many of those which eventually escaped were so badly holed as to be virtually unseaworthy.[67] Of the men, probably over 1,000 were killed and 800 badly wounded. One ship alone lost 330 of its crew of 457.[68] Also, in spite of coming in close, the English were far too canny to allow themselves to be boarded, or to attempt to board their victims. The Spanish soldiers did what they could with their arquebuses, but were consistently denied the opportunity which they craved for hand-to-hand fighting. The English kept tantalisingly out of reach, and blasted them with their guns. At such short range, the Spanish guns should have been almost as effective, but their crews were inept, and often the ammunition did not fit, so the response was at best sporadic. English casualties were light, and no ships were lost – or even badly damaged. At about five in the afternoon the English began to run out of ammunition, and the wind changed to blow from the south. That evening the remains of the Armada ran out into the North Sea, and Medina Sidonia could only struggle to return his scattered ships into some semblance of a fleet.[69] There was no longer an objective for which to fight, and all thoughts turned to the problems of escape.

There were some among the English commanders who feared that the Armada would retreat to Norway to effect repairs before trying again, but this, it soon transpired, was to place too high a value on Medina Sidonia's determination. There could be no question of returning by the way he had come. The winds were unfavourable, and he was not to know that the English fleet was plague-stricken and desperate to disband. So he decided to go north, around the north of Scotland, which was a route already familiar to some of his seamen who had been involved in importing naval stores from Scandinavia. Once he got past the Tyne, the English pursuit slackened off. Of the 130 ships which had set out from Lisbon in May only fifty-nine had made it back to Spain by the beginning of November.[70] As we have seen, two had been taken in the Channel, and another ten or a dozen lost at Gravelines. The remainder were littered along the coasts of Scotland and Ireland, although a few of the commandeered merchantmen may simply have slipped off home without leaving any record.[71] At the very least a third of the Armada had been lost, and as many as 15,000 men may have perished, the vast majority by shipwreck. The only coherent part of the fleet which returned with any dignity was the eight ships which Medina Sidonia managed to bring into Santander on 21 September. It had been a total disaster, and made worse for the king because he had invested so much faith in the Divine nature of his mission. It does not seem to have occurred to Philip that if he had trusted more in his specialist advisers and less in God, some of the more crucial errors could have been avoided. Instead he consoled himself with the thought that so great a punishment could only have been inflicted on him for his sins, and his pride having been humbled, he would not need to be chastised again.[72]

Meanwhile, English euphoria was put on hold, because the demobilisation of the fleet was a sad story indeed. By the time that he called off the pursuit of the Armada, plague was raging in Howard's fleet, and it became imperative to get the men ashore as quickly as possible. Ships were evacuated in a variety of east coast ports from Newcastle southwards, and the wretched seamen were literally dying in the streets. Many of them had neither proper clothing nor medical care. Nor did they have any money, partly because Burghley had not expected them to come ashore so soon, but more particularly because the system could not cope with so many different venues. If the ships had been discharged in due order at Deptford or Woolwich in late September, there might perhaps have been the money available to pay them off, but the mechanism simply did not exist to transport specie to so many locations at such short notice. The Admiral and his captains did their best, using their own resources of money and credit, but it was nowhere near enough.[73] It has been estimated that as many as 8,000 of the 16,000 or so men who had served in the fleet died, either on board ship or shortly after landing – a casualty rate which compares with that of the defeated Armada. By contrast only a few dozen had died in the actual fighting.[74] The Lord Admiral was appalled by this outcome. 'It would grieve any man's heart to see them that had served so valiantly die so miserably', he wrote in early September.[75] The queen and Burghley have both been accused of callous indifference to the mariners' plight, but that is beside the point. Burghley did his best, and certainly knew what was going on, but after the huge effort required to mobilise the fleet and get it to sea, the administrative machinery simply broke down. The crisis had been so urgent and the threat so real, that proper steps had not been taken to clear up afterwards.

The Council also had to think of what might happen next. Even when the scale of the victory became clear, Elizabeth knew perfectly well that the Spanish threat was not ended. Enraged by his failure, Philip might very well try again – and that sooner rather than later. She did not know that the Armada had cost the king the equivalent of £2.5 million, and well nigh bankrupted him. She only knew that his resources were infinitely greater than hers. Opposing him had cost no more than £200,000, but that was also a vast sum for a navy which normally cost no more than a tenth of that.[76] That she had been able to do so at all was thanks partly to the efficiency of the Admiralty, which had been built up over the years, and partly to the public-spirited co-operation of the maritime community. It is perhaps not surprising that Elizabeth was thinking more of the need to safeguard against the next Armada than of the present needs of her seamen. After all, nearly half her fleet had been contributed voluntarily, and paying the seamen from those ships was the responsibility of the owners, not of the queen. What proportion of the plague victims came from that part of the fleet we do not know, but caring for them and recovering their ships must have presented a serious headache, particularly to the City of London. Money was not a problem there, but getting it to where it was needed took time, and much of it must have arrived too late. Meanwhile thousands of men had to make their way home without their proper conduct money, and paid only in IOUs which they frequently had to discount. At the same time, as Hawkins wrote to Burghley on 4 September, '… our ships [are] utterly unmeet and unfitted to follow any enterprise without a thorough new trimming, refreshing and new furnishing …'.[77] Elizabeth's fleet may have been victorious, but it was exhausted, and nobody knew how soon it might have to be called into service again.

Meanwhile, among those not particularly affected by the woes of the seamen, or indeed much concerned with restoring the fleet, the euphoria of victory was beginning to build. Almost before the sounds of battle had died away, Thomas Delony had entered 'Three ballads of the Armada fight' at the Stationers' Hall.[78] Their message was clear and unequivocal – God fought for England.

> *O Noble England,*
> *fall down upon thy knee!*
> *And praise thy GOD with thankful heart,*
> *Which still maintaineth thee!*
> *The foreign foes that seek thy utter spoil,*
> *Shall then, through His especial grace,*
> *Be brought to shameful foil ….*

A highly coloured and imaginative account of the heroics of the English navy then follows, and after thirteen stanzas of celebration, he concludes:

> *Lord GOD Almighty*
> *(which hath the hearts in hand,*
> *Of every person to dispose)*
> *Defend this English land!*
> *Bless Thou our Sovereign*
> *With long and happy life!*
> *Endue her Council with Thy grace!*
> *And end this mortal strife!*
> *Give to the rest*
> *Of Commons more and less,*
> *Loving hearts! Obedient minds!*
> *And perfect faithfulness!*
> *That they and we,*
> *And all with one accord*
> *On Sion's hill may sing the praise*
> *Of our most mighty Lord.*

Public rejoicing began almost at once, and built to a climax three months later. Thanksgiving services proclaimed the victory, and propagated the same message: the Protestant God had triumphed over the tyrannous and Antichristian ambitions of the pope and the Spaniards. Alexander Nowell preached at St Paul's on 20 August giving thanks for the great overthrow of God's enemies.[79] A national thanksgiving was ordered by the Council at the end of September, and 17 November (the commemoration of the queen's accession) was kept 'almost as a Holy day', with sermons and bonfires 'for joy and thanksgiving unto God for the overthrow of the Spaniards, our enemies, upon the sea …'. Spenser's *Faerie Queene*, published in 1590, contains allegorical scenes in which the evil Souldan (representing Philip) is overcome by Prince Arther (England) in the service of Mercilla (Queen Elizabeth).[80] By then the theme had become a trope. All this rather contrived ecstasy was naturally accompanied by a mythology which served to magnify the threat. The Armada had been deemed invincible; its ships were enormous in size, and covered the sea to the horizon; Spanish soldiers had been equipped with whips of exceptional cruelty with which to subdue their wretched English victims – and so on.[81] All of which legendary accretions have tended to disguise the fact, which was well enough known to Elizabeth and her Council, that the war was not over, and that there was an urgent need for a counter-stroke before the Spanish navy – and equally important, Spanish morale – could recover from a blow which had been real enough both in material and in psychological terms.

CHAPTER 9 NOTES

1. Rodger, *Safeguard of the Sea*, pp. 256–7.
2. Parma knew perfectly well that the plans were aimed against England, and that Philip would never countenance any deal. Parker and Martin, *The Spanish Armada*, p. 151.
3. Monson, *Tracts,* I, p. 141.
4. BL Lansdowne MS 52, f.93.
5. Ibid., ff.92–3.
6. J.H. Pollen, 'Mary Queen of Scots and the Babington Plot', *Scottish Historical Society*, 3rd series, III (1922). For a full discussion of this plot and its implications, see Conyers Read, *Mr Secretary Walsingham and the Policy of Queen Elizabeth* (1925), II, p. 44.
7. J.A. Williamson, *The Age of Drake* (1946), pp. 291–2.
8. Kelsey, *Sir Francis Drake*, pp. 285–6.
9. 'Sir Francis Drake's agreement with Thomas Cordell, John Watte and others …', BL Lansdowne MS 56, no. 52, f.175, transcribed in Julian Corbett, ed., *Papers Relating to the Navy during the Spanish War, 1585–1587* (Navy Records Society, 1898), pp. 105–6.
10. Ibid., p. 104.
11. TNA SP12/102, no. 2. Transcribed in Corbett, *Papers Relating to the Navy*, pp. 103–4.

12. Drake to Walsingham, 27 April 1587. TNA SP12/200, no. 46. M.-J. Rodriguez Salgado, 'Philip II and the Great Armada of 1588', in *Armada, 1588–1988. An International Exhibition to Commemorate the Spanish Armada*, p. 22.

13. Parker and Martin, *The Spanish Armada*, p. 128.

14. Corbett, *Papers Relating to the Navy*, p. 117.

15. Peter Pierson, *Commander of the Armada. The Seventh Duke of Medina Sidonia* (1989), pp. 69–70.

16. Kelsey, *Sir Francis Drake*, pp. 292–4.

17. Parker and Martin, *The Spanish Armada*, p. 164. One, the *Bazana*, was wrecked at the entrance to Bayonne.

18. Robert Leng, 'The True Description of the last voiage of that worthy Captayne Sir Francis Drake', ed. Clarence Hopper, *Camden Miscellany*, 5 (1864), p. 17.

19. Corbett, *Papers Relating to the Navy*, p. 131.

20. Borough to Drake, 30 April 1587. TNA SP12/200, no. 57, and 202, no. 14/2. For a full discussion of this fracas, see Kelsey, *Sir Francis Drake*, pp. 294–5.

21. 'Borough's affidavit in reply', TNA SP12/203, no. 1, transcribed in Corbett, *Papers Relating the Navy*, pp. 183–4.

22. Leng, 'The True Description …', p. 22. For various parts of the declared lists, see TNA SP12/202, no. 53, and SP12/204, no. 8.

23. M.A.S. Hume, *Calendar of Letters and Papers [at] Simancas, Elizabeth*, IV, p. 130.

24. Burghley to De Loo, 28 July 1587. *Calendar of State Papers, Foreign … of the reign of Elizabeth*, ed. A.J. Butler (1913–21), XXI, iii, p. 186.

25. Parker and Martin, *The Spanish Armada*, p. 135.

26. Ibid., p. 137 and n. 11, for a discussion of the significance of Margate.

27. Ibid., pp. 140–1.

28. Loades, *The Tudor Navy*, pp. 242–3.

29. AGS Estado 431, ff.124–6, cited by Parker and Martin, *The Spanish Armada*, p. 146.

30. Pierson, *Commander of the Armada*.

31. Parker and Martin, *The Spanish Armada*, p. 148. Medina Sidonia wrote an uncompromising assessment of the Armada's chances to Don Juan da Idiaquez on 18 February.

32. Leicester had become heavily involved in the internal politics of the Netherlands, and accepted the title of Governor General against the queen's wishes. For the expression of her indignation, see her letter to Leicester of 10 February 1586. BL Cotton MS Galba C.VIII, f.27, printed in *Elizabeth I: Collected Works*, ed. L.S. Marcus etc. (2000), p. 273.

33. Parker and Martin, *The Spanish Armada*, p. 147.

34. Ibid., p. 156.

35. I.A.A. Thompson, 'Spanish Armada Guns', *Mariners Mirror*, LXI, 1975, pp. 355–71.

36. Parker and Martin, *The Spanish Armada*, p. 55.

37. Bertendona to the King, 15 February 1588, cited by Garrett Mattingly, *The Defeat of the Spanish Armada* (1959), p. 202.

38. For example, AGS Estado 165/104–14. *Calendar of State Papers, Spanish, Elizabeth*, IV, pp. 245–50.

39. Parker and Martin, *The Spanish Armada*, p. 158.

40. Loades, *Tudor Navy*, p. 247.

41. Parker and Martin, *The Spanish Armada*, p. 162.

42. Petruccio Ubaldino, 'Comentario della Impressa Fatta contra il Regno D'Inghilterra del Re Catholica L'Anno 1588' (BL Royal MS 14.A.XI). D.W. Waters, *The Elizabethan Navy and the Armada of Spain* (National Maritime Museum, 1975), pp. 69–100.

43. C. Fernandez Duro, *La Armada Invencible* (1884–5), II, pp. 101–5.

44. Kelsey, *Sir Francis Drake*, pp. 323–4.

45. Parker and Martin, *The Spanish Armada*, p. 165.

46. J. Charnock, *The History of Marine Architecture* (1802), p. 63.

47. BL MS Royal 14 B.XIII, printed by Charnock, *History of Marine Architecture*, pp. 59–72.

48. Loades, *Tudor Navy*, p. 248.

49. E.K. Thompson, 'English and Spanish Tonnage in 1588', *Mariners Mirror*, 46, 1959. W. Salisbury, 'Early Tonnage Measurements in England', *Mariners Mirror*, 52, 1966.

50. Rodger, *Safeguard of the Sea*, pp. 263–71.

51. Deposition of James Baron, 7 October 1605. TNA E133/47/3.

52. Ibid. See also Howard to Walsingham, 27 August 1588. TNA SP12/215, no. 59(i), f.105.

53. Parker and Martin, *The Spanish Armada*, p. 171.

54. The second messenger did not reach Parma's headquarters until 4 August. See Parma's letter of 12 August, *Calendar of State Papers, Venetian*, IX, f.382.

55. Pierson, *Commander of the Armada*, p. 153.

56. Parker and Martin, *The Spanish Armada*, p. 178.

57. Ibid., pp. 176–7.

58. Corbett, *Drake and the Tudor Navy*, pp. 235–41.

59. Parker and Martin, *The Spanish Armada*, p. 181 and n. 3.

60. Rodriguez Salgado, *Armada*, pp. 233–42.

61. J.B. van Overeem, 'Justinus van Nassau en de Armada (1588)', *Marineblad*, LIII, 1938, pp. 821–31, cited by Parker and Martin, *The Spanish Armada*, p. 287.

62. For a discussion of this breakdown and its consequences, see Parker and Martin, *The Spanish Armada*, pp. 183–5.

63. Federico Giambelli, who had been responsible for the fireship attack on Antwerp, had moved to England, and it was feared (falsely) that he might have devised these ships.

64. Oppenheim, *History*, p. 163.

65. In fact no ship of the Armada was damaged in this attack, as the fireships drifted innocuously ashore. Loades, *Tudor Navy*, p. 252. Parker and Martin, *The Spanish Armada*, p. 187.

66. Pierson, *Commander of the Armada*, p. 162. Kelsey, *Sir Francis Drake*, p. 334.

67. M.-J. Rodriguez Salgado and Simon Adams, eds, *England, Spain and the Gran Armada, 1585–1604* (1991).

68. The *San Felipe*. Parker and Martin, *The Spanish Armada*, p. 192.

69. Ibid.

70. Ibid., p. 258. C. Martin, *Full Fathom Five; Wrecks of the Spanish Armada* (1978).

71. This is pure speculation, but a number of these ships are unaccounted for in the Spanish records, which are very full in respect of their own ships.

72. For a consideration of Philip's reaction to this disaster, and of the gout which had afflicted him throughout the year, see Henry Kamen, *Philip of Spain* (1997), pp. 270–7.

73. R.B. Wernham, *The Expedition of Sir John Norris and Sir Francis Drake to Spain and Portugal, 1589* (Navy Records Society, 1988), pp. xii–xv.

74. Loades, *Tudor Navy*, p. 253.

75. Ibid.

76. I.A.A. Thompson, 'The Invincible Armada', in *Royal Armada* (Manorial Research, 1988), p. 172.

77. TNA SP12/216, no. 3.

78. Reprinted in A.F. Pollard, *Tudor Tracts* (1903), pp. 485–502.

79. Peter Sinclair, 'Notes on the Spanish Armada', in Jeff Doyle and Bruce Moore, eds, *England and the Spanish Armada* (1990), pp. 3–11.

80. Marion Campbell, 'Writing the Armada: The Representation of an Event in Spenser's Faerie Queene', in Doyle and Moore, *England and the Spanish Armada*, pp. 35–56.

81. Jeff Doyle, 'The Factional Use of the Iconography of the Spanish Armada in English Art and Literature, 1580–1603,' in Doyle and Moore, *England and the Spanish Armada*, pp. 57–78.

CHAPTER TEN

Epilogue

By August 1588 the English Exchequer was empty. Expenditure had risen from a pre-war average of £168,000 to £367,000 in 1587 and £420,000 in 1588. The war chest was exhausted and the parliamentary taxation inadequate. Subsidies to the Dutch alone were costing £313,000 a year.[1] So it is not surprising that Elizabeth's first thought, when the initial sounds of rejoicing had died away in the autumn of 1588, was that now was the time to intercept the *flota*, which must be worth at least £2 million. It would take months before the battered remains of the Armada could be fit for service again, and in the meantime the Atlantic Guard would have been seriously weakened. However, although the queen's ships and the others which had served against the Spaniards had not been knocked to pieces, it would be many months before they could be ready for use again. Some of them had been at sea for five or six months, and all were in urgent need of careening and caulking. They also needed fumigating to get rid of the infections which had played such havoc with the crews at the end of the campaign.[2] By the time that all this had been done, and the ships had actually got themselves to the Azores, the *flota* would long since have been safe in Lisbon or Cadiz. Yet to do nothing would have been to throw away the golden opportunity which had been created. By 1590 Philip would not only have had time to repair and refurbish the Armada survivors, he would also have been able to hire – or even build – replacements. Given the scale of Spanish resources, the window of opportunity was not large.

So on 20 September the Council met to decide what could be done with the resources which they could reasonably expect to be available. Their first thought was to destroy the remains of the Armada, then believed to be either at Lisbon or at Seville; the second was to take Lisbon (which was rather less realistic); and the third was to take the Azores (which was not realistic at all).[3] A pretext already existed for an attack on Lisbon, and that was certainly in the minds of some councillors. Dom Antonio still lurked around the court, and was currently negotiating for financial support from another enemy of Philip II, the Sharif of Morocco. Dom Antonio had approached the Sharif during the summer, and by 10 September Elizabeth had written in his support.[4]

However, this was an indication that Lisbon was not high on her own agenda. What was on the agenda was a suggestion which had probably originated in unrecorded discussions held in early September, for a co-operative venture, of the kind which had been launched against Cadiz and Sagres in the previous year. Sir Francis Drake and Sir John Norris had undertaken to lead such an expedition, and that was an option which appealed to queen and Council alike. The original suggestion had been that the queen should contribute £20,000, six ships 'of the second sort' and a variety of guns and ammunition.[5] These proposals were clarified and modified at the meeting on the 20th. The crews of the queen's ships were to be paid by the other 'adventurers'; the number of troops involved was set at 8,000; and the Dutch were to be invited to provide logistical support. At the same time, Norris, Drake and their backers would raise £40,000.

This method of proceeding was fine, in so far as it relieved pressure on Elizabeth's overstretched resources, but it also meant that she had no more than a 50 per cent say in determining the expedition's aims. This did not matter as long as it was agreed that the main objective would be the shipping in Lisbon harbour, followed by an attempt on Philip's treasure fleet. However by mid-October it had become clear that the remains of the Armada were not at Lisbon, but at San Sebastian and Santander on the Biscay coast. This meant that Drake and Norris would have to make a difficult, and financially unrewarding, detour on their way to Lisbon if they were to destroy them.[6] Meanwhile Drake had become thoroughly convinced by the persuasive Dom Antonio that he would only have to sail into the Tagus for the whole country to rise up spontaneously and throw off the Spanish yoke. Powerful merchant interests in London, which were due to provide most of the backers' money, were also convinced by this propaganda and looked forward eagerly to gaining control of the lucrative Portuguese trade to the Far East. This ambition was also fuelled by Thomas Cavendish, who returned at this time from another voyage of circumnavigation with news from the East Indies that 'our countrymen may have trade as freely as the Portuguese, if they will'.[7]

All this built up pressure on Drake and Norris to disregard the queen's instructions and to sail straight to Lisbon. Throughout the winter, preparations proceeded, although not without difficulties. As early as the middle of October the queen was forced to advance most of her promised contribution to get Drake through a crisis in the provision of victuals. Then in November Sir John Norris went to the Low Countries to persuade the Estates General to release some of the English footmen currently serving there. Norris's method of negotiating was described as 'manly and brave, but much too arrogant', and he was soon at cross-purposes with Lord Willoughby, the General of the English forces.[8] However, by the beginning of December the Estates had given him all that he was asking for – permission to withdraw 2,000 footmen and 200 horse, and leave to purchase arms and munitions. They also agreed to provide five of their own warships, and ten companies of infantry, with the transports to carry them – all to be ready by the end of December.[9]

Norris and Drake should thus have been greatly strengthened as a result of the former's mission, but at the cost of adding yet another agenda to the determination of objectives. However that was not the only difficulty. Expenses continued to run ahead of provision. By January £65,000 had been committed against a provision of £54,000. Moreover in the Netherlands a bill for £18,500 had been incurred for which no provision had been made at all, and the Dutch authorities absolutely refused to allow English troops to be withdrawn from the garrisons of Ostend and Bergen-op-Zoom. Willoughby was reduced to despair, claiming that he would be left without sufficient field troops to be of any use, and the queen's ingenious attempt to find a way around the dilemma was rejected.[10] By February the Dutch had gone off the whole idea, and eventually provided only six of the promised ten bands of soldiers, and none of the warships or munitions. So difficult did relations with the Estates General become that only six of the thirteen English companies which should have been released actually appeared, and the expedition which eventually set off in April was not at all strengthened as a result of all this to-ing and fro-ing. This breakdown also caused delays in England. The assembly of troops was put back to 1 February, and the queen was forced to pick up further substantial bills.[11] The normal campaigning season was coming on, so that the element of surprise would be lost, and Drake still did not have enough transports for his soldiers. While their frustrations were thus growing, the idea of using an attack on Lisbon to seat Dom Antonio on the Portuguese throne was growing on the two commanders, and on their financial backers. Knowing this, at the end of February Elizabeth reiterated her original instructions:

> before you attempt anything either in Portugal or in the said Islands [Azores], our express pleasure and commandment is that you first distress the ships of war in Guipuzcoa, Biscay [or] Galicia … to the end that they may not impeach you in such enterprises as you are to execute ….[12]

These orders the commanders were solemnly sworn to obey, but so little faith did the queen place in their oaths that shortly after, in early March, she appointed Anthony Ashley, one of the Clerks of the Privy Council, to accompany the expedition and to report on their actions.

Her fears were fully justified. Having had its budget topped up yet again, and survived an attempt by the earl of Essex to join it, the expedition eventually set off on 18 April. The commanders made not the slightest attempt to go to

Santander or San Sebastian, but set course instead for Coruna, having heard that a rich fleet of 200 merchantmen was lying there. A clearer statement of their true intentions could hardly have been made – and Coruna was on the direct route to Lisbon. On 23 April they took the town by surprise, but found no rich merchantmen. Instead they took the lower town after a sharp fight, but to no purpose. Some plunder and some victuals were secured, but nothing like what might have been hoped for.[13] Norris then insisted upon attacking the upper town, which was much stronger but where he hoped for better pickings, and while the siege was going on he defeated a Spanish relieving force at Puente de Burgos, just along the coast. However the attack on the citadel of Coruna made no progress at all, and after setting fire to the lower town, on 8 May the troops re-embarked and set out again – southwards, towards Lisbon. Alerted by Ashley's dispatches, the queen became increasingly angry, and rejected a hopeful request for reinforcements which the commanders dispatched on 16 May.[14]

The tactics of what then transpired are easy to follow but hard to understand. Before they reached Lisbon the earl of Essex had succeeded in joining them, but he brought nothing by way of reinforcements, and that was a serious omission.[15] Desertion and sickness had reduced Norris's force to about 10,000 men by this time, and that alone should have given him pause. However, so high was his confidence in Dom Antonio's promises that he landed the bulk of his force at Paniche, 45 miles north of Lisbon, on 18 May, in the expectation that he would sweep up a fresh army of the Pretender's enthusiastic supporters on his march to the Tagus. Drake meanwhile was to proceed with his ships, and rendezvous with Norris just outside the city. When it came to the point, however, the Admiral decided to wait at Cascais several miles down the river. He had arrived there on 20 May, but apparently found his welcome less warm than he had been led to expect, and decided not to venture further without news of the army's success.[16] It was 25 May before word reached him that Norris was in the suburbs of Lisbon, and he prepared to move part of his fleet to support the expected capture of the town. However this never happened because Norris, finding Lisbon strongly held against him, and no sign of Dom Antonio's supporters, had already given up. On 26 May he led his army down to Cascais, where the captains then dithered for two weeks, trying to decide whether to try again. On the one hand, they had encountered no serious resistance – even the nearby fort of St Julian had offered to surrender on demand – but on the other hand no acceptance either. It remained to be seen what would happen if they were to mount a serious attack, but with their numbers dwindling all the time, it was decided that such a risk could not be justified. On 3 June it was decided to sail for the Azores. The troops were embarked, the Dutch flyboats paid off, and the earl of Essex sent home.[17]

The fleet never reached its destination. Blown north by contrary winds, on 19 June the main group of ships found themselves among the isles of Bayona, and several had already departed for home. In a fit of frustration they attacked the neighbouring town of Vigo, but found it deserted and stripped of all its valuables. The expedition then became divided, more by accident of weather than intention, and Drake set off, ostensibly for the Azores, on 22 June. At that point Norris, who had control of thirty-three of the fifty or so ships still with them, decided that he was so far depleted that he could accomplish nothing more, and sailed for home. When he returned to Plymouth on 2 or 3 July, he was astonished to find Drake already there, having been ostensibly overcome by adverse weather, but in reality having decided that his mission was no longer possible with the diminished force under his control. At first the queen's reaction to this expensive fiasco was surprisingly mild. On 7 July the Council informed the commanders that Her Majesty 'did take their service and good endeavours in very acceptable part ...'.[18] However, when the accounts were called for and the scale of the losses and muddle became more clear, her tone changed. It was 1591 before the accounts were finally made up, and by that time it was clear that everyone who had invested in the Lisbon voyage was heavily out of pocket. Then the commanders' failure to obey the queen's original orders was remembered, to their discredit. Sir Francis Drake apparently got most of the blame, and his favour at court, once so high, never fully recovered.

Drake and Norris, however, were not the only captains at sea in this post-Armada year. It would have been surprising if they had been, given the constant need for defence and the uncertainties over Philip's intentions. In September 1589, soon after Drake and Norris's return, and long before their business was cleared, Martin Frobisher led another squadron to the Portuguese coast. This had some success, in the sense that it took some well freighted merchantmen, but the treasure fleet had long since arrived, and if it had any more ambitious purpose, that was not realised.[19] At the same time the earl of Cumberland was also privateering, and also enjoying some success, but since his exploits did not pass through the naval accounts, we know relatively little about them. On the strength of these achievements, Hawkins became more ambitious, and during the winter of 1589–90 drew up a scheme for maintaining a long-term blockade of the Spanish coast. As a first step in that direction, early in 1590 he began to prepare a squadron of six ships, to take up position as soon as the weather should improve.[20] In the event, this did not happen because Elizabeth decided to send an expeditionary force to France in support of Henry of Navarre, the Huguenot leader who had become King Henry IV in 1589, and was struggling to impose himself on his kingdom. The Council decided that it could not have a significant portion of the navy wandering the ocean while the

EPILOGUE   211

queen had forces pinned down in Brittany, and liable to need naval support, so Hawkins's initiative was cancelled, much to his chagrin. Later in the summer, when the situation in Brittany had stabilised, or at any rate was accorded a lower priority, he did, however, get his way – up to a point. He was sent out with a number of ships, ostensibly to watch for Spanish troop movements into Brittany, but in fact to maintain a more general blockade, which he did for some weeks. At the same time, Frobisher was sent to the Azores, with the usual instructions to watch out for Spanish treasure ships. Neither of these voyages was particularly successful, in the sense that neither returned a profit, but what they did prove was that the English navy was capable of maintaining a long-term presence in hostile waters, and effectively strangling enemy commerce.[21] Only the well guarded *flota* managed to get through, and Spanish military operations in northern Europe were seriously impeded. Strategically the sea war of 1590 was drawn, but that meant that the English, whose focus was the more specific, were the more successful.

While Sir John Hawkins was preoccupied with events at sea, his kinsman by marriage, Edward Fenton, became Deputy Treasurer. He was originally appointed for a year, from February 1589 to February 1590, but as Sir John's preoccupations continued, that was extended for a second year. Fenton kept a running account of his expenditure, with costing estimates for building, maintenance and provisioning, which now survives in the Pepys Library at Magdalene College, Cambridge, and this enables a summary analysis of naval activity for those two years to be made.[22] In January 1591, at the end of his period of responsibility, he recorded expenditure over the whole period on ships in the Narrow Seas, under various commanders and at regular intervals. This squadron was on duty throughout the year, and was replaced whenever the ships and men needed refreshing. The same entry also records payments made to named captains for specific ships, but without noticing where they were serving. On 12 May 1589 an expenditure of £406 was recorded for bringing 'Don Pedro's ship' (the *Nuestra Senora del Rosario*) from Dartmouth, where she had been in the custody of Sir John Gilbert, round to the Thames in accordance with the Council's instructions.[23] The receipt and disbursement of Exchequer warrants, both ordinary and extraordinary, is similarly noted. Strenuous efforts were being made to pay off the debts accumulated in 1587 and 1588, and in March 1590 the Ordinary was increased from £5,714 to £8,973, in response to several representations from Hawkins.[24] Building and 'new building' records go back to December 1588, when the *Bear*, the *Mary Rose*, the *Hope* and the *Bonaventure* were docked for refurbishment which it was estimated would cost £6,000. In 1590 Mathew Baker was working at Woolwich, building the *Merhoneur*, the *Quittance*, the *Answer*, and two 'great longboats', for which payment of £5,200 was recorded. At the same time

Peter Pett (another royal shipwright) was building the *Defiance* at Deptford (£3,000), and Richard Chapman the *Garland* and the *Crane* 'in his own dock at Deptford' (£4,100).[25] All the warrants covering this expenditure were duly noted, and the money dispensed on preparing ships for the seas on special missions – like that of Norris and Drake to Lisbon.

In August 1590 Fenton made a complete survey of the queen's ships then in service – forty-four vessels with a total tonnage of 23,705. These ranged from the massive *Triumph* of 1,000 tons down to the *Cygnet* of 20 tons. Six of them were of 800 tons or more, but only one – the *Bonavolia* – was a galley and none appear to have been galleasses.[26] The best equipped fleet in Europe had by this time abandoned oar power almost entirely. When in service the greatest of these ships carried 500 men, of whom 340 were seamen, and if they had all been at sea at the same time, 7,830 men would have been required, while in harbour 441 shipkeepers would have been sufficient to ensure their security. Of course at times of real emergency, such as the Armada, the royal navy was only the spearhead of national defence. In 1582 176 civilian vessels of 100 tons and more had been listed as available, and that number would certainly have increased ten years later.[27] If a second Armada had appeared at this time, as was generally feared, Elizabeth could probably have mustered upwards of 200 ships to send against it, and these would have been equipped with the finest guns and the most skilful sea gunners in the world. All together twelve ships were built or rebuilt between 1586 and 1592, and a further two purchased, so Fenton's list was work in progress. All together his notes disclose an expenditure of about £120,000 over these two full years, which was good value for money, considering what the armies in France and the Low Countries were costing at the same time. In spite of Philip's superior resources, and the manner in which he learned the lessons of his failure in 1588, the war at sea continued to be finely balanced. Only in privateering did the English still retain a clear advantage. Spain had no equivalent of the earl of Cumberland, nor of Raleigh, Drake and Hawkins in their private capacities. England's secret was the unique partnership between the queen and her subjects – a partnership well expressed when the *Madre de Dios* was taken in 1592, as we have already seen.[28]

Of course not all voyages were successful. Not only was the Lisbon expedition of 1589 a failure, and the attempts of 1590 unproductive, but Lord Thomas Howard's presence in the Azores in 1591 proved to be equally futile. Howard's objective was once again the *flota*, but he lacked sufficient power to tackle the escort which Philip was by this time able to provide. He was dislodged from his position even before the treasure fleet appeared, and his enterprise is best remembered for the quixotic self-sacrifice of the *Revenge*, surely one of the most heroic and pointless actions ever fought at sea.[29] Howard took a few small ships, but what his adventure had demonstrated conclusively was that only a large fleet kept on station for many weeks would have any chance of capturing this enormous and elusive prize. Elizabeth drew in her horns and in 1593 only routine patrolling and escort work was attempted. Expenditure over the next three years averaged no more than £27,000. In 1594 another Armada was feared, but all that demonstrated was the imperfections of the English intelligence system, which had declined in efficiency since Sir Francis Walsingham's death in 1590. What actually transpired was worrying rather than threatening. Newlyn and Penzance in Cornwall were burned and some of the inhabitants carried off in a small-scale galley strike, launched from Brittany.[30] The raiders were fortunate with the weather, and managed to sneak in between the regular naval patrols, but their exploit was a sufficient warning against complacency. The main naval operation of the year was the attack on the Spanish fort of Crozon, which had been built to command the harbour of Brest. Since 1590 Sir John Norris had maintained a fluctuating presence in Brittany in support of the duc de Dombes, who was Henry IV's governor. Once Henry had converted to Catholicism in 1593, his position became much stronger, and in the following year he was able to give priority to dislodging the Spaniards from their position in the province.[31] With this Elizabeth was in complete agreement, and Norris's troops were reinforced. At the end of August Sir Martin Frobisher led a squadron of four warships and various auxiliaries to support his operation, and siege was laid to the fort, which was also known as 'El Leon'. The warships landed additional soldiers, and bombarded the Spanish positions from the sea. Eventually on 7 November Crozon was taken by assault, and the Spanish threat to south-west England thereby markedly diminished.[32] Frobisher subsequently died of wounds suffered in the assault, but otherwise the operation, although small-scale, was completely successful.

Frobisher's operation had been entirely a Crown project. No plunder was expected (or obtained) and private investment was not invited. Elizabeth nevertheless remained wedded to the idea of co-operative enterprises, and when Drake and Hawkins came up with another proposal towards the end of 1594, Lisbon was forgotten, and they were told to go ahead. The idea was the same as ten years earlier, a plundering attack on Spain's colonies in the New World, particularly Panama. The queen was to provide six ships, £30,000, and a commission authorising the whole operation, while the 'adventurers' (mainly Hawkins and Drake themselves) were to find £60,000 and twenty-one ships.[33] Unfortunately the principals were at cross-purposes from the start. Elizabeth treated it as though it were an entirely naval operation and (as with Lisbon six years earlier) issued orders for a raid on the Spanish coast, to be followed by the interception of the *flota,* while Drake and Hawkins pointed out that their understanding was that an attack on the Caribbean had been agreed. A compromise was then reached; Elizabeth modified her instructions, and the adventurers ignored them. In this state of mutual misunderstanding, the expedition set out from Plymouth on 28 August 1595.[34] The fleet was well found and well victualled, but the Spaniards knew more about its true objectives than the queen did, and Drake and Hawkins were ill-suited to co-operation. They bickered endlessly, particularly about tactics, and when they eventually arrived at San Juan de Puerto Rico, they found the Spanish expecting them and the town heavily fortified. In late November the English attacked with their customary panache, but were driven off with heavy losses, including Sir Nicholas Clifford who was in command of the soldiers.[35] Hawkins was already a sick man, and died at sea the same day. These deaths resolved any possible issues of command, but Drake, now in sole charge, was unable to do much better. He was able to take La Hacha (on the mainland) on 1 December and Nombre de Dios on the 28th, but the plunder in both cases was disappointingly small. The Spaniards had learned not to leave valuables in weakly defended settlements, and the places which would have been worth taking (like Puerto Rico) were now heavily fortified. There were no more easy pickings in the Caribbean. Drake in turn died, a disappointed and frustrated man, while the fleet was off Porto Bello on 28 January 1596, and it was left to Sir Thomas Baskerville to bring the expedition back to Plymouth in May.[36] Off Cuba, on their way back, they were attacked by a Spanish squadron, but managed to drive it off with losses. There was no plunder in such an achievement, but it was a victory of a sort. However, by the summer of 1596 England had lost three of its most feared 'sea-dogs', and it remained to be seen whether a new generation could repeat their exploits in the new situation which now appertained in the New World. The man who thought he knew the answer was the earl of Essex.

Since his not particularly glorious participation in the Lisbon expedition, Essex had been hankering to prove himself as a soldier, and for the last six months had been agitating for another attempt to be made. Since the beginning of 1596, while Drake was still off the coast of America, plans had been taking shape, and in early April they were given fresh point when Spanish troops from the Netherlands suddenly seized Calais. Since the death of the duke of Parma in 1593, the Spaniards had not been doing very well in the Low Countries, so this coup was something of a surprise. It also brought the enemy within twenty miles of England, and meant that a riposte of some kind was not only desirable but necessary.[37] Plans which had been germinating for months were brought to rapid fruition during April. A joint Anglo-Dutch attack at some unspecified place on the coast of Spain was decided upon, and this time the Dutch participation was to be substantial. Within a matter of weeks eighteen royal ships, sixty-eight auxiliaries, eighteen hoys and flyboats, and twenty-four Dutch men-of-war had been assembled.[38] The Lord Admiral, Lord William Howard, was to be in overall command; the Dutch ships were led by Jan van Duijvenvoorde, the Admiral of Holland; and the soldiers (7,000 in number) were to be captained by the earl of Essex. Perhaps because the Dutch were participating, or perhaps because the queen had learned a painful lesson at Lisbon, this was to be a purely military operation, uncomplicated by private agendas or investment.[39] The auxiliaries had been taken up in the traditional fashion, and not voluntarily contributed by their owners, so that this time there could be no excuse for disobeying orders. The objective was simply and only to 'annoy' the king of Spain:

> ... by burning of [his] ships of war in his havens before they could come forth to the seas, and therewith also destroying his magazines of victuals and his munitions for the arming of his navy, to provide that neither the rebels in Ireland should be aided and strengthened, nor yet the king be able, of long time, to and have any great navy in readiness to offend us ...[40]

Lord Thomas Howard, Sir Walter Raleigh, Sir Francis Vere, Sir Conyers Clifford and Sir George Carew were appointed to 'aid and assist' the generals, and also (probably) to ensure that their inevitable disagreements did not ruin the whole enterprise. As the queen knew only too well, the earl of Essex could be a difficult colleague.

Having got their ships and men to Plymouth at the end of April, Howard and Essex were itching to be off – not least because there were well founded rumours that Elizabeth might be about to change her mind. In fact she did just that, not once but twice, and ended up where she had started out, so the Admiral was not recalled, and his commission was not revoked.[41] On 1 June the 'counter Armada' as it has been called, got to sea. No objective had been declared, and the decision to attack Cadiz was apparently known to only a very few. Howard had no desire to make the mistake that Hawkins and Drake had made in the previous year, when leaky communications had resulted in the Spaniards being as well briefed on the objectives of the voyage as the captains themselves. A few days later, off Cape Ortegal, Howard divided his ships into five battle squadrons, and issued sealed instructions to his captains.[42] Only then did the nature of the task before them become fully clear. As a result of these precautions, when he reached Cadiz on 20 June, the surprise was complete. The English did not in fact attack until the following day, but the respite was too short for the defenders to be able to do anything to strengthen their positions. As Howard swept into the harbour, the guns of Fort San Felipe, and of the galleys which were moored nearby, opened up, but without the slightest effect. Driven steadily further into the narrowing harbour, the Spanish ships began to impede each other and become entangled. A few managed at first to escape down a narrow channel to the south of the Isle of Leon, but the *Vanguard* soon blocked off that way of retreat, and the cornered shipping was almost totally destroyed.[43] The flagship of the Spanish Admiral, the *San Felipe*, blew up with great loss of life, and two other galleons, the *San Mateo* and the *San Andres*, were captured. The rest were burned, sunk or driven ashore.

While the main naval forces had been occupied in this way, the other elements of the expedition had not been idle. The Dutch attacked and captured Puntal, on the seaward side of Cadiz, and a force of English soldiers under the command of Sir Conyers Clifford had destroyed the bridges leading from the island of Cadiz to the mainland, thus inhibiting any possible relief. At the same time the main army, under the earl of Essex, attacked the city itself, which was walled but only lightly defended. The garrison surrendered on terms, the bulk of the civilian population was then evacuated, and the city was ransomed for 520,000 ducats (£180,000).[44] Hostages were duly given for the delivery of this very large sum. While these negotiations were still going on Howard sent Raleigh with a squadron of warships to deal with the secondary harbour of Puerto Reale, which was also crammed with merchant shipping. Thinking that they had the measure of their assailants, the authorities there offered a ransom of 2 million ducats. This time they miscalculated, because Raleigh responded that his instructions were to destroy — which was correct — and he proceeded to do just that. By the time that he had finished, and taking into account what had happened earlier, two galleons had been captured, and thirteen men-of-war, eleven Indiamen and upwards of a hundred miscellaneous traders had been sunk or burned. The Spaniards later calculated their losses at over 20 million ducats (£6,800,000), or more than three times the cost of the Armada.[45] The victory had been complete, and executed with remarkable efficiency, given the notorious proneness of English troops to drunken indiscipline, and of English commanders to quarrel among themselves.

The quarrels came later, because Essex and van Duijvenvoorde wanted to retain control of the city, and to garrison it as a base for future operations on the Spanish coast. Howard and the other members of the Council disagreed, pointing out that it would only be a matter of time before the Spaniards counter-attacked in overwhelming force. Having inflicted a humiliating defeat and devastating losses, the only sensible course was to get out while the going was good, and so they did, to the earl's bitter chagrin.[46] In spite of the ransom, the fortifications of Cadiz were razed, several of its principal buildings destroyed, and the rest systematically pillaged. The English left on 5 July. They called at Faro and Coruna on the way back, but found both virtually deserted, and the Council swiftly prohibited the commanders from attempting any other enterprise — even an ambush in the Azores. They had no intention of spoiling the moment, because not only had Howard and Essex secured a victory which made all sorts of points about the state of the war, they had also secured an enormous booty which would go straight into the royal coffers. There was no point in taking further risks. The fleet returned in triumph, and the only person not happy with the outcome was the earl of Essex, who felt that his achievements had been disparaged and his counsel ignored. A victory which filled his countrymen with patriotic pride and religious enthusiasm served only to fuel his growing paranoia — but that is a story which falls outside the scope of this study. The duke of Medina Sidonia, who had ridden to the rescue when Cadiz had been attacked by Drake eleven years earlier, could only wring his hands over this latest disaster: 'It is plainly a chastisement from our Lord', he wrote, 'and His will alone. Blessed be his name, although the loss has been very heavy ....'[47] His king, meanwhile, already in failing health, was left to wonder what further sins he could have committed to deserve this bitter chastisement. The English, of course, knew the answer to that one.

The taking of Cadiz was in many ways a greater victory than that over the Armada. It is quite possible to argue that bad weather and defective logistics would have frustrated Medina Sidonia even if the English fleet had been a hundred miles away, but Cadiz was a positive triumph. It was an amphibious combined operation in which English and Dutch, soldiers and seamen, operated in perfect harmony, and the bile of the earl of Essex should not be allowed to conceal that. It is also a fitting point at which to conclude this survey of the development of the English navy, because thereafter the queen's advancing age, and national war-weariness meant that control began to relax, money began to be wasted, and there were no more great victories. Lord Howard was created earl of Nottingham in 1597, and remained Lord Admiral until 1618, but his later years in office were overshadowed by corruption and nepotism.[48] The earl of Essex ended on the block in 1601, having convinced himself that the world was conspiring his downfall. In spite of dutifully lamenting his sins, Philip was quick to organise a counter-stroke after the humiliation of Cadiz, and the Admiral of Castile had assembled 100 ships and 16,000 men at Ferrol by the end of September. It is unlikely that this was intended to be more than an exemplary strike, and may have been aimed at Ireland, but it was in any case dispersed by autumn gales off the Cape of Finisterre.[49] In 1597 it was resolved to try again, and this time the creaky English intelligence service picked up reports of the intention. When the earl of Essex was allowed to try his hand at repeating the exploits of Drake, the first instructions for what was later known as 'the islands voyage' involved an attack on this Spanish preparation. It was then believed that the weather had intervened again, and that part of Essex's instructions was cancelled.[50] In fact the Spaniards had scaled down their ambitions, aiming merely to raid Falmouth, and the two fleets passed at sea without seeing each other. The islands voyage went on its futile way, and the Spanish raid on Falmouth was again frustrated by a gale, so it would be difficult to say which side was more disappointed by the waste of time, money and effort which the campaigns of 1597 had involved. The Spaniards did manage to land a small force at Kinsale in Ireland in 1601, but it was too little and too late for the earl of Tyrone, and having been cut off by the navy was easily contained and defeated by Lord Mountjoy, then the Royal Deputy.[51]

The navy had come a long way in fifty years, and had changed dramatically since Lord Lisle had led out his fleet against the French in 1545. Then the strategic aims of the navy had been almost entirely defensive. Supplementary ships had been taken up for 'wafting' or escort duties, but the ambitions of the royal navy proper did not extend much beyond fighting the French in the Channel. The tactical boundaries within which the navy operated extended from Brest in the south-west to the Firth of Forth in the north-east, and its notion of aggressive warfare was confined to coastal raiding and the burning of small places like Tréport.[52] Formation fighting was a new idea, adopted from the Spaniards, and both the synchronised broadside and the line-ahead tactic were still in the future. Big English ships were either carracks, like the *Mary Rose*, or galleys like the *Subtle*. Privateering was in its infancy, and the guns of the fleet were a miscellany of old serpentines, English cast bronze and imported cast iron. The casting of iron guns in England had begun only three years earlier and hardly any were in service. Fifty years later, although there were still a couple of galleys in service, the carrack had almost completely disappeared. In 1600 Sir William Monson wrote:

> There are two manner of ships built; the one with a flush deck, fore and aft, snug and low by the water, the other lofty and high charged, with half deck, forecastle and cobridge heads. The ship with a flush deck I hold good to fight in, if she be a fast ship by the wind and keep herself from boarding ....[53]

The flush-decked ship was the galleon, with lines modelled on those of the earlier galleass, but without oars, while the high-charged ship was the direct descendant of the carrack, a style no longer favoured except for the very largest vessels, where speed and manoeuvrability were hardly factors.[54] The average sailing speed of a warship was much higher in 1600 than it had been in 1545, and her guns were far more lethal. In place of the earlier miscellany, the warship of the 1590s was equipped with matching sets of culverins and demi-culverins, which had both longer range and higher muzzle velocity. They were also much more likely to have been made in England, because English gunfounding had developed by leaps and bounds after about 1550, and the need for imported weaponry had virtually disappeared. Even a private warship, like that which foundered off Alderney in 1592, and which displaced no more than about 150 tons, was equipped with a matching set of guns, all of English manufacture.[55] Many of these developments, both of tactics and of gunnery, had been initiated by the privateers before they were adopted by the navy. A privateer's success would depend upon its ability not only to out-sail its prey, but also to escape from hostile warships if any pursuit should be attempted; and its guns were essential items of equipment, upon which captures depended. It was no accident that men like Drake, Hawkins and Frobisher had many years of privateering experience behind them before they entered the queen's service.

At the same time the strategic range of the navy had also been transformed. Again this owed much to the privateers, or pirates as they should more properly be termed. Ambiguous operations like those of John Hawkins in the 1560s introduced the ships of the royal navy to the Caribbean, and to other parts of the New World where they would never legitimately have come. Henry VIII had never been much interested in long-distance voyages, and the so-called Merchant Adventurers had been more concerned with defending their position in Antwerp, and in bickering with the Hanseatic League. Sir Thomas Spert had been to Brazil in 1526, William Hawkins in 1530 and 1531, Robert Reniger and William Hawkins again in 1540, and one Pudsey had even built a fort there in 1542.[56] However, none of these ventures had attracted either royal or corporate backing, and apart from Hawkins's voyage of 1540 are poorly documented. There seem to have been other voyages to the west coast of Africa, and there was a regular trade with the Levant before it was cut off by Ottoman expansion in the early years of the century. Sebastian Cabot had wanted to maintain his father's links with England, but the king gave him no encouragement, and he entered the service of the Emperor Charles V in the 1520s. Henry was deeply interested in warships, and was at war with France until almost the end of his life, but he showed no interest in the merchant marine. He leased out some of his ships to merchants in the traditional manner, if they were not otherwise in use, and took up merchantmen for victualling and other support roles as they might be needed, but it does not seem to have occurred to him that he could 'invest' either ships or money in private enterprises. He was also very much concerned that sea-power should be a state monopoly, and the private war ship, which had been such a feature of the civil wars of the fifteenth century, did not return during his lifetime.

However, no sooner was Henry dead than the seascape began to change. Even the conservative Merchant Adventurers were beginning to get uneasy about their dependence upon Antwerp, and that unease was increased when the religious policies of the Protectorate (which were generally popular in

London) led inevitably to strained relations with the Emperor. In 1548 the ageing but still active Sebastian Cabot came back to England. He may have fallen out with the Inquisition in Spain, but it is more likely that he was invited, either by the earl of Warwick, the Lord Admiral or by an anonymous group of London merchants.[57] Charles V was most upset by the loss of his Pilot Major, and refused at first to believe that he had come of his own free will. He brought with him all the secrets of the *Casa de Contratacion*, and that was a serious blow to Spanish Imperial interests. It is unlikely that his invitation could have come directly from the king or the Lord Protector, who were showing at this stage no more interest in commercial affairs than Henry VIII had done. However in October 1549 the duke of Somerset fell from power, and after a few months the earl of Warwick replaced him. Sebastian Cabot was given a pension, and encouraged to begin re-directing the energies of the London merchants. In this he was greatly assisted by events in Antwerp, where the English cloth market had seriously overheated. The debasement of the English currency by Henry VIII and Somerset had made the cloth 'good cheap', and dramatically increased demand. Overstimulated, the industry had increased production to the point at which the market had become saturated, and at that point attempts to redeem the English coinage had caused an increase in prices. The result was a temporary collapse, and a trade which had been worth £300,000 a year went into sharp recession.[58] This was Cabot's chance to make his point about the need for diversification, and he did so to good effect.

The result was the Willoughby/Chancellor voyage of 1553, which was funded by a mixture of London merchants and courtiers, led by the earl of Warwick. After Warwick's death the Muscovy Company was founded in 1555 on the basis of Chancellor's success, and Sebastian Cabot become the governor. Had he lived, Edward VI might well have become personally involved, but he died in July 1553 and his sister and successor, Mary, was no more interested in commerce than her father had been. However, a fuse had been lit in London which was burning steadily. The Muscovy Company was small beer. Much more promising were the prospects of trade with Portuguese Guinea and with the Spanish New World, opened up by Mary's marriage to Philip of Spain. Unfortunately, Philip did not see things in that light. He forbade access to the American colonies, and did his best to prevent trade with Guinea, which was not under his direct control. This attitude, among other things, made him seriously unpopular in London, and inhibited commercial and political relations between the City and the Crown.[59] What might have resulted if Mary had lived we do not know, but she died in her turn on 17 November 1558, and her successor Elizabeth immediately returned relations with London to where they had been under Edward and the earl of Warwick (or duke of Northumberland as he eventually became). Sir William Cecil, the new Principal Secretary, had strong City links, and a new direction of royal policy was soon apparent. As we have seen, this resulted in unprecedented partnership arrangements between the queen, her courtiers and the London merchants. Royal ships began to be used, not on a hiring basis, but as part of an investment. Captains had always been amphibians between royal and private service, and Sir Thomas Wyndham, the Master of Naval Ordnance had died in the course of a private trading voyage to West Africa in 1553, but their status now became even more ambiguous. It became quite normal for officers in charge of the queen's warships to have experience of long-distance oceanic voyages in a way which they would never have done in earlier generations.

Experience of 'adventuring' also expanded in other ways. Royal captains who were also merchants had been common for years, but men like John Hawkins were not merchants in any normal sense. They were pirates, and contributed substantially to that deterioration in relations with Spain which Elizabeth seemed at the same time so anxious to prevent. They were also master navigators and great sea fighters. So the first twenty-five years of Elizabeth's reign saw not only a radical diversification of English trade, but also the flourishing of a new sort of semi-recognised pirate, and the return of the private warship which Henry VIII had been so concerned to eliminate. The queen's capacity to sustain such apparently contradictory policies over so many years was a mark of her greatness as a ruler. It is also probable that only a woman could have done it, making skilful use, as she did, of contemporary gender stereotypes.[60] As a result, when war came, the navy had the ability and the capacity to think both expansively and aggressively. Drake's expedition to the West Indies in 1585 was the first time that the royal navy had been deployed officially outside European waters, but it was an experience which must have seemed familiar to many of those who took part. Similarly, when he attacked Vigo on the same voyage, it was the first time that the ships of the navy had attacked the coast of Europe without a military presence. By 1590 a wholly separate naval strategy had been evolved to control the Atlantic – one which in the near future would be known as 'blue water' – which depended entirely upon ships and guns. In 1601 Sir William Monson presented to Sir Robert Cecil, by that time Principal Secretary, an exposition of this strategy, entitled 'A project how to make war upon Spain'.

'Our only security', he wrote,

> must be to cut off Spain's forces by sea seeing their means of invasion and strength of defence depends upon their shipping .... First and principally, we must keep employed two main fleets upon the coasts of Spain eight months of the year, that is, from March to November.

> Every fleet to consist of 45 ships, be divided into three squadrons, one to lie off the Rock [Cape Roca] to intercept all traders of Lisbon; the second off the South Cape to stop all intercourse to San Lucar and Cadiz, and to and from the Indies; the third to the [Canary] Islands .... Our fleet being thus divided, no army at sea can be prepared, or at least gathered to a head, but we shall intercept them. We shall not only debar the Spaniards and Portuguese their own trade, but all nations to them ....[61]

In other words, a blockade. Not of the partial sort envisaged by John Hawkins in 1590, but a full blockade. As Sir William admitted, such a policy might turn out to be too ambitious for the queen's resources, but the fact that he was thinking in that way was significant. Even Drake and Hawkins had not been so ambitious as to think that they could sever all Spain's communications by sea, but Monson was right – that was the way to victory over such a powerful adversary.

The early seventeenth century was not to be a flourishing time for the royal navy, but when commerce and politics again united to give a priority to the fleet, under the protectorate of Oliver Cromwell, the Admiralty was able to pick up the threads where Howard and Drake, and Hawkins and Monson, had laid them down.[62] By then Spain was not the Great Enemy, but that was not the point. In the reign of Elizabeth England had briefly been a great naval power, and when that momentum was renewed in the time of Samuel Pepys, Britannia began to rule the waves.

CHAPTER 10 NOTES

1. TNA SP12/218, nos 51–2. F.C. Dietz, *English Public Finance, 1559–1641*, pp. 439–41.
2. R.B. Wernham, *The Expedition of Sir John Norris and Sir Francis Drake to Spain and Portugal, 1589* (NRS, 1988), p. xiii.
3. 'Notes of the charge of Sir John Norris journey, and Sir Francis Drake, at St. James's', 20 September 1588. TNA SP12/216, no. 33.
4. BL Harley MS 296, f.203. Wernham, *Expedition*, pp. 7–8.
5. 'A proportion to be furnished by Her Majesty of all sorts of provision for the enterprise of Portugal', September 1588. TNA SP12/217, no. 69.
6. *Calendar of State Papers, Venetian*, VIII, pp. 394–6. See also Edmund Palmer to Sir Francis Walsingham, 29 September 1588, Wernham, *Expedition*, p. 15.
7. Richard Hakluyt, *The Principal Navigations ... of the English Nation* (edn. 1927), VIII, p. 279.
8. Wernham, *Expedition*, p. xxiii.
9. *Historical Manuscripts Commission*, Ancaster MSS (1907), p. 227.
10. She sent a revised list for the withdrawals to Willoughby on 27 January. Wernham, *Expedition*, pp. 73–4.

11. She paid Norris £11,678 for five months' victuals and summer apparel. Ibid., pp. 90–1.
12. 'Instructions for Sir John Norris and Sir Francis Drake', 23 February 1589. TNA SP12/222, no. 89.
13. Wernham, *Expedition,* pp. xxxix–xl.
14. Anthony Ashley to the Council, 7 May 1589. TNA SP12/224, no. 14. The queen's response, written on 20 May, did not reach the commanders until 6 June.
15. See the earl of Essex's 'Apology'. TNA SP12/269, f.103.
16. 'The charges against Norris and Drake and their answers', 23 October 1589. TNA SP12/227, no. 35.
17. Wernham, *Expedition,* p. liv.
18. Queen to Norris and Drake, 7 July 1589. TNA SP12/225, no. 15. It was not until October that the extent of the failure became clear. See 'The charges against Norris and Drake …'.
19. Loades and Knighton, *Elizabethan Naval Administration,* section 8, Introduction.
20. The *Ark Raleigh, Mary Rose, Nonpareil, Rainbow, Swiftsure* and *Foresight.* TNA SP12/230, no. 35.
21. Hawkins to Burghley, 31 October 1590. TNA SP12/233, no. 118. See also Monson, *Tracts,* I, p. 250.
22. PL MS 513. See also Loades and Knighton, *Elizabethan Naval Administration,* section 8.
23. PL 513. *ENA,* 8(a).
24. TNA SP12/230, no. 66. SP15/13, no. 132.
25. PL 513, *ENA,* 8(a).
26. Ibid.
27. TNA SP12/156, ff.88–90. *British Naval Documents,* pp. 1207–9.
28. See above, p. 141. 'The taking of the Madre de Dios, Anno 1592', ed. C.L Kingsford, *Naval Miscellany,* II (NRS, 1912), pp. 85–122.
29. Peter Earle, *The Last Fight of the Revenge* (1992) gives a comprehensive account of this incident.
30. Robert Dickinson, 'The Spanish Raid on Mount's Bay in 1595', *Journal of the Royal Institution of Cornwall,* ns X (1987–90), pp. 178–86.
31. For a full account of Norris's campaigns in Brittany, see John S. Nolan, *Sir John Norreys and the Elizabethan Military World* (1997), pp. 180–217.
32. Ibid., pp. 216–17. See also the map drawn by Norris. TNA, MPF 278 A.
33. Loades, *Tudor Navy,* p. 262. For a full account of this last expedition, see Kelsey, *Sir Francis Drake,* pp. 377–91.
34. Kelsey, *Sir Francis Drake,* p. 381.
35. Richard Hakluyt, *The Third and Last Volume of the Voyages … of the English Nation* (1600), p. 585. 'The voyage truly discoursed'.
36. Loades, *Tudor Navy,* p. 263.
37. Stephen and Elizabeth Usherwood, *The Counter Armada, 1596* (1983), pp. 22–3.
38. Ibid., pp. 39–42.
39. Loades, *Tudor Navy,* p. 263.
40. BL Cotton MS Otho E.IX, f.313. Usherwood, *The Counter Armada,* p. 18.
41. Usherwood, *The Counter Armada,* pp. 30–2.
42. W. Laird Clowes, *The Royal Navy. A History,* I (1897), p. 512.

43. Lambeth Palace Codex 250, ff.352–3. Usherwood, *The Counter Armada*, pp. 68–9.
44. Usherwood, *The Counter Armada*, pp. 84–6.
45. Loades, *Tudor Navy*, p. 265. Parker and Martin, *The Spanish Armada*, pp. 133–56.
46. Laird Clowes, *The Royal Navy*, p. 516.
47. Usherwood, *The Counter Armada*, p. 94.
48. A.P. McGowan, *The Jacobean Commissions of Enquiry, 1608 and 1618* (NRS, 1971), Introduction.
49. Loades, *Tudor Navy*, p. 266 and note.
50. Ibid.
51. J.J. Silke, *Kinsale: The Spanish Intervention in Ireland at the End of the Elizabethan Wars* (1970).
52. These burning forays characterised all of Henry VIII's wars, but in each case the ships were used simply to carry the troops to the point of operations. These raids were never resisted at sea.
53. From 'How to fight at sea, one ship with another …', by Sir William Monson. M. Oppenheim, *The Naval Tracts of Sir William Monson*, IV, pp. 91–3.
54. The *Prince Royal*, built by Phineas Pett in 1610, which was a heavily armed three-decker, was a good example of these later 'high charged' ships. Rodger, *Safeguard of the Sea*, pp. 386–8.
55. Jason Monaghan and Mensun Bound, *A Ship Cast Away about Alderney* (2001), pp. 65–76; and subsequent work.
56. R.G. Marsden, 'The Voyage of the Barbara to Brazil, Anno. 1540'. *Naval Miscellany*, II, p. 3.
57. *ODNB*.
58. Loades, *England's Maritime Empire* (2000), pp. 53–5. R. Davis, *English Overseas Trade, 1500–1700* (1973).
59. Loades, 'Philip II as King of England', in *Law and Government under the Tudors: Essays Presented to Sir Geoffrey Elton*, ed. C. Cross et al. (1988).
60. For Elizabeth's gender manipulations, see Philippa Berry, *Of Chastity and Power: Elizabethan Literature and the Virgin Queen* (1989).
61. Oppenheim, *The Naval Tracts of Sir William Monson*, V, pp. 53–6. *British Naval Documents*, pp. 75–6.
62. Bernard Capp, *Cromwell's Navy* (1989).

Bibliography

Standard Abbreviations

AGI	Archivo de Indias, Seville
AGS	Archivo General, Simancas
AHN	Archivo Historico Nacional, Madrid
APC	*Acts of the Privy Council*
BL	The British Library
Bod	The Bodleian Library, Oxford
Cal. Span.	*Calendar of State Papers, Spanish*
ENA	*Elizabethan Naval Administration*
HMC	Historical Manuscripts Commission
NRS	Navy Records Society
ODNB	*Oxford Dictionary of National Biography*
PL	The Pepys Library, Magdalene College, Cambridge
RSTC	*Revised Short Title Catalogue*
TNA	The National Archives

Manuscripts

The National Archive, Kew
AO1
C47, C66
E28, E36, E101, E133, E403
MPF 278A
PC2
SP1, SP10, SP11, SP12, SP47, SP50, SP62, SP68, SP69, SP94

The British Library
Add. 9294, 11405, 22047, 32654, 48126
Arundel 97
Cotton Otho E.VIII, E.IX; Galba C.VIII
Harley 280, 284, 296, 540, 2202, 7383,
Lansdowne 52, 62, 70, 145, 157, 1225,
Royal 7C, 14A, 14B

The Bodleian Library, Oxford
Ashmole 861
Rawlinsion A.192, A.200, A.201, A.202, A.203, C.171
Tanner 241.

Pepys Library, Magdalene College, Cambridge
513, 1266, 2820, 2875, 2876, 2991

Lambeth Palace Library
605, Codex 250.

CONTEMPORARY PRINTED WORKS

Walter Bigges, *A Summarie and True Discourse of Sir Francis Drakes West Indian Voyage* (London, 1589) [*RSTC* 3056]

John Dee, *General and rare monuments pertaining to the perfect Arte of Navigation* (London, 1577) [*RSTC* 6459]

Richard Hakluyt, *The Principall navigacions, voyages, and discoveries of the English Nation* (London, 1589) [*RSTC* 12625]

Richard Hakluyt, *The Third and Last volume of the voyages ... of the English Nation* (London, 1600) [*RSTC* 12626]

Edward Hall, *The Union of the two noble and illustre houses of York and Lancaster* (London, 1548) [*RSTC* 12721]

John Hawkins, *A True Declaration of the Troublesome Voyadge to the parties of Guynea and the West Indies* (London, 1569) [*RSTC* 12961]

Raphael Holinshed, *Chronicles etc.* (London, 1577, 1587) [*RSTC* 13568, 13569]

Job Hortop, *The Rare Travails of Job Hortop* (London, 1591) [*RSTC* 13827.5]

William Patten, *The Expedition into Scotland of the most worthily fortunate Prince, Edward, Duke of Somerset* (London, 1548). Reprinted in A.F. Pollard, *Tudor Tracts* (London, 1903), pp. 53–157 [*RSTC* 19476.5]

John Stow, *The Annals of England, Faithfully Collected ....* (London, 1592) [*RSTC* 23334]

The Late Expedition in Scotland ... the year of our Lord God 1544 (London, 1544). Reprinted in Pollard, *Tudor Tracts*, pp. 37–51 [*RSTC* 22270]

The World Encompassed by Sir Francis Drake (London, 1628) [*RSTC* 7161]

CALENDARS AND PRINTED DOCUMENTS

S. Adams, ed., 'New Light on the "Reformation" of John Hawkins: The Ellesmere Naval Survey of 1584', *English Historical Review*, 105, 1991, pp. 97–111.

S. Adams and M-J. Rodriguez Salgado, eds, 'The Count of Feria's Despatch of 14th November 1558', *Camden Miscellany*, XXVIII, 1984.

Acts of the Privy Council, ed. J.R. Dasent (London, 1890–1907).

The Anthony Roll of Henry VIII, ed. D. Loades and C.S. Knighton (NRS, Aldershot, 2000).

B.L. Beer and S.M. Jack, eds, *The Letters of William, Lord Paget of Beaudesert, 1547–1563*. Camden Society, 4th series, XIII, 1974.

F.B. Bickley, ed., *The Little Red Book of Bristol* (Edinburgh, 1900).

British Naval Documents, 1204–1960, ed. J.B. Hattendorf et al. (NRS, Aldershot, 1993).

Calendar of State Papers, Domestic, Edward VI, ed. C.S. Knighton (London, 1992).

Calendar of State Papers, Domestic, Mary ed. C.S. Knighton (London, 1998).

Calendar of State Papers, Foreign, Edward VI, and Mary (London, 1861–3).

Calendar of State Papers ... of the reign of Elizabeth (London, 1913–21).

Calendar of State Papers Spanish, Elizabeth (London, 1892–9).

Calendar of State Papers, Venetian (London, 1864–98).

Calendar of the Patent Rolls, Edward VI (London, 1924–9).

Calendar of the Patent Rolls, Philip and Mary (London, 1936–9).

William Cobbett, *State Trials* (London, 1816–98).

The Debate Between the Heralds of England and France, ed. Henry Pyne (London, 1870).

Elizabeth Donno, ed., *An Elizabethan in 1582: The Diary of Richard Maddox, Fellow of All Souls*. Hakluyt Society, 2nd series, 147, 1976.

Elizabeth I: Collected Works, ed. L.S. Marcus, J. Mueller and M.B. Rose (Chicago, 2000).

Fighting Instructions, 1530–1816, ed. Sir Julian Corbett (NRS, London, 1905).

Hale and Fleetwood on Admiralty Jurisdiction, ed. M.J. Pritchard and D.E.C. Yale (Selden Society, London, 1993).

S. Haynes, *State Papers of William Cecil, Lord Burghley* (London, 1740–59).

Historical Manuscripts Commission, 13th and 17th Reports. Ancaster MSS (London, 1907).

Clarence Hopper, ed., 'Robert Leng's True Description of the last voiage of that Worthy Captayne Sir Francis Drake', *Camden Miscellany*, V, 1864.

P.L. Hughes and J.F. Larkin, *Tudor Royal Proclamations* (New Haven, Yale University Press, 1964–9).

W.K. Jordan, *The Chronicle and Political Papers of King Edward VI* (London, Allen & Unwin, 1966).

C.L. Kingsford, ed., 'The Taking of the Madre de Dios, Anno 1592', in *Naval Miscellany*, II, ed. J.K. Laughton (NRS, London, 1912).

Letters and Papers ... of the Reign of Henry VIII, ed. J. Gairdner *et al.* (London, 1862–1910).

Letters and Papers Relating to the War with France, 1512–1513, ed Alfred Spont (NRS, London, 1897).

David Loades and C.S. Knighton, 'Lord Admiral Lisle and the Invasion of Scotland, 1544', *Naval Miscellany*, VII, ed. Susan Rose (2008).

David Loades and C.S. Knighton, *Elizabethan Naval Administration* (NRS, forthcoming).

D. MacCulloch, ed., 'The Vitae Mariae Angliae Reginae of Robert Wingfield of Brantham', *Camden Miscellany*, XXVIII, 1984.

A.P. McGowan, ed., *The Jacobean Commissions of Enquiry, 1608, 1618* (NRS, London, 1971).

R.G. Marsden, ed., 'The Voyage of the Barbara to Brazil, Anno 1540', in *Naval Miscellany*, II, ed. J.K. Laughton (NRS, London, 1912).

G.P. Naish, 'Spanish Documents Relating to the Armada', *Naval Miscellany*, IV (NRS, London, 1952).

Naval Accounts and Inventories of the Reign of Henry VII, ed. M. Oppenheim (NRS, London, 1896).

The Navy of the Lancastrian Kings, ed. Susan Rose (NRS, London, Allen & Unwin, 1982).

J.G. Nichols, ed., *The Chronicle of Queen Jane and of the first two years of Mary*, Camden Society, XLVIII, 1850.

J.G. Nichols, ed., *The Diary of Henry Machyn*, Camden Society, XLII, 1848.

Zelia Nuttall, ed., *New Light on Drake: A Collection of Documents relating to his Voyage of Circumnavigation, 1577–1580*, Hakluyt Society, 2nd series, 34, 1914.

M. Oppenheim, ed., *Sir William Monson's Naval Tracts* (NRS, London, 1902–14).

Papers Relating to the Navy during the Spanish War, 1585–1587, ed. Sir Julian Corbett (NRS, London, 1898).

D.L. Potter, 'Documents concerning the Negotiation of the Anglo-French Treaty of March 1550', *Camden Miscellany*, XXVIII, 1984, pp. 59–180.

Revised Short Title Catalogue of Books Printed in England, Scotland and Ireland, and of English Books Printed Abroad, 1475–1640, ed. W.A. Jackson, F.S. Ferguson and K.F. Pantzer (London, 1976–86).

W.C. Richardson, ed., *The Report of the Royal Commission of 1552* (Morganstown, WV, 1974).

The State Papers of Henry VIII (London, 1830–52).

Statutes of the Realm, ed. A. Luders *et al.* (London, 1810–28).

J. Strype, *Ecclesiastical Memorials* (Oxford, 1822).

E.G.R. Taylor, ed., *The Troublesome Voyage of captain Edward Fenton, 1582–3*, Hakluyt Society, 2nd series, 113, 1959.

R.B. Wernham, ed., *The Expedition of Sir John Norris and Sir Francis Drake to Spain and Portugal, 1589* (NRS, Aldershot, 1988).

I.A. Wright, ed., *Discourses concerning English Voyages to the Spanish Main, 1569–1580* (Hakluyt Society, 1932).

Irene Wright, ed., *Further English Voyages of Spanish America*, Hakluyt Society, 2nd series, 99, 1951.

Secondary Works: Books

K.R. Andrews, *Elizabethan Privateering* (Cambridge, Cambridge University Press, 1964).

K.R. Andrews, *Drake's Voyages: A Reassessment of their Place in England's Maritime Expansion* (London, Weidenfeld and Nicholson, 1967).

Philippa Berry, *Of Chastity and Power: Elizabethan Literature and the Virgin Queen* (London, Routledge, 1989).

J.B. Black, *The Reign of Elizabeth* (Oxford, Oxford University Press, 1959).

Dorothy Burwash, *English Merchant Shipping, 1460–1540* (Newton Abbot, David & Charles, 1947/1969).

M.L. Bush, *The Government Policy of Protector Somerset* (Manchester, University Press, 1975).

Bernard Capp, *Cromwell's Navy* (Oxford, Oxford University Press, 1989).

J. Charnock, *The History of Marine Architecture* (London, 1802).

W. Laird Clowes, *The Royal Navy: A History from the Earliest Times to the Present* (London, Little, Brown and Low, 1897–1903).

D.C. Coleman, *The Economy of England, 1450–1750* (Oxford, Oxford University Press, 1977).

H.M. Colvin, *The History of the King's Works* (Oxford, Oxford University Press, 1963–76), Vol. IV.

G. Connell-Smith, *Forerunners of Drake* (London, Longman, Green and Co., 1954).

Ralph Davis, *English Overseas Trade, 1500–1700* (London, Macmillian, 1973).

J.E.A. Dawson, *The Politics of Religion in the Age of Mary Queen of Scots* (Cambridge, Cambridge University Press, 2002).

F.C. Dietz, *English Public Finance, 1558–1640* (New York/London, Frank Cass, 1932/1964).

J. Doyle and B. Moore, *England and the Spanish Armada* (Canberra, A.C.T., 1990).

Peter Earle, *The Last Fight of the Revenge* (London, Collins and Brown, 1992).

C. Fernandez Duro, *La Armada Invencible* (Madrid, 1884–5).

M.C. Fissell, *English Warfare, 1511–1642* (London, Routledge, 2001).

Sir William Foster, *England's Quest of Eastern Trade* (London, A. and C. Black, 1933).

P.J. French, *John Dee: The World of an Elizabethan Magus* (London, Routledge, 1973).

Cheryl A. Fury, *Tides in the Affairs of Men: A Social History of Elizabethan Seamen, 1580–1603* (Westport, Conn., 2002).

J.F. Guilmartin, *Gunpowder and Galleys: Changing Technology and Mediterranean Warfare at Sea in the Sixteenth Century* (Cambridge, Cambridge University Press, 1974).

P. Gwyn, *The King's Cardinal* (London, Barrie & Jenkins, 1990).

Jonathan Isreal, *The Dutch Republic ...1477–1806* (Oxford, Oxford University Press, 1995).

W.K. Jordan, *Edward VI: The Young King* (London, Allen & Unwin, 1967).

W.K. Jordan, *Edward VI: The Threshold of Power* (London, Allen & Unwin, 1970).

Harry Kelsey, *Sir Francis Drake: The Queen's Pirate* (New Haven, Yale University Press, 1998).

Harry Kelsey, *Sir John Hawkins: Queen Elizabeth's Slave Trader* (New Haven, Yale University Press, 2003).

Peter Kirsch, *The Galleon* (London, Conway, 1990).

C.S. Knighton and D. Loades, *Letters from the Mary Rose* (Stroud, Sutton, 2002).

D. Loades, *Two Tudor Conspiracies* (Cambridge, Cambridge University Press, 1965).

D. Loades, *The Reign of Mary Tudor* (London, Longmans, 1991).

D. Loades, *The Tudor Navy* (Aldershot, Scolar, 1992).

D. Loades, *John Dudley, Duke of Northumberland* (Oxford, Oxford University Press, 1996).

D. Loades, *England's Maritime Empire ... 1490–1690* (London, Longmans, 2000).

D. Loades, *Elizabeth I* (London, Hambledon, 2003).

D. Loades, *The Cecils: Privilege and Power behind the Throne* (London, TNA, 2007).

D. Loades, *Henry VIII: Court, Church and Conflict* (London, TNA, 2007).

D. Loades, *The Life and Career of William Paulet, First Marquis of Winchester* (Aldershot, Ashgate, 2008).

Wallace Maccaffrey, *Queen Elizabeth and the Making of Policy, 1572–1588* (Princeton, 1981).

D. MacCulloch, *Thomas Cranmer* (New Haven, Yale University Press, 1996).

C. Martin, *Full Fathom Five: Wrecks of the Spanish Armada* (London, Chatto and Windus, 1978).

Garrett Mattingly, *Catherine of Aragon* (London, Cape, 1963).

Garrett Mattingly, *The Defeat of the Spanish Armada* (London, Cape, 1959).

Marcus Merriman, *The Rough Wooing* (East Linton, 2003).

J. Monaghan and M. Bound, *A Ship Cast Away about Alderney* (Alderney, The Trustees, 2001).

B. Murphy, *Bastard Prince: Henry VIII's Lost Son* (Stroud, Sutton, 2001).

J.S. Nolan, *Sir John Norreys and the Elizabethan Military World* (Exeter, University Press, 1997).

M. Oppenheim, *A History of the Administration of the Royal Navy, 1509–1660* (London, Temple Smith, 1896/1988).

Oxford Dictionary of National Biography (2004).

Peter Padfield, *Guns at Sea* (London, H. Evelyn, 1973).

G. Parker and C. Martin, *The Spanish Armada* (London, Hamish Hamilton, 1988).

Gervase Phillips, *The Anglo-Scottish Wars, 1511–1550* (Woodbridge, Boydell & Brewer, 1999).

Peter Pierson, *Commander of the Armada: The Seventh Duke of Medina Sidonia* (New Haven, Yale University Press, 1989).

Conyers Read, *Mr. Secretary Walsingham and the Policy of Queen Elizabeth* (Oxford, Oxford University Press, 1925).

Conyers Read, *Mr. Secretary Cecil and Queen Elizabeth* (London, Cape, 1955).

W.C. Richardson, *Stephen Vaughn* (Baton Rouge, Louisiana State U.P., 1953).

N.A.M. Rodger, *The Safeguard of the Sea* (London, HarperCollins, 1997).

M.-J. Rodriguez Salgado, *Armada, 1588–1988: An International Exhibition to Commemorate the Spanish Armada* (London, National Maritime Museum, 1988).

M-J. Rodriguez Salgado and Simon Adams, *England, Spain and the Gran Armada, 1585–1604* (Edinburgh, Donald, 1991).

Margaret Rule, *The Mary Rose* (London, Conway, 1982).

J.J. Silke, *Kinsale: The Spanish Intervention in Ireland at the End of the Elizabethan Wars* (Liverpool, University Press, 1970).

R.T. Spence, *The Privateering Earl* (Stroud, Sutton, 1995).

N.M. Sutherland, *Princes, Politics and Religion, 1547–1589* (London, Hambledon, 1984).

Stephen and Elizabeth Usherwood, *The Counter Armada, 1596* (London, Bodley Head, 1983).

H. Van der Wee, *The Growth of the Antwerp Money Market and the European Economy* (The Hague, Nijhoff, 1963).

Retha Warnicke, *The Marrying of Anne of Cleves* (Cambridge, Cambridge University Press, 2000).

D.W. Waters, *The Elizabethan Navy and the Armada of Spain* (London, National Maritime Museum, 1975).

N.J. Williams, *The Maritime Trade of the East Anglian Ports, 1550–1590* (Oxford, Oxford University Press, 1988).

J.A. Williamson, *The Age of Drake* (London, Black, 1946).

Derek Wilson, *Sweet Robin: A Biography of Robert Dudley, Earl of Leicester, 1533–1588* (London, Hamish Hamilton, 1981).

Allegra Woodworth, *Purveyance for the Royal Household in the Reign of Queen Elizabeth* (Transactions of the American Philosophical Society, 1945).

J. Wormald, *Mary Queen of Scots: A Study in Failure* (London, Philip, 1988).

Gaston Zeller, *Les Institutions de la France au XVIe siecle* (Paris, 1948).

Articles and Papers

J.D. Alsop, 'The Revenue Commission of 1552', *Historical Journal*, 22, 1979, pp. 511–33.

J.D. Alsop, 'A Regime at Sea: The Navy and the 1553 Succession Crisis', *Albion*, 24, 1992, pp. 583–8.

R.C. Anderson, 'Henry VIII's Great Galley', *Mariners Mirror*, 6, 1920, pp. 274–81.

K.R. Andrews, 'The Aims of Drake's Expedition of 1577–80', *American Historical Review*, 73, 1968, pp. 724–41.

Richard Boulind, 'Ships of Private Origin in the Mid-Tudor Navy', *Mariners Mirror*, 59, 1973, pp. 385–408.

R. Pearce Chope, 'New Light on Sir Richard Grenville', *Transactions of the Devon Association*, 49, 1917, pp. 210–82.

C.S.L. Davies, 'The Administration of the Royal Navy under Henry VIII: The Origins of the Navy Board', *English Historical Review*, 80, 1965, pp. 268–88.

C.S.L. Davies, 'England and the French War, 1557–9', in *The Mid-Tudor Polity, 1540–1560*, ed. J. Loach and R. Tittler (1981).

Robert Dickinson, 'The Spanish Raid on Mounts Bay in 1595', *Journal of the Royal Institution of Cornwall*, n.s. 10 (1987–90), pp. 178–86.

B. Dietz, 'The Royal Bounty and English Shipping in the Sixteenth and Seventeenth Centuries', *Mariners Mirror*, 77, 1991, pp. 5–21.

F.E. Dyer, 'Reprisals in the Sixteenth Century', *Mariners Mirror*, 21, 1935, pp. 187–97.

T. Glasgow jnr, 'The Navy in Philip and Mary's War', *Mariners Mirror*, 53, 1967, pp. 321–42.

T. Glasgow jnr, 'The Navy in the Le Havre Campaign, 1562–4', *Mariners Mirror*, 54, 1968, pp. 281–96

T. Glasgow jnr, 'The Maturing of Naval Administration, 1556–1564', *Mariners Mirror*, 56, 1970, pp. 3–26.

J.A. Guy, 'The Privy Council; Revolution or Evolution?' in *Revolution Reassessed: Revisions in the History of Tudor Government and Administration*, ed. C. Coleman and D. Starkey (Oxford, Oxford University Press, 1986).

E.W. Ives, 'Henry VIII's Will: A Forensic Conundrum', *Historical Journal*, 35, 1992, pp. 779–84.

D. Loades, 'Philip II as King of England', in *Law and Government under the Tudors*, ed. C. Cross, D. Loades, and J. Scarisbrick (Cambridge, Cambridge University Press, 1988).

D. Loades, 'The King's Ships and the Keeping of the Seas, 1413–1480', *Medieval History*, 1, 1991, pp. 93–104.

R.G. Marsden, 'The Vice Admirals of the Coasts', *English Historical Review*, 22, 1907, pp. 468–77.

Graham Nicholson, 'The Act of Appeals and the English Reformation', in *Law and Government under the Tudors*, ed. C. Cross, D. Loades, and J. Scarisbrick (Cambridge, Cambridge University Press, 1988).

J.H. Pollen, 'Mary Queen of Scots and the Babington Plot', *Scottish Historical Society*, 3rd series, 3, 1922.

M. Prestwich, 'Calvinism in France, 1559–1629', in *International Calvinism, 1541–1715*, ed. M. Prestwich (Oxford, Oxford University Press, 1985).

Conyers Read, 'Queen Elizabeth's Seizure of Alba's Pay Ships', *Journal of Modern History*, 5, 1933, pp. 443–64.

C.F. Richmond, 'The Keeping of the Seas during the Hundred Years War', *History*, 49, 1964, pp. 283–98.

C.F. Richmond, 'English Naval Power in the Fifteenth Century', *History*, 52, 1967, pp. 1–15.

M.H. Rule and C.T.C. Dobbs, 'The Tudor Warship Mary Rose: Aspects of Recent Research', in *The Archaeology of the Ship*, ed. M. Bound (London, 1995), pp. 26–9.

W. Salisbury, 'Early Tonnage Measurements in England', *Mariners Mirror*, 52, 1966.

G.V. Scammell, 'Manning the English Merchant Service in the Sixteenth Century', *Mariners Mirror*, 56, 1970, pp. 131–54.

R.D. Smith, 'Artillery and the Hundred Years War. Myth and Interpretation', in *Arms, Armies and Fortifications during the Hundred Years War*, ed. Anne Curry and Michael Hughes (Woodbridge, Boydell, 1994).

E.K. Thompson, 'English and Spanish Tonnage in 1588', *Mariners Mirror*, 46, 1959.

I.A.A. Thompson, 'Spanish Armada Guns', *Mariners Mirror*, 61, 1975, pp. 355–71.

I.A.A. Thompson, 'The Invincible Armada', in *Royal Armada* (Manorial Research, 1988).

H.C. Tomlinson, 'The Ordnance Office and the Navy', *English Historical Review*, 90, 1975, pp. 19–39.

S.M. Vine, 'Some Aspects of Deck Construction in the Mary Rose', *Proceedings of the Third Annual Conference for New Researchers in Maritime History* (London, 1995).

Index

Admiralty court 1, 20, 110, 112, 115, 116, 138, 139, 141
   lawful prize in 138, 141
   solicitor of 139
Alderney, Isle of 219
Allen, Thomas 159
Anian, Strait of (mythical) 168
Ancrum Moor, battle of 25
Anne of Cleves, Queen of England 12
Antwerp 32, 74, 75, 113, 198, 219, 220
Anthony, Anthony 33, 34
   Anthony Roll 33, 34, 35, 65, 72
Anthony, William 34
Antonio, Dom, Portuguese Pretender 171, 173, 206, 207, 208, 209
   his supporters 209
Arran, Isle of 96
Armada of Spain 52, 121, 130, 140, 149, 150, 151, 152, 180, 181, 185, 187, 190–7, 199, 200, 202, 206, 212, 213, 217
   cost of 216
   guns of 192
   India Guard 191
   logistics 192
   soldiers 192, 199
   urcas or hulks 193, 194
Ashton, Christopher 87, 88
Ashley, Anthony 208, 209
Atlantic, control of 93, 221
Audley, Sir Thomas 30, 94

Baeshe, Edward, Surveyor General of the Victuals 46, 49, 50, 51, 71, 79, 81, 85, 91, 94, 120, 134, 136, 146, 147, 150, 151, 152, 157
   extraordinary payments to 136
   his contract 135, 137 147
   his 'Opinion' 134
Bayona 174, 180, 210

Beaton, David, Cardinal Archbishop of St. Andrews 15, 23, 25, 57
Baker, James, Master Shipwright 36, 125
Baker, Mathew, Master Shipwright 125, 147, 148, 157, 160
   his 'Fragments' 160
Baltic, sea 32, 75
Barlow, Roger 74
Baskerville, Sir Thomas 214
Bazan, Don Alvaro de, Marquis of Santa Cruz 171, 180, 181, 185, 187–91
Bergen-op-Zoom 208
Berwick on Tweed 23, 36, 38, 59
Blackness, fort 59
Blount, Charles, Lord Mountjoy 218
Boleyn, Anne, Queen of England 11
Bond, William 39
Boqueron, fort 176
Borobuta 114
Borough, Stephen, navigator 97
Borough, William 155, 189
Boulogne 24, 25, 26, 29, 32, 33, 41, 57, 63, 68, 69, 161, 197
   Treaty of 46
Bourbon, Louis de, Prince of Conde 108
Brandon, Charles, Duke of Suffolk 14, 15. 21, 26, 40
Brest 7, 95, 218
Brighton 29
Bristol 3, 25, 36, 73, 74, 112, 124, 127
   merchants of 74
Brittany 24, 94, 211
Broke, William 42, 49, 120
Brooke, George, Lord Cobham 68
Brooke, Richard 76
Brygandyne, Robert, Clerk of the Ships 6, 9, 10, 39
Buckland abbey 170
Burgh, Sir John 141

INDEX

Cabot, John 74
Cabot, Sebastian 74, 75, 219, 220
Cadiz, 161, 186, 187, 189, 215, 216, 217
   Puntal 216
   Puerto Reale 188, 216
   'The counter Armada' 215
Calais 4, 5, 16, 20, 23, 24, 25, 80, 83, 92, 94, 105, 108
   castle 93
   pale 92, 93
   roads 197. 214
Callis, a pirate 117
Canary Islands 112
Cape Finisterre 193
Cape of Good Hope 169
Cape Verde Islands 175
Capo San Antonio 177
Capo Blanco 166
Carew, Sir George 28, 215
Carew, Sir Peter 87, 117
Carey, Henry, Lord Hunsdon 151, 152
Carliell, Christopher 175, 176
Carrickfergus 86
Cartagena 114, 174, 176
Casa de Contratacion, Seville 74, 97, 220
Cateau Cambrecis, Peace of 104
Catherine of Aragon, Queen of England 6
Catherine de Medici, Regent of France 107, 108, 109
Cavendish, Sir Richard 79
Cavendish, Thomas 207
Ceasar, Dr. Julius, Judge of Admiralty 139
Cecil, Sir Robert, Principal Secretary 141, 154, 221
Cecil, Sir William, Lord Burghley 44, 49, 52, 100, 101, 105, 108, 116, 150, 154, 172, 173, 185, 190, 201, 221
Chain defence across the Medway 159
Chamberlain, Ralph 111
Chancellor, Richard 75, 76
Chapman, Richard 212
Chapuys, Eustace, Imperial Ambassador 1, 12, 16 20
Charles II, King of England 34
Charles V, Holy Roman Emperor 13, 15, 31, 33, 34, 56, 69, 72, 74, 80, 82, 83, 219, 220
Charles IX, King of France 107

Cheney, Sir Thomas 68, 88
Chichester, Sir John 117
China 74
   Cathay Company 75
Cinq Ports 2, 90
Clark, Francis 110
Clement VII, Pope 11
Clerk, or Keeper, of the Ships, Office 1, 3, 4, 39, 40, 50, 101
Clere, Sir Thomas 41, 47, 91, 92
Clerk Controller, Office 9, 40
Clermont, Rene de, Admiral of France 7
Clifford, Sir Conyers 215
Clifford, George, Earl of Cumberland 138, 140–42, 179, 210, 212
Clifford, Sir Nicholas 214
Cockpool 61
Cole, a pirate 87
Coligny, Gaspard, Sieur de Chataillon 68, 108
Colonies, English 165
   Roanoake 178
Colonies, Spanish 220
Commissions, Royal 114, 154
Community, maritime 125, 129, 131
   fisherman's Guilds 130
   of Array 26
   of Enquiry, into finances, 1552 71
   of Oyer and Terminer 117
   of recruitment 127, 131, 132
      compulsion under 132
   other crafts 126–7
   shipwrights 125, 126, 157, 158
Cortes, Martin 97
   his *Arte de Navegar* 97
Cotton, Sir Thomas 96, 102, 107
Council, the kings, or Privy 12, 13, 15, 19, 23, 42, 43, 46, 56, 64, 75, 76
   Henry VIII's executors 56
   of Edward VI 56, 67, 69, 70, 71
   of Elizabeth 108, 111, 117, 118, 130, 134, 137, 138, 145, 147, 148, 159, 171, 178, 181, 187, 200, 206, 210
   of Mary 79–84, 86, 88, 89, 90, 93, 95
   Privy Seal Loan 146
   select 82

Council for Marine Causes 9, 41, 43, 44, 46, 48, 51, 52, 66, 70, 71, 79, 81, 101, 131, 134, 154, 156, 200, 217
  accounts 74
  Book of Sea Causes 101, 103, 145
  corruption in 217
  investigation into 84
  ordinances 48
  pay and expenses 42, 120, 150
Council of War 191
Court, a pirate 117
Crane, William 39
Cranmer, Thomas, Archbishop of Canterbury 11
Cromwell, Oliver 222
Cromwell, Thomas, Lord Privy Seal 11, 12, 13, 40, 41, 52
Crosse, Robert 142
Crozon, Brittany 213

D'Annebault, Claude, Admiral of France 26–33, 36, 52, 53
Danzig 40, 82
Darrell, Marmaduke 153, 155
Da Silva, Nino, Portuguese pilot 167
Dartmouth 141, 211
De Bidoux, Pregent, Galley Commander 8
Dee, John 130, 131
  his 'Perfect Arte of navigation' 130
Deloney, Thomas 201
Devereux, Robert, Earl of Essex 150, 208, 209, 214–17
Devon 124
Dieppe 89
Dockyards 1, 5, 11, 66, 185
  Colne (Harwich) 19, 21, 36, 65, 66, 73, 155
  Clerk of the Yard 126
  Deptford 1, 7, 8, 33, 39, 45, 49, 64, 65, 66, 71, 72, 76, 83, 101, 102, 124–8, 134, 146, 155–8, 159, 200, 212
  Erith 9, 39
  forges 66
  Gillingham (Chatham) 49, 66, 70, 71, 101, 103, 110, 131, 146, 156–8, 159
  Portsmouth 1, 5, 7, 9, 26, 27, 29, 30, 33, 39, 45, 46, 49, 64, 65, 66, 70, 71, 76, 83, 90, 92, 94, 96, 100, 101, 102, 103, 106, 110, 125, 134, 137, 146, 156, 157, 161
  private 66
  Rotherhithe 124–7
  Ratcliffe 127, 134, 151
  shipkeepers 85, 212
  storehouses 66
  Tower Hill (Chatham) 49, 52, 66, 134, 151
  Woolwich 1, 39, 64, 65, 66,71, 72, 76, 80, 101, 102, 126, 155–8, 159, 200
  workforce 66, 85
Douglas, Archibald, Earl of Angus 21, 26
Doughty, Thomas 167, 169, 189
Dover 71
Downs, the 15
Drake, Sir Francis 138, 141, 165–171, 173–180, 186–190, 193, 194, 207–10, 212–15, 219
  knighted 170
  protestant hero 178
  the 'Summarie and true Discourse' 178
Dreux, battle of 109
Dudley, Ambrose, Earl of Warwick 109
Dudley, Sir Andrew 57, 60
Dudley, Lady Amy 107
Dudley, Edmund 6
Dudley, John, Viscount Lisle, Earl of Warwick, Duke of Northumberland, Lord Admiral 14, 15, 16, 19, 20, 22, 24, 27–33, 36, 41, 43, 45, 47, 56, 58, 61, 67, 68, 69, 72, 75, 76, 79, 94, 104, 218, 220, 221
Dudley, Henry 87
Dudley, Lord Robert, Earl of Leicester 107, 108, 112, 179, 191
Duijvenvoorde, Jan van, Dutch Admiral 215, 216
Dunbar 58, 62,106
Dundee 60, 61
Dunkirk 198

Eden, Robert 97
Edinburgh 21, 23, 26
  Treaty of, 1560 106, 107
Edward III, King of England 20

INDEX

Edward IV, King of England 4
Edward VI, King of England 14, 46, 56, 70, 72, 75, 220
  coronation of 56
  his journal 68, 70
  his religious settlement 68
Egmont Lamoral, Count of 96
Elizabeth I, Queen of England 44, 49, 52, 64, 75, 85, 93, 97, 100, 104, 105, 107, 108, 110, 112, 113, 116, 118, 119, 125, 130, 134, 139, 140, 141, 145, 150, 155, 164, 165, 166, 169–72, 178, 185, 186, 195, 200, 201, 206, 207, 209, 211, 212, 213, 220, 222
  religious settlement 104
  Protector of Scotland 105
  'fasting days' 129
  plots against 171, 180
  resources 172
  Accession Day 202
  her instructions 207, 208
  co-operative enterprises 213 221
  Privy Purse 146
Elizabeth of York, Queen of England 5
Elliott, John 135
Elmes, William 57
Empson, Sir Richard 6,
Enriquez, Don Martin 115
'Espagnols sur mer' battle of (1350) 2
Etaples 24, 32
Eure, Sir Ralph, Lord Eure 23, 25
Exeter 67
Eyemouth 106

Falmouth 89, 166, 218
Farnese, Alexander, Duke of Parma 171, 172, 180, 181, 185, 190–94, 196, 197, 198, 214
Fenner, Thomas 142
Ferrol 217
Fenton, Edward 170, 211, 212
Fiennes, Edward, Lord Clinton, Lord Admiral 58–65, 70, 79, 80, 91, 93, 95, 100, 106, 110, 112, 137, 138, 139, 154
Ferrers, Walter, Lord 47
Figueroa, Don Gomez Soarez de, Count of Feria 95, 96, 164

Firth of Forth 59, 62, 63, 65
Fishing fleet, English 119, 129
Fitzroy, Henry, Duke of Richmond 10, 11, 12, 47
FitzWilliam, William, Earl of Southampton, Lord Admiral 12, 41,
Flanders banks 197, 198
Flicke, Robert 185
Flodden, battle of (1513) 8, 14
Flota (Spanish treasure fleet) 174, 185, 186, 206, 207, 211, 212, 213
Forts, Artillery 12, 185
Framlingham 79
France 6, 57, 79, 82, 119, 164, 210, 212
  friendship with 72
  Huguenots 165, 179
    colony in Florida 165
    Treaty of Richmond 108
  navy of 105
  threat from 84
  Tumult of Amboise 105
  war with 1, 14, 15, 24, 89
Francis I, King of France 13, 32, 52, 56
Francis II, King of France 104, 105, 107
Friesland 68
Frobisher, Sir Martin 140, 141, 161, 196, 210, 211, 213, 219

Galicia 115
Galleys, 27, 28, 30, 32, 58, 62, 70
  Celtic 86
  Spanish 176
Gardiner, Stephen, Bishop of Winchester 21, 22, 43, 45, 81
Gilbert, Sir John 211
Gloucester 125
Gomez, Ruy, Secretary to King Philip 88
Gonson, Benjamin, Treasurer of the navy 41, 42, 44, 47, 48, 49 67, 71, 72, 80, 81, 84, 85, 90, 100, 107, 111, 112, 119, 120, 133, 134, 135, 146, 147, 155, 159, 161
  his Quarter Books 50, 51, 66, 111, 125, 126, 132, 134, 145, 151, 153, 154, 156, 157
  declared accounts 145
Gonson, William, Keeper of the Storehouses 10–13, 16, 40–43
Gray, Patrick, Lord 60

Granvelle, Antoine Perrenot de, Bishop of Arras 69, 89
Graynfield, John 64
Grenville, Sir Richard 165, 166
Greenwich 9, 68, 89
  Treaty of (1543) 15, 19, 58
Gresham, Sir Thomas 95,
Gresham College, London 128
Greville, Fulk 153, 154
Grey, Thomas, Marquis of Dorset 7
Grey, William, Lord Grey of Wilton 57, 60, 62, 106
Grice, Gilbert 79
Guidotti, Antonio 68
Guise, Henry, duke of 92, 107, 108, 109, 171
Guisnes 93
Guns 218
  gunfounding 120, 218
  'habillaments' 33, 49
  small 2

Haddington 62, 63, 67
  Convention of (1548) 62
Hales, James 81
Hall, Edward, Chronicler 15
Hamburg 113
Hamilton, James, Earl of Arran 14, 19, 21, 25, 26, 57
Hanseatic League 4, 138, 219
Harford, James 66
Havana 177
Hawkins, John, Treasurer of the navy 48, 112–116, 119, 120, 138, 140, 147, 150, 153, 154, 155, 158, 160, 161, 164, 173, 179, 195, 201, 210, 213, 214, 215, 219, 221, 222
  accused of negligence 148
  his 'bargains' 146-9, 153, 154.
Hawkins, William 53, 74, 219
Haynes, Thomas 66
Henry (Dauphin) II, King of France 32, 64, 79, 87, 88, 89, 164
Henry III, King of England 1, 20
Henry IV, King of France 210, 213
Henry V, King of England 2, 3, 4, 8
Henry VI, King of England 3, 4
Henry VII, King of England 4, 5, 6, 39, 52, 74

Henry VIII, King of England 1, 6–10, 12, 15, 20, 22, 25, 26, 31, 33, 34, 39, 52, 53, 54, 56, 70, 103, 120, 161, 219, 220
  his 'Great matter' 11
  journey to France, 1544 23
Hepburn, Patrick, Earl of Bothwell 23
Herbert, William, Earl of Pembroke 90, 92, 112
Hoby, Sir Philip 68
Holstock, William 66, 120
Holy Island 20, 57, 62, 63, 106
Holy League (1511) 6
Hopton, John, Clerk Controller 9, 10, 39
Howard, Lord, of Bindon 140
Howard, Sir Edward, Lord Admiral 7, 8, 47
Howard, Thomas, third Duke of Norfolk, Lord Admiral 8, 10, 14, 24, 26, 45, 47
Howard, Thomas, fourth Duke of Norfolk 105
Howard, Sir Thomas 212, 215
Howard, Lord Charles, Lord Admiral 194, 196, 198, 200, 215, 216, 217
Howard, Lord William, Lord Admiral 80, 81, 83, 85, 90
Howlett, Richard, Clerk of the Ships 42, 48, 49, 120
Hull 3, 91, 128
Hume, Lord 23
Humphreys, James 131, 133

Inchcolm 60, 61
Inchgowrie 23
Inchkeith 22
Ipswich 3, 91
Ireland 85, 86, 199, 109, 150, 159, 217
  Irish Sea 111
  Kinsale 218
  Ulster 85, 86, 96, 107
    Fishing the Bann 85, 86
Islands Voyage (1597) 217, 218

Jackson, John 34
James IV, King of Scotland 14
James VI of Scotland 171
Java 169

INDEX

Jermyn, Thomas, Clerk of the Ships 10, 11
Jerningham, Henry 76
John, King of England 1
John of Calais 25
Johnson, Henry 34
Johnson, William 46
Joinville, Treaty of (1585) 178

Keeper of the Storehouses, Office 40
Keeping the Seas 68, 82, 83
   licences and indentures 4
   private fleets 4
Kent, Thomas 86
Killigrew, family 117, 140
   Pendennis Castle 140
Killigrew, Sir John 139
Killigrew, Sir Peter 87, 88, 91
Kinghorn 59
Kings Bench, Court of 116
   Felony 116
Kings Lynn 127, 129
Kintyre 96

La Coruna 193, 194, 216
Lane, Ralph, 178
La Rochelle 179
Lauder 60
Le Conquet 95
Le Havre (Newhaven) 26, 52, 89, 90, 109, 110, 111, 145, 146, 147, 164
Legge, Robert, Treasurer of the navy 41, 43, 47, 58, 65
Leicester 11
Leith 22, 23, 59, 62, 63, 105, 106, 119, 133
Levello, Augustino, Venetian shipwright 156
Lima 118
Lisbon 185, 186, 187, 190, 191, 206, 207, 209, 212
   expedition to 212
Liverpool 73
Lizard, William 156
London, City of 3. 48, 56, 102, 124, 129, 140, 141, 173, 185, 186, 194, 195, 200
   The Tower 49, 81, 121
   ships of 112

Levant Company 170
livery companies 53
maritime culture 74
Merchant Adventurers 113, 119, 219
Muscovy Company 75, 128, 220
Longford, Roger 153
Louis XII, King of France 6, 14,
Lovell, John 113, 138,
Low Countries (Netherlands) 69, 82, 83, 85, 92, 95, 113, 147, 150, 164, 166, 205, 207, 208, 212, 214
   estates general 186
   navy 180, 197, 209
   the Dutch 113, 207, 214
   United Provinces 180
Lutterell, Sir John 59-63
Luxan, Francisco de 115

Magdalene College, Cambridge 34, 211
Magellan, Straits of 166, 167
Malen, John, sea captain 96
Manners, Henry, Earl of Rutland 92
Manners, Thomas, Earl of Rutland 14
Mansell, Sir Rhys 15, 16, 19, 20
Mansell, Sir Robert 154
Margaret of Anjou, Queen of England 4
Margaret of Parma, Regent of the Low Countries 113
Margarita, Island 114
'Margate Head' 193
Marillac, Claude de, French Ambassador 53
Mariners 125, 127, 129
   bargemen 125
   boys 128
   demobilisation 132
   grommets 128
   shipkeepers 158, 159
   shipmen's guilds 127
   wages 25, 53, 102, 132, 133, 150
   wherrymen 125
Mary I, Queen of England 31, 33, 69, 75, 76, 79, 80, 95, 97, 100, 164
   her marriage 164
   her pregnancy 82
Mary of Guise, Regent of Scotland 25, 104, 106
Mary of Hungary, Regent of the Low Countries 56, 69

Mary, Queen of Scots 58, 62, 67,
    105–108, 118, 171, 186
  her 'rough wooing' 14, 58
Master gunners 132
Mediterranean sea 75
Mendoza, Bernardino de, Spanish
    Ambassador 170, 171
Merchant Guilds, general 133
Middleton, Miles 20, 31, 33
Militia, English 173
Mocha, Island 168
Moluccas 169
Monasteries, dissolution of 32
Monson, Sir William 218, 221, 222
Montgomery, John 118
Montalembert, Andre, Sieur d'Esse 62,
    63
Montreuil 24
More, Edmund 11, 13
Morley, Thomas 66,
Musgrave, Sir William 14
Mussleborough 59

Navy 124, 130
  auxilliaries 72
  costs of 32
    bounties 52, 53
    ordinary 36, 42, 43, 85, 101–04,
        135, 145, 147, 149, 157, 211
    prest and conduct money 131
    sea causes extraordinary 157, 159
    warrant dormant 145, 146, 149
  deployment 100, 101, 106, 172, 180
    'blue water' strategy 222
    'en ala' 195
    fireships 198
  Channel Guard 8, 9, 25, 95
  Winter Guard 65, 88
  Summer Guard 70, 103, 107
  fighting instructions 94
  routine patrols 108, 146, 213
  private warships 140, 194, 221
  North Sea squadron 172
  Atlantic Guard 206
Navigation, celestial 127
Neville, Henry, Earl of Westmorland 89
Neville, Richard, Earl of Warwick 4
Newcastle upon Tyne 15, 19, 21, 25, 36,
    58, 71, 91, 124, 128

Newfoundland Banks 129
Newhaven, Sussex 29, 135
Newlyn, Cornwall 213
Nombre de Dios 165, 177, 214
Nonsuch, Treaty of (1585) 172
Norris, Sir John 150, 207–10, 213
North East passage 74
North Sea 111
Norway 199
Nowell, Alexander 202
Norwich 125

O'Neill, Hugh, Earl of Tyrone 218
Ordnance, Office of 13, 41
Orkney, Isles 92
Osbourne, John 48
Ostend 208
Ottoman Empire 219
Oxenham, John 165

Paget, Sir William, Lord Paget 29, 31,
    32, 33, 69
Palma 174
Palmer, Sir Henry 155, 179
Palmer, Sir Thomas 61
Panama 177, 213
Parliament 11, 56, 83, 150, 179
  subsidy from 150, 172, 206
Parr, Catherine (Lady Latimer) Queen of
    Henry VIII 64
Parr, William, Lord of Kendal 15
Patch, William 132
Patten, William 59
Paulet, Sir Hugh 11
Paulet, William, Lord St. John, Marquis of
    Winchester, Lord Treasurer 21, 22,
    43–6, 70, 71, 84, 85, 91, 94, 108,
    145, 153
Peckham, Sir Edmund 81
Penzance 213
Pepys, Samuel 34, 156, 202
Perez da Guzman, Alonso, Duke of
    Medina Sidonia 188, 191, 193–9,
    217
Perth 60
Perrot, Sir John 139
Petre, Sir William 32, 90
Pett, Peter, Master Shipwright 147, 148,
    160, 212

INDEX

Philip II of Spain, King of England 31, 33, 82, 83, 87, 88, 90, 93, 94, 95, 97, 103, 106, 118, 165, 166, 170, 171, 174, 178, 181, 185, 186, 190, 191, 199, 210, 212, 220
   resources 172
Philippines 169
Piers, William 86
Pilgrimage of Grace 40
Pinkie Cleugh, battle (1547) 62
Piracy 53, 63, 69, 73, 79, 86, 87, 88, 95, 108, 109, 112, 116, 118, 137, 139, 170, 177, 180, 219
   Barbary corsairs 72
Pius V, Pope 165, 166
   Regnans in Excelsis 118
Plague 110, 199, 200
Plantagenet, Arthur, Viscount Lisle 34
Plymouth 53, 88, 91, 126, 169, 178, 187, 189, 194, 210, 214, 215
Porter, William 141
Portland Bill 196
Portugal 113, 140, 207, 208
   Carracks of 140
Poynings, Sir Adrian 109
Poynings, Thomas 24
Privateering 25, 31, 32, 33, 69, 110, 116, 132, 133, 137, 138, 139, 210, 212, 218, 219
   Letters of Marque 95, 110, 138
   reprisals 20, 116

Quarles, James, Surveyor General of the Victuals 137, 152

Radcliffe, Henry, Earl of Sussex 96
Raleigh, Walter, senior 94, 140
Raleigh, Walter, junior 94, 140, 179, 212, 215, 216
Rathins 86
Rebellions (1549) 67
Rebellion in the north (1569) 118, 147
Recalde, Juan Martin de 187, 189, 195
Renard, Simon, Imperial Ambassador 31, 33
Reneger, Robert 219
Ribault, Jean, French adventurer 74
Richard III, King of England 4
Rio de la Hacha 114

Rochester 134, 151
Rogers, Thomas, Clerk of the Ships 4
Rome, reconciliation of the English Church with 82
Ropes and cables 126
Rous, Sir Edmund 85, 86
Roxborough 60
Russell, John, Lord 13, 29
Ruthven, Lord 63
Ruysbank, fort 92, 93
Rye 32, 110
Ryther, John 45

Sackville, Sir Thomas 154
Sadler, Sir Ralph 41
Sagres, castle 189
St. Christopher Island 175
St. Katherines 151
St. Quentin, battle of (1557) 92
San Juan de Puerto Rico 214
San Juan d'Ulloa 114, 115, 116
San Julian, port of 167
San Lucar 31, 33
Santander 209
San Augustin, Florida 178
San Sebastian 209
Santo Domingo 174–7
Scarborough 89
Scheyfve, Johan, Imperial Ambassador 69, 74
Scotland 19, 21, 41, 56, 57, 58, 65, 73, 82, 86, 91, 105, 118, 139, 164, 199
   Ayton Castle 61
   Broughty Crag 60–63, 67, 68
   Council of 14
   French presence in 33, 49, 62, 106, 119
   garrisons 134
   land border 5
   nobility 91, 104, 105, 107
   reformers 69
   St. Andrews castle 57, 58
   war with 1, 14
Sebastian, King of Portugal 171
Selsey Bill 197
Seymour, Edward, Earl of Hertford, Duke of Somerset, Lord Protector 21, 22, 23, 32, 33, 45, 56 57, 58, 59, 60–64, 67, 68, 220

Seymour, Lord Henry 194, 197
Seymour, Sir Thomas 24, 25, 56, 63, 64, 65, 69
Sharif of Morocco 206
Sheerness 103, 159
Ships (English)
  design 120, 160, 218
  fireships 188
  maintenance of 51
  royal, lists of 97, 101, 124, 129, 212
  rowbarges 35, 67, 103
  tonnage 133
Ships names (English)
  Achates 158
  Adventure 160
  Aid 174
  Anne Gallant 72, 111, 133
  Answer 160, 211
  Antelope 157, 158
  Anthony 59
  Ark Royal 161
  Artigo 64
  Bark Aucher 57, 60, 64
  Bark of Bullen 70, 73, 84
  Bark Hawkins 195
  Bonavolia 212
  Bona Speranza 75
  Bosse 59
  Brygandyne 73, 112
  Bull 157
  Christopher 73
  Confidencia 75
  Crane 212
  Cygnet 212
  Dainty 140
  David of Lubeck 111, 133
  Deadnought 158, 159, 187
  Defiance 212
  Double Rose 65, 86
  Edward Bonaventure 75, 188, 211
  Elizabeth 167, 168, 174
  Elizabeth Bonaventure 174, 187
  Elizabeth Jonas 102, 111, 157
  Falcon 101, 101
  Fleur de Luce 65, 86, 112
  Foresight 156, 159
  Gabriel Royal 7
  Galleon Dudley 195
  Galley Eleanor 156, 158
  Galleon Leicester 174, 195
  Galley Mermaid 67, 73
  Galley Subtill (Subtle) 35, 60, 218
  Garland 212
  George 73
  Gerfalcon (Jerfalcon) 70, 72, 86
  Golden Lion 187, 189
  Grace Dieu 2, 3, 5
  Grand Mistress 35, 73
  Great Bark 61, 81, 91, 131
  Great Galley 9, 12, 35
  Great Pinnace 64
  Greyhound 79, 81, 157
  Hart 146
  Hare 100, 101
  Henry Grace a Dieu 8, 33, 35, 39, 64, 80, 101, 120
  Jennet 81, 100, 101, 157, 158
  Jesus of Lubeck 61, 72, 112, 114–6
  Judith 115
  Katherine Fortileza 7
  Katherine Pleasaunce 9
  Less Galley 20
  Lion 101, 159, 160
  Marigold 167, 168
  Mary Hamborough 60, 64. 65
  Mary James 64
  Mary and John 6
  Mary Rose (I) 6, 8, 12, 28, 29, 34, 35, 36, 39, 46
  Mary Rose (II) 83, 101, 211, 218
  Mary Thomas 64
  Mary Willoughby 13, 59, 64, 67, 70, 72, 86, 96, 109, 146
  Mathew 72, 174
  Merhonoeur 160, 211
  Minion 20, 57, 89, 91
  Moon 67
  New Bark 96
  New Hope 176
  New Years Gift 176
  Nonpareil (Philip and Mary) 158, 160
  Pauncey 57, 65
  Pelican (Golden Hind) 166, 170
  Peter 100
  Peter Pomegranate 6, 8, 12, 39, 84
  Philip and Mary 83, 101, 111

INDEX

Phoenix 60, 82, 101, 109
Primrose 70, 82, 83, 101, 102, 112, 157, 174
Quittance 160, 211
Rainbow 187
Regent 5, 7,
Revenge 120, 158
Saker 109
Santa Maria 167
Sea Dragon 160
Seven Stars 67
Scourge of Malice 140, 179
Scout 158
Sovereign 5, 7
Speedwell 106, 160
Sun 33, 82
Swallow 111, 146
Swan 167
Sweepstake 22, 101, 112, 114, 115, 101
Swiftsure 159
'The Venetian' 89
Tiger 61, 89, 157, 174
Trego Reneger 70
Trinity Henry 10. 73, 101, 155
Triumph 109, 120, 158, 159, 160, 196
Tryright 106, 160
Victory 109, 111, 120, 212
White Bear 158, 211
William and John 114
Ships names (French)
  Cordeliere 7
  Grande Maitresse 27
  Philippe 27
  Sacre 19
  Sacrette 87, 88
Ships names (Scottish)
  Salamander 23
  Unicorn 23, 72
Ships names (Spanish)
  Neustra Senora del Rosario 195, 211
  San Andres (St. Andrew) 160, 216
  San Felipe (St Philip) 150, 161,190
  San Juan 195
  San Lorenzo 198
  San Martin 198, 216
  San Mateo (St.Mathew) 160, 216
  San Salvador 31, 33, 195
  Santa Cruz 141

Ships name (Portuguese)
  Madre de Dios 140, 141, 150, 161, 212.
Sierra Leone 169
Sixtus V, Pope 180, 202
Sluys 191, 192
Solent 26, 27, 196
Solway Moss, battle (1542) 14, 15
Southampton 46
Southwell, Richard 45
Spain 113
  galleys 188
  relations with 31, 81, 115, 164, 170, 202, 221
  soldiers of 199
  war with 172, 188

Spert, Sir Thomas, Clerk Controller 10, 11, 13, 219
Spenser, Edmund 202
  his 'Faerie Queene' 202
Spert, Sir Thomas 10. 11, 13
Star Chamber, Court of 117
Stafford, Thomas 89
Stevenson, a pirate 86, 87
Strozzi, Leo, galley commander 58
Stuart, Mathew, Earl of Lennox 2, 26
Suffolk 124

Terciera, 174
  Battle of 171
'The Debate between the Heralds of England and France 3
Thorne, Robert 74
Throgmorton, Francis 171
Throgmorton, Sir Nicholas 107, 108
Timber, supplies of 50
Toledo, Frenando Alvarez de, Duke of Alba 92, 113, 116, 118, 165, 166
  his payships 116
Toledo, Treaty of 12
Tournai 8
Tremayne, Nicholas 87, 88, 117
Treport 30, 218
Trinity House 128
Tyrell, Sir William 79, 88

Upnor 49, 103, 155, 159
Ushant 83,194,

Valdes, Don Pedro 195
Valois, Francis, Duke of Anjou 172, 178
Valparaiso 168
Van der Delft, Francis, Imperial Ambassador 29, 31, 33, 69
Vaucelles, truce of (1556) 87, 88
Vaughn, Stephen 36, 40
Venice 185
Vere, Sir Francis 215
Vice Admirals of the coasts 64, 118, 139
Victualling 44, 50, 51, 59, 70, 71, 84, 85, 90, 134, 137
  Commissions of Purveyance 70, 152
  complaints 137
  daily allowance 136
  dead pays 46, 135
  purveyors 44, 70, 134, 137
  quota system 134
  supplements 136
  the king's price 44, 51
Vigo 115, 174, 210, 221

Walsingham, Sir Francis 213
Warfare, cost of 100, 111, 120, 130, 149, 206, 211
Waterford 133
Waters, Edward 13
Watson, William 82
Wattes, Richard 46, 71
Wentworth, Lord Thomas 89, 92, 93
Wharham, William, Archbishop of Canterbury 11
Wharton, Sir Thomas 14

Wight, Isle of 27, 28, 196
William the Silent, leader of the Dutch 172
Willoughby, Lord 207, 208
William IV, King of Great Britain 34
Willoughby, Sir Hugh 75, 76
Winnington, Robert 3
Winter, George 49, 120, 131
Winter, John 41, 42, 43, 47
Winter, Sir William 48, 49, 72, 81, 94, 95, 105, 106, 111, 112, 119, 120, 132
Winter, William, junior 142
Wynter, Thomas 168
Wogan, Sir John 139
Wolsey, Thomas, Cardinal Archbishop of York 10, 11, 40, 52
Woodless, Thomas 131
Woodhouse, Sir William, Vice Admiral 19, 47, 49, 90, 91, 92, 94, 109, 111, 119, 120, 155
Works, Office of 13, 41
Wotton, Edward, Ambassador in France 87
Wriothesley, Sir Thomas 41
Wyatt, Sir Thomas, his rebellion 81, 87
Wyndham, Sir Thomas 47, 48 61, 80, 221

Yarmouth, Norfolk 79, 91
York 127

Zuniga, Juan de 181, 185